THE EUROPEAN UNION'S SHAPING OF THE INTERNATIONAL LEGAL ORDER

The European Union undoubtedly plays an important role in the formation of international law. This takes place through a number of avenues ranging from the simple existence of this supranational legal order within the sphere of international law to the actual influencing of international legal order. With contributions by leading scholars, this collection of essays constructs and analyses a new and stimulating approach in which the European Union is perceived as an active co-creator of the international legal order on a variety of planes. Providing concrete examples of the European Union's approach to the international legal order in different policy fields, this book will be a key reference point for a new active paradigm of EU external relations law.

DIMITRY KOCHENOV is Professor of EU Constitutional Law at the Department of European and Economic Law, University of Groningen. He consulted for the Government of the Netherlands on the application of EU law in the overseas territories of the Kingdom. He is also a regular contributor to a number of leading periodicals in law and political science.

FABIAN AMTENBRINK is Professor of European Union Law at Erasmus University, Rotterdam and a visiting professor at the College of Europe, Bruges. His teaching specializes in constitutional, institutional and substantive law of the European Union. He has published widely in books and journals and serves on the editorial boards of, among others, *European Law Review* and *European Journal of Consumer Law*.

THE EUROPEAN UNION'S SHAPING OF THE INTERNATIONAL LEGAL ORDER

Edited by

DIMITRY KOCHENOV

and

FABIAN AMTENBRINK

CAMBRIDGE
UNIVERSITY PRESS

CAMBRIDGE
UNIVERSITY PRESS

University Printing House, Cambridge CB2 8BS, United Kingdom

Published in the United States of America by Cambridge University Press, New York

Cambridge University Press is part of the University of Cambridge.

It furthers the University's mission by disseminating knowledge in the pursuit of education, learning and research at the highest international levels of excellence.

www.cambridge.org
Information on this title: www.cambridge.org/9781107033337

First published 2014

Printed in the United Kingdom by CPI Group Ltd, Croydon CR0 4YY

A catalogue record for this publication is available from the British Library

Library of Congress Cataloguing in Publication data
The European Union's shaping of the international legal order / Dimitry Kochenov, Fabian Amtenbrink.
pages cm.
ISBN 978-1-107-03333-7 (Hardback)
1. International law. 2. Law–European influences. 3. International law–European Union countries. I. Kochenov, Dimitry, 1979– editor of compilation. II. Amtenbrink, Fabian, editor of compilation.
KZ3410.E925 2013
341.242′2–dc23 2013018616

ISBN 978-1-107-03333-7 Hardback

Does Europe not, now that it is finally unified, have a leading role to play in a new world order, that of a power able both to play a stabilising role worldwide and to point the way ahead for many countries and peoples?

Laeken Declaration on the Future of the European Union, 2001

CONTENTS

CONTRIBUTORS

FABIAN AMTENBRINK is Professor of European Union Law at Erasmus University, Rotterdam and a visiting professor at the College of Europe, Bruges.

STEVEN BLOCKMANS is a senior research fellow and Head of the Foreign Policy Unit at the Centre for European Policy Studies (CEPS), Brussels and Professor of External Relations Law and Governance at the Faculty of Law, University of Amsterdam.

ANATOLE BOUTE is a lecturer in the School of Law, University of Aberdeen and legal adviser to the IFC Russia Renewable Energy Programme (World Bank Group).

GRÁINNE DE BÚRCA is Florence Ellinwood Allen Professor of Law, New York University School of Law.

LAURE DELCOUR is the Research Director of the Institut de Relations Internationales et Stratégiques (IRIS), Paris.

CHRISTINA ECKES is Associate Professor, Amsterdam Centre for European Law and Governance, University of Amsterdam and Emile Noël Fellow-in-residence 2012/2013, New York University School of Law.

ESTER HERLIN-KARNELL is Senior Lecturer in EU Law and Co-Director of the Centre for European Legal Studies, VU University Amsterdam.

DIMITRY KOCHENOV is Professor of EU Constitutional Law at the Department of European and Economic Law, University of Groningen.

TILMAN KRÜGER is a doctoral candidate at the Collaborative Research Centre 597 'Transformations of the State', University of Bremen.

JORIS LARIK is a postdoctoral fellow at the Leuven Centre for Global Governance Studies, KU Leuven.

CHRISTOPH OHLER is Professor of Public Law, European Law, International Law and International Business Law, Faculty of Law, Frederic Schiller University of Jena.

LAURENT PECH is Professor of EU Law, School of Law, Middlesex University.

THOMAS RAMOPOULOS is a research fellow at the Leuven Centre for Global Governance Studies and PhD candidate at the Institute for International Law, KU Leuven.

PETER VAN ELSUWEGE is Professor of European Union Law at the Faculty of Law, University of Ghent.

SVEN VAN KERCKHOVEN is a research fellow at the Leuven Centre for Global Governance Studies and a PhD candidate at the Faculty of Business and Economics, KU Leuven.

BART VAN VOOREN is Senior Associate in the EU Regulatory and Trade Practice Group at Altius Brussels and Adjunct Associate Professor of EU Law at the University of Copenhagen.

ANDREW T. WILLIAMS is Professor of Law and Director of the Centre for Human Rights in Practice, Warwick University.

JAN WOUTERS is Professor of International Law and the Law of International Organizations, and Jean Monnet Chair *ad personam* EU and Global Governance, KU Leuven.

PREFACE

This book is an attempt to approach the European Union (EU) as an active co-creator of international law alongside a number of other actors. It thus embraces an active rather than a passive approach to the study of EU external relations and the EU's role in the world, building on a starting assumption – well founded, we claim – that co-shaping international law has been a notable *raison d'être* of the EU from the first days of integration. This vision is tested against the ethical premise of the feasibility of justice claims beyond the state and put within a continuum of the opposition between the familiar *Realpolitik* and the idea of delivering on the messianic promise of peace and prosperity for all, underpinning the European integration project.

Applying the proposed approach along these lines in the context of a dynamic legal analysis of a number of different fields of regulation – from international migration, energy efficiency, global warming and state creation to international financial stability – the volume largely comes to mixed conclusions: the EU is not yet a fully fledged trendsetter – not even an efficient problem-solver at the international level, notwithstanding the fact that it is (co)responsible for the generation and the launch of a number of fundamentally important initiatives, from *Kyoto* to the financial transaction tax, undoubtedly influencing the international legal order to a great degree. Behind all the EU's moves aiming at impacting the international legal order is a mix of *Realpolitik* and idealism – boasting a much larger share of the former, in fact, than the EU institutions would probably be in the position to admit. Most importantly, however, the active paradigm of the study of the law of the EU's external relations is certainly viable and is here to stay.

Drafts of the majority of the contributions to this volume were presented at a conference convened by the editors at the Egmont Palace in Brussels in May 2011 to test the active approach to the study of EU external relations law in preparation of this volume. The editors would like to thank all the participants of the conference, including those who made valuable contributions to the debate without, however, contributing chapters, such as Christophe Hillion and Panos Koutrakos, as well as the Centre for the Law of EU External Relations (CLEER) for the generous support of the initial event.

This book would not have been possible without the constant friendly support of Sinéad Maloney of Cambridge University Press and the dedication of our editorial assistants Martijn van den Brink, Justin Lindeboom and, especially, Suryapratim Roy, graduate students in Groningen, who achieved wonders, working to impossible deadlines.

ABBREVIATIONS

ACP	African Caribbean and Pacific
ACTA	Anti-Counterfeiting Trade Agreement
AHLC	Ad Hoc Liaison Committee
ASEAN	Association of Southeast Asian Nations
ATAA	Air Transport Association of America
BCBS	Basel Committee of Banking Supervision
BIT	bilateral investment treaty
BVerfGE	*Bundesverfassungsgerichtsentscheidungen* [Decisions of the German Federal Constitutional Court]
CAIT	Climate Analysis Indicators Tool
CDM	Clean Development Mechanism
CDRRC	Common but Differentiated Responsibilities and Respective Capabilities
CFSP	Common Foreign and Security Policy
CLEER	Centre for the Law of EU External Relations
CPM	Civil Protection Mechanism
CSCE	Conference on Security and Cooperation in Europe
CSDP	Common Security and Defence Policy
DCI	Development Cooperation Instrument
DG	Directorate-General
DG Clima	Directorate-General for Climate Change
DIIS	Danish Institute of International Studies
DSU	Dispute Settlement Understanding
EAC	European Atomic Energy
EC	European Community/European Communities
ECB	European Central Bank
ECHO	European Community Humanitarian Office
ECHR	European Convention on Human Rights
ECJ	Court of Justice of the European Union
Ecofin	Economic and Financial Affairs
ECSC	European Coal and Steel Community
ECT	Energy Charter Treaty

ECtHR	European Court of Human Rights
EEA	European Economic Area
EEAP	Energy Efficiency Action Plan
EEAS	European External Action Service
EEC	European Economic Community
EESC	European Economic and Social Committee
EFSF	European Financial Stability Facility
EFTA	European Free Trade Association
EIDHR	European Instrument for Democracy and Human Rights
EMAA	Euro-Mediterranean Association Agreement
EMP	Euro-Mediterranean Partnership
EMU	Economic and Monetary Union
ENP	European Neighbourhood Policy
ENPI	European Neighbourhood and Partnership Instrument
EnCT	European Energy Community Treaty
EPC	European Political Cooperation
EPE	Energy Policy for Europe
ERM II	Exchange Rate Mechanism between the euro and other participating EU currencies
ERTA	Economic Recovery Tax Act
ESM	European Stability Mechanism
ETS	emissions trading scheme
EU	European Union
EU ETS	European Union Emissions Trading Scheme
EUBAM Rafah	European Union Border Assistance Mission at the Rafah Crossing Point
EUMM	European Union Monitoring Mission
EUPOL COPPS	European Union Co-ordinating Office for Palestinian Police Support
EURIMF	European Union representatives to the IMF
EU-SILC	European Union Statistics on Income and Living Conditions
FAO	Food and Agriculture Organization
FRY	Federal Republic of Yugoslavia
FSB	Financial Stability Board
FTT	financial transaction tax
GATS	General Agreement on Trade in Services
GATT	General Agreement on Tariffs and Trade
GDP	gross domestic product
GEC	Global Economic Council
GEGO	Global Economic Governance Organization
GHG	greenhouse gas
GMO	genetically modified organism
GRECO	Group of States against Corruption

HiiL	Hague Institute for the Internationalisation of Law
IAIS	International Association of Insurance Supervisors
ICC	International Criminal Court
ICJ	International Court of Justice
ICSID	International Convention for the Settlement of Investment Disputes
IDA	International Development Association
IEA	International Energy Agency
IFFI	International Finance Facility for Immunisation
IFIC	international financial institutions and conferences
ILM	International Legal Materials
IMF	International Monetary Fund
INOGATE	Interstate Oil and Gas Transportation to Europe
IOSCO	International Organization of Securities Commissions
IPA	Instrument for Pre-Accession Assistance
IPEEC	International Partnership for Energy Efficiency Cooperation
KFG	Kolleg-Forschergruppe
MoU	memorandum of understanding
NGO	non-governmental organization
OECD	Organization for Economic Co-operation and Development
OIRA	Office of Information and Regulatory Affairs
OJ	*Official Journal of the European Union*
OPT	Occupied Palestinian Territories
OSCE	Organization for Security and Co-operation in Europe
OTC	over the counter
PA	Palestinian National Authority
PCA	Partnership and Cooperation Agreement
PCA	Permanent Court of Arbitration
PCIJ	Permanent Court of International Justice
PEEREA	Protocol on Energy Efficiency and Related Environmental Aspects
PPA	Power Purchase Agreement
REIO	Regional Economic Integration Organisation
REMEP	Rome Euro-Mediterranean Energy Platform
RIAA	United Nations Reports of International Arbitral Awards
ROD	Reporting Obligations Database
RSCAS	Robert Schuman Centre for Advanced Studies
SCIMF	Sub-committee on IMF [under the Ecofin Council]
SFRY	Socialist Federal Republic of Yugoslavia
SZRF	Sobranie Zakonodatel'stva Rossijskoj Federatsii
TEC	Treaty Establishing the European Community
TESB	Treaty Establishing the European Stability Mechanism
TEU	Treaty on European Union

TFEU	Treaty on the Functioning of the European Union
TSCG	Treaty on Stability, Coordination and Governance
UAR	United Arab Republic
UN	United Nations
UNCITRAL	United Nations Convention on International Trade Law
UNESCO	United Nations Educational, Scientific and Cultural Organization
UNFCCC	United Nations Framework Convention on Climate Change
UNGA	United Nations General Assembly
UNHRC	United Nations Human Rights Committee
UNSC	United Nations Security Council
UNTS	United Nations Treaty Series
US	United States of America
WTO	World Trade Organization

TABLE OF CASES

Court of Justice of the European Union

General Court

International Court of Justice

Permanent Court of International Justice

The International Criminal Tribunal for the former Yugoslavia

World Trade Organization

International Centre for Settlement of Investment Disputes

Decisions of Arbitration Courts and Tribunals

Bundesverfassungsgericht

Conseil constitutionnel

Introduction: the active paradigm of the study of the EU's place in the world

DIMITRY KOCHENOV AND FABIAN AMTENBRINK

1 The active paradigm to study the EU's engagement with the world

This book zooms in on the EU's active engagement with the international legal order. It aims at analysing how the EU shapes its environment and creates rules and practices for the world, reshaping – or at least attempting to reshape – international law. The book does more than simply visiting a range of essential fields of the EU's engagement. It offers an ethical perspective on the Union's actions, shedding light on some underlying motivations, which are at times more complex than the official documents would suggest.

This collection advocates what we refer to as an 'active paradigm' of the study of the EU in the international legal context, approaching the Union as an active co-creator of the international legal order,[1] as opposed to emphasizing the perspective of the reception of international law in the EU,[2] the latter's legal interconnectedness with the rest of the world,[3] its role in emergencies[4] or the soft

[1] See J. Frowein, 'The Contribution of the European Union to Public International Law', in A. von Bogdandy, P. Mavroides and Y. Mény (eds.), *European Integration and International Coordination: Studies in Honour of Claus-Dieter Ehlermann* (The Hague: Kluwer Law International, 2002), p. 171; B. de Witte, 'The Emergence of a European System of Public International Law', in J. Wouters, A. Nollenkaemper and E. de Wet (eds.), *The Europeanisation of Internationational Law* (The Hague: TMC Asser Press. 2008).

[2] For a classical authoritative account of EU external relations law, see P. Eeckhout, *EU External Relations Law*, 2nd edn (Oxford University Press, 2012). Specifically on the role of international law within the EU legal order, see E. Cannizzaro, P. Palchetti and R. Wessel (eds.), *International Law as Law of the European Union* (Leiden: Martinus Nijhoff, 2011).

[3] M. Evans and P. Koutrakos (eds.), *Beyond the Established Legal Orders: Policy Interconnections between the EU and the Rest of the World* (Oxford: Hart Publishing, 2011).

[4] A. Antoniadis, R. Schütze and E. Spaventa (eds.), *The European Union and Global Emergencies: Law and Policy Aspects* (Oxford: Hart Publishing, 2011).

'governance' approaches to EU's global influence, prevalent in the literature.[5]

The analysis reveals that embracing the 'active paradigm', while at times overambitious, overall is well justified in a wide array of areas. Indeed, the EU's global legal influence is not only rooted in its very *raison d'être*[6] – it is much more significant and consequential than many would expect. In fact what is presently suggested is that the standard approach of locating the EU *within* the international legal order should coexist with a different one: the shaping of the international legal order *by* the EU. It is this unorthodox approach, which lies at the core of the active paradigm of approaching the study of the EU in the international legal context, that takes centre stage in this edited volume. Crucially, it opens the way to assess the Union's future role in the world re-imagined under its influence.

The EU plays an important role in the formation of international law. This takes place through a number of avenues ranging from the consequences of the mere existence of this supranational legal order within the sphere of international law[7] – providing a model way of thinking about an alternative approach to the prevalent practice of framing international relations, thus inciting actions of others and providing a point of inspiration[8] – to the attempts by the Union to engage in a proactive co-shaping of the international legal order alongside other actors. Such co-shaping, too, takes a wide array of forms, ranging from simply

[5] See e.g. G. de Búrca, 'EU External Relations: The Governance Mode of Foreign Policy', in B. Van Vooren, S. Blockmans and J. Wouters (eds.), *The EU's Role in Global Governance: The Legal Dimension* (Oxford University Press, 2013).

[6] See the chapter by Gráinne de Búrca in this volume as well as the concluding chapter by the editors.

[7] See e.g. R. Petrov and P. Van Elsuwege (eds.), *The Application of EU Law in the Eastern Neighbourhood of the European Union* (London: Routledge, 2013); Evans and Koutrakos, *Beyond the Established Legal Orders.*

[8] This is an important consideration to take into account, which underlies the successes of the export of the EU's *acquis* to third countries, as well as the attractiveness of the block explaining the successes of its steady growth through history. On the latter, see C. Hillion (ed.), *EU Enlargement: A Legal Approach* (Oxford: Hart Publishing, 2004); M. Cremona (ed.), *The Enlargement of the European Union* (Oxford University Press, 2003); A. Ott and K. Inglis, *Handbook on EU Enlargement: A Commentary on the Enlargement Process* (The Hague: TMC Asser Press, 2002). On the former, see I. Govaere, et al. (eds.), *The European Union in the World: Essays in Honour of Marc Maresceau* (Leiden: Brill, 2014); L. Delcour and E. Toulmets (eds.), *Pioneer Europe? Testing EU Foreign Policy in the Neighbourhood* (Baden-Baden: Nomos, 2008); A. Magen, 'The Shadow of Enlargement: Can the European Neighbourhood Policy Achieve Compliance?' (2006) 12 *Columbia Journal of European Law* 384; M. Maresceau and E. Lannon (eds.), *The EU's Enlargement and Mediterranean Strategies: A Comparative Analysis* (Basingstoke: Palgrave, 2001).

pursuing internal EU objectives with clear implications for the neighbourhood and trading partners,[9] to the active involvement in international organizations,[10] coupled with exporting its own approaches to the functioning of international law,[11] as well as international agenda-setting[12] and the solving of specific problems in the spirit of the values enshrined in the Treaties.[13] Add to this the promotion of particular principles in its external relations[14] and the involvement in the formulation of the essential rules at the international plane, including those governing the creation and recognition of states[15] and those ensuring international financial stability[16] – and a picture of EU's shaping of the international legal order emerges in all its complexity.

The EU's engagement with the international legal order has been most intimate from the Union's very inception and, especially, from the Court of Justice's (ECJ) clarification that EU law is, as such, not international law.[17] Not a simple international organization,[18] the EU ensured that its law 'is dressed in the constitutional gowns of supremacy and direct

[9] As it happens in the area of migration, for instance, as described by Laure Delcour in this volume.

[10] S. Blavoukos and D. Bourantonis (eds.), *The EU Presence in International Organisations* (London: Routledge, 2010); M. Rasch, *The European Union at the United Nations* (Leiden: Martinus Nijhoff, 2008).

[11] As explained by Tilman Krüger in relation to WTO law later in this volume.

[12] As with the global financial transactions tax, analysed by Bart Van Vooren in his contribution to this collection.

[13] M. Cremona, 'Values in EU Foreign Policy', in M. Evans and P. Koutrakos (eds.), *Beyond the Established Legal Orders: Policy Interconnections between the EU and the Rest of the World* (Oxford: Hart Publishing, 2011), p. 275; S. Lucarelli, 'Values, Principles, Identity and European Union Foreign Policy', in S. Lucarelli and I. Manners (eds.), *Values and Principles in European Union Foreign Policy* (London: Routledge, 2006). See also the chapter by Ester Herlin-Karnell in this volume.

[14] As explained by Laurent Pech in this volume, using rule of law as an example. Classical case studies usually focus on the promotion of democracy and human rights worldwide, e.g. L. Bartels, *Human Rights Conditionality in the EU's International Agreements* (Oxford University Press, 2005). See also L. Ogerschnig, 'EU Democracy Assistance: An Analysis of Theory and Practice 1991–2011', PhD thesis, European University Institute, Florence, 2013.

[15] As analysed by Steven Blockmans in this volume.

[16] As analysed by Christoph Ohler in this volume.

[17] Case 26/62 *Van Gend en Loos*64/64 *Flaminio Costa* v. *ENEL* [1964] ECR 585. See on the nature of EU law: R. Schütze, *From Dual to Cooperative Federalism* (Oxford University Press, 2009); K. Lenaerts and K. Gutman, '"Federal Common Law" in the European Union: A Comparative Perspective from the United States' (2006) 54 *American Journal of Comparative Law* 1.

[18] A. Somek, 'On Supranationality' (2001) 5 *European Integration Online Papers*, available at http://eiop.or.at/eiop/pdf/2001-003.pdf.

effect'.[19] The distinction between EU law and international law is of essential importance for the functioning of the former in the Member States, but it also has broader implications. In fact, one of the main achievements of the Union to date remains the substitution of what Philip Allott characterized as 'diplomacy' in the relations between the Member States of the Union with 'democracy':[20] the very logic of inter-state relations within the Union has thereby been transformed entirely.[21] Instead of acting in the interests of 'own peoples'[22] no matter what, the Member States are ready to take the interests of others (both states and, necessarily, peoples of other states) into account, when decisions are taken. The key implication of this transformation is the demonstration that an *ethos* of interstate relations different from the familiar de Vattelian dogma, which has been holding our minds hostage for centuries, is feasible.[23] Put differently, by distancing itself from the reigning paradigm of international relations internally, the EU has undergone a remarkable transformation, becoming a success story in the eyes of its neighbours.

The idea of distancing the EU legal space from classical international relations also helps in explaining the successes of the EU's enlargements, widely regarded as the main foreign policy achievements of the EU to date. By socializing new Member States into the constitutionalized space of the Union where Allott's 'diplomacy' is not the main *modus operandi*, any enlargement[24] – from the EU's internal perspective at least – is a move from 'diplomacy' to 'democracy'.

Yet, the impact of such consitutionalization on the *ethos* of the Union's external action has been minimal, as Andrew Williams's scholarship

[19] P. Eeckhout, 'A Panorama of Two Decades of EU External Relations Law', in A. Arnull, P. Eeckhout and T. Tridimas (eds.), *Continutity and Change in EU Law: Essays in Honour of Sir Francis Jacobs* (Oxford: Hart Publishing, 2008), p. 329. For a magisterial analysis of EU constitutionalism, see J. H. H. Weiler, *The Constitution for Europe* (Cambridge University Press, 1999).

[20] P. Allott, 'The European Community Is Not the True European Community' (1991) 100 *Yale Law Journal* 2485.

[21] E. Basheska, 'The Principle of Good Neighbourly Relations in European Union Law', PhD thesis, University of Groningen, 2013.

[22] On the 'container theory of society', see U. Beck, *What Is Globalisation?* (Cambridge: Polity Press, 2000), p. 23.

[23] For a powerful plea to move away from the de Vattelian reality of international relations, see P. Allott, *The Health of Nations: Society and Law beyond the State* (Cambridge University Press, 2002). See also I. Scobbie, 'Slouching towards the Holy City: Some Weeds for Philip Allott' (2005) 16 *European Journal of International Law* 299.

[24] On the connection between EU enlargements and the development of European constitutionalism, see W. Sadurski, *Constitutionalism and the Enlargement of Europe* (Oxford University Press, 2012).

demonstrates with remarkable clarity. Having ensured peace internally, the EU is not a peacemaker externally[25] – and understanding its engagement with human rights in the wider world has rightly been called a 'study in irony'.[26] EU's dealing with the conflict in the former Yugoslavia provides but one vivid example of the remarkable inability to deal with outstanding problems even in the closest proximity to the Union. Regrettably, to agree with an authoritative study by Urfan Khaliq, as far as the actual promotion of values and principles by the EU is concerned, it is rooted in policies which are 'neither consistent nor coherent, but need to be'.[27] Even the pre-accession value-promotion context leading to the EU's enlargements allows coming to the same conclusion.[28]

The internal success story of the EU is essentially different from the external disappointments and is rarely questioned.[29] It provides a vivid example of how much can be achieved by departing from the classical dogmatics of international relations and mainstream international law in interstate relations in a given region. In Europe *le droit de l'intégration* has been born,[30] potentially providing a way out from the shadow of at least the most disappointing side-effects of de Vattelianism through the constitutionalization of interstate relations and thereby – essentially – the departure from international law as we know it outside the Union.

Quite naturally, the constitutionalization of EU law led to the emergence of the questions concerning international law's functioning within the supranational EU legal order.[31] Although openness to international law is the prevalent vision,[32] whether international law should function in the EU internally depends on the blessing of the Union, which can also be withheld, should it contradict the EU's policy, objectives, rationale or principles. Numerous examples of such situations can be given, from the

[25] A. Williams, *The Ethos of Europe* (Cambridge University Press, 2010), pp. 22–69.

[26] A. Williams, *EU Human Rights Policies: A Study in Irony* (Oxford University Press, 2004).

[27] U. Khaliq, *Ethical Dimensions of the Foreign Policy of the European Union* (Cambridge University Press, 2008), p. 447.

[28] D. Kochenov, *EU Enlargement and the Failure of Conditionality: Pre-Accession Conditionality in the Areas of Democracy and the Rule of Law* (The Hague: Kluwer Law International, 2008).

[29] For exceptions, see I. Ward, *The Margins of European Law* (Basingstoke: Macmillan, 1996); G. de Búrca, D. Kochenov and A. Williams (eds.), *Europe's Justice Deficit?* (Oxford: Hart Publishing, 2014 (forthcoming)).

[30] P. Pescatore, *Le droit de l'intégration* (Leyden: A. W. Sijthoff, 1972).

[31] E.g. C. W. A. Timmermans, 'The EU and Public International Law' (1999) 4 *European Foreign Affairs Review* 181.

[32] For the basic principle, see Case 104/81 *Hauptzollamt Mainz* v. *Kupferberg* [1982] ECR 3641. But see Joined Cases 21–24/72 *International Fruit Company* v. *Produktschap voor Groenten en Fuit* [1972] ECR 1219.

enforceability of WTO law[33] in the EU to *Micheletti*,[34] and, more recently, *Kadi*,[35] to mention just a few. The EU undoubtedly does not regard itself as an emanation of ordinary international law at work and is ready to defend itself – also against international law, if needed.[36] Just as the strategies deployed by the Member States in the context of the establishment of supranational legal principles internally,[37] such defence can take at least two forms. The first consists in tweaking international law internally in the context of (dis-)applying it within the Union legal order (*Kadi* provides a valuable example of this). The second relates to the (co-)creation of the international law jointly with other actors with the aim of ensuring that the result is compatible with (internal) EU law. While the Union can be seen using both strategies, the second is of particular importance everywhere outwith the Union, not merely within – international law affecting all actors is thereby transformed.

This edited volume focuses on this second field, that is the active (co-)shaping of the international legal order by the EU. As such this collection departs from the majority of the existing studies focusing either on the functioning of international law within the EU or on the role of the EU in implementing international law, where little light is shed on the active role played by the EU in shaping the international legal order. In contrast, in this book the Union is perceived to take on an active rather than a passive role. The key task of this work is to adopt this active perspective in reflecting on EU's achievements and outlining the avenues for the future development of the international legal order. The latter has

[33] A. Tancredi, 'On the Absence of Direct Effect of the WTO Dispute Settlement Body's Decisions in the EU Legal Order', in E. Cannizzaro, P. Palchetti and R. Wessel (eds.), *International Law as Law of the European Union* (Leiden: Martinus Nijhoff, 2011); A. Tancredi, 'EC Practice in the WTO: How Wide Is the "Scope of Manoeuvre?"' (2004) 15 *European Journal of International Law* 933.

[34] Case C-369/90 *Mario Vicente Micheletti and others* v. *Delegación del Gobierno en Cantabria* [1992] ECR I-4239. For an analysis in the context of international law, see e.g. D. Kochenov, '*Ius Tractum* of Many Faces: EU Citizenship and a Difficult Relationship between Status and Rights' (2009) 15 *Columbia Journal of European Law* 169 (181–2).

[35] Case C-402/05 P and C-415/05 P *Kadi and Al Barakaat International Foundation* v. *Council and Commission* [2008] ECR I-6351. J. Kokott and C. Sobotta, 'The *Kadi* Case – Constitutional Core Values and International Law – Finding the Balance?' (2012) 23 *European Journal of International Law* 1015.

[36] For criticism, see e.g. G. de Búrca, 'The European Court of Justice and the International Legal Order after *Kadi*' (2010) 51 *Harvard International Law Journal* 44.

[37] J. H. H. Weiler, 'The Community System: The Dual Character of Supranationalism' (1981) 1 *Yearbook of European Law* 267.

been changed profoundly, we argue, since the moment the EU assumed an active role on the international scene.

It is submitted that the role of the EU is only likely to increase in this regard: the Union's mission and economic power – it is still the largest economy in the world by all counts, the times of crisis notwithstanding – all suggest that its influence as a shaper of the international legal order is bound to grow. In particular, its reluctance (or incapacity) to rely on raw power, leaves it with one option: like the Low Countries of the time of Hugo Grotius, to reshape the legal field. Indeed, the EU's very *raison d'être*, rooted in the history of the European integration project and aptly expressed in the objectives of the Treaties and the principles establishing its place in the world,[38] seem to suggest – quite strongly and convincingly – that a more important engagement with the development of international law could be expected of it.

2 Structure of the work

The task given to the authors contributing to this book was not to construct, but to analyse. The main premise, which the editors defend, is that the new, active approach to the role played by the EU in the international legal order flows naturally from the current position of the Union in the world, and is particularly visible in the context of the EU's external action during the last two decades, as Gráinne de Búrca explains in her contribution. The book's structure sets out to illustrate and to test the idea of the EU's active engagement with the world. Correspondingly, the work splits into three Parts. Part I provides some theoretical background for the special role played by the Union in the context of international relations and law, focusing on the Union's potential and means to function as an active co-shaper of its international environment. It is demonstrated that expecting just outcomes of the Union (its *nature non-Étatique* notwithstanding) – including redistributive ones – is not only possible and logically sound, but also necessary[39] – and that the Union's very *raison d'être*, particularly as rethought and reassessed during the ongoing economic crisis, supports this vision.[40] Moreover, this is also reflected in numerous provisions of the Treaties, analysed in a

[38] For a meticulous study of these in a comparative context, see the chapter by Joris Larik in this volume.
[39] See the chapter by Andrew Williams in this volume.
[40] See the chapter by Gráinne de Búrca in this volume.

comparative perspective.[41] To be sure, whether the Union actually lives up to this vision is a different matter open for debate.[42]

Part II supplies eight concrete case studies of the EU's activities in the context of its attempts to shape the international legal order in a wide array of diverse areas of importance. Such case studies are intended to test the active paradigm of the EU's external relations, including the scrutiny of the ethical side of the EU's action in areas such as development of international law on the recognition of states,[43] international approaches to energy law[44] and climate change,[45] including energy sustainability,[46] WTO dispute resolution[47] and patterns of global migration.[48]

Part III, which is a natural continuation of the Part II, is distinguished for its special focus: it examines the world financial architecture and some steps the Union attempted to take in order to promote world financial stability in the time of crisis.[49] The crisis, as often happens, offers plentiful opportunities besides triggering negative consequences. EU institutions are very well aware of this: essentially important proposals of a systemic nature are being circulated now, in times of crisis, which will be shaping the Union for the years to come.[50] The EU's external engagement is not an exception in this regard. So besides the Fiscal Compact,[51] which, as of itself, will also have external implications, important reform suggestions are tabled belonging de facto, if not *de jure*, to the field of world economic and financial governance,[52] such as the introduction of a tax on financial transactions.[53] At the same time, the

[41] See the chapter by Joris Larik in this volume.
[42] See the concluding chapter in this volume.
[43] See the chapter by Steven Blockmans in this volume.
[44] See the chapter by Peter Van Elsuwege in this volume.
[45] See the chapter by Christina Eckes in this volume.
[46] See the chapter by Anatole Boute in this volume.
[47] See the chapter by Tilman Krüger in this volume.
[48] See the chapter by Laure Delcour in this volume.
[49] See the chapter by Jan Wouters, Sven Van Kerckhoven and Thomas Ramopoulos in this volume.
[50] E.g. M. Poiares Maduro, 'A New Governance for the European Union and the Euro: Democracy and Justice', Robert Schuman Centre for Advanced Studies (RSCAS) Policy Papers No. 2012/11 (2012).
[51] Treaty on Stability, Coordination and Governance in the Economic and Monetary Union, signed 2 March 2012. See e.g. P. Craig, 'The Stability, Coordination and Governance Treaty: Principle, Politics and Pragmatism' (2012) 37 *European Law Review* 231.
[52] See the chapter by Christoph Ohler in this volume.
[53] See the chapter by Van Vooren in this volume.

crisis has also brought the redistributive function of the EU back on the agenda, creating tensions between the Member States and questioning some the assumptions of solidarity taken for granted until very recently.

2.1 The Mechanics of the active paradigm

The basic idea of the EU's shaping of the international legal order, embracing an active paradigm of the study of this organization's engagement with the world, can only be accepted once three questions are answered. The first is what is the *raison d'être* of the EU – and how far the organization is designed to take on such an active role? The second is whether taking up such a role can seriously be expected at all of the Union, which is not a state, thus facing numerous issues related to the feasibility of conceiving it as a space of justice and expecting ethical outcomes of its activities. The third concerns the black-letter law of the EU itself: once its rationale in the context of external action, as well as its ability, from a legal–philosophical point of view, to generate just outcomes and to be a space of justice are proven, turning to the Treaties is indispensable. Part I of the book focuses on these three issues, preparing the ground for the case studies that follow.

In Chapter 1 Gráinne de Búrca traces the main lines of development of EU law with one main question in mind: what is the EU for? The answer has been evolving rapidly as the Union moves from crisis to crisis. All the story of European integration can be presented as Europe's gradual opening up to the world: from an inward-looking, purely regional organization aiming at achieving concrete objectives for the Member States to the current state of integration where the external component is rapidly gaining in importance both internally – as a potential provider of legitimacy – and externally. It took the EU fifty years to mature to occupy the position of a potential shaper of the international legal environment – and its influence will only grow when the current economic crisis – the most problematic in the Union's history – is overcome.

Once the essential place of the external dimension at the current stage of the Union's development has been clarified, an array of theoretical and also practical issues arises. In Chapter 2 Andrew Williams addresses some of these outstanding issues and approaches the EU from a legal–philosophical perspective to demonstrate that it is possible to theorize this organization as a plausible vehicle of interim global justice, viewing it as being capable of playing a role of a primary agent of justice with the capacity to assume distributive duties. Indeed, defending the EU's capability to be viewed in this light opens up the way to expect of it the openness to the idea of justice, which can alone – raw power and pure *Realpolitik* aside – establish the EU as a determining force in the development of the international legal order. Williams chooses distributive justice as a starting point to demonstrate that the EU can indeed be so regarded. Besides the underlying philosophy of EU law, the chapter is perceptive of the practice of the EU's Institutions, and is thus fully grounded in reality. The chapter builds a continuum of stages of interim global justice, proceeding from Thomas Nagel's 'political' understanding of distributive justice on to the 'cosmopolitan' idea in the vein of Kwame Anthony Appaiah. Crucially, so theorized, the EU is much closer to the 'cosmopolitan' understanding than many critics would presume, raising our expectations of it as a promoter of justice on the world stage.

In Chapter 3 Joris Larik examines the primary law of the EU, analysing the legal effects of the binding objectives directly related to the EU's activities vis-à-vis the international legal order deploying a comparative perspective of the scrutiny of such objectives in modern jurisprudence in Europe and beyond. The chapter demonstrates beyond any reasonable doubt that shaping the international legal order is among the legal foundations of the integration project as it stands to date, thus amounting to one of its *raisons d'être*. Moreover, the growing number, as well as the detailed nature, of the Treaty provisions with external implications in the EU is fully in line with the legal developments in other jurisdictions. Particular attention in the chapter is paid to the analysis of the German and French doctrines regarding the legal effects and nature of such constitutional norms – *Staatszielbestimmungen* and *objectifs de valeur constitutionnelle* – only to demonstrate that dismissing them as pure declarations would be entirely premature. They play an essential role in the functioning of the respective legal systems and the EU is not an exception, merely reflecting a global phenomenon in the constitutionalization of external action and influence. Crucially, the chapter makes it clear that the pursuit of the external objectives is binding on the Union, which places its external influence at the core of the *acquis*: the Union is *obliged by law* to strive to shape the international legal order along the lines of its own principles and values.

2.2 The case studies

Parts II and III essentially set out to test the robustness of the theoretical evidence provided in favour of the active paradigm for the study of the

EU's engagement with the world by analysing the EU's actual role in a number of vital fields of international law and policy, examining whether and to what extent the actual influence of the EU in the international sphere coincides with what may be expected against the background of the multifaceted legal–theoretical analysis offered in Part I. Both institutional and substantive aspects of the EU's engagement with international law and policies are covered.

The testing of the main hypothesis starts off with Chapter 4, where Ester Heriln-Karnell scrutinizes the EU's role and ability in projecting its values to the international legal order – an activity that the Union views as closely related to its greater ambition of ensuring justice in its neighbourhood and beyond. The chapter approaches the EU's function as a global agent of values both from a theoretical and from a purely practical perspective, by looking at the values-related provisions in primary law and their deployment by the ECJ. The value promotion is theorized in the context of global constitutionalism. The role of the Lisbon Treaty, which reinforced the normative legal framework of the EU's values-promotion, is particularly underlined.

The embrace of value-laden approaches by the EU in its external relations might seem problematic from the point of view of justice, as it essentially blurs the lines between what is external and what is internal, thus threatening to result in a simple export of the *acquis*, albeit spiced-up with value-rhetoric, to third countries, having no regard to their approaches to the moral–political issues, which the EU value system touches upon. In this context – from the abolition of the death penalty to a particular vision of human rights protection – the EU has no claim to neutrality. What we are frequently dealing with is the use of values as a vehicle to transplant European vision and approaches to the international scene. While this is not necessarily a bad thing, the fact that values rhetoric might be an inadequate reflection of the ongoing processes should nevertheless be taken into account. The EU thus acts as a norm entrepreneur, at times fusing the internal and the external aspects of its law under the guise of values, using them as a potent tool to transform the international legal order.

In Chapter 5 Laurent Pech continues the values story by providing a detailed case study of the EU's external engagement with one central value, namely the rule of law. Pech argues that although the EU did not actually shape the global formulation of the rule of law, it plays an essential part in its global promotion, having adopted a broad, holistic understanding of the principle. Although the norm building as such in this particular case is not a success story, its diffusion at the global scene is a different matter and deserves equal attention. What is of particular importance in Pech's analysis is the demonstration that the rule of law as promoted and embraced by the Union goes beyond a formalistic vision, thus taking on a tint of value when its substance is scrutinized. A number of legal principles are promoted by the EU as essential elements of the rule of law concept, including legality, respect and protection of human rights, non-discrimination and others.

Testing the EU's involvement in other areas demonstrates, however, that the EU is not only good with the diffusion of rules – like in the case of the rule of law – but also shapes them in the context of the international legal order quite efficiently. The Union's involvement in the shaping of the international rules on the recognition of states, analysed by Steven Blockmans in Chapter 6 is a perfect illustration of this claim. Blockmans shows that the EU, through its law and practice, has directly affected the current international legal rules on statehood. In other words, the active paradigm of the EU's external relations law reaches as far as the creation of the primary subjects of international law, i.e. states. Notwithstanding the fact that the EU, as an international organization, is not directly involved in the recognition or non-recognition of states, it has been taking part in shaping the international rules on statehood at least since the disintegration of the Soviet Union and the armed conflict in the former Yugoslavia.

The Union introduced additional conditions for the entities seeking recognition as states, which are not only reflected in political documents such as its Guidelines on the Recognition of New States and the Declaration on Yugoslavia but have been applied in practice by the ad hoc Badinter Arbitration Commission, dealing with the claims to recognition by the states of the former Yugoslavia. Besides the additional criteria, which the EU de facto added to the Montevideo Convention rules – including minority protection and good neighbourly relations – the Union also *de jure* recognized the right of federal entities to secession, which is of essential importance in the context of the development of international law of statehood. The chapter tests its claims in the contemporary context of EU relations with Abkhazia, South Ossetia and the Palestinian Authority, coming to a conclusion that the rules formulated by the Badinter Arbitration Commission hold, making them part of international law. The EU has thus been very successful in the promotion of what Blockmans regards as the 'Europeanization' of the international law on statehood, standing behind the new 'Montevideo-plus' conditions. The EU's engagement with the international law on statehood is thus an ideal example of a successful shaping of the international legal rules by the Union.

Another such example – and another way in which the Union deploys active engagement to promote its vision of the international legal order – is assessed by Tilman Krüger in Chapter 7, which focuses on the Union's efforts of judicialization of international trade through strategic litigation behaviour in the World Trade Organization (WTO). The chapter demonstrates that acting as a litigant the EU is very successful in reshaping the organization in the context when further multilateral negotiations are unlikely to bring desired outcomes. To come to the conclusions concerning the EU's effective involvement in the rule development at the WTO through litigation, Krüger analyses two examples: the recognition of precedent within the WTO system and opening the Appellate Body hearings to the public. Both demonstrate that the EU made important contributions to the institutional evolution of the WTO and to the judicialization of world trade, thus, arguably, attempting to reshape the WTO in its own image. The fact that the EU selects its arguments with the shaping of long-term systemic outcomes for the build-up of the WTO in mind proves the long-term vision demonstrated by the EU when acting within the WTO context.

A trio of case studies that follows concentrates on global EU leadership in environmental and energy matters providing a complex but telling example of the active engagement paradigm at work. Chapter 8 deals with the EU's global climate change policy. Christina Eckes explains in detail how the EU emerged as a leading actor in this field on the international stage. From Kyoto on, the EU made numerous attempts to promote climate change mitigation globally, embracing a number of modi operandi – from multilateral negotiations to the familiar de facto export of the *acquis* through the European Union Emissions Trading Scheme (EU ETS). As a result, besides some controversies that arose in front of the ECJ, the EU ensured that first important steps are taken in the direction of addressing the negative consequences of climate change through a 'unilateral way to multilateralism', as Eckes calls it. Undoubtedly, the EU has been the leading force behind the establishment of the international greenhouse reduction regime, thus opening up a new vista of international law, which is not only of overwhelming importance, but also of great moral appeal, as the only reason behind it is the prevention of a climate disaster. The design of the scheme of international regulation, which emerged from EU efforts, is very much reminiscent of the EU's internal approaches to solving outstanding problems, i.e. governing through targets and technocratic market regulation. Although numerous burning issues remain unsolved, including the problem of 'carbon debt' and finding the right balance between idealistic and economic factors in climate mitigation policies, the role played by the EU in the global climate law field is absolutely crucial.

A similar vector of the EU's engagement – probably with less articulated global results – emerges also in the context of the establishment of international approaches to energy law analysed by Peter Van Elsuwege in Chapter 9, which argues that the EU adopted a 'rule-based market approach'. As in the context of climate change mitigation and WTO judicialization, the Union went to great lengths to ensure that a binding legal regime is in place. In promoting such a regime, great emphasis was put by the Union on the export of the *acquis* to neighbouring countries and further afield, with the aim of developing legally binding rules based on the EU's approaches and ideology. While this works well with relatively weak countries and with nations sharing the essential constitutive values of the EU, in the context of other states important problems arise, subjecting the dominant approaches embraced by the Union to the test.

The Russian Federation – the EU's crucial and inescapable energy partner – is an almost proverbial example of how this happens in practice. Refusing to be on the receiving end of the EU's norm transplantation exercise, Russia poses an important challenge, which is one of the focuses of Van Elsuwege's case study. More important still, the EU's engagements in the field of energy also cause *internal* frictions, which have implications for the external energy policy of the Union and the shaping of the international legal order in this field. Lastly, the energy field also opens a Pandora's box of ethical problems – particularly when achieving the EU's objectives of energy security, no matter what is laid bare, which is too evident in its relations with the energy-rich Central Asian dictatorships, such as Turkmenistan or Azerbaijan. Human rights concerns and the idea of the promotion of EU values clearly take a back seat, and standard EU approaches do not work. All in all, Russia, Turkmenistan, Saudi Arabia etc. apart, the EU has been struggling to upload its own *acquis* to the international level where regulation in the energy field has been scarce.

Anatole Boute, in Chapter 10 continues the energy–climate theme, bridging the perspectives presented by Eckes and Van Elsuwege through focusing on the issue of energy efficiency. Given that the amount of energy wasted – particularly outside of the EU – defies imagination, undermining climate change mitigation efforts and European energy security concerns, this field plays an increasingly important role. In addition, here the EU is actively shaping international law at a number of levels, from its activities within the G8 to constant attempts to upload its *acquis* to the international level, besides de facto introducing this issue to the global agenda. The beauty of the stated goals notwithstanding, the EU's *Realpolitik* constantly shines through, which does not undermine the fact that energy efficiency policy, if efficiently and consistently implemented on the global stage, could help bridge the divide between the developed and developing worlds and assist climate change mitigation. An essential point to be kept in mind when discussing all the energy- and climate change-related aspects of the EU's global engagement is the issue of the EU's carbon debt to the rest of the world, introducing a huge moral responsibility into the picture.

While acting in line with what moral considerations demand yet reaching geo-strategic goals could be legitimately expected of the Union in light of the findings of Part I, the EU equally demonstrates an ability to act almost entirely ignoring its own proclaimed principles and values for the sake of short-term political considerations with no greater interests in mind. The EU does this too. Chapter 11 focuses on a field where this is the case: Laure Delcour analyses the EU's influence on global migration regulation. Although the EU is active in attempting to shape migration law mostly in its periphery, in particular in the Eastern Partnership countries and the Southern Mediterranean, its policies have immediate implications for global approaches to migration. This area, which is overwhelmingly politicized, offers an example of the most ethically problematic and morally unjustifiable engagement of the Union with the world and has only one goal: to ensure that no migrants from the third world reach its shores. This policy, besides damaging the development of 'fortress Europe' as such, also costs many lives and is responsible for unreasonable multiplication of human misery in the EU's periphery and beyond. Worse still, in its external relations the EU does not appear to tolerate approaches to migration that are more liberal than its own, thus requiring its neighbouring countries to alter their regulation of migration in the direction of intolerance and closed borders.

Delcour's analysis builds on the example of Georgia to illustrate this point and comes to a conclusion that the EU assigns a clear function to the poor countries in its periphery, using them as a *cordon sanitaire* and a 'dumping ground' for unwanted human material – frequently in violation of the European Convention on Human Rights (ECHR) and its own human rights obligations as well as the values its Treaties proclaim.

The EU's influence on global migration rules is thus a purely negative one, securitizing borders and stigmatizing migrants from the global south, combined with the uploading of such approaches to the legal systems of the countries in the EU's neighbourhood. In essence, however, just as in the cases of energy law and climate change mitigation the EU's approaches to global migration evolve around the idea of the export of the *acquis*.

While it may be envisaged that the inclusion of such diverse policy fields will result in a rather mosaic-like picture, the outcome of the sectorial assessment of the EU's engagement with particular parts of the international legal order clearly allows for the conclusion that the hypothesis offered in Part I stands not only from a theoretical perspective, but also in practical terms.

2.3 Europe's stance on the global economic and financial crisis

The contributions of the last part of the book focus on the EU's role in the shaping of global economic and financial (market) governance. Indeed, the global economic and financial crisis and the subsequent euro area debt crisis have dragged the external dimension of economic and monetary union and financial market regulation from the shadows of other policy areas traditionally more directly linked to external relations and put them right at the centre of the EU's activities. Given the vast economic and societal implications of the global financial instability, as well as the apparent difficulties arising in the context of the attempts to tame the crisis, the question that arises is whether the EU is punching at its weight.

Christoph Ohler in Chapter 12 examines the role of the EU in standard setting in the field of international financial regulation. The challenges, which the EU and its Member States, as well as all other countries forming part of the global financial marketplace face, have clearly surfaced in the wake of the global economic and financial crisis. As Ohler points out, the international scope, the network nature and the risks involved make financial markets a natural arena for international standard setting. While the liberalization of the free movement of capital lagged behind, already in the past the European Community could be seen taking a keen interest, albeit with an observer status, in international standard-setting networks. With the establishment of an internal financial (service) market and the founding of the Economic and Monetary Union the EU has become a major factor contributing to the (in)stability of the global financial system. Ohler's contribution clearly makes the case for financial stability as an international public good, whereby he readily admits that agreeing on the principles is easier than agreeing on the actual path effectively to implement it. This is not only because of the frequent disagreements on the economic effects of certain measures, or because of conflicts of (economic) interests, but at the EU level is also due to what Ohler refers to as 'the limits of the (European) regulatory state'.[54] What is more, Ohler argues, integrated global financial markets are not matched by a system of international burden sharing, a problem he also diagnoses for the EU. In other words, while the EU's (de-)stabilizing global influence here is overwhelming, its actual role in solving the problems that arise leaves much to be desired.

Wouters, Van Kerckhoven and Ramopoulos in Chapter 13 dive deeper into the active role of the EU in international economic governance thereby focusing on the International Monetary Fund (IMF). Their contribution examines the leeway that primary Union law, as amended by the Treaty of Lisbon, gives in pursuing Union or euro area interests at the level of the IMF. The authors examine whether the EU is equipped with 'the legal tools to improve the effectiveness, visibility and coherence of its external representation'[55] that is currently hampered by the individual representation of EU Member States at the level of the IMF. With regard to the latter, the authors argue that the EU is overrepresented in terms of voting share, but underrepresented in terms of impact and effectiveness. Primary Union law in the view of the authors may provide the possibilities for a single euro area representation. However, the IMF Articles of Agreement, geared towards the participation of countries, constitute a major obstacle for such a development, if upheld in their present form. In this context, the authors cast doubts on the legal feasibility of a single euro area seat that would improve the visibility and negotiation position of the European single currency area.

Bart Van Vooren in Chapter 14 completes the *tour d'horizon* of the EU's role in global economic and financial governance by focusing on the EU's activities in one area of international financial regulation that has recently resulted in heated debates of an at times dogmatic nature, that is the initiative for the establishment of a global or at least European financial transaction tax (FTT). Van Vooren highlights the EU's initial efforts towards the establishing of such a tax across the whole territory of the EU and the plans to make use of the momentum arising from such an

[54] Ohler's chapter in this volume, p. 301.
[55] The chapter by Wouters, Van Kerckhoven and Ramopoulos in this volume, p. 307.

initiative to push for a global legal regime. However, despite the potentially positive impact of such a tax on legitimizing the EU both internally and externally as an international value-inspired actor, the contribution draws the picture of a highly politicized and controversial issue that has driven a wedge not only between the EU and its international counterparts but also between the Member States that are split about the costs and benefits of such a measure. For Van Vooren the FTT serves as an example of the ambitious political agenda embraced by the EU with regard to the shaping of the international legal order. If this is so, what derives from his analysis is that such aspirations do not necessarily receive undivided backing from the Union's Member States, nor from the international community.

PART I

The EU's shaping of the international legal order: the mechanics

1

Europe's *raison d'être*

GRÁINNE DE BÚRCA

1 Introduction

What is the *raison d'être* of the European Union? Does it still make sense to ask this question today? Launched in 1952 as a kind of pilot project of limited economic integration with a view to securing greater peace and prosperity for its Member States, the EU has evolved into something much larger, more complex and more ambitious. This chapter argues, contrary to the recent suggestion of an influential commentator,[1] that the question of the EU's mission or *raison d'être* still matters today, and not only because of the serious economic crisis in which it has been mired since 2007. I argue that while the European Union at its origin was primarily inwardly focused on repairing and strengthening a damaged continent so as to deliver internal peace and prosperity, it has become as much or more concerned today with its external dimension, namely with enhancing Europe's global economic and political influence and role. That is not to say either that the external dimension of European integration was unimportant at the time the Community was first created or that internal peace and prosperity have ceased to be central concerns in the present day. Far from it. Nevertheless, the last two decades in particular have brought a more sustained focus on the external and global significance of European integration. When the question of Europe's *raison d'être* is raised today, the importance of having a relatively unified European political system to counterbalance the influence of other existing and rising powers has become a more significant part of the answer than was ever previously the case.

An earlier version of this chapter was delivered as the John Maurice Kelly Memorial Lecture at University College Dublin in May 2012, at the Academy of European Law in July 2012 and the workshop of the European Constitutional Law Network at NYU in October 2012. Thanks are due to the participants at those events for their input and feedback, and also to Kalypso Nicolaïdis and Dimitry Kochenov for their comments.

[1] J. H. H. Weiler '60 Years since the First European Community: Reflections on Messianism' (2011) 22 *European Journal of International Law* 303.

2 After the economic crisis

It is just over sixty years since the coming into being of the European Coal and Steel Community when the first foundation stones of the European Union were laid. During that time, the EU has enjoyed periods of success as well as periods of stagnation or decline, and an uneven if always dynamic process of transnational integration. The term 'crisis' has been applied at many points in time to describe the state of affairs in the EU, including the 'empty chair' policy of 1965 when France abandoned its seat in the Council of Ministers for six months, the severe economic impact of the Arab oil embargo on European states in 1973, the first Danish 'no' vote in a referendum on the Maastricht Treaty in 1992, and the rejection by the French and Dutch populations of the Constitutional Treaty in referendums in 2005. Yet few would disagree that the crisis which began to unfold in the European Union from 2007 on has been of a different scale and severity than any previous crisis.

The economic maelstrom convulsing the EU since that time has unquestionably been the most severe and profound crisis which the European integration project has confronted in its sixty years of existence. It has even been framed at various stages as an existential crisis: a question of whether not only Europe's currency, the euro, but even the EU itself could survive the wrenching economic circumstances brought about by a banking crisis followed by a sovereign debt crisis. And the unfolding of the crisis, with all the uncertainty, has brought doubts about the viability of the single currency and the future of the European Union; and all the economic pain and hardship it has brought has focused attention again on the original question of what purpose the EU actually serves.

For many decades before that, the European Union experiment, despite its various challenges, was widely considered to represent a significant achievement on many levels. In Joseph Weiler's terms, it had delivered on its most important foundational goals: primarily those of bringing peace and prosperity to the European continent.[2] In terms of peace, not only had it bound the states of Europe post-Second World War into a close political compact which made war between them virtually impossible, but it had also by the end of the century achieved another of its early goals, namely

[2] J. H. H. Weiler, 'Europe after Maastricht: Do the New Clothes Have an Emperor?', Jean Monnet Working Paper No. 12 (1995). Weiler also referred to 'supranationality' as the third of the EU's foundational ideals, by which he meant a notion of community rather than 'unity', a novel transnational arrangement that is neither state nor international organization, and that avoids many of the vices of statehood.

the reuniting of Eastern and Western Europe after the fall of the Iron Curtain. In terms of prosperity, it had, through the single European market and greater mobility of labour, goods and capital – as well as its cohesion funds – improved the standard of living for many Europeans and strengthened the economies of EU Member States.[3] It had also challenged the unbridled European nationalism of the first half of the twentieth century by introducing a novel form of transnational cooperation. It was something, which was neither as thin as traditional international co-operation and diplomacy nor as demanding as a unified federal state, which would encourage the development of political trust, common interests and the habits of constant close cooperation between European states even while not subduing their individual national identities.[4]

The path of European integration was far from smooth, although it has been suggested that it was precisely the kinds of ongoing crises mentioned above – the empty-chair policy, the political stagnation of the 1970s, the failure of the Constitutional Treaty and so on – that galvanized other important reforms. Thus the political crisis and the empty-chair policy of the 1960s may have encouraged the ECJ to continue promoting the ideas of direct effect and primacy which have been central to the European legal construction.[5] The period of legislative and policy stagnation of the 1970s arguably galvanized plans for the Single European Act and later economic and monetary union; the coming to power of Jörg Haider and his extremely right-wing Freedom Party in Austria in 1999 helped to catalyse the beginnings of a real EU human rights policy; the failure of the Constitutional Treaty in 2005 led to stronger political resolve on the adoption of the Lisbon Treaty and so on. But the past decade and a half has seen more fundamental and persistent challenges, particularly

[3] For an influential argument that the real motivating factor behind the process of European integration was its 'rescue' of economically damaged nation states, see A. Milward, *The European Rescue of the Nation State* (Abingdon: Routledge, 1994).

[4] This was what Weiler referred to as the European ideal of supranationality. J. H. H. Weiler, '60 Years since the First European Community'. Philip Allott, in turn, described the real achievement of the European Community as its 'democratizing of the international relations of Western Europe' whereby 'international relations would be transcended, surpassed, and replaced with a new kind of democratic process. The essence of the European Community is not a federalizing of the Member States, still less a confederalizing endeavour. The essence is the democratizing, that is to say the communalizing, of the *inter se* relations of the peoples of Europe'. P. Allott, 'The European Community is not the True European Community' (1991) 100 *Yale Law Journal* 2485.

[5] P. Craig, 'Once Upon a Time in the West: Direct Effect and the Federalization of EC Law' (1992) 12 *Oxford Journal of Legal Studies* 453 (456–70).

the spread of Euroscepticism, the emergence of anti-European parties and the marked rise of the extreme right across Europe.

But it has been the severity of Europe's current economic crisis that has particularly focused attention again on the underlying question of what the European Union and the European integration project is for today. If it was clear in the post-war period that the goals of economic revival and peaceful cooperation underpinned the project, it seems much less evident, sixty years on, how the *raison d'être* of the EU today should be articulated. And that seems particularly stark in the present circumstances, given that the complex and painful task of pulling the EU and the Member States out of the present crisis will be an even more difficult one to accomplish if the various peoples of Europe and the citizens of EU Member States lack a sense of what the EU and the process of integration are for.[6] Instead of a focus on what kinds of policies and changes are needed to move the EU forward and out of its present economic distress and instability, the question that many of Europe's citizens have been asking during the last three years of hardship, austerity and political conflict has been: why should such changes be made? Why should people suffer unemployment, economic hardship and austerity in order to 'save' the euro and the European Union? In this way, the economic crisis has brought the question of the EU's *raison d'être* into focus.

When the Schuman Declaration was signed in 1950 and when the European Coal and Steel Treaty was drafted, the project of European integration had a conventionally understood political, economic and security dimension. The political dimension, the idea of having a more united European continent, was in part a response to the wars which had divided and shattered Europe – the idea of binding France and Germany together into a close and irreversible political community; the *economic* impetus was to stimulate and reinvigorate the damaged post-war economies of Europe, to bring about the benefits of closer trade and shared

[6] Kalypso Nicolaïdis and Justine Lacroix in the Introduction to their book *European Stories* have pointed out that Europe as a continent and an idea has quite distinct meanings for the various peoples of Europe, and that the intellectual debates on the European Union take a very different shape in different Member States. Yet, despite this undeniable and rich diversity of narratives about the meaning and significance of Europe and the EU within different states and amongst different communities, it is nonetheless the case that there has been a general broadly shared understanding across much of Europe that the political purpose of the post-war project of integration was about securing a degree of peace and economic prosperity for the continent. K. Nicolaïdis and J. Lacroix, *European Stories* (Oxford University Press, 2011).

markets and to benefit from the economies of scale of a single market. And there was a *security* (and hence at least partly external) dimension too, including the construction of a united Europe in the face of the perceived threat of the Soviet Union at the time. The benefit of each of these three dimensions was felt to varying degrees over the sixty years since the ECSC treaty was signed. Ireland, Greece, Spain, Portugal and other states enjoyed some of these benefits for many years before their economic woes of recent years erupted. Europe, for all its troubles and challenges, became a more prosperous, peaceful and politically integrated continent than it had been for many centuries.

3 Questioning the *raison d'être* of the EU

There are three related reasons why the EU's *raison d'être*, which seemed relatively clear and uncontroversial for much of its early history – even if it did not spark great enthusiasm amongst the European population – seems to be in question again today:

(a) The first concerns the relative success of the EU in delivering peace and prosperity for some years. It seems that some of these achievements of European integration – and particularly the 'peace dividend' – came to be taken for granted, perhaps not even really associated any longer with the existence of the EU. Consequently, the EU may no longer be seen as important for ensuring peaceful relations between European states.

(b) The second and related reason is that this taken-for-grantedness of the EU and what it has achieved has not sufficed to give the EU the kind of legitimacy that states (whose achievements are arguably also taken for granted) enjoy. There are times when the people are angry with conditions within their nation state, but the anger is generally directed at the government of the day, and not at the existence of the state itself. States as political entities generally enjoy a basic degree of popular support and legitimacy. The reason for their existence is normally taken for granted in the absence of some major calamity, or a call for secession or independence, as for example in the case of Scotland, Quebec or Kosovo. States are political communities whose legitimacy and *raison d'être* are not generally called into question. The attachment felt by citizens to their national political communities does not, however, seem to apply to their relationship as citizens of the EU, perhaps in part because of the recently created and rather formal legal status of

EU citizenship. For all that EU integration may have delivered in the past on various dimensions of peace and prosperity, its existence and its desirability as a political entity has not been accepted or internalized by the peoples of Europe. On the contrary, the questions what it is for, why it exists, why states should adopt European policies or citizens should follow EU laws, remain very much alive. The EU's legitimacy seems to remain a kind of performance-based legitimacy, deriving from its ability to 'deliver the goods'. Rather than gaining political legitimacy and acceptance as an entity which has helped to create a peaceful and united continent, it has remained a political entity always in question; always required to justify its existence.

(c) The third and related reason for the EU's *raison d'être* being in question again today is what has been outlined above: namely the nature and severity of the crisis in which the EU finds itself at present. The situation today is one in which the 'prosperity' enjoyed for some decades by many EU Member States has been severely undermined. More specifically, it is not just that the EU is failing to deliver prosperity, but on the contrary it is seen to be actively imposing austerity and hardship. The EU is perceived today as one of the agents of socio-economic distress, and a significant causal factor in the nature and degree of economic and social pain being felt in many European states, including Spain, Greece, Ireland and others. By iron-casting the requirements of balanced budgets and debt-reduction, and in the absence of deflationary options, EU policies strictly limit the options of states facing growing unemployment and low or no growth, and the EU is seen to be worsening the social and economic conditions of its citizens.

In other words, the EU has moved from its founding period during which the *raison d'être* question could be clearly and relatively uncontroversially answered (the delivery of peace and prosperity) to one in which it is considerably less clear. Not being a nation state, and lacking the common bonds of culture, history and language enjoyed by many states, the EU has also not evolved into the kind of cohesive political community whose polity legitimacy has been put beyond question. And, finally, the current economic crisis has put the process of European integration in question again in a different and more acute way. At the current time, European integration is seen to have become the problem or at least a part of the problem, both for those who are suffering from the social and economic effects of austerity policies and for those in more prosperous states who are concerned that they will be expected to bail out indebted countries. To quote the words of Finnish Foreign Minister Alexander Stubb, who pointed out that the crisis has certainly brought the EU closer to its citizens, but not in the way it had always hoped to do: 'when [the euro crisis] hits your wallet and when you're going to have to bail out other countries, then suddenly the EU becomes a hell of a lot more interesting!'[7]

It might be argued in response that although the German-, IMF- and ECB-driven austerity policies adopted to respond to the banking and sovereign debt crises in various EU Member States has exacerbated significant social and economic pain, this is not the same thing as identifying the EU or European integration itself as the primary cause of the current crisis. The causes of the crisis are complex and multiple, and they include inadequate regulation of the banking sector, excessive speculation, in some cases significant public sector overspending and a lack of trust in relation to the compliance by some states with the stability pact rules underlying the euro. Yet even if the root causes of the economic crisis lie in part elsewhere, it is incontrovertible that the EU has now significantly limited the remedial measures (such as deflation which is impossible due to euro membership) that the hardest hit states can take to improve their economic situation, and that it is the EU which is imposing significant fiscal austerity.

We seem to be confronted with at least two different possible directions ahead. One is the path of closer integration, and at the other end of the spectrum is the possibility of gradual disintegration. The disintegration option includes the default scenario where the conditions imposed by the EU or the IMF would become impossible or unacceptable to a state and it leaves the euro, with all the consequences that that would have for the state in question and for the rest of the EU (and beyond). Greece certainly hovered for many months during 2011 and 2012 on the brink of this option, and the political and social reaction within Greece to the extreme consequences of the austerity policy may even now still push the country towards exit. The closer integration option, on the other hand, which is the path that has so far been tentatively pursued by the EU, is to move further in the direction of fiscal and political union

[7] See The Brookings Institution, Will Europe Survive the Crisis?: A Statesman's Forum with Alexander Stubb, Finnish Minister for European Affairs and Foreign Trade, Washington, DC, 12 March 2012, Proceedings available at www.brookings.edu/~/media/events/2012/3/12%20stubb/20120312_stubb.

with the declared aim of building common safeguards against the occurrence of the kinds of situation, which gave rise to the crisis in the first place. Thus the Fiscal Treaty was adopted to give the Commission a stronger monitoring and supervisory role in relation to national fiscal policies,[8] the European Stability Mechanism was established as a lender-of-last-resort for EU Member States in financial trouble,[9] and steps towards banking union have been taken with the decision on the creation of a single banking supervision mechanism in December 2012. So far they have been incremental rather than dramatic steps, with significant opposition remaining to the idea of a stronger political union or a fiscal transfer union.

Yet even as the starkest disintegration/default option has become less of an immediate prospect, the likelihood of fragmentation and further weakening of the European project remains a very real one despite these gradual moves towards closer forms of integration. It may be true that for many Europeans the disintegration option would be an unwelcome one, not only because of the likely undoing of the whole project of European integration and the good that it brought, but also because of the immediate and medium-term economic upheaval and pain that the break-up of the EU would bring. Yet, on the other hand, the proposal to move instead towards closer integration, the idea of strengthening the EU by establishing a genuine fiscal and political union, brings us back to the question of the EU's legitimacy and its *raison d'être*. The desire to avoid short- or medium-term economic pain does not furnish a good enough reason in itself to create a permanently closer European political and fiscal union, with all the compromise of national and local autonomy which that would involve. There may be degrees of economic desperation within several European states at present, but that does not provide a compelling enough reason for people to choose deeper and closer European integration. There must be something more to the project of European integration than the avoidance of short-term economic pain if the requisite public support and political justification for closer union

[8] Treaty on Stability, Coordination and Governance in the Economic and Monetary Union, 3 March 2012 (not yet ratified), available at www.european-council.europa.eu/media/579087/treaty.pdf.

[9] Treaty Establishing the European Stability Mechanism, 2 February 2012 (not yet ratified), available at www.european-council.europa.eu/media/582311/05-tesm2.en12.pdf; European Council, Decision of 25 March 2011 amending Article 136 of the Treaty on the Functioning of the European Union with regard to a Stability Mechanism for Member States whose Currency is the euro OJ (2011) L 91.

is to exist. Yet the growth of Euroscepticism and disaffection with the process of European integration even before the economic crisis arose suggests that there is little popular or public consensus on the value of European integration or the *raison d'être* of the EU today.

So let me here identify two different albeit related issues. The first relates to the immediate steps being taken to move forward out of the current crisis. The second concerns the deeper challenge of articulating a broadly shared conception of what the purposes and goals of European integration are in the present day. These are related for the reasons discussed above, namely that it is difficult in the context of the current crisis to contemplate steps towards closer European integration when there is little public acceptance or agreement on what the EU is actually for. As far as the immediate steps out of the crisis are concerned, however, it seems clear that it is damaging for the EU to be associated only or mainly with policies which bring intolerable economic and social hardship for domestic populations, even if these policies are supposedly intended to right some of the wrongs and the mistakes which gave rise to the crisis.[10] It seems very likely that the path of unrelenting austerity, which has so far been pursued, will continue to undermine the prospects for the EU's future as a legitimate political system. Not only does this strategy risk accelerating the process of alienating voters and citizens from the EU, but it also arguably undermines the global perception and reputation of Europe as offering a distinctive and alternative model of welfare capitalism to the variety of deregulated capitalism represented by the US and the other rising model of state capitalism in China and other parts of Asia.[11] In that sense, the current programme of closer European fiscal and political integration, even if incremental as at present, is unlikely to gain public and hence political support if there is not a move away from an unrelieved focus on austerity, and there is not a greater focus on growth, investment and welfare.

Yet even if there is some softening of the strict fiscal discipline pursued by the EU at present, and a greater focus on growth, investment and welfare is introduced, with the EU setting itself on a more publicly

[10] See the recent Caritas report for an account on the socio-economic effects of the crisis in five of the hardest-hit Member States. A. Leahy, et al., *The Impact of the European Crisis* (Brussels: Caritas Europa, 2013), available at www.caritas-europa.org/module/FileLib/CaritasCrisisReport_web.pdf.

[11] For a recent analysis of the prospects for European welfare capitalism, see C. Hay and D. Wincott, *The Political Economy of European Welfare Capitalism* (Basingstoke: Palgrave Macmillan, 2012).

supported path out of the crisis, the position remains as described above. In other words, at best the EU finds itself in a situation where it is not on the brink of disintegration or collapse but where the reason for its existence remains significantly in question. The rise of Euroscepticism and anti-European parties is not the only manifestation of the lack of social support for the EU: also voter apathy, the lack of interest in EU policies and institutions and the ever-decreasing turnout for European Parliament elections testify to the same phenomenon.[12]

4 The sources of polity legitimacy: input, output and mission legitimacy

Let us move, then, from the immediacy of the current crisis to this longer-term, more continuous and underlying malaise of the EU: its weak legitimacy and the lack of a clear *raison d'être*.

In an editorial comment in the *European Journal of International Law* in 2011, Joseph Weiler presented the EU's three major failings as the lack of strong democracy, the lack of capacity and resolve, and the slide in the legitimacy and mobilizing force of the EU and its institutions.[13] He argued that the European Community's founding tendency was to legitimate itself by 'political messianism'. He explained political messianism as the pursuit of a mission (in this case, the Community's three ideals of peace, prosperity and supranationalism) articulated by an elite but not originating in popular consent or ordinary political processes. He compared this founding tendency of the EU to legitimate itself by the pursuit of a mission with the ordinary democratic constitutionalism of modern nation states. The gist of his argument is that this kind of political messianism, however necessary it may have seemed at the outset of the European integration project, is always doomed to collapse, and that if Europe cannot shift the foundations of its legitimacy from the pursuit of ideals to regular process-democracy then it, too, will continue its downward slide. Thus the contrast he draws is between the ordinary democratic constitutionalism of modern states, and the elite ideal-driven project of the European Union polity. His conclusion is that the European Union is doomed to fail if it does not

[12] For a recent analysis, see the special issue of *Journal of Common Market Studies*: S. Usherwood, N. Startin and S. Guerra (eds.), 'Confronting Euroscepticism' (2013) 51 *Journal of Common Market Studies* 1.

[13] Weiler, '60 Years since the First European Community'.

transform itself – or rather, if it does not transform its mode of legitimation – into that of modern democratic constitutional states.

The part of Weiler's argument that is unquestionable is that the EU lacks the robust democratic legitimacy of a nation state and indeed that its popular and social legitimacy has continued to slide over the last two decades. It is also unquestionable, despite the inevitable complications that greater politicization would bring,[14] that the EU needs to strengthen its democratic foundations and processes. What is mistaken, however, in my view, is the idea that the EU's legitimacy should and could be based today simply or primarily on democratic-process legitimacy.

Let me explain why. I suggest that there are three main sources of polity legitimacy on which political systems generally draw.[15] The primary source is input legitimacy (democratic processes), the second is output legitimacy (effective delivery of outcomes), and the third is mission legitimacy. The balance between these three sources varies at different points in time and depending on the characteristics and circumstances of the political system in question. In the case of established democratic states, input legitimacy generally dominates, and the legitimacy of the state rests largely on its democratic political system. Output legitimacy is not, however, irrelevant: it remains in the background mainly because it is generally taken for granted that an effectively functioning democratic political system will deliver the basic security and welfare needs of its members. If this ceases to be the case, however, and a political system's capacity to ensure these basic needs no longer exist or is severely undermined (as for example in Weimar Germany), input legitimacy is unlikely to suffice and the overall legitimacy of the polity will suffer. In other words, states draw on both input and output legitimacy, even if input legitimacy (ordinary process democracy, in Weiler's terms) is generally the dominant source. But there is also a third source of legitimacy on which political systems implicitly draw, and that is what Weiler terms 'mission legitimacy'. Mission legitimacy refers to the foundational commitments of a particular state or political system, or the ideals for which it stands. While mission legitimacy is normally even less

[14] For a discussion of the pros and cons of greater politicization of the EU, see the exchange between Simon Hix and Stefano Bartolini published by Notre Europe in 2006. S. Hix, 'Politics: The Right or the Wrong Sort of Medicine for the EU?' and S. Bartolini, 'Should the European Union Be Politicised?: Prospects and Risks', http://personal.lse.ac.uk/hix/Working_Papers/NotreEurope_Hix%20_Bartolini.pdf.

[15] The relationship between input and output legitimacy in the EU context is the subject of Fritz Scharpf's excellent book *Governing in Europe* (Oxford University Press, 1999).

evident than output legitimacy as an everyday source of polity legitimacy, it nevertheless comes to the fore at times of crisis or celebration in the life of states, for example during wartime when sacrifices are called for, or at certain ceremonial moments such as presidential elections and inaugurations. It may refer to a commitment to certain substantive values or objectives, and it may be more abstractly or more concretely defined. Think for example of the United States' foundational commitment to the inalienable right to life, liberty and the pursuit of happiness, and to limited government under law; of France's founding ideals of 'liberty, equality, fraternity'; or of Canada's ideal of multicultural confederation. Founding commitments, ideals or missions often endure, but they do not necessarily remain unchanged. Indeed, they are regularly invented and re-invented as history unfolds, and as states undergo upheaval and change. In the case of many modern democratic states, their missions or founding ideals do not play a significant everyday role in establishing the ongoing legitimacy of the polity, and ordinary process democracy is the most prominent source of their legitimacy. Nevertheless, the founding ideals or mission supply a further implicit source of polity legitimacy which can play an important role, from time to time, in enhancing the legitimacy even of long-established democratic states.

The EU, however, is not in the same position as most modern democratic states, and the distribution of its reliance on the three sources of polity legitimacy is correspondingly different from that of most states. Despite six decades of existence, the EU remains significantly different from a nation state in many important respects. It remains composed of twenty-seven separate states, with their distinct identities, histories and languages. It has evolved a complex process of transnational politics and transnational governance with various democratic elements, but it has not developed a thick democratic process, a strong collective identity or a cohesive political unity. Contrary to Weiler, I suggest that the EU cannot, in its present state of development, seek to rely primarily on ordinary democratic processes to ground its legitimacy as a polity. Whether the EU does eventually evolve into a more closely integrated federal system that could base its primary source legitimacy on the ordinary processes of constitutional democracy remains to be seen, although there are currently many challenges to that deeper vision of political integration. For the moment, however, the EU is very far from being able to do so. Instead, the EU continues to draw its legitimacy as much from its performance and output (effective delivery of policy) and from its perceived mission (*raison d'être*), as it does from its every-day political processes (or ordinary process democracy).

In short, I suggest that at its current stage of evolution the EU still needs to articulate a convincing *raison d'être* if it is to generate the kind of popular support and legitimacy which a powerful transnational economic and political system of this kind requires for its survival, and which captures why this regional system of transnational governance actually matters. The peace dividend seems no longer sufficient for younger generations to whom the virtues of European integration are not evident, who have no memory of war, and who today confront a bleak economic future. And while the democratic character of the EU clearly needs to be significantly strengthened, the EU cannot rely primarily on the kind of thick social solidarity and deep democratic consent for its legitimacy that states can. Mission legitimacy, along with democratic legitimacy and output legitimacy, continues to play an important role.

5 The EU's *raison d'être* today

While the term 'political messianism' used by Weiler may have unattractive connotations, the same idea – namely that the EU's founding ideals and mission continue to play an important role today – has been expressed more positively by others. Martin Wolf in 2012 argued in the *Financial Times* that the fact that the EU is based on an ideal helps to explain its survival and resilience in the face of such strong economic and political centrifugal forces.[16] In trying to explain what forces account for the political commitment to the survival of the euro, despite the enormous economic struggle that it currently entails for all countries of the Eurozone, he wrote:

> The principal political force is the commitment to the ideal of an integrated Europe, along with the huge investment of the elite in that project. This enormously important motivation is often underestimated by outsiders. While the Eurozone is not a country, it is much more than a currency union. Also for Germany, much the most important member, the Eurozone is the capstone of a process of integration with its neighbours that has helped bring stability and prosperity after the disasters of the first half of the 20th century.

[16] M. Wolf, 'Why the Eurozone May Yet Survive: Members Remain Absolutely Committed to the Idea of an Integrated Europe', *Financial Times*, 17 April 2012.

Wolf's argument is that this underlying political commitment (what Weiler calls the messianic) is what fundamentally and most powerfully continues to drive the European integration process. He then elaborates further on the EU's original mission of bringing peace and prosperity to the continent, asserting that 'the big idea that brings the members [of the EU] together is that of their place within Europe and the world'.

There are two important insights in this brief commentary. The first is the emphasis on the continued salience of the EU's founding ideal, or mission. But the second is the reframing of the EU's founding ideal (bringing a degree of peace and prosperity to the continent) in a way that emphasizes the external as well as the internal relevance of European integration. In the remainder of this chapter I will elaborate on this idea, namely that what explains the continuing commitment to European integration in the face of such powerful centripetal economic and political forces is both the relationship of states and their citizens within the EU political system *and* the place of the European Union in the world. I suggest that this dual-facing mission – the development of a novel transnational relationship between the Member States, their citizens and the EU on the one hand, and the development of the EU's situation and role within the broader global context on the other, provides a better articulation of the EU's *raison d'être* today.[17]

While the founding ideas of integration as a way of bringing stability and prosperity to the European continent had at least an implicit external dimension – which asserted itself over time not only through repeated enlargements but also through the development of EU external policies – nevertheless the first four decades of the European project were to a great extent inwardly focused on matters such as the establishment of the internal market and the creation of an effective regulatory and political system. With time, however, the external dimension of integration became more prominent, and a major focus of the EU since the time of the Maastricht Treaty in 1993 has been with Europe's global role. The Lisbon Treaty most recently and notably contained

[17] For an argument that the EU's foreign policy mode mirrors in various respects the 'governance mode' of transnational relations that it has developed internally, see G. de Búrca, 'EU External Relations: The Governance Mode of Foreign Policy', in B. Van Vooren, S. Blockmans and J. Wouters (eds.), *The EU's Role in Global Governance: The Legal Dimension* (Oxford University Press, 2012), pp. 39–58.

many high-profile reforms aimed at strengthening the values, institutions and actors shaping EU international relations.[18]

While it may seem implausible to suggest that what might generate stronger citizen support for the EU is its global role rather than its internal capacity to deliver social and economic welfare, my argument is that these two dimensions are increasingly connected. The internal and external dimensions of EU action are connected in a range of relevant ways. In the first place, the EU increasingly claims to act (and is expected by Europeans to act) so as to manage the effects of globalization.[19] Secondly, many of the ways in which the EU has projected itself as an international actor reflect the modes of transnational governance it has developed in its internal domain. A third way in which the internal and external dimensions of European integration are related is in the potential capacity of the EU to represent an alternative geopolitical model to that of other major powers, whether the US on the one hand, or China and other emerging economies on the other. For all its current woes, the EU remains the largest market in the world, and a major exporter of regulatory standards as well as a major trade partner.[20] A particularly powerful critique of the EU's primary focus on austerity throughout the economic crisis has been that 'it bears negative consequences for Europe and the world [. . .] [T]he politics of austerity prevents Europe from offering an alternative vision of capitalism and globalization to that put forward by the United States. Gone is the idea of Europe leading a global third way between laissez-faire capitalism and managed socialism'.[21] This EU capacity to offer a third-way model of social democracy as an alternative means of managing economic globalization is relevant both internally and externally.

In an increasingly interdependent world, the EU's potential to exercise global leadership on a range of crucial matters which states cannot address alone, including climate change, migration, internet governance,

[18] See P. Koutrakos (ed.), 'The European Union's External Relations a Year after Lisbon', Centre for the Law of EU External Relations Working Paper 2011/3 (2011), available at www.asser.nl/upload/documents/772011_51358CLEER%20WP%202011-3%20-%20KOUTRAKOS.pdf.

[19] See the special issue of the *Journal of European Public Policy*: S. Meunier and W. Jacoby (eds.), 'Europe and the Management of Globalization' (2010) 17 *Journal of European Public Policy* 299–448. For a discussion of apparent public expectations that the EU should fulfill this role, see p. 302.

[20] See A. Bradford, 'The Brussels Effect' (2012) 107 *Northwestern University Law Review* 1.

[21] A. Newman, 'Austerity and the End of the European Model', *Foreign Affairs*, 1 May 2012.

financial regulation and terrorism, to mention just a few, is just as relevant to the lives of EU citizens as the EU's internal social and economic policies. Writing in 2011 in *the Financial Times*, Giuliano Amato and Federico Ghizzoni drew on Ian Morris's magisterial historical work to suggest that the need to tackle Morris's 'five horsemen of the apocalypse' (climate change, famine, migration, disease and state failure)[22] provides a powerful reason for the EU's continued existence.[23] All of these challenges will affect the lives of both European citizens and others, and are not merely the remote foreign policy concerns of elites. The EU has experience, internally, of coordinating the different interests of sovereign states with a view to addressing common problems, and this experience equips it well to promote and support similar collective problem-solving processes internationally.[24] Further, the EU has sought to develop and project a distinctive character as a global actor in fields such as climate change, development, human rights and democracy-promotion, and as an actor which is committed to pursuing collective, coordinated, as well as multilateral solutions to global problems.[25]

In conclusion, while agreeing that the EU unquestionably needs continued democratic reform and strengthening, this chapter has set out to refute the argument that the EU must henceforth seek to legitimate itself only by the ordinary processes of democracy and must abandon its 'messianic' origins. I have argued that the EU in its current state of evolution remains significantly dependent not just on input and output legitimacy, but also on its mission legitimacy. This means that the question of the EU's *raison d'être* remains salient today, and not only because of the deep economic crisis in which it has been mired. And what then is the EU's *raison d'être*? I have argued that the EU's founding mission of delivering peace and prosperity is no longer only or mainly internally focused, as the external dimension of European integration has

[22] I. Morris, *Why the West Rules – For Now* (New York: Farrar, Straus & Giroux, 2010)

[23] G. Amato and F. Ghizzoni, 'Why It's Worth Keeping the EU Dream Alive', *Financial Times*, 31 October 2011

[24] See de Búrca, 'EU External Relations'.

[25] The European Council on Foreign Relations in its annual scorecards on European foreign policy has indicated that even where it is weak in bilateral relations with powerful states such as China and Russia, the EU has scored well on a broad range of important multilateral and global issues, notably climate change, crisis management, Bretton Woods reform, non-proliferation, human rights at the UN, international criminal court policy, development aid and global health. See www.ecfr.eu/content/entry/european_foreign_policy_scorecard_2012 and www.ecfr.eu/content/entry/european_foreign_policy_scorecard_2013.

become increasingly prominent. In other words, the EU's capacity to manage globalization and its potential to exercise international leadership on a range of crucial global challenges are important aspects of its *raison d'être* today. The EU's capacity to provide its Member States and citizens with collective power and a coordinated problem-solving capability, to offer an alternative socio-economic and geopolitical model to those of other existing and rising powers, and to offer global leadership on some of the most pressing transnational challenges, provides a powerful rationale for the EU's existence today.

2

The EU, interim global justice and the international legal order

ANDREW T. WILLIAMS

1 Introduction

How should redistributive justice operate beyond the state? This is one of the most significant questions for political philosophy and those who seek some ethical core to any international legal order.[1] It is an underlying theme for those who seek to make moral sense of the mechanisms and purpose of institutional relationships between peoples and is the crux of 'global justice' accounts. It is particularly important, I suggest, for the EU in these times of prolonged economic adversity. Should it adopt a redistributive role in its own right, where it oversees, perhaps provokes, the transfer of resources across state borders *within* its territory to assist those people in greatest need? Or should it leave individual Member States to assume responsibility for its citizens and in particular the human consequences of their own economic troubles? Should it be obligated to redistribute wealth to the global poor *outside* its territory and assume greater responsibility for fairer international rules of trade? Or should it only recognize a limited humanitarian role based on charity not duty?

These are the vital ethical and legal questions that this chapter aims to consider. This is with the view that current economic crises provide an ideal test for assessing the relevance of global justice theory (as it relates to the distribution of wealth) to the EU in its internal as well as external operations.[2] If obligations to assist the poor within its borders and

[1] The rise of transnational constitutionalism as a subject worthy of analysis is one manifestation of this concern. For a useful introduction to the role of the EU within general international debates, see N. Tsagourias (ed.), *Transnational Constitutionalism: International and European Perspectives* (Cambridge University Press, 2007).

[2] Global justice is considered here from the perspective of socio-economic or distributive justice. This encompasses those actions intended to narrow the benefit and burden gap between people and peoples so as to address the condition of severe poverty that is

outside find purchase at these times of austerity, then their applicability when a general surplus of wealth is the norm must be more convincing. The extent of any obligations assumed by or imposed on the EU will have considerable bearing on the nature of its relationship with (and shaping of) the international legal order that might be said to exist. For if it can be recognized that the EU owes a deep institutional duty (respected and enforced in law) in relation to the distribution of wealth, a duty perhaps enshrined in its legal system, then the precedent it offers to other regional or international regimes could be highly influential. Equally, any weak (or even no) duty might reduce or negate the prospect of international legal commitments to assist the global poor. There is thus a need to consider both the underlying philosophy of EU law *and* the practice of EU institutions. The former will help decide whether the EU *should* be engaged in redistribution across borders (the ethical question), the latter whether it *can* or *does* so engage (the empirical question).[3]

My starting argument is that it would be wrong to dismiss the EU as a polity incapable of acting as a primary agent of justice.[4] Although a relational idea of distributive justice remains dominant in much current political philosophy (where distribution requires shared social and political institutions, usually in the form of the state), the non-relational belief that a duty of distribution is nevertheless owed to those worse off who are *not* members of those shared institutions should not be ignored. In other words, the formation of the shared institution is never a precondition for distributive justice in theory. It is therefore wrong to label interstate cooperative institutions, such as the EU, as simply 'unjust' and thus discounted in global justice terms. Rather, the EU represents a plausible vehicle of *interim* global justice. This reflects an understanding that *all* accounts of distributive justice are premised on an ultimate position, which might one day be reached; a position whereby inequalities of benefits and burdens are eradicated and the unmerited suffering of the

experienced by so many in the world today. It is not to preclude or deny the relevance or importance of other forms of justice. However, to avoid becoming overwhelmed by a categorisation of the various potential components of global justice, this chapter is restricted to the moral demand for greater distributive fairness across borders and between peoples.

[3] Of course, neither of these aspects can be resolved in the short space available here. However, it is the subject of a wider and enduring project of the author. See, in particular, A. Williams, *The Ethos of Europe: Law, Values and Justice in the EU* (Cambridge University Press, 2010) and A. Williams, 'Promoting Justice after Lisbon: Groundwork for a New Philosophy of EU Law' (2010) 30 *Oxford Journal of Legal Studies* 663 (663–93).

[4] I have discussed this claim in the works cited above.

powerless is addressed. However, these accounts are 'interim' because the ultimate destination is recognized as unlikely to be reached except in theory. Consequently, *any* cooperative institutional endeavour (whether or not in the form of the state) operates as an interim global justice actor. It is inappropriate, therefore, to dismiss interstate ventures merely because of weak shared social and political institutions (weak that is in comparison to those commonly associated with the 'state'). Rather, it makes vital the need to assess all cooperative ventures in order to determine the depth and breadth of commitment to distribution internally and externally.

The recognition that the EU may be called an institution of 'interim global justice' leads on to the second argument made in this chapter. Given the spectrum of global justice accounts between what Thomas Nagel calls the 'political' and the 'cosmopolitan'[5] it is appropriate to assess the EU according to *stages* of interim global justice. These serve as rough guides in determining where on this spectrum the EU currently sits. Critically assessing the EU's 'justice balance' in interim global justice terms with a view to recognizing its current condition and future trajectory may therefore release a practical engagement with the institution vis-à-vis its distributive obligations.[6] Knowing where the institution stands must be the first step in advocating for greater or lesser responsibility and, indeed, establishing the value of the EU for the shaping of the international legal order in global justice terms. Although it is not possible to conduct this audit in full here, some assessment of the EU and the stage of interim global justice inhabited is possible. This is addressed in section 3.

2 The concept of interim global justice

The cosmopolitan approach to global justice may be typified as an equal concern for our fellow human beings no matter where they are located.[7]

[5] Adopted here is Thomas Nagel's polar distinction between the political approach to global justice, which seriously restricts the obligation of any state or polity to owe duties of distribution beyond its borders and the cosmopolitan which denies the moral relevance of state boundaries when it comes to responding to the plight of those worst off in the world. These offer plausible extremes within which a spectrum of responsibility may be judged. See T. Nagel, 'The Problem of Global Justice' (2005) 33 *Philosophy and Public Affairs* 113 (113–47).

[6] It is plausible that this method has equal applicability when assessing any legal institution whether national or international.

[7] See e.g. K. A. Appiah, *Cosmopolitanism: Ethics in a World of Strangers* (London: Penguin Books, 2007) and P. Singer, *The Life You Can Save: Acting Now to End World Poverty* (Oxford: Picador, 2009).

To pursue, if not fulfil, that moral obligation more effectively, institutions may be constructed on a global scale. An internationally 'common system of institutions' is often presented as a pragmatic solution to the theoretical problem of greater distribution between peoples, provided always that what Thomas Pogge has called 'covert arbitrary discrimination in favour of the wealthy societies and against the global poor' is avoided.[8]

At the other end of the spectrum, the political conception (as described by Thomas Nagel for instance) denies that any moral obligation owed to others should be as strong as cosmopolitan thinking would have it.[9] Distributive justice is only comprehensible in the political view as a value *within* sovereign states. It is only then assumed that citizens 'have a duty of justice to one another through the legal, social, and economic institutions that sovereign power makes possible'.[10] But rather than preclude global or international institutions, this conception accepts their creation albeit with severe ethical restraints imposed. The duty to others beyond one's sovereign state is limited to a minimal humanitarianism, Nagel suggests, and the function of international institutions is restricted 'to enable us to fulfil the duty of rescue toward people in dire straits all over the world'.[11]

The admission of a duty of rescue, however, provides a basis for connection rather than disjuncture between the political and cosmopolitan extremes. It is the foundation upon which much attachment to global justice as an ideal of whatever persuasion is based. For is there really a significant moral distinction between recognizing a duty to help others who are suffering as a result of an acute crisis and a duty to help those who are suffering as a result of chronic conditions of poverty – the first prompting rescue, the second prompting at best charity? If suffering is the moral trigger (which is the tenor of humanitarianism as a concept), then the cause of that suffering must have little if any importance. Even if causation were deemed an issue, few would argue against the duty to rescue those 'innocents' who suffer as a result of an individual government's action or neglect. Consequently, the lines between the acute and the chronic will inevitably be blurred.

[8] T. Pogge, *World Poverty and Human Rights* (Cambridge: Polity Press, 2002), p. 117

[9] See, typically, H. Morgenthau, *Politics Among Nations: The Struggle for Power and Peace*, 6th edn (New York: McGraw-Hill, 1985).

[10] Nagel, 'The Problem of Global Justice', p. 121.

[11] *Ibid.*, p. 132. This would suggest the EU should only be considered in these very limited terms. The argument would be that it is not a sovereign state and therefore should possess no distributive obligations either within or outside its borders.

There is good reason to suppose, therefore, that the spectrum of global justice accounts is premised on the acceptance that *some* duty to others *should* be assumed. What one can be expected to do faced by widespread suffering is determined less on moral and more on practical grounds. Most accounts are premised with an ideal of global justice, perhaps unreachable but nonetheless desirable, in mind. In other words, containment of a distributive duty is fixed by reference to a limit of equal distribution of resources between people wherever they may live in the world. This limit is often described as cosmopolitan even though there are a variety of global justice theories that have attached themselves to that term.[12] Nonetheless, even those who speak of equality or distributive duties being restricted to the state define those obligations in terms of those who are excluded by political boundary (a matter of practice), rather than moral principle. It may well be, as David Miller argues, a greater responsibility should be reserved for those *within* a community (which may in theory encompass a polity beyond the nation state), but that does not vitiate a (sometimes substantial) residual or parallel duty owed to the distant needy.[13]

All this suggests that global justice accounts between an extreme political conception (no duty owed to anyone anywhere) *and* the cosmopolitan are 'interim' in nature. Accounts are premised on the plausibility of a cosmopolitan redistributive ideal as a legitimate moral goal without necessarily accepting that it will ever be reached or, indeed, ever accepting expressly a duty to bring it about. Indeed, any acknowledgement of some form of moral obligation to others (which is a position few would deny)[14] is inherently interim in character.

On the presumption that most accounts of global justice accept at least some duties towards others in 'dire straits' or suffering 'dire plight' (the relative nature and practical reality of which suggest an elasticity that is forever stretched), the enquiry moves on to determine *who* owes this duty and to what extent it can be fulfilled.

[12] For an analysis of cosmopolitan thinkers, see, for instance, S. Caney, *Justice beyond Borders: A Global Political Theory* (Oxford University Press, 2005), pp. 1–24.

[13] D. Miller, *National Responsibility and Global Justice* (Oxford University Press, 2007).

[14] It is hard to countenance a moral–philosophical position whereby *as a matter of fundamental principle* a state or people would refuse to come to the aid of those in desperate and immediate need when practicably able to render assistance at no significant cost to itself. There may be many reasons for not doing so in practice, however, but this would represent an exception to the basic moral principle and would need to be weighed against the moral responsibility engaged.

As has been pointed out above, it is assumed that distributive justice duties can be owed both by individuals and institutions set up to organize our societies and their relations with others internally and externally. Limiting duty-holders to the state would strike a false position in these circumstances. But can we then move from states axiomatically being primary agents of justice to other institutional cooperative ventures which do not have global scope or pretension?

The notion of the interim in global justice terms explicitly allows this extension. Many justice theories identify the need for institutions to assume the responsibilities for coordinating activity beyond the state designed to give effect (at least in part) to appropriate principles of justice.[15] Such institutions provide the *loci* for implementation of the individual ethic of distribution in either weak or strong form. It is implausible in this respect to discount the EU as one such venture. Simply as a vehicle for interstate cooperation it assumes this character.

There is good reason therefore to identify the EU as an institution, if only in theory and in the first instance, capable of being a primary agent of justice with the capacity to assume distributive duties. If this is accepted, the EU (or, indeed, any international institution) should not be assessed in simplistic terms as being either 'just' or 'unjust'. Rather, it should be seen as an '*interim*' global justice institution, which should be assessed in terms of its actual and potential engagement in the distribution of wealth both within and outside its boundaries given that both dimensions are international in character.

It is this assessment to which I now turn. If the sense of the interim captures distributive justice as a value to be sought through ethical design and institutional action then there is a need to evaluate the extent to which the EU (and any international institution for that matter) acknowledges (through constitution) and acts (through policy and practice) with distributive justice in mind. The next section is an attempt to provide a framework for this analysis.

3 The EU and the stages of interim global justice

If the concept of interim global justice represents a spectrum of distributive duty (from the political to the cosmopolitan), where within that range has the EU been constituted? What precedent does it offer in

[15] See Nagel, 'The Problem of Global Justice'; C. Beitz, *Political Theory and International Relations* (Princeton, NJ: Princeton University Press, 1999).

ethical design and practical action for the international order? To assist in this evaluation it is proposed to examine the EU in relation to five plausible interim stages or junctures within the global justice spectrum. They are: the intra-state (3.1); the intra-state+ (3.2); the community of states (3.3); the community of states+ (3.4); and the guarded cosmopolitan (3.5). These are not intended to be exhaustive descriptions but rather interpretative and representative of stages of thought as regards global justice.

Below, each stage is first explained before a brief assessment of the EU (in relation to that stage's applicability) is made. Thus an initial evaluation of the EU's precedent for global justice is possible, providing some sense of a 'justice audit' in the making.

3.1 *The intra-state stage*

It is a common perception that states operate in accordance with egoistic principles.[16] The fundamental condition is that the maintenance of a state's sovereignty is non-negotiable from a contractual point of view. Even if practical realities may cause us to question the depth of sovereignty actually exercised today, national integrity underpinned by national sovereignty are preconditioning principles.[17] Other principles then revolve around that basic position. Non-intervention in the affairs of other sovereign states (based on a notion of reciprocity), the pre-eminence of financial and physical security of the state and the lawful power to determine the conditions of citizenship are all recognizable from international law.[18] Whatever justice principles are adopted internally, no non-negotiable obligation to external others is accepted.

In this stage, any cooperation between states must be contractual in nature. And being contractual, any interstate institutions to operate the cooperative arrangements would have their powers and duties restricted to the achievement of those basic principles and in accordance with agreed terms. Mutual benefit may require mutual burden, but this would be contingent on not jeopardizing the basic principles of state. There would be no recognition of any non-negotiable obligation to those living outside the borders of contracting states beyond this self-interested limit.

The intra-state stage reflects political realist position such as proffered by Hans Morgenthau, although there is some hint of the interim even

[16] See Morengthau, *Politics Among Nations*. [17] *Ibid*.

[18] See e.g. Malcolm Shaw, *International Law*, 6th edn (Cambridge University Press, 2008).

in his work. He recognizes that moral values should influence the foreign affairs of states even though that might conflict with rational self-interest.[19] Still, the basic observation holds good: states are deemed the primary agents of justice, justice is an internal affair if anything, and no obligation is owed to anyone or any state beyond the provisions of agreed laws.

Undoubtedly, many may identify the EU with this stage. In its formative period there was clear preference in design (if not underlying philosophy) for a venture which preserved and promoted the interests of its Member States. We do not need to rehearse the history of the EU to know that the early prevailing wisdom was that the EU then represented a vehicle for enhancing the economic development of its Members through the construction of a limited common market.[20] Internally, the contractual nature of arrangements between states was not accompanied by any great desire to redistribute wealth. The Treaty Establishing the European Community (TEC) may have contained preamble statements regarding laying the 'foundations of an ever closer union among the peoples of Europe' and confirming the 'solidarity which binds Europe and the overseas countries [i.e. colonies and ex-colonies of Member States]' but these were not accompanied by constitutional provisions designed to address inequalities of resources.[21] Of course, in the 1950s and 1960s the concern was internal reconstruction not redistribution. Equally, there was no perceived need for a foreign policy, ethically devised or not.

Despite the evident original intra-state nature, the EU has dramatically developed constitutionally and institutionally suggesting that whatever its initial character vis-à-vis any ethical commitment this might have altered. Indeed, it was not long before European law ensured that the project acknowledged the surrender of some state sovereignty and emphasized the collective interests *in tandem with* individual state interests. Those iconic decisions in *Van Gend en Loos*[22] and *Costa* v. *ENEL*[23] provided the basis for the EU as an evolving polity. There may have been

[19] H. Morgenthau, *Human Rights and Foreign Policy* (New York: Council on Religion and International Affairs, 1979).

[20] See the chapter by Gráinne de Búrca in this volume.

[21] On 'Eurafrica', see e.g. D. Custos, 'Implications of the European Integration for the Overseas', in D. Kochenov (ed.), *EU Law of the Overseas* (The Hague: Kluwer Law International, 2011), p. 91.

[22] Case 26/62 *NV Algemene Transport- en Expeditie Onderneming van Gend and Loos* v. *Netherlands Inland Revenue Administration* [1963] ECR 1.

[23] Case 6/64 *Flaminio Costa* v. *ENEL* [1964] ECR 585.

no philosophy of Community law at the time which promoted the idea of distributive obligations owed beyond Member States borders, but successive expansions from 1972 onwards and the construction of a form of foreign policy presence at the same time changed the legal and constituting environment. The EU may still have been generally constrained by a political philosophy and practice that preserved power in the Member States, but the acceptance of a distribution of sovereignty in theory allowed distributive justice type initiatives to be contemplated. We therefore need to look beyond the intra-state stage as a useful descriptor of the EU.

3.2 The intra-state+ stage

The intra-state+ stage accepts the basic premises of the previous position but reflects the influence of the changing nature of politics and polities in an era of globalization. Although much sovereign power still rests in the state, new technologies and modes of business have diffused this significantly. They have also brought peoples closer together, providing both greater knowledge about the plight of distant others and the technical resources to do something meaningful in response.

The intra-state+ position recognizes this contemporary condition and accepts that the suffering experienced in the world merits *some* response from those states (and their agents) which have resources to assist. This is less a matter of obligation and more an acknowledgement, in principle, of 'humanitarian appeal'. The phrase 'in principle' implies a belief that there can be *no* automatic response to humanitarian disaster for the very reason that no fixed obligation to come to the rescue of others is accepted. The donor state is always in a position to refuse appeals for help on the basis of its own administrative determination of whether an event merits response *as* a humanitarian disaster. Any assistance is therefore charitable, an option that can be exercised or not at the total discretion of the donor. Thomas Nagel identifies this humanitarian duty as one restricted to 'some minimal concern' owed 'to fellow human beings threatened with starvation or severe malnutrition and early death from easily preventable diseases'.[24] This is not a matter of justice, according to Nagel. Ultimately, humanitarian duties are not associated with any desire to distribute wealth. They persist because of a possible

[24] Nagel, 'The Problem of Global Justice', p. 118.

humane response to the crises of others. Individual ends do not need to coincide with the ends of those experiencing acute suffering.

The main distinction between the intra-state and the intra-state+ stages arises not through principle, therefore. Even in the intra-state stage, which it occupied in its early period, the EU might have coordinated interventions both within its Member States and beyond to help people in dire need. But it did not have a constitutional authority to do so. Any development assistance had to be negotiated separately with beneficiary states and agreed by the Member States.[25] The intra-state+ stage intimates a difference in contemporary practice rather than principle. If polities with resources habitually provide assistance in response to humanitarian pleas and make this a coordinated practice then one could claim a customary obligation, perhaps habit, has been forged.

Nevertheless, the recognition that there is a changing international environment (as technological and economic capacity enables polities to provide assistance where humanitarian disaster has occurred) has framed some contemporary interstate cooperation initiatives.[26] These ventures operate under a contractual framework which sets the parameters for that collectively agreed purpose including interstate humanitarian responses. This makes administrative sense in that by pooling resources and appointing managers to oversee any relief when assistance is agreed it can be done effectively and efficiently.

The EU could be said to reflect these attributes in some of its operations. The nature of its interstate institutions remains essentially contractual. Resources are only provided for the purposes designed. Consent is required for variation of behaviour and any membership is voluntary. But both in constitution and in practice there is evidence that the EU has assumed humanitarian responsibilities. Externally, successive treaties since 1957 have recognized the obligation to assist the developing world. This may have been confined to ex-colonies initially but successive agreements with those independent states in Africa, the Caribbean and the Pacific have acknowledged a commitment to provide aid.[27] Admittedly, this has not necessarily always been entirely benevolent. Tied as it was in

[25] For a brief review of the history of this development policy, see A. Williams, *EU Human Rights Policies: A Study in Irony* (Oxford University Press, 2004), pp. 16–52.

[26] Most notably the UN Development Programme and its humanitarian operations sanctioned by the UN Security Council have demonstrated the recognition that some action to relieve acute suffering should be undertaken.

[27] See Williams, *EU Human Rights Policies.*

many bilateral aid agreements to conditions which ensured any distribution of funds benefited the interests of the EU's Member States, it would be difficult to establish that even a humanitarian obligation was truly embraced.[28] Still, from the early 1960s the Community and later the EU facilitated the construction of the agreements which can be reasonably interpreted as reflecting some form of obligation to assist the economic and social development of countries in the global South.[29]

However, it was the establishment of the European Community Humanitarian Office (ECHO) in 1992 which suggested a change in the EU's humanitarian intent.[30] The Joint Declaration issued in 2008 claiming a European consensus on humanitarian aid explicitly accepted such aid to be a 'fundamental expression of the universal value of solidarity between people and a moral imperative'.[31] ECHO's annual expenditure of approximately €1 billion would at least imply a substantial realization of this ethical position.

Internally, the humanitarian obligation also appears within the structure of the EU, although this is undoubtedly only a relatively recent phenomenon. In 2001 ECHO introduced the Civil Protection Mechanism (CPM), now made up of thirty-two states (the EU Member States plus Croatia, Macedonia, Iceland, Liechtenstein and Norway), which is supposed to facilitate co-operation in responding to significant natural or man-made disasters occurring either inside or outside the EU. There have been few opportunities internally, but it has nevertheless been deployed for the earthquake in Italy in 2009 and a toxic sludge disaster in Hungary in 2010.[32]

Of course, it seems unlikely that the EU would fail to respond to great catastrophe should one occur within one of its Member States. And this

[28] OECD reported in 1988 on the deleterious effects of tying aid by requiring donee countries to use aid provided to purchase goods from the donor country. See OECD, *The Tying of Aid* (Paris: OECD, 1988).

[29] See M. Holland, *The European Union and the Third World* (Basingstoke: Palgrave, 2002), which remains a good source of reference for the history of this topic. See also K. Arts and A. K. Dickson (eds.), *EU Development Cooperation: From Model to Symbol* (Manchester University Press, 2010).

[30] Council Regulation (EC) No. 1257/96 of 20 June 1996 concerning humanitarian aid, OJ [1996] L163 of 2 July 1996.

[31] Art. 1, Joint Statement by the Council and the Representatives of the Governments of the Member States Meeting within the Council, the European Parliament and the European Commission 2008/C 25/01.

[32] See http://ec.europa.eu/echo/aid/europe_caucasus/italy_en.htm for a report on the Italian earthquake response and http://ec.europa.eu/echo/aid/europe_caucasus/hungary_en.htm for one on the Hungarian situation.

is perhaps the hallmark of a developed sense of commitment to others which the EU has provoked during its evolution into its current form. But does *chronic* suffering (evident through the effects of relative poverty, for instance) qualify in the same way? One only has to look at the EU's response to poverty within its borders to see how coming to the aid of the 'internal other' may be structurally constricted. Recent initiatives responding to economic adversity, particularly the European Platform against Poverty and Social Exclusion, appear limited to encouraging growth, flexible employment practices, and better education or training, which all place the emphasis on state-based self-help rather than any direct distribution of resources from the wealthy to the poorest.[33]

3.3 *The community of states stage*

The community of states stage also rests on the presumption that states are necessary constructions for the establishment of any form of just global order. The basic principles of the intra-state position (non-intervention and state sovereignty) remain apt. The difference lies in the notion of responsibilities assumed to be owed by states to other states. Taking some cue from intra-state arrangements, where communities of individuals aspire to do justice to each other, the community of states stage attempts analogous arrangements *between* states.

One of the primary rules in this regard is the humanitarian obligation to come to the assistance of a state whose people are suffering catastrophe. However, the moral claim does not rest there. There is also recognition that states operating together can improve the general fortunes of less wealthy states through cooperation and the development of institutions designed to promote individual human rights and perhaps a fairer trade system (whatever this might imply). As far as human rights are concerned, the obligation is generally limited to a narrow band of civil (and perhaps political) rights which impose a negative, not positive, duty upon states.[34] The assumption is that although the community of

[33] See in particular the communication from the Commission to the European Parliament, the Council, the European Economic and Social Committee and the Committee of the Regions, 'The European Platform against Poverty and Social Exclusion: A European Framework for Social and Territorial Cohesion', (2010) 0758 final.

[34] Rawls identifies these key rights as the right to life, to liberty, freedom of conscience and thought, to property and formal equality. See J. Rawls, *The Law of Peoples* (Cambridge, Mass.: Harvard University Press, 1999), p. 65.

states should not generally interfere in the internal affairs of its Member States, there is nonetheless a collective recognition that certain oppressive behaviour will not be tolerated.

Underlying this community of states stage (just as with the intra-state versions) is the absence of an explicit acceptance that distributive duties are owed to distant others, the hallmark of any cosmopolitan expression. Rather, any ethical claims to distribution remain restricted to *within* states. Nonetheless, the humanitarian vision, which enables us to sympathize with others, cannot be blind to the plight of those suffering abroad nor to the recognition that certain systemic conditions (in particular concerning trade and finance) contribute to distant suffering. The response though is limited. Any sense of obligation is channelled into a collective duty which attaches only to states not to individuals living in wealthy countries. Thus, it is the community of states which must come to the aid of people known to be enduring immediately relievable suffering.

The implication is that any global justice demands, such as they are, are best organized and managed by cooperative institutions. These may acquire some apparent autonomy but it is of a technical character, limited to how they can operate effectively within defined parameters. Like the intra-state stages, they remain creatures of state-to-state agreement.

It is at least arguable that the modern human rights movement has fixed itself to this community of states stage. Any sense of distributive justice is limited by design and practice. It may be that the principle of non-intervention is punctured but the hole created is miniscule. It remains the exception for the community to interfere effectively in the affairs of one of its members. The reasons for intervention are deliberately restricted. Legal rules are constructed to ensure that this is so. Over time there may be a relaxation of these restrictions, to enable more frequent interventions, but these require considerable and prolonged contractual negotiations for very small gain. As it is, the principle of non-intervention may have been relaxed in detail but the acceptance that a state which engages in inflicting deliberate harm on its subjects through its agents is interpreted through a very narrow lens. There have to be identifiable victims, harms suffered by them, state agent perpetrators evidentially responsible for those individual harms, and an available remedy (cessation of harmful practices, punishment, compensation etc.). Even then, the scale has to be considered egregious (gross and systematic abuses, in the lexicon of global human rights institutions). The result is that intervention is likely to be far outweighed by inaction. That is the condition preserved by the community of states stage.

One might suppose that this is little different from the intra-state+ stage. However, the distinction relates to the nature of association. In the intra-state+ stage, states engage with each other on a purely voluntary basis. Any institution created cannot capture a state in perpetuity. Exit is always an option as a necessary condition of the sovereignty principle. In the community of states stage, this may also hold true of particular institutions in theory, but there is no escape from the 'community of states' as a whole; if a state exists it is a member of the community of states by definition. Particular states may be 'exiled' (if one can use such an expression) or labelled 'rogue' but they cannot escape the very limited duties imposed.

On first blush it is here that the EU displays many relevant characteristics. We have already seen the general commitment to humanitarian issues both internally and abroad. But the adoption of respect for human rights as a central value, worthy of promotion and coordinated action across internal and external borders, the development of which has gradually occurred over forty years, demonstrates a deeper sense of obligation. This is not to say the human rights commitment within and outside the EU borders has been parallel.[35] Internally, human rights have undoubtedly assumed increasing influence. There is no need to rehearse this story in detail here. Suffice it to say that the commitment to human rights is important to EU policy and EU law, at least rhetorically and, since the Lisbon Treaty, constitutionally.[36] There is evidence of some adherence to both the negative (protecting the rights of individuals from the power of states and institutions) and positive (promoting those rights through practical and legislative measures) aspects of rights. It remains arguable, however, as to whether the EU represents a cooperative venture which has made respect for human rights a pre-eminent condition of all its actions and those of its members. The procedure under Article 7 of the Treaty on European Union for imposing meaningful sanctions against Member States has yet to be used despite the saga of extraordinary rendition, the expulsion of Roma from France, the insidious discrimination against minorities and migrants.[37] These illustrate the impotence

[35] The bifurcation of human rights policies was excavated in depth by the author; the critique fashioned then still holds good. Williams, *EU Human Rights Policies*.

[36] This was also the subject of Williams, 'Promoting Justice after Lisbon'.

[37] On extraordinary rendition, see the Dick Marty Report; Committee on Legal Affairs and Human Rights, Council of Europe Parliamentary Assembly, 'Alleged Secret Detentions in Council of Europe Member States', Information Memorandum II, AS/Jur (2006) 03 rev., 22 January 2006, available at http://assembly.coe.int/main.asp?link=/committeedocs/2006/20060124_jdoc032006_e.htm; on the continuing policy of

of the EU when faced with Member State-inflicted abuse. Instead, human rights have only been selectively promoted (often in narrowly defined areas such as employment and migration) with their role in the market seemingly the determining factor.[38]

In contrast, general foreign policy, development policy and (after 1992) accession policy, have all embraced the influence of a wider view of human rights.[39] They have all encompassed negative action through sanctions and positive action through enticement (provision of aid and for some states the promise of accession). There is now a sophisticated range of methods available and multiple examples of their application.[40] However, despite the 'ethical' nature of these initiatives the community of states ideal only requires *some* acknowledgement of a slightly enhanced humanitarian obligation. There is surely sufficient evidence to suggest the EU is recognizable in this respect. The question, though, is whether the greater claims can be made for the EU as regards distributive justice.

3.4 *The community of states+ stage*

The foundational conditions of the community of states stage do not promote any meaningful alteration in the structures of global relations which might significantly alleviate the suffering of the poor. But what may be called the community of states+ stage represents an attempt to

expulsion of Roma, see 'France's "scandalous" expulsion of Roma camps resumes', *Daily Telegraph*, 27 August 2012, available at www.telegraph.co.uk/news/worldnews/europe/france/9502160/Frances-scandalous-expulsion-of-Roma-camps-resumes.html; and on continuing discrimination, see e.g. the Fundamental Rights Agency report. European Union Agency for Fundamental Rights, 'Migrants, Minorities and Employment – Exclusion and Discrimination in the 27 Member States of the European Union. Update 2003–2008', FRA Report, 2010, available at http://fra.europa.eu/en/publication/2011/migrants-minorities-and-employment-exclusion-and-discrimination-27-member-states.

38 J. Coppel and A. O'Neil, 'The ECJ: Taking Rights Seriously' (1992) 12 *Legal Studies* 227 argued many years ago that the then European Court of Justice's support of fundamental rights was merely a way of shoring up the idea of a single market. Individual rights per se were not interpreted as worthy of independent value. Some contemporary support for this interpretation might also be fashioned from the decisions of the ECJ in *Viking* and *Laval*, which have attracted significant criticism for their seeming failure to take rights seriously. See C-438/05 *The International Transport Workers' Federation and The Finnish Seamen's Union* v. *Viking Line ABP and OÜ Viking Line Eesti* [2007] ECR I-10779; C-341/05 *Laval un Partneri Ltd.* v. *Svenska Byggnadsarbetareförbundet, Svenska Byggnadsarbetareförbundets avd. 1, Byggettan, Svenska Elektrikerförbundet* [2007] ECR I-11767.

39 These were charted in Williams, *EU Human Rights Policies*.

40 See, in particular, the EU's annual Human Rights reviews.

impute a higher responsibility for distribution which may develop out of a geographically defined voluntary association of states. In other words, the construction of a regional rather than global cooperative interstate venture, which seeks nonetheless to place itself within the general community of states but provide for enhanced responsibilities within its borders, might represent an extension of the previous stage.

Such an advanced version retains the founding principles of sovereignty and non-intervention but amends them *within* the cooperative venture not outside. This is pursued through institutions which adopt distributive aims if only to reflect the interests of all in the regional association in moving towards the equalization of wealth. Although the 'collective within a collective' remains contractual and superficially voluntary, just as with the preceding stages institutions created to manage the venture develop so as to make it difficult for any member to exit in practice. An enhanced responsibility is assumed albeit still limited by the founding principles. Thus, Nagel's criteria for socio-economic justice, which require a society to be 'fully associative' and dependent upon 'positive rights' arising 'only because we are joined together with certain others in a political society under strong centralized control', would be met by such a regional association of states.[41] We might argue about whether a 'political society' exists and whether it is a voluntary association or not, but these are empirical matters to be determined. They do not in themselves require the presence of the state. Only if one defines 'a political society under strong centralized control' as a 'state' (and only a 'state') can one escape the possibility that states coming together in some cooperative venture may fulfil the definition and thus release distributive justice duties.

The community of states+ stage avoids the circularity of such a flawed definition by recognizing that a greater degree of obligation *can* exist between states as well as within them. Through strong institutions, developing autonomous powers, a transnational political society can be constructed which makes association practically compulsory. The discourse of human rights can be particularly useful in supporting such a move away or parallel to the state. It can suggest that members of such an association are not only states but also the peoples who are citizens of those states, obligations thus flowing amongst and between both. Thus, not only are civil rights encompassed but also potentially

[41] Nagel, 'The Problem of Global Justice', p. 127.

political and socio-economic rights. The institutions of the cooperative venture can therefore make 'exceptional demands' on its individual and state members producing 'exceptional obligations' through the avenue of rights and the political determination that those rights should be 'promoted' by institutions constructed for that purpose. Positive standards of justice may thus have a meaningful presence in theory even though there may be restrictions placed on them constitutionally and in practice.

The community of states+ stage may still operate with contractual interstate arrangements similar to the intra-state or political conception, but the combination of a functional/constitutional determination to develop cooperation through rights *and* a practical assumption of power to fulfil that design may develop an institutional ethos that is independent and dependent simultaneously. The balance may shift from time to time, of course, but the possibility of addressing inequalities so as to contribute to socio-economic justice is at least plausible. The degree of political strength may develop so as to make exit unrealistic albeit still feasible.

The institutionalization of a 'community' is, of course, one of the historic hallmarks of the EU. It remains an example par excellence of an interstate cooperative venture constructed through law. This has given the project a quality which almost transcends state-based politics. By bringing the 'peoples of Europe' closer together, suppressing conflict, creating mutual interest, valorizing mutual values, and developing a law which provides a degree of binding positive rights for the benefit of individuals, a common identity has, arguably, been forged. Such a common identity, if truly in place, must have pretensions to an 'associative political society'. There would be little value in the venture otherwise. The question, however, is whether such a community spirit (as it might be called) has any real purchase beyond the humanitarian obligation.

Internally, we have already seen the influence of human rights acquire some depth. Member States whether they like it or not have had their sovereignty restricted and their laws changed as a result of legislative and judicial action. The Commission has, for instance, embarked on an unprecedented programme of human rights promotion through policy and law.[42] Constitutionally, the Lisbon Treaty released the EU from a

[42] For an overview of intent, see European Commission, 'Strategy for the Effective Implementation of the Charter of Fundamental Rights by the European Union', COM (2010) 573 final; Report from the Commission to the European Parliament, the Council the European Economic and Social Committee and the Committee of the Regions, '2011 Report on the Application of the EU Charter of Fundamental Rights', COM (2012) 169 final.

legal straitjacket; the promotion of human rights is a goal which the Union is obliged to pursue under Article 3 TEU, the Charter of Fundamental Rights is now legally binding, and accession to the ECHR has been sanctioned. This is an unprecedented human rights agenda for an interstate enterprise, developing a legal regime which is positive in its remit. Coupled with an external promotion of human rights (as previously noted) the EU demonstrates a significant public commitment to this matter.

The associative nature of the community can also be detected in some longer-lasting policies. The EU's internal regional policy, present since the Union's inception but vastly expanded in recent years, is arguably a vehicle for redistribution although it is difficult to make this connection in anything other than theory. Cohesion policy oversees a complex allocation of funds which on the face of it appear considerable. During the budget period 2007–13 the sum of €308 billion was due to be allocated.[43] Externally, too, the development policy budget is impressive. The EU provides over 50 per cent of international development aid and some €22.7 billion was allocated to the European Development Fund for the period 2008–13. The primary aim is to 'eliminate extreme poverty and hunger' in line with the Millennium Development Goals.[44]

These contributions all suggest a community of states+ level of commitment. Some caution is called for, however. First, the monies provided to aid the global poor is a fraction of that applied internally and barely scratches the surface of the problem of enduring poverty for the world's poorest. Claims that there has been meaningful distribution within the EU are also weak. Although the EU proclaims a determination to strengthening 'economic and social cohesion by correcting imbalances' and promoting solidarity amongst regions through the provision of centrally administered funds, the Union's language is limited to 'reinforcing economic competitiveness, creating jobs and strengthening internal cohesion'.[45] Even the

[43] Of that, Poland received €67 billion, Spain €34 billion and Italy €27 billion. Germany received €25 billion.

[44] Joint statement by the Council and the representatives of the governments of the Member States meeting within the Council, the European Parliament and the Commission on European Union Development Policy: 'The European Consensus', C 46/01, OJ C 46 of 24 Februray 2006.

[45] Commission Regulation setting out rules for the implementation of Council Regulation (EC) No. 1083/2006 laying down general provisions on the European Regional Development Fund, the European Social Fund and the Cohesion Fund and of Regulation (EC) No. 1080/2006 of the European Parliament and of the Council on the European Regional Development Fund, (EC) 1828/2006, OJ [2006] L 371/1

European Social Fund is devoted to matters of 'improving employment and job opportunities, encouraging a high level of employment and more and better jobs'.[46] There is an assumption that wealth can somehow trickle down to those least well off in the EU. As long as the workforce is 'adaptable', 'economically inactive persons' are encouraged to 'enter the labour market', and 'human capital' can be developed through increasing 'quality and productivity at work' then social exclusion (in other words, those who are the poorest) *might* be reduced.[47] But the poverty indicators within the EU belie any such impact. Eurostat released data showing that 'persistent-at-risk-of-poverty' rates across the EU were increasing from 2008 until 2010.[48] It is doubtful, given the current economic problems, that this will have improved.

Empirically, therefore, there is little evidence to show that any effective redistribution has taken place internally or externally. Of course, the complexities of the integrated market mean that it is difficult to conclude the effects one way or another. Some, no doubt, could claim that countries such as Ireland and Greece and those in Central and Eastern Europe did benefit greatly through membership of the EU and that this could represent a form of distribution. But whether this has contributed to distributive justice, where the poorest in societies have benefited rather than a small elite, is doubtful. The poverty indicators referred to above suggest any distribution is hard to detect.

What might be claimed, however, is that the EU has constructed the trappings of global justice commitments for moving wealth across borders and to assist the most deprived. It has also developed a legal framework for this to occur. But this commitment remains weak and contingent. Funds do not flow easily from Member State to Member State for *any* purpose let alone to help the needy. Nor do they flow outside the EU in any quantities truly to change the life chances of those in extreme poverty. This may nonetheless place the EU at an early community of states+ stage of the spectrum of global justice.

[46] Regulation (EC) No. 1081/2006 of the European Parliament and of the Council of 5 July 2006 on the European Social Fund and Repealing Regulation (EC) No. 1784/1999, OJ [2006] L 210/12

[47] *Ibid*., Preamble.

[48] http://epp.eurostat.ec.europa.eu/tgm/table.do?tab=table&init=1&language=en&pcode=tessi020&plugin=1; see also S. Jenkins and P. van Kerm, 'Patterns of Persistent Poverty: Evidence from EU-SILC', Institute for Social and Economic Research Working Paper No. 2011–30 (November 2011), available at https://www.iser.essex.ac.uk/publications/working-papers/iser/2011-30.pdf.

3.5 *The guarded cosmopolitan stage*

The guarded cosmopolitan stage is founded on the principle that obligations owed to others should be similar regardless of whether they are members of the same political community or not. If a case can be made that an obligation is owed to others within one's own national community to reduce or eradicate unequal distribution of benefits and burdens then there is no plausible moral reason why that obligation should not be owed to those outside our community. In other words, the community border is a largely irrelevant moral concern.

There is no need to debate the rights and wrongs of this position. It exists as an ethical imperative for many political philosophers of varying dispositions.[49] Suffice it to say that the potential for proceeding far beyond a purely humanitarian commitment is the core attraction of this guarded cosmopolitan stage. The moral tripartite position (as expressed by Thomas Pogge) of (a) individualism, where the unit of concern is the individual human being, (b) universality, where concern for each individual should be equal, and (c) generality, where 'persons are ultimate units of concern for everyone' not just their national or group compatriots, provides the basis for then asking: what should be owed to those suffering intolerable poverty?[50] Invariably, this provokes debates about minimum obligations. And therein lies the guarded nature of this stage of global justice. There are no mainstream commentators who argue that full equality of resources and benefits are the minimum. Even if, as Pogge advocates, the guiding principle is that '*we*' should recognize that support for others should not only be through aid but also through changing the global institutional order that perpetuates or accentuates poverty, the demands of this stage are minimal rather than maximal.[51] Important as reforming the global economic order may be, initiatives are designed to reduce the harm done to the global poor rather than fulfil the cosmopolitan ideal of equality. In these theoretical and very real senses, we are still dealing with a perpetual interim. When constructing international cooperative institutions with the guarded cosmopolitan stage they may therefore operate so as to enhance equality, solidarity, respect for rights,

[49] See Caney, *Justice beyond Borders*.
[50] T. Pogge, 'Cosmopolitanism and Sovereignty' (1992) 103.1 *Ethics* 48–75.
[51] T. Pogge, '"Assisting" the Global Poor', in D. K. Chatterjee (ed.), *The Ethics of Assistance: Morality and the Distant Needy* (Cambridge University Press, 2004), pp. 260–80.

unconditional hospitality etc., but they will do so with constraint and not as global justice institutions per se.

If we apply this to the EU it is possible to see some aspects which perhaps suggest the guarded cosmopolitan stage is descriptive of where the EU is placed. Ulrich Beck and Edgar Grande sum up the possibility when they declare that the EU was 'marked from the outset by the fact that the fundamental principle of cosmopolitanism was politically *institutionalized*, though at the same time *deformed* in the most diverse ways'.[52] The idea of a European Union was always cosmopolitan in theory, they argue, but that idea has been warped by the intervention of state self-interest (particularly but certainly not exclusively economic) and a top-down approach to integration. These 'deformations' provide the guarded character referred to above. Others think the same way. Gerard Delanty and Chris Rumford point to the development of the European Social Model, European citizenship (however weak), a construction of porous borders and a nascent European identity projected externally as well as across internal boundaries to suggest the promise of some form of cosmopolitanism.[53]

There is significant optimism in these accounts. They imply that cosmopolitan thinking not only gives form to the European project as it has developed but also provides a basis for future evolution. By applying a sense of cosmopolitan ethic to the operation of the EU, the hope is that people of the world as well as those in Europe will benefit. Thus, the notion of 'interim' global justice even in these hopeful stories is reinforced. Ultimately, though, these accounts look for justice where there is scant evidence to be found. The EU has simply failed to construct suitable credentials of any form of cosmopolitanism that oversees a realized commitment to help the most in need wherever they live. If anything, the political failure to see the economic crises post-2009 as a matter of collective responsibility (as opposed to a matter of collective regulation of the banking system) demonstrates the inherent antipathy towards cosmopolitan ideals. Distribution may occur and social justice may be advanced through EU action, but there is no clear structural or philosophical commitment to ignore borders in any serious attempt to address gross inequality and deep poverty.

[52] U. Beck and E. Grande, *Cosmopolitan Europe* (Cambridge: Polity Press, 2007), p. 5.

[53] G. Delanty and C. Rumford, *Rethinking Europe: Social Theory and the Implications of Europeanization* (London: Routledge, 2005).

4 Conclusion

The undercurrent message in this chapter is that regular evaluation of distributive justice credentials for the EU is both plausible and necessary. This begins with the acknowledgement of global justice as a practically interim subject. Nothing is to be gained by dismissing the EU as 'unjust' or 'just'. That is too simplistic an analysis. Rather, the notion of the interim is a reflection of the processual nature of global justice demands, which requires an assessment of the EU's decision-making and policies, leaving open the determination of a balance of justice indicators. We might then be better placed to decide what the EU *is* in global justice terms before deciding what it *should* be, how it *does* impact upon the international legal order in this respect and how it *should* and how it *can* do so in the future.

This task requires the accumulation of economic, legal and sociological evidence which is lacking at present. It would be insufficient to focus only on measuring *injustice* in the sense of the harm that the EU may or may not do, however important a task this may be.[54] Such an evaluation would also have to examine the EU's contribution, or lack of contribution, to socio-economic justice both as a cross-border project *within* the bounded Union *and* as a globally impactful enterprise through specific policy construction and implementation.[55] In short, a 'justice audit' is required, one which can be considered then in the light of the stages of justice presented above, so as to provide a significantly better political sense of global justice claims and critiques.

This is undoubtedly a complex job but perhaps no more so than judging 'freedom' indicators, as some organizations and analysts want to do.[56] Nonetheless, it would be warranted to establish more precisely what the EU has contributed to the attainment of global justice goals and which stage(s) it reflects. Admittedly, in the EU context, some authors have tried to introduce a more nuanced examination of 'justice' (without

[54] Sionaidh Douglas-Scott reminded the author of the importance of assessing injustice at the conference. Her article solidifies this strong argument. S. Douglas-Scott, 'Justice and Pluralism in the EU' (2012) 65.1 *Current Legal Problems* 83.

[55] It would be wrong to ignore the internal dimension. Even though, for some, the EU is tantamount to a state, the fact remains that for international law purposes at least it does not possess that character. Thus if the EU has been shown to distribute resources on the basis of addressing inequalities then such a factor should not be ignored.

[56] See the annual Freedom House reports. Freedom House, *Freedom in the World* (Washington, DC: Freedom House, 2013), available at www.freedomhouse.org/report-types/freedom-world.

defining its parameters), with Jürgen Neyer and Danny Nicol recently swapping positions on the question.[57] However, the basis upon which this discussion has developed has been by juxtaposition with the tendency to assess the EU and its legitimacy primarily in relation to its democratic credentials. This is too narrow a scope (which Nicol accepts) given the range of possible distributive justice stages sketched in the previous section.

In particular, there is a need properly to assess those policies and practices in terms of the transfer of funds to (or away from) the poorest across the Member States to determine whether there are measurable net gains. Accurate economic data and analysis are needed to establish what has happened to, as well as the impact of, these monies and the flow of funds in general.[58] It is also necessary to consider the effect and impact of those stability programmes which have aimed at influencing economic policies of struggling Member States in the Eurozone. Successive bail-out arrangements come with conditions that are unlikely to benefit the poor and may even cast more people in Europe into poverty. Consequently, a deep evaluation of these deals from a justice perspective would be necessary if a full justice audit was to be conducted.

The external behaviour of the EU must be similarly assessed. Any audit would have to consider, again empirically, the various flows of funds with a significant degree of sophistication. Limiting consideration to the amount of development aid which the EU is apt to valorize in its self-assessments is insufficient. By applauding its status as the largest aid donor in the world, it forgets the complexity of economic relations that exist between itself and impoverished countries (affected by trade preferences, tariffs, corporate exploitation, land grabbing, tied aid) which may well suggest a net loss for those supposed beneficiary states. Pogge has for some time highlighted the adverse effect of trade policies on the

[57] J. Neyer, 'Justice, Not Democracy: Legitimacy in the European Union' (2010) 48 *Journal of Common Market Studies* 903; D. Nicol, 'Can Justice Dethrone Democracy in the European Union? A Reply to Jürgen Neyer' (2012) 50 *Journal of Common Market Studies* 508. For a longer debate, see Gráinne de Búrca, et al., 'Debating Europe's Justice Deficit: The EU, Swabian Housewives, Rawls and Ryanair', European University Institute Working Papers (2013) (forthcoming).

[58] M. Antuofermo and E. Di Meglio, '23% of EU Citizens were at Risk of Poverty or Social Exclusion in 2010', EuroStat Report on Population and Social Conditions, September 2012, and the European Commission's report: European Commission, 'Study on the Measurement of Extreme Poverty in the European Union' (2010), p. 6.

developing world although the story does not end there.[59] Corporations based in the EU cannot be taken entirely out of the equation merely because we are examining the EU as a primary agent of justice in its own right. If it possesses the power to regulate and affect the behaviour of such corporations then that provides another element for consideration in the ways it chooses to act or not.

By addressing all these aspects in breadth and depth we might then be better placed to judge the EU in global justice terms. A holistic picture placed within the general modal framework proposed, would provide significantly greater scope for political and indeed philosophical examination and response. Then, perhaps, a full holistic evaluation of the EU's global justice pretensions and its ability to shape the international legal order in this respect can be undertaken. It is a necessary step if the EU is to know itself sufficiently to decide how it can engage with and influence the wider world in distributive justice terms.

[59] Pogge, *World Poverty and Human Rights.*

3

Shaping the international order as an EU objective

JORIS LARIK

1 Introduction

While views differ on the success of the European Union as an international actor,[1] its ambition can hardly be denied. It endeavours to be a global leader in various areas, including the promotion of the rule of law, state-building, migration, environmental sustainability, energy and championing international economic and financial governance.[2] These ambitions to shape the international order in ways consistent with the Union's own values and interests have been made explicit in numerous policy documents, such as the Laeken Declaration of 2001 and the European Security Strategy of 2003. While the former proclaimed the Union to be a 'power seeking to set globalization within a moral framework',[3] the latter declared the overarching purpose of EU external relations to be the 'development of a stronger international society, well-functioning international institutions and a rule-based international order'.[4]

With the entry into force of the Lisbon Treaty, the EU has gone even further to exhibit its global aspirations. It has introduced more streamlined and extensive language into its primary law on what can be called the Union's 'external objectives'.[5] In these provisions, we find

[1] For an overview, see C. Hill and M. Smith, 'Acting for Europe: Reassessing the European Union's Place in International Relations', in C. Hill and M. Smith (eds.), *International Relations and the European Union*, 2nd edn (Oxford University Press, 2011).

[2] See the contributions in Parts II and III of this volume.

[3] European Council, Presidency Conclusions, European Council meeting in Laeken 14 and 15 December 2001, SN 300/1/01 REV 1, p. 20.

[4] European Council, 'A Secure Europe in a Better World, European Security Strategy', Brussels, 13 December 2003, p. 9; see also European Council, 'Report on the Implementation of the European Security Strategy: Providing Security in a Changing World', S 407/08, Brussels, 11 December 2008.

[5] The general Union objectives can be found in Art. 3 TEU, with para. 5 defining the objectives of the Union '[i]n its relations with the wider world'. These are elaborated upon in Art. 21 TEU, which is part of the 'General Provisions on the Union's External Action'. There are also policy-specific objectives, for example, Art. 206 TFEU on the Common

commitments both to substantive goals for EU external action and to procedural aspects on how to shape the international legal order. In terms of substance, the Union pledges 'to uphold and promote its values and interests and contribute to the protection of its citizens'[6] while being 'guided by the principles which have inspired its own creation'.[7] These include, amongst others, democracy, human rights, sustainable development, free and fair trade and the eradication of poverty. In terms of procedures and frameworks to be utilized to meet these ends, the Treaties commit the Union to 'the strict observance and the development of international law',[8] to 'promote multilateral solutions to common problems, in particular in the framework of the United Nations'[9] and to foster 'an international system based on stronger multilateral cooperation and good global governance'.[10] In these provisions, the 'active paradigm' of EU external relations converges on an emphasis on value promotion on a global scale as well as on approaching the EU's active engagement with the world as an inherent legitimizing part of its *raison d'être*.[11]

These norms have received thus far a rather mixed welcome in scholarship. Some commentators heralded the bundling together of these principles and objectives as a 'major innovation' and forming the 'spinal column' of EU external action.[12] Others, by contrast, dismiss them as a mere 'wish list for a better world',[13] observe 'an almost epidemic proliferation of objectives of the Union',[14] and ridicule them

Commercial Policy and Art. 208 TFEU on development cooperation, which are to be pursued in the context of the general objectives and principles.

6 Art. 3(5) TEU. 7 Art. 21(1) TEU. 8 Art. 3(5) TEU.

9 Art. 21(1)(2) TEU. 10 Art. 21(2)(h) TEU.

11 See the introduction to this volume and the contributions by Gráinne de Búrca and Andrew Williams.

12 C. Kaddous, 'External Action under the Lisbon Treaty', in I. Pernice and E. Tanchev (eds.), *Ceci n'est pas une Constitution – Constitutionalisation without a Constitution?* (Berlin: Nomos, 2009), p. 178; regarding the Constitutional Treaty, see M. Cremona, 'The Draft Constitutional Treaty: External Relations and External Action' (2003) 40 *Common Market Law Review* 1347.

13 In the original: 'Wunschzettel für eine bessere Welt'; W. Drescher, 'Ziele und Zuständigkeiten', in A. Marchetti and C. Demesmay (eds.), *Der Vertrag von Lissabon: Analyse und Bewertung* (Berlin: Nomos, 2010), p. 68.

14 In the original, 'eine geradezu epidemische Ausbreitung von Unionszielen'; J. Terhechte, 'Kommentierung zum Art. 3 EUV (Ziele der Union)', in E. Grabitz, M. Hilf and M. Nettesheim (eds.), *Das Recht der Europäischen Union*, 41st supplement (loose-leaf) (Munich: C. H. Beck, 2010), marginal no. 63, arguing in the context of objectives of the Common Foreign and Security Policy (CFSP).

as 'redolent of motherhood and apple pie'.[15] Generally, these remarks might well fit the criticism by de Witte of the 'relentless accumulation of constitutional law',[16] having led to 'too much confusing and unhelpful constitutional law of foreign relations in the EU'.[17] Would these broadly formulated external objectives then qualify as particularly 'confusing and unhelpful'? After all, these provisions do not establish as such either competences or individual rights.

The aim of this contribution is to put the EU's external objectives, as legal norms, into a comparative perspective. It endeavours to answer the following question: how unusual is it really for a constitutional document to exhibit a polity's ambition to shape the international order? To this end, the chapter will contextualize external objectives with the general trends in comparative constitutional law as well as doctrinal approaches developed to grasp constitutional objectives as a norm category. In Europe, the latter can be found in both the German and French legal traditions. Far from any claim of exhaustiveness, the examples selected here, of both textual and doctrinal nature, serve to demonstrate that the criticisms referred to above tend to be too harsh. In fact, the EU Treaties are not at all that unusual in this regard. From a German or French perspective, constitutional objectives – also in the field of foreign policy – are to be considered legally binding norms performing important functions within a given legal order, including that of the European Union.

To elaborate on these points, section 2 will present evidence of an overall 'dynamic internationalization' in constitutional law around the world, which reveals that the codification of external objectives into national constitutions is rather commonplace. Section 3 will subsequently show that German and French legal doctrines approach such objectives as legally binding norms of constitutional law, serving primarily as an interpretive tool that makes it possible to round off otherwise unclear public powers and to justify certain limits to individual rights. It is argued here that there are no cogent reasons to exclude foreign policy-related objectives from this category. Section 4 will return to EU

[15] A. Dashwood, et al., *Wyatt and Dashwood's European Union Law*, 6th edn (Oxford: Hart Publishing, 2011), p. 903, referring to Art. 21(1) TEU.

[16] B. de Witte, 'Too Much Constitutional Law in the European Union's Foreign Relations', in M. Cremona and B. de Witte (eds.), *EU Foreign Relations Law: Constitutional Fundamentals* (Oxford: Hart Publishing, 2008), p. 10.

[17] *Ibid.*, p. 12.

primary law, apply the previous findings to the Union legal order and thereby situate its codified objectives, including the external ones, as norms of its constitutional law. The chapter concludes in section 5 that both the overall trends in contemporary constitutional law and related doctrinal debates should caution us against dismissing the external objectives codified in the EU Treaties. Instead, provisions on how to shape the international order are an increasingly important part of constitutional law.

2 Dynamic internationalization in constitutional law

At the outset, it is worthwhile to take stock of the general trends in comparative constitutional law. De Witte observed that, generally, 'values and objectives that must inspire the country's foreign policy' are a common feature in contemporary European constitutions.[18] This section not only confirms this, but also shows that it is not merely a European phenomenon, but indeed a global one. However, at the same time, de Witte admonished EU primary law for dealing with foreign policy issues 'in a much more detailed way than national constitutions'.[19] This statement is to be qualified with respect to external objectives. It is true that after the Lisbon reform the EU Treaties are certainly amongst the most verbose constitutional documents when it comes to external objectives, but they do not appear excessive or unusual when compared with many contemporary national constitutions.

Recent decades have seen a considerable amount of constitution drafting. As Sartori observed, writing in 1997, of 'the 170 or so written documents called constitutions in today's world, more than half have been written since 1974'.[20] This constitutional innovation was marked by two important trends: the 'internationalization' of constitutional law[21] and the codification of objectives of the state, which has been termed the 'dynamisation of constitutional law'.[22]

[18] *Ibid.* [19] *Ibid.*, p. 10.

[20] G. Sartori, *Comparative Constitutional Engineering*, 2nd edn (Basingstoke: Palgrave Macmillan, 1997), p. 197.

[21] See e.g. H. Tourard, *L'internationalisation des constitutions nationales* (Paris: Librairie générale de droit et de jurisprudence, 2000).

[22] In the original, 'Dynamisierung des Verfassungsrechts'; K.-P. Sommermann, *Staatsziele und Staatszielbestimmungen* (Tübingen: Mohr Siebeck, 1997), p. 374; similarly, P. de Montalivet, *Les Objectifs de valeur constitutionnelle* (Paris: Dalloz, 2006), p. 67, who speaks of a 'dynamic conception of law' (in the original, 'une conception dynamique du droit').

Regarding 'internationalization', as Wilson noted already in 1964, following each World War 'there was a wave of effort to include in national constitutions provisions whereby the law of nations would be made a part of municipal law'.[23] This trend has continued especially after the end of the Cold War in constitutional drafting processes in the formerly Eastern bloc countries, which now tend to include next to provisions on the incorporation of international law also other aspects such as universal value statements and guiding principles on foreign policy.[24] In this context, Kotzur discerns a trend that the more recent a constitution is, the stronger its references to a globalized world beyond the nation state usually are.[25]

As to 'dynamisation', provisions that mandate the state to pursue certain objectives have equally proliferated in constitutional documents around the world. The modern constitution, in addition to its traditional function of establishing the rules and limits of government,[26] also sketches out a certain future which is to be strived towards through the means of this very constitutional framework. Already in the 1970s, Scheuner described constitutional objectives as indicative of a contemporary trend towards the socially active polity and transnational integration.[27] According to De Montalivet, these provisions are nothing less than the constitutional response to 'a post-modernity characterised by complexity, disorder, indetermination and uncertainty'.[28] In view of such uncertainties, Sommermann sees constitutional objectives as a way of allaying the need for orientation and a 'hunger for values' of a political community.[29]

Both these trends can be detected today in almost all modern constitutions and represent the constitutional reflection of the provident social welfare state (note also the French term *l'État providence*)[30]

[23] R. Wilson, 'International Law in New National Constitutions' (1964) 58 *American Journal of International Law* 432.

[24] V. Vereshchetin, 'New Constitutions and the Old Problem of the Relationship between International Law and National Law' (1996) 7 *European Journal of International Law* 1.

[25] M. Kotzur, 'Weltrechtliche Bezüge in nationalen Verfassungstexten: Die Rezeption verfassungsrechtlicher Normen durch das Völkerrecht' (2008) 39 *Rechtstheorie* 191 (213).

[26] See e.g. L. Henkin, *The Rights of Man Today* (London: Stevens and Sons, 1979), pp. 31–2, who argues that, for historical reasons, the US constitution was primarily concerned with limiting government power.

[27] U. Scheuner, *Staatstheorie und Staatsrecht – Gesammelte Schriften* (Berlin: Duncker and Humblot, 1978), p. 242.

[28] In the original: 'une post-modernité marquée par la complexité, le désordre, l'indétermination et l'incertitude', de Montalivet, *Les Objectifs de valeur constitutionnelle*, p. 571.

[29] In the original: 'Wertehunger'; Sommermann, *Staatsziele und Staatszielbestimmungen*, p. 1.

[30] De Montalivet, *Les Objectifs de valeur constitutionnelle*, p. 68.

acting in a globalized and interdependent world. The codification of internationally oriented objectives into a constitution is the most visible expression of the convergence of these two trends. As Röben underlines, constitutional law in the area of foreign relations is a means of the modern state and its legal order to adapt to the pressures created by globalization and global law-making processes. Constitutional law, in reaction to these pressures, turns to and embraces the external.[31] Thus, 'internationalization' is not only about the role of international law in the domestic legal order, just as 'dynamization' is not just about the pursuit of constitutional objectives domestically. Externally oriented constitutional objectives indicate that constitutional law not only regulates how external influences are to be reacted to internally, but that it also provides guidance for a state's own input into shaping these influences, thus bearing witness to an 'active paradigm' for the conduct of foreign relations in national constitutional law.

Even though spatial constraints will not allow a comprehensive analysis of all such constitutional provisions, a selection of pertinent examples for this double trend will be provided from around the world.[32] Starting in Europe, the Portuguese constitution is most extensive in this regard. It contains an article with seven paragraphs devoted to the substantive principles guiding the external relations of the country.[33] These include national independence, human rights, sovereign equality, the peaceful settlement of international disputes, non-interference in internal affairs, the abolition of imperialism, colonialism, aggression, domination and exploitation, disarmament, the dissolution of political-military blocs, and collective security. Furthermore, it commits Portugal to the right to self-determination and insurrection against oppression, the maintenance of a bond of friendship with other Portuguese-speaking countries as well as European integration. Finally, the transfer of powers to the EU and acceptance of the jurisdiction of the International Criminal Court (ICC) are included as well.

The German Basic Law also devotes various provisions to foreign policy guidance, albeit in a more scattered and, at times, implicit way. A normative statement with an external dimension is made already in the first article following the famous evocation of the inviolability of human

[31] V. Röben, *Außenverfassungsrecht* (Tübingen: Mohr Siebeck, 2007), foreword.

[32] For English-language translations of national constitutional provisions, the Oceana Law® database 'Constitutions of Countries of the World' has been used (www.oceanalaw.com).

[33] Art. 7 Portuguese constitution.

dignity, according to which 'the German people therefore acknowledge inviolable and inalienable human rights as the foundation of *every* community, of peace and justice *in the world*'.[34] Human rights are thus asserted as universally valid norms and an explicit nexus with international peace and justice is established.[35] In addition, one can derive foreign policy objectives from the permissions granted by the Basic Law for the Federal Republic to participate in the European Union along certain normative lines,[36] as well as to transfer powers to international organizations, accede to a system of collective defence and compulsory international dispute settlement.[37] These put an emphasis on the objectives of international cooperation, security and the international rule of law, especially when read in conjunction with the clause in the preamble that expresses 'the will to promote world peace as an equal partner in a united Europe'.[38]

In a less extensive manner, the constitution of Bulgaria also devotes an article to foreign policy. First, it posits international law as the guideline of Bulgaria's foreign policy,[39] which shows again that the promotion of international law is not simply a matter of internal incorporation and compliance. Secondly, it stipulates as the 'highest objective' of Bulgarian foreign policy, the country's security, independence and the protection of its citizens' well-being and rights, as well as 'the promotion of a just international order'.[40]

The proliferation of such provisions is by no means confined to Europe. Two examples of this are the constitutions of the rising powers, Brazil and the People's Republic of China. In the case of Brazil, its constitution lists principles that govern the country's international relations, those being national independence, prevalence of human rights, self-determination of peoples, non-intervention, sovereign equality, the defence of peace, peaceful resolution of conflicts, repudiation of terrorism and racism, cooperation amongst people for the progress of humanity, as well as recognition of political asylum.[41] In addition, the sole paragraph

[34] Art. 1(2) German Basic Law (emphases added).
[35] Röben, *Außenverfassungsrecht*, pp. 197–8.
[36] Art. 23(1) German Basic Law, which premises such participation on democratic, social and federal principles, the rule of law, subsidiarity, and fundamental rights protection; similarly Art. 7(6) Portuguese constitution.
[37] Art. 24 German Basic Law. See for a similar provision, Art. 29 Irish constitution.
[38] Preamble, German Basic Law.
[39] Art. 24(1) Bulgarian constitution.
[40] Art. 24(2) Bulgarian constitution; similarly, Art. 135(1) Lithuanian constitution.
[41] Art. 4 Brazilian constitution; see for a similar list of principles, Art. 51 Indian constitution.

of the article to which these principles are attached mandates Brazil to 'seek the economic, political, social and cultural integration of the people of Latin America, with a view toward forming a Latin-American community of nations'.[42] This shows that regional integration as a subject for constitutional law is not a European monopoly either.[43]

The most extensive language on foreign affairs in a national constitution can arguably be found in the preamble of the constitution of China, which was adopted in 1982. It stresses the importance of global interdependence, acknowledging that '[t]he future of China is closely linked with that of the whole world'. This is followed by an enumeration of the principles that are to guide Chinese foreign policy. Those include mutual respect for sovereignty and territorial integrity, mutual non-aggression, non-interference in each other's internal affairs, and peaceful coexistence in developing diplomatic relations and economic and cultural exchanges with other countries.[44] This reflects a rather traditional, Westphalian understanding of the international (legal) order. In addition, the constitution expresses opposition to imperialism, hegemonism and colonialism, and mandates the state to show solidarity to people in other countries in their struggle for independence and to strive 'to safeguard world peace and promote the cause of human progress'.[45] While one may question the degree of actual 'constitutionalism' underpinning the legal order of the People's Republic, especially in view of the lack of judicial review,[46] it is nonetheless noteworthy that its constitutional document eagerly partakes in the trend of 'dynamic internationalization'.

In sum, we can observe that external objectives, as the expression of the dynamic internationalization of constitutional law, exist in many constitutions today. An active approach to foreign policy, codified in the highest laws of a country, providing guidance in terms of both substance (for example, human rights, human dignity or self-determination) and governance (for example, peaceful dispute settlement, international law and regional integration) is thus nothing unusual. Consequently, the

[42] Art. 4 Brazilian constitution.

[43] On the European constitutional dimension, see C. Grabenwarter, 'National Constitutional Law Relating to the European Union', in A. von Bogdandy and J. Bast (eds.), *Principles of European Constitutional Law*, 2nd edn (Munich: C. H. Beck, 2010).

[44] Twelfth paragraph of the preamble of the Constitution of the People's Republic of China, which has not been amended since the adoption of the constitution.

[45] Ibid.

[46] See e.g. Q. Zhang, 'A Constitution without Constitutionalism? The Paths of Constitutional Development in China' (2010) 8 *International Journal of Constitutional Law* 950.

post-Lisbon EU Treaties appear less objectionable, and also somewhat less original. The alleged 'epidemic' of external objectives in EU primary law thus turns out to be a 'pandemic' given the global scale of this trend. Disproving the uniqueness of these provisions of course does not in itself entail a judgment as to their legal value and function. In order to tackle these issues, it is necessary to look beyond the constitutional texts and draw on doctrinal approaches that have been elaborated in order to situate constitutional objectives as norms in a given legal order. While constitutional provisions in this area abound, there are only few doctrines of sufficient sophistication to grasp them.

3 Doctrinal approaches: *Staatszielbestimmungen* and *objectifs de valeur constitutionnelle*

Two important legal traditions in Europe have devoted considerable attention to constitutional objectives as a norm category. These are the German doctrine of *Staatszielbestimmungen* and its French counterpart of *objectifs de valeur constitutionnelle*. In both jurisdictions, codified objectives are recognized as a category of binding norms of constitutional value committing all state organs and serve as a tool to interpret the constitution as a whole.

3.1 Staatszielbestimmungen

The legal tradition in Europe showing the keenest interest in constitutional objectives is arguably the German one. *Staatsziele* (state objectives) are understood as specific goals that the state sets itself in the pursuit of the common good.[47] German scholarship speaks of *Staatszielbestimmungen* (constitutional provisions on state objectives) where those are codified. The notion of 'state objective' was coined by Hans Peter Ipsen in 1949 by defining the concept of the 'soziale Rechtsstaat'[48] (a compound of the rule of law and the social state) as a *Staatsziel*.[49]

[47] See e.g. J. Isensee, 'Staatsaufgaben', in J. Isensee and P. Kirchhof (eds.), *Handbuch des Staatsrechts der Bundesrepublik Deutschland*, vol. 4, 3rd edn (Heidelberg: C. F. Müller, 2006), p. 121; and Sommermann, *Staatsziele und Staatszielbestimmungen*, pp. 3–4.

[48] The term is used in Arts. 20 and 28 German Basic Law.

[49] See Sommermann, *Staatsziele und Staatszielbestimmungen*, p. 5; Scheuner, *Staatstheorie und Staatsrecht – Gesammelte Schriften*, p. 226.

Tellingly, within the German discourse, constitutional objectives have been criticized for reasons very similar to those voiced against the external objectives of the EU now. The gist of these criticisms is that the rather vague, soft character of constitutional objectives is alien to the original characteristic style of the Basic Law, which owed its success to dependable legal guarantees that can be invoked in court,[50] and not to the kind of provisions that serve 'as a people's catechism or credo of a civic religion'.[51] Moreover, such objectives have been admonished for raising expectations that will be difficult to satisfy, challenging ultimately the effectiveness of constitutional law as a whole.[52]

Generally, however, they are well-received and are regarded as legally binding norms of constitutional rank which commit the entirety of state organs, but without establishing competences or individual rights.[53] Objectives are understood to be primarily addressed to the legislator.[54] The German Federal Constitutional Court (*Bundesverfassungsgericht*), although it has never used the term *Staatszielbestimmung* in its case law, has nonetheless used provisions understood as such by scholars on various occasions when interpreting the Basic Law.

For instance, the *Bundesverfassungsgericht* has referred to the principle of social justice as a goal (without, however, calling it a *Staatsziel*) entailing 'the obligation of the state to provide for a just social order'.[55] Even though this was broadly defined leaving the legislator with a wide margin of manoeuvre, the court ruled that the duty to provide for

[50] Isensee, 'Staatsaufgaben', p. 144.

[51] In the original: 'als Volkskatechismus und zivilreligiöses Glaubensbekenntnis'; *ibid.*; also D. Merten, 'Über Staatsziele' [1993] *Die Öffentliche Verwaltung* 368 (373).

[52] P. Badura, 'Arten der Verfassungsrechtssätze', in J. Isensee and P. Kirchhof (eds.), *Handbuch des Staatsrechts der Bundesrepublik Deutschland*, vol. 7 (Heidelberg: C. F. Müller, 1992), p. 41.

[53] Sommermann, *Staatsziele und Staatszielbestimmungen*, p. 5; B. Plecher-Hochstraßer, *Zielbestimmungen im Mehrebenensystem: Die Verzahnung der Staatszielbestimmungen im GG mit den Zielbestimmungen im EUV, EGV, EuratomV und EUVV* (Meidenbauer, 2006), p. 23, who draws on the definition of the 1983 Expert Commission, Bundesministerium des Innern und der Justiz, *Staatszielbestimmungen/Gesetzgebungsaufträge*, Bericht der Sachverständigenkommission, Staatszielbestimmugen/Gesetzgebungsaufträge, Bonn, 1983, p. 5.

[54] Sommermann, *Staatsziele und Staatszielbestimmungen*, pp. 383–7; Plecher-Hochstraßer, *Zielbestimmungen im Mehrebenensystem*, p. 26; Badura, 'Arten der Verfassungsrechtssätze', p. 41.

[55] In the original: 'die Pflicht des Staates, für eine gerechte Sozialordnung zu sorgen'; *BVerfGE* 59, 231, para. 68 (decision of 13 January 1982 concerning freelancers).

minimum conditions for a dignified life was 'compelling'.[56] Similarly, in its famous judgment on the Lisbon Treaty of 2009, the court stressed that participation in the EU was not at the discretion of German constitutional organs, as such participation represents a 'constitutional mandate'.[57] However, it should be stressed that apart from such core duties, the attainment of the objective is not required, but only its active pursuit.[58] This qualification of the scope of this obligation is well captured in the German literature by the notions of *Vorbehalt des Möglichen*, i.e. the bounds of possibility,[59] and Alexy's optimization requirement (*Optimierungsgebot*),[60] i.e. 'norms that require that something be realized to the greatest extent possible given the legal and factual possibilities'.[61] Vice versa, only in extreme cases where the objective had been disregarded in a manifest way could the German Constitutional Court find that an organ of the state had acted unconstitutionally.[62] For example, the court ruled in the context of the objective of reunification (*Wiedervereinigungsgebot*) that given the wide discretion of the legislature, the judiciary will only step in once the former acts in a way that is obviously opposed to reunification from a legal or factual point of view.[63] Thus, generally, the *Bundesverfassungsgericht* did not find actual violations through manifest disregard of constitutional objectives.

As a more tangible function, objectives can help to authorize certain conduct by the state, above all when other constitutional norms on competence or individual rights are being interpreted. Wherever in the constitution a particular branch of government is mandated to act, competence questions become intertwined with objectives. While objectives do not establish competence as such, they help to justify the exercise of power by public

[56] In the original: 'zwingend'; *BVerfGE* 82, 60, para. 88 (decision of 29 May 1990 concerning tax-free minimum living wage).

[57] In the original: 'Verfassungsauftrag'; *BVerfGE* 123, 267, para. 225 (decision of 30 June 2009 concerning approval of the Lisbon Treaty).

[58] Isensee, 'Staatsaufgaben', p. 121; Plecher-Hochstraßer, *Zielbestimmungen im Mehrebenensystem*, pp. 32–3.

[59] Sommermann, *Staatsziele und Staatszielbestimmungen*, p. 224.

[60] *Ibid.*, pp. 360–1, who calls state objectives optimization requirements '*par excellence*' (at 361); also Isensee, 'Staatsaufgaben', p. 126.

[61] R. Alexy, *A Theory of Constitutional Rights* (Oxford University Press, 2010), p. 47.

[62] Sommermann, *Staatsziele und Staatszielbestimmungen*, pp. 429–36; Scheuner, *Staatstheorie und Staatsrecht*, p. 236.

[63] *BVerfGE* 36, 1, para. 80 (decision of 31 July 1973 concerning the Basic Treaty (*Grundlagenvertrag*) between the Federal Republic and the German Democratic Republic).

bodies in case of uncertainty.[64] Objectives can also serve to justify derogations from constitutionally protected rights.[65] However, the pursuit of objectives and the corresponding constitutional interpretation are only permitted to the extent that they do not undermine the structural principles (*Strukturprinzipien*)[66] which are enshrined in the constitution, such as democracy, federalism and effective fundamental rights protection.[67] In the decision on the Lisbon Treaty, the *Bundesverfassungsgericht* decided that such structural limits also apply to the pursuit of European integration.[68]

With particular regard to external objectives, German scholarship accepts them as belonging to the overall category of constitutional objectives and provides a number of additional features to be taken into account. Conceptually, as *Staatsziele* represent specific manifestations of the pursuit of the common good by the state, adding the external dimension leads to an intertwining of the ideas of the national, regional and global common goods.[69] Institutionally, while the legislator is primarily concerned with the pursuit of state objectives internally, in foreign affairs the executive – as the international representative of a country[70] – becomes the co-protagonist in the pursuit of such objectives.[71]

As to the legal force of external objectives, further insights can be drawn from the case law of the *Bundesverfassungsgericht*. While the court, as Thomas Franck argues, has refused to abdicate its jurisdiction over foreign affairs,[72] it has acknowledged at the same

[64] Scheuner, *Staatstheorie und Staatsrecht*, pp. 234–5.

[65] Plecher-Hochstraßer, *Zielbestimmungen im Mehrebenensystem*, pp. 40–1; Sommermann, *Staatsziele und Staatszielbestimmungen*, pp. 422–5, who refers to a German Constitutional Court decision on freelancers, where it ruled that social justice (*Sozialstaatsprinzip*) as a state objective can only restrict fundamental rights by further concretization through law, *BVerfGE* 59, 231, para. 68 (decision of 13 January 1982 on freelancers).

[66] Unlike state objectives, they establish the basic characteristics of the state, i.e. what it *is*, not what it should *strive for*. Sommermann, *Staatsziele und Staatszielbestimmungen*, p. 373; Merten, 'Über Staatsziele', p. 370.

[67] This relates to the broader question to which extent the interest of the individual can be trumped by the 'common good'. See J. Isensee, 'Gemeinwohl im Verfassungsstaat', in J. Isensee and P. Kirchhof (eds.), *Handbuch des Staatsrechts der Bundesrepublik Deutschland*, vol. 4, 3rd edn (Heidelberg: C. F. Müller, 2006), pp. 8 and 19–22.

[68] *BVerfGE* 123, 267, para. 340.

[69] Isensee 'Gemeinwohl im Verfassungsstaat', p. 9, also pp. 20–1.

[70] See C. Calliess, 'Auswärtige Gewalt', in Isensee and Kirchhof, *Handbuch des Staatsrechts der Bundesrepublik Deutschland*, vol. 3, p. 590.

[71] Sommermann, *Staatsziele und Staatszielbestimmungen*, p. 387.

[72] T. Franck, *Political Questions/Judicial Answers: Does the Rule of Law Apply to Foreign Affairs?* (Princeton, NJ: Princeton University Press, 1992), pp. 107–25.

time the enhanced limitations of the government in pursuing external objectives and thus grants it an even wider margin of discretion than it usually has internally. In an early judgment, the *Bundesverfassungsgericht* underlined that in reviewing the constitutionality of an international agreement, the court concedes to the treaty-making organs of the Federal Republic of Germany a large measure of discretion, recognizing that 'the circle of solutions theoretically available to draw up the agreement is in practice narrowed down to what is politically achievable vis-à-vis the respective contractual partner'.[73]

As a result, the bounds of possibility have to be considered as generally narrower in the foreign affairs domain, as in addition to the legal constraints, political willingness and material resources within a state one has to take into account the legal requirements of the international system, those within other states, the political conditions present in other states, as well as the allocation of resources outside one's own borders. In short, external objectives have to be pursued through playing according to the manifold rules of a multilevel legal system and the volatile political opportunities of a multilevel game.[74] As a consequence, the already limited role of the judiciary in monitoring objectives is restrained further.

With this reasoning, the Federal Constitutional Court was in fact applying multilevel logic par excellence. Nevertheless, the interpretive function of objectives, and an ensuing role to be played by the judiciary, continue to apply in the external domain. This is illustrated, for instance, by the decision of the *Bundesverfassungsgericht* in which it ruled that collective security as mentioned in the German Basic Law[75] also covered collective defence arrangements, thus allowing the Federal Republic to participate in operations of the latter.[76]

[73] In the original: 'zumal der Kreis der an sich zur Wahl stehenden vertraglichen Lösungen sich praktisch auf das dem jeweiligen Vertragspartner gegenüber politisch Erreichbare verengt'; *BVerfGE* 4, 157 para. 37 (decision of 4 May 1955 concerning the Status of the Saar Agreement).

[74] For the concepts, see, respectively, I. Pernice, 'The Global Dimension of Multilevel Constitutionalism: A Legal Response to the Challenges of Globalisation', in P. M. Dupuy, et al. (eds.), *Common Values in International Law: Essays in Honour of Christian Tomuschat* (Kehl: N. P. Engel, 2006); and R. Putnam, 'Diplomacy and Domestic Politics: The Logic of Two-Level Games' (1988) 42 *International Organisation* 427.

[75] Art. 24(2) German Basic Law.

[76] *BVerfGE* 90, 286 para. 236 (decision of 12 July 1994 concerning 'out of area' operations).

3.2 *Objectifs de valeur constitutionnelle*

French doctrine has devoted particular attention to constitutional objectives as well, which are known there as *objectifs de valeur constitutionnelle*. Their origin and history, however, are markedly different from their German counterpart. While German jurists claim authorship of the concept based on scholarly interpretation of the Basic Law, the French doctrine emanated directly from the case law of the *Conseil constitutionnel*. This notion was introduced by a decision of the *Conseil* from 1982 on a law concerning the freedom of audio-visual communication, in which it declared safeguarding public order, respect for the freedoms of others and the preservation of sociocultural pluralism to be *objectifs de valeur constitutionnelle*.[77] De Montalivet submits that the *Conseil* was most likely influenced by the previous case law of none other than the Court of Justice of the EU (ECJ),[78] in particular the *Nold* judgment of 1974 in terms of restrictions of fundamental rights.[79]

The *objectifs* have received criticism in French scholarship comparable to that in Germany and the EU. It has been argued that the vague concept of an objective is 'unheard of' and 'foreign' to the French legal tradition,[80] potentially even risking the 'desecration'[81] of the French constitution and the judicialization of politics (*gouvernement des juges*).[82]

Overall, current French scholarship deems the *objectifs* a norm category of constitutional law (i.e. as part of the so-called *bloc de constitutionnalité*), which have their source either in the text of the French constitution, the Preamble of the constitution of the Fourth Republic or the 1789 Declaration of the Rights of Man and of the Citizen (to both of which reference is made

[77] Décision n° 82-141 DC du 27 juillet 1982, *Loi sur la communication audiovisuelle*, Recueil, p. 48, para. 5. More objectives have been added in later judgments, see F. Luchaire, 'Brèves remarques sur une création du Conseil constitutionnel: l'objectif de valeur constitutionnelle' (2005) 64 *Revue française de droit constitutionnel* 675 (676–7).

[78] De Montalivet, *Les Objectifs de valeur constitutionnelle*, pp. 7 and 47–53; also Luchaire, 'Brèves remarques sur une création du Conseil constitutionnel', p. 675.

[79] Case 4/79 *Nold* v. *Commission* [1975] ECR 491, para. 14.

[80] In the original: 'inédite' and 'étrangère', respectively; C. Vimbert, 'L'Ordre public dans la jurisprudence du Conseil constitutionnel' (1994) 3 *Revue du droit public et de la science politique en France et à l'étranger* 693 (712).

[81] In the original: 'désacralisation'; P. Pactet, 'La Désacralisation progressive de la Constitution de 1958', in *La République: Mélanges en l'honneur de Pierre Avril* (Paris: Montchrestien, 2001), p. 389.

[82] See de Montalivet, *Les Objectifs de valeur constitutionnelle*, pp. 64–9, who rejects that such a judicialisation has occurred.

in the preamble of the current constitution).[83] De Montalivet concludes that the *objectifs* are in themselves legally binding norms, obliging the entirety of state power, with the prime addressee being the legislature.[84] According to him, they perform the three basic functions of prohibition, obligation and permission. As we will see, the *objectifs* operate in a manner much akin to German *Staatszielbestimmungen*.

In terms of the obligatory force of objectives, the *Conseil constitutionnel* has stated, for instance, that 'it is incumbent upon the legislator' to implement the constitutional objective of making decent accommodation available for each person.[85] In another case, the *Conseil* ruled that it falls to the legislature and competent regulatory authorities to decide on appropriate rules aimed at the 'realization' of the objective to provide health protection.[86] However, despite this strong wording, the scope of the obligation is in fact limited here as well, as objectives cannot be invoked directly by individuals in court but impose only a best endeavours obligation (*obligation de moyens*).[87]

Closely related is the function of prohibition, where the German and French approaches converge as well. According to French doctrine, a law that manifestly disregards a constitutional objective is forbidden,[88] which *in extremis* could lead to declaring that law unconstitutional through judicial review. For instance, concerning the constitutionality of the French ratification of the Schengen Agreement,[89] the *Conseil* ruled that the law approving the agreement could not be considered as 'disregarding' the constitutional objective of safeguarding public order.[90] While usually

[83] Luchaire, 'Brèves remarques sur une création du Conseil constitutionnel', pp. 677–8; Bertrand Faure, 'Les Objectifs de valeur constitutionnelle: une nouvelle catégorie juridique?' (1995) 21 *Revue française de droit constitutionnel* 47 (63–6); in detail, see de Montalivet, *Les Objectifs de valeur constitutionnelle*, pp. 72–105.

[84] De Montalivet, *Les Objectifs de valeur constitutionnelle*, p. 459.

[85] In the original: 'il appartient au législateur'; Décision n° 98-403 DC du 29 juillet 1998, *Loi d'orientation relative à la lutte contre les exclusions*, Recueil, p. 276, para. 7.

[86] In the original: 'réalisation'; Décision n° 89-269 DC du 22 janvier 1990, *Loi portant diverses dispositions relatives à la sécurité sociale et à la santé*, Recueil, p. 33, para. 26. For further case law, see de Montalivet, *Les Objectifs de valeur constitutionnelle*, p. 357–64.

[87] *Ibid.*, p. 561. [88] *Ibid.*, p. 528.

[89] The Schengen *acquis* – Agreement between the Governments of the States of the Benelux Economic Union, the Federal Republic of Germany and the French Republic on the Gradual Abolition of Checks at their Common Borders, OJ (2000) L 239, 22 September 2000, pp. 13–18

[90] In the original: 'méconnaissant'; Décision n° 91-294 DC du 25 juillet 1991, *Loi autorisant l'approbation de la convention d'application de l'accord de Schengen*, Recueil, p. 91, para. 17. For further case law, see de Montalivet, *Les Objectifs de valeur constitutionnelle*, pp. 334–40.

the *Conseil* concludes that no violation has occurred,[91] it did rule in one decision that a contested provision of a law was contrary to, inter alia, the objective of the intelligibility and accessibility of the law.[92] The prohibition function of *objectifs* is thus not merely a theoretical construct.

Lastly, as to the permissive function, which is closely linked to constitutional interpretation, the French debate is focused on the extent to which *objectifs* can justify limitations of individual rights,[93] rather than the question of competence allocation. Nonetheless, the *Conseil* has been prudent to point to the limits of competences that apply in the pursuit of constitutional objectives. For example, the court made explicit that the modalities in the pursuit of the objective of public health are to be determined by the state organs 'according to their respective competences'.[94] In terms of restricting individual rights, scholars stress that *objectifs* also help to reconcile different rights and to mark their limits vis-à-vis the public common good.[95] For instance, in the decision on the objective to provide decent housing, the *Conseil* ruled that the legislator is allowed to apply limitations to the right to property to this end, as long as it does not undermine the core of that right.[96] Furthermore, it stressed that individual rights and constitutional objectives pursued by the state are also mutually reinforcing. For example, the *Conseil* stated in another decision that in the absence of public order 'the exercise of individual freedoms could not be guaranteed'.[97] De Montalivet therefore concludes that the most important function of the *objectifs* resides in their contribution to the effectiveness of individual rights.[98]

[91] Luchaire, 'Brèves remarques sur une création du Conseil constitutionnel', p. 678.

[92] Décision n° 2003-475 DC du 24 juillet 2003, *Loi portant réforme de l'élection des sénateurs*, Recueil, p. 397, para. 26.

[93] Faure, 'Les Objectifs de valeur constitutionnelle', p. 63; de Montalivet *Les Objectifs de valeur constitutionnelle*, p. 399.

[94] In the original: 'selon leurs compétences respectives', Décision n° 89-269 DC du 22 janvier 1990, *Loi portant diverses dispositions relatives à la sécurité sociale et à la santé*, Recueil, p. 33, para. 26.

[95] De Montalivet, *Les Objectifs de valeur constitutionnelle*, p. 586; B. Genevois, *La jurisprudence du Conseil constitutionnel: Principes Directeurs* (Paris: Éditions Sciences et Techniques Humaines, 1988), p. 342; Faure, 'Les Objectifs de valeur constitutionnelle', pp. 63–6.

[96] Décision n° 98-403 DC du 29 juillet 1998, *Loi d'orientation relative à la lutte contre les exclusions*, Recueil, p. 276, para. 7; also Décision n° 90-283 DC du 08 janvier 1991, *Loi relative à la lutte contre le tabagisme et l'alcoolisme*, Recueil, p. 11, para. 8.

[97] Décision n° 85-187 DC du 25 janvier 1985, *Loi relative à l'état d'urgence en Nouvelle-Calédonie et dépendances*, Recueil, p. 43, para. 3. For further case law, see de Montalivet, *Les Objectifs de valeur constitutionnelle*, p. 400 et seq.

[98] De Montalivet, *Les Objectifs de valeur constitutionnelle*, p. 454.

With regard to the external dimension, however, French scholarship is not as outspoken. The most likely reason for this is that French legal writing focuses on the *objectifs* as established in the case law of the *Conseil constitutionnel*, some of which are rather specific, such as combating fiscal fraud. To date, the *Conseil* has not pronounced an explicitly external *objectif*, which may be seen either as a denial of their existence or simply as reflective of the fact that the *Conseil* has not yet had the opportunity to rule on them. It should be recalled here that the *Bundesverfassungsgericht* has never adopted the notion of *Staatsziel* itself, and speaks generally of 'principles' or simply 'goals'. Instead, academic commentators started theorizing about constitutional objectives, with German scholars having readily accepted the existence of a wide range of constitutional objectives including external ones.

To conclude that the French legal order and doctrine decidedly reject the existence of external objectives as such seems unwarranted. For a start, the French constitution contains provisions with explicit external objectives, such as developing the international *Francophonie*[99] and participation in the European Union.[100] Moreover, the *Conseil* has issued decisions in cases with a foreign policy dimension from which we can discern at least an external dimension to the existing *objectifs*. It ruled, as we have seen, that the conclusion of the Schengen agreement by France was not unconstitutional, as approval of that treaty did not disregard the objective of public order. This can be taken as indicating that the pursuit of internal *objectifs* cannot be undermined through international commitments, arguably in the pursuit of implicit external objectives such as international cooperation and integration.

4 External objectives as EU primary law

It emerges from the previous sections that external objectives are textually neither unusual, nor, as part of the norm category of constitutional objectives, legally negligible. Put differently, the contemporary constitution indeed expresses itself as to how the international order ought to be shaped. This is of legal significance for the interpretation of the constitutional law as a whole. The last bastion of the harshest critics of EU external objectives would be then to set the EU legal order and its objectives apart from the findings presented above. In other words, while

99 Art. 87 French constitution. 100 Art. 88(1) French constitution.

'ordinary' national constitutional orders may well have such objectives operating within them, a similar approach to the EU would be inappropriate in view of its different nature. As will be argued here, even this last line of defence does not hold. In the following, the preceding findings will be applied to EU primary law as reformed by the Lisbon Treaty, taking into account the peculiar features of the Union.

As a preliminary observation, it should be noted that while external relations law of the EU has received considerable scholarly attention, particularly for questions of conferred powers, competence and legal basis, the external objectives of the Union, on the contrary, have led a rather shadowy existence. There is, however, a certain amount of literature on Union (and former Community) objectives in general.[101]

Of course, caution must be exercised with regard to the transferability of national constitutional law concepts to the supranational level given the *sui generis* character of the Union and its legal order.[102] Nonetheless, there has been a persistently strong current in EU legal scholarship that considers it appropriate to approach EU primary law in constitutional terms.[103] The main difference with regard to objectives found in national constitutions and those of the EU results from the fact that the Union is not a state with all-encompassing competence (*Kompetenz-Kompetenz*)

[101] e.g. C. Calliess, 'Kollektive Ziele und Prinzipien im Verfassungsrecht der EU – Bestandsaufnahme, Wirkungen und Perspektiven' (2003) 92 *Archiv für Rechts- und Sozialphilosophie-Beihefte*, pp. 85–111; F. Reimer, 'Ziele und Zuständigkeiten: Die Funktionen der Unionszielbestimmungen' (2003) *Europarecht* 992; M. Kotzur, 'Die Ziele der Union: Verfassungsidentität und Gemeinschaftsidee' (2005) *Die Öffentliche Verwaltung* 313; Sommermann, *Staatsziele und Staatszielbestimmungen*, pp. 280–96; Plecher-Hochstraßer, *Zielbestimmungen im Mehrebenensystem*, pp. 105–54; earlier, notably P. Pescatore, 'Les Objectifs de la Communauté européenne comme principes d'interprétation dans la jurisprudence de la Cour de justice', in *Miscellanea W. J. Ganshof van der Meersch* (Brussels: Bruylant 1972); and H. P. Ipsen, *Europäisches Gemeinschaftsrecht* (Tübingen: Mohr Siebeck 1972), pp. 545–67.

[102] A. von Bogdandy, 'Zur Übertragbarkeit staatsrechtlicher Figuren auf die Europäische Union', in M. Brenner, P. Huber and M. Möstl (eds.), *Der Staat des Grundgesetzes – Kontinuität und Wandel: Festschrift für Peter Badura zum siebzigsten Geburtstag* (Tübingen: Mohr Siebeck 2004).

[103] See e.g. A. von Bogdandy and J. Bast, 'The Constitutional Approach to EU Law – From Taming Intergovernmental Relationships to Framing Political Processes', in von Bogdandy and Bast, *Principles of European Constitutional Law*; P. Craig, 'Constitutions, Constitutionalism, and the European Union' (2001) 7 *European Law Review* 125; and seminally E. Stein, 'Lawyers, Judges, and the Making of a Transnational Constitution' (1981) 75 *American Journal of International Law* 1; with particular regard to EU external relations law as constitutional law, M. Cremona and B. de Witte, 'Introduction', in Cremona and de Witte, *EU Foreign Relations Law: Constitutional Fundamentals*, pp. xi–xv.

but instead remains an entity of conferred powers aimed at certain goals. Therefore, the codification of specific goals of the European project was a feature present from the very outset in the founding treaties of the Communities.[104] As Ipsen aptly observed in 1972, the Union and its predecessors have an actual *Zielbedarf*, i.e. a need for goals.[105] However, having been through various amendment rounds, this need has been amply satiated in view of the many and very broad objectives the Union is to pursue today.[106]

As we have seen from the developments in comparative constitutional law, states, although they do not *need* to codify objectives to justify their actions or even existence, apparently now *perceive* a need to do so. In German, one could thus speak of states having a *Zielbedürfnis*, i.e. the urge to enshrine objectives in their constitutional documents. A theoretical difference between *Zielbedarf* and *Zielbedürfnis* remains, but the result is the same: the codification and entrenchment of objectives in a foundational document, including goals related to external relations, and their subsequent factoring into the overall legal order. Hence, while keeping the particular features of the EU and its legal system in mind, a constitutional law approach to EU primary law amenable to comparison with national constitutional orders is indeed possible with regard to objectives. In this way, it is legitimate to draw on 'the repertoire of established doctrines'[107] in order to come to terms also with the external objectives in EU primary law.

Authors commenting on Union (and former Community) objectives, even before the Lisbon Treaty, generally assert that these, too, are legally binding, in principle justiciable norms,[108] but with limited justiciability due to the discretion granted to the EU organs in pursuing these objectives.[109] This conclusion draws on the case law of the Court of Justice,

[104] Art. 2 ECSC Treaty; Art. 1(2) EAC Treaty; Art. 2 EEC Treaty.

[105] Ipsen, *Europäisches Gemeinschaftsrecht*, p. 995.

[106] In particular, Art. 3(1) TEU on the promotion of peace, the Union's values and the well-being of its peoples or Art. 3(2) on the area of freedom, security and justice.

[107] A. von Bogdandy, 'Founding Principles', in von Bogdandy and Bast, *Principles of European Constitutional Law*, p. 24.

[108] Reimer 'Ziele und Zuständigkeiten: Die Funktionen der Unionszielbestimmungen', p. 1000; Plecher-Hochstraßer, *Zielbestimmungen im Mehrebenensystem*, p. 112; and P.-C. Müller-Graff, 'Verfassungsziele der EG/EU', in Manfred Dauses (ed.), *Handbuch des EU-Wirtschaftsrechts*, 27th edn (loose-leaf) (C. H. Beck 2010), marginal no. 176.

[109] M. Ruffert, 'Art. 3 (ex-Art. 2 EUV) [Ziele der EU]', in C. Calliess and M. Ruffert (eds.), *EUV/AEUV Kommentar*, 4th edn (Munich: C. H. Beck, 2011), marginal no. 5; and Calliess, 'Kollektive Ziele und Prinzipien im Verfassungsrecht der EU', p. 94.

which rejected, with regard to former Article 3(f) TEC on ensuring competition as a Community task, that such a goal was 'devoid of legal effect'.[110] Following the entry into force of the Lisbon Treaty and the disappearance of the pillar structure, the former distinction between Community and Union objectives has disappeared as well. Today, there remain only Union objectives.[111]

In terms of the addressees of Union objectives, these include a priori all Union organs. An emphasis on the legislative branch can also be assumed here, even though the peculiar legislative powers of the Commission, next to the co-legislators the European Parliament and Council, need to be accounted for.[112] The issue of the Member States as addressees of Union objectives, however, is more complex. With regard to Article 2 TEC on the tasks of the former Community, the Court of Justice denied that these could 'have the effect either of imposing legal obligations on the Member States or of conferring rights on individuals'.[113] Of course, Member States are bound by Union law, but they are more than mere 'Union organs', not least in the field of foreign policy.[114] The objectives are applied to them via the 'duty of sincere cooperation', which states that '[t]he Member States shall facilitate the achievement of the Union's *tasks* and refrain from any measure which could jeopardize the attainment of the Union's *objectives*'.[115]

As to the legal functions of Union objectives, in analogy to the German and French doctrines, we can also distinguish instances where they either oblige, prohibit and permit. As to the first, the Court has underlined the 'obligatory force' of objectives.[116] Regarding the scope of such an obligation, it is again the pursuit of the objective that is binding, not its

[110] Case 6/72 *Europemballage Corporation and Continental Can Company Inc.* v. *Commission of the European Communities* [1973] ECR 215, para. 23.

[111] This is of course notwithstanding institutional and procedural differences, which set the CFSP apart from other Union policies, Art. 24(1)(2)TEU; further P. Van Elsuwege, 'EU External Action after the Collapse of the Pillar Structure: In Search of a New Balance between Delimitation and Consistency' (2010) 47 *Common Market Law Review* 987.

[112] Art. 17(1) and (2) TEU; further P. Craig and G. de Búrca, *EU Law: Text, Cases and Materials*, 5th edn (Oxford University Press, 2011), pp. 36–9.

[113] Case C-339/89 *Alsthom Atlantique SA* v. *Compagnie de construction mécanique Sulzer SA* [1991] ECR 1991 I-107, para. 9.

[114] Note in this context Declarations Nos. 13 and 14 on 13 concerning the common foreign and security policy that were annexed to the Lisbon Treaty.

[115] Art. 4(3)(3)TEU (emphases added). See also Müller-Graff, 'Verfassungsziele der EG/EU', marginal no. 4; Ruffert, 'Art. 3 (ex-Art. 2 EUV) [Ziele der EU]', marginal no. 4.

[116] Case 6/72 *Continental Can* [1973] ECR 215, para. 25.

actual realization, coupled with a margin of discretion for the political branches.[117] In the words of the court, 'those are broad objectives in the sense that it must be possible for the measures required for their pursuit to concern a variety of specific matters'.[118] In this vein, Kotzur's (otherwise rather complex) definition of Union objectives rightly draws again on the Alexyian notion of optimization.[119]

Union objectives also entail prohibitions, that is actions which manifestly disregard these objectives. But, given the breadth of the current objectives, this question has become increasingly hypothetical.[120] Especially where several objectives are at stake, the court has awarded wide discretion to the institutions.[121] However, the notion of prohibition appears more rigid as well as judicially enforceable when coupled with the duty of cooperation. The case law of the Court of Justice reveals that it is often Member States that are condemned for having acted in a way jeopardizing Union objectives, not least in the area of external relations.[122]

In terms of authorization, also, Union objectives operate as an interpretive tool to clarify competences and justify restrictions on individual rights.[123] Concerning the former, this raises an intricate connection to the issue of conferral of powers and the lack of a *Kompetenz-Kompetenz*. As such, objectives cannot establish competence for the Union.[124] Nevertheless, they serve an important function in framing competence as well

[117] Case 1/69 *Italy* v. *Commission* [1969] ECR 277, para. 5, where the court urges the Commission 'to exercise its discretionary powers in accordance with the objectives of the Community'.

[118] *Ibid.*, para. 37; also L. Azoulai, 'Article I-3', in L. Burgorgue-Larsen, A. Levade and F. Picod (eds.), *Traité établissant une Constitution pour l'Europe*, vol. 1 (Brussels: Bruylant 2007), pp. 75–6.

[119] Kotzur, 'Die Ziele der Union: Verfassungsidentität und Gemeinschaftsidee', p. 315.

[120] Müller-Graff 'Verfassungsziele der EG/EU', marginal no. 178; Reimer, 'Ziele und Zuständigkeiten: Die Funktionen der Unionszielbestimmungen', pp. 992–3.

[121] Case 112/80 *Firma Anton Dürbeck* v. *Hauptzollamt Frankfurt am Main-Flughafen* [1981] ECR 1095, para. 44, which concerned measures which would have adversely affected trade objectives, but were conducive to the Common Agricultural Policy.

[122] For example, Case C-246/07 *Commission* v. *Sweden (PFOS)* [2010] ECR I-3317; further A. Delgado Castelleiro and J. Larik, 'The Duty to Remain Silent: Limitless Loyalty in EU External Relations?' (2011) 36 *European Law Review* 522.

[123] Calliess, 'Kollektive Ziele und Prinzipien im Verfassungsrecht der EU', p. 92; K. Lenaerts and P. Van Nuffel, *European Union* Law, 2nd edn (London: Sweet & Maxwell, 2011), p. 111, who argue that the legal impact of Union objectives is in fact 'limited to guiding the interpretation of Union law'.

[124] Art. 3(6) TEU. Calliess 'Kollektive Ziele und Prinzipien im Verfassungsrecht der EU', p. 89; Ruffert, 'Art. 3 (ex-Art. 2 EUV) [Ziele der EU]', marginal no. 12.

as in shaping the exercise thereof.[125] This is important with regard to establishing additional powers under what is now Article 352 TFEU, which requires action 'within the framework of policies defined by the Treaties' as well as the pursuit of at least 'one of the objectives set out in the Treaties'.[126] A pre-Lisbon example for the prominent role of objectives in this context, also with an external dimension, is the legal basis question for cross-pillar sanctions against individuals in the *Kadi* case.[127] The court found that the Union had competence by virtue of a generous interpretation of the notion of Community objectives.[128] The Court's negative opinion on the accession to the European Convention on Human Rights from 1996, however, shows that also in EU law there are structural limits to deriving competence in connection with the pursuit of objectives.[129] In addition, in the particular context of the Union, objectives are significant in determining not simply any, but the proper legal basis for the use of Union competence, which has important institutional and procedural consequences (voting requirements). The *Small Arms* decision serves as a prominent example for this from the external relations sphere.[130]

Regarding authorization to limit fundamental rights, the Court of Justice has also made a number of important pronouncements. As was mentioned earlier, the *Conseil constitutionnel* was most likely inspired by ECJ rulings such as *Nold*. In this case, the court ruled that fundamental rights may 'be subject to certain limits justified by the overall objectives pursued by the Community, on condition that the substance of these rights is left untouched'.[131] This issue was also raised in cases with an

[125] Müller-Graff, 'Verfassungsziele der EG/EU', marginal nos. 180-18; Calliess 'Kollektive Ziele und Prinzipien im Verfassungsrecht der EU', pp. 89–90; Azoulai, 'Article I-3', pp. 73–5; Reimer 'Ziele und Zuständigkeiten: Die Funktionen der Unionszielbestimmungen', pp. 1001–2.

[126] Art. 352(1) TEU.

[127] Joined Cases C-402/05 P and C-415/05 *P. Kadi and Al Barakaat* v. *Council and Commission* [2008] ECR I-06351.

[128] *Ibid.*, para. 235; M. Cremona, 'External Relations and External Competence of the European Union: The Emergence of an Integrated Policy', in P. Craig and G. de Búrca (eds.), *The Evolution of EU Law*, 2nd edn (Oxford University Press, 2011), p. 264. Note that the current version, Art. 352(1) TFEU, refers to 'the objectives set out in the Treaties', while the previous reference to 'the operation of the Common Market' has been dropped.

[129] Opinion 2/94 [1996] ECR I-1759, paras. 35–6. After the Lisbon reform, the Union's accession to the Convention is now explicitly provided for in Art. 6(2) TEU.

[130] Case C-91/05 *Commission* v. *Council* (Small Arms) [2008] ECR I-3651.

[131] Case 4/79 *Nold* v. *Commission* [1975] ECR 491, para. 14.

external dimension. In *Bosphorus*, the ECJ considered that a measure restricting property rights was not disproportionate in view of 'an objective of general interest so fundamental for the international community', i.e. responding to the war and the massive human rights violations in Bosnia at the time.[132] Similarly, the *Kadi* judgment can be seen as an attempt to find the right balance between fundamental rights protection and the compliance with international law, in particular the United Nations. However, it is striking that the court did not refer in either case to the provisions in the Treaties that actually codify these objectives. Even after the Lisbon reform, the General Court, in its 2010 decision concerning Mr Kadi, made a rather obscure reference to the external objectives contained in the TEU. It referred there to 'certain doubts [that] may have been voiced in legal circles as to whether the judgment of the Court of Justice in *Kadi* is wholly consistent' with requirements of international law as well as a number of provisions from EU primary law, including Articles 3(5) and 21(1) and (2) TEU.[133]

Importantly, with regard to the 'bounds of possibility', the broadened discretion of the political branches in the field of external relations could be seen as even more accentuated in the EU. Internally, it has to rely on the political will of its Member States to act internationally *at all* in the first place, and furthermore to act *through* the Union in areas of non-exclusive external competence. Externally, the EU depends also on the willingness of the outside world to interact *with* an actor so unusual as the Union. The former problem applies particularly to the Common Foreign and Security Policy, where unanimous voting applies and, in case of the Common Security and Defence Policy, where the Union has to rely on 'capabilities provided by the Member States'.[134] The latter issue arises, for instance, when the Union is faced with international organizations whose charters do not allow it to become a member.[135] In all these cases, the infamous 'capabilities-expectations gap'[136] is prone to be widened through raising expectations by legally entrenching ambitious foreign policy objectives into the primary law in areas where many constraints

[132] Case C-84/95 *Bosphorus* [1996] I–3953, para. 36.

[133] Case T-85/09 *Kadi* v. *Commission* [2010] ECR II-5177, para. 115.

[134] Art. 42(1) TEU.

[135] See I. Govaere, J. Capiau and A. Vermeersch, 'In-Between Seats: the Participation of the European Union in International Organizations' (2004) 9 *European Foreign Affairs Review* 155.

[136] C. Hill, 'The Capability-Expectations Gap, or Conceptualising Europe's International Role' (1993) 31 *Journal of Common Market Studies* 305.

apply, both internal and external. The EU Treaties boldly posit that the Union will 'consolidate and support democracy, the rule of law, human rights and the principles of international law'.[137] Yet it often appears incapable of asserting itself, not least owing to diverging Member State views, as was illustrated by the 2003 Iraq War, the recognition of Kosovo or Palestine or the Libyan revolution. From a legal point of view, this serves as the clearest illustration of the challenges to the effectiveness of constitutional law to deliver on its promises.

5 Conclusion

Three conclusions can be made regarding the appraisal of the external objectives contained in the EU Treaties. First, constitutional law around the world has witnessed a significant amount of innovation in the recent past, an undeniable feature of which is its 'dynamic internationalization' through the codification of external objectives. These include both guidance in terms of substance as well as governance. Against this backdrop, the inclusion of (more) external objectives in EU primary law by Lisbon is thus neither unheard of nor exceptional. On the contrary, by ranking itself amongst the constitutions that are the most explicit in their global 'mission statements', the reformed EU Treaties are not the odd ones out, but instead find themselves in the vanguard of a worldwide trend attesting to an 'active paradigm' in constitutional foreign relations law.

Secondly, it is furthermore possible to embed the analysis of external objectives of the Union into the overall appreciation of constitutional objectives as a norm category. As was sketched above, the German and French legal traditions provide sophisticated approaches in this regard. Both conclude overall that such objectives constitute legally binding and in principle justiciable norms of constitutional value, in the light of which the constitution as a whole is to be interpreted. It is within this norm category that also external objectives are at home, not somewhere outside of the 'actual' constitution. As, at the same time, they belong to the foreign relations constitution, certain specific features apply to external objectives. The executive branch becomes the co-protagonist next to the legislature, while the margin of discretion in pursuing these objectives widens. However, these features do not justify denying to these objectives their constitutional rank and their legal functions, not least their interpretive function.

137 Art. 21(2)(b) TEU.

Thirdly, even though scholarship on EU external relations law has not yet devoted significant attention to external relations objectives per se, these objectives are clearly present in the primary law and have figured in the judgments of the ECJ. Moreover, there is an increasing amount of scholarship addressing Union objectives in general as a legally relevant norm category. This case law and the emerging scholarly discourse point in the direction of also characterizing the external objectives of the Union as veritable constitutional norms performing the functions of constitutional objectives.

Looking to the future, it remains to be seen how the Court of Justice, as the prime interpreter of EU law, will receive the streamlined and expanded external objectives in its post-Lisbon case law. Since these now appear more prominently than ever within the Union's 'basic constitutional charter',[138] one would hope that the court, as well as other institutions and scholars, will join the 'legal circles'[139] that take EU external objectives seriously. Just as Treaty objectives have been drawn upon time and again to advance the *internal* order of the Union towards a community based on rules and values, an approach which was legally endorsed – if not encouraged – by the hallmark 'teleological' approach of the Court of Justice itself,[140] the external objectives of the Union call for nothing other than the active shaping of the *international* order along the same lines.

[138] Case 294/83 *Les Verts* [1986] ECR 1339, para. 23.
[139] Case T-85/09 *Kadi* v. *Commission* [2010] ECR II-5177, para. 115.
[140] Calliess, 'Kollektive Ziele und Prinzipien im Verfassungsrecht der EU', p. 85.

PART II

The EU's shaping of the international legal order: the evidence

4

EU values and the shaping of the international legal context

ESTER HERLIN-KARNELL

1 Introduction

The international arena is increasingly important in EU legal discourse. The EU seeks to promote its values abroad by shaping the world stage. The EU was born from the ashes of a less than ideal world and its normative core starts from what Europeans wanted to escape.[1] Several EU law scholars recognize the genesis of the EU as a peace project: European history forms the initial foundation stone of the EU's integration enterprise where values have always played an important role and has had a clear effect on the external sphere.[2] There is thus an inherent dynamic in the use of values on the EU scale, which is closely connected to the constitutional question of what kind of Europe the EU and its Member States are seeking to achieve. This chapter takes its starting point in the claim that Europe's *raison d'être* depends largely on the ability of the EU to uphold its values internally before these values are exported externally. Moreover, the chapter argues that the EU's promotion of values is closely connected to the bigger ambition of ensuring justice and good global governance.

More deeply, the question of the EU as a promoter of values is reflected in the greater debate on the future of European integration.

This contribution is a revised version of an article initially published as E. Herlin-Karnell, 'The EU as a Promoter of Values and the European Global Project' (2012) 13 *German Law Journal* 1225. Thanks go to the editors of this book for their very helpful comments on this chapter. The usual disclaimer applies.

[1] K. Nicolaïdis, 'The Idea of European Democracy', in J. Dickson and P. Elefteriades, *The Philosophical Foundation of EU Law* (Oxford University Press, 2012), p. 247.

[2] See e.g. P. Eleftheriadis, *Cosmopolitan Law* (2003) 9 *European Law Journal*, 241. See also Robert Schuman, 'Declaration of 9 May 1950', in P. M. R. Stirk and D. Weigall, *The Origins and Development of European Integration: A Reader and a Commentary* (London: Pinter, 1999), p. 76

After all, already the Laeken declaration discussed the EU's future as a promoter of values beyond the EU borders.[3] Famously, Laeken asked:

> What is Europe's role in this changed world? Does Europe not, now that is finally unified, have a leading role to play in a new world order, that of a power able both to play a stabilising role worldwide and to point the way ahead for many countries and peoples?

The purpose of this chapter is to investigate the notion of EU values and their adjudication in the international domain. The contribution assesses the theoretical framework for understanding the EU's function as an agent of values – both internally and externally by addressing the issue of how the EU shapes the international discourse by insistence on values. It cautiously asks to what extent the different – and new – strands of constitutionalism in EU law, such as pluralism, global constitutional law and cosmopolitan law, are all fragments or expressions of the same constitutional message at the global level: how to ensure increased legitimacy as well as 'good governance' in terms of a proper transnational balance. Thereafter, the contribution sets out to look at the area of environmental protection as representing an area where the EU is currently very active, and where the question of EU values as well as the desirability of EU action is put to the test on a global scale, thus anticipating and reconfirming the conclusions reached by Christina Eckes in her chapter later in the volume. As witnessed in the recent judgment on the validity of the European Union Emissions Trading Scheme (EU ETS), the EU's values may sometimes spill over to the global level and hence become a mechanism for shaping the external stage.[4] As such it represents a good test case for understanding the EU's normative mission and green entrepreneurship.

The chapter proceeds in three stages. The first section expands the formal analysis provided by Joris Larik in this volume and discusses what the EU's values are, and how the EU's mission as a promoter of these values in the legal context has intensified with the adoption of the Lisbon Treaty. Secondly, the chapter looks at the normative framework to understand the EU's function as a promoter of values in the transnational – and increasingly global – setting. In doing so, the focus comes to rest on the EU's 'missionary' principle as stipulated in Article 3(5)

[3] 'Laeken Declaration on the Future of the European Union', annexed to the Presidency Conclusions of the European Council summit, 14–15 December 2001, available at http://european-convention.eu.int/pdf/lknen.pdf.

[4] Case C-366/10 *Air Transport Association of America* v. *Secretary of State for Energy and Climate Change* [2011] I-1133.

TEU, specifically, the EU's tendency to promote its values not only within, but also outside of, Europe. Thirdly, the chapter considers the viability of the EU becoming a successful actor in the global sphere. In doing so, the chapter focuses on the protection of the environment through the ETS, and on EU security regulation. These two areas represent important elements of what could arguably be referred to as global constitutionalism. Hence, the contribution will discuss not only the EU global concern for the protection of the environment, as demonstrated in a recent ETS case.[5]

The chapter investigates different manifestations of EU values in the constitutional context. It explores how global law is linked not only to the external dimension of EU law but also to the core of the EU constitutional narrative. It will be shown that the EU's stance in relation to the rest of the world is framed in a bold rhetoric with a touch of what Joseph Weiler has characterized as European 'messianism'.[6]

2 The plethora of EU values

The constitutional objectives of the EU are intimately connected to the normative question of what values the Union should protect.[7] The notion of shared values has made a remarkable journey in the EU. The identification of common values and the recognition of the need for such values has been a reoccurring European theme ever since the Enlightenment, a time where the move towards a more humane system emerged in Europe, particularly with regard to the national criminal law justice system.[8] Several centuries later, the conception of a 'normative European power', although contested, has become an increasingly popular starting point in the discussion of the EU's involvement in external relations and foreign policy issues through which Europe's global position is often understood.[9]

[5] See the chapter by Christina Eckes in this volume for an analysis of this case.

[6] J. H. H. Weiler, 'Deciphering the Political and Legal DNA of European Integration', in J. Dickson and P. Eleftheriadis, *The Philosophical Foundations of European Union Law* (Oxford University Press, 2012).

[7] On the legal value of EU objectives, see the chapter by Joris Larik in this volume.

[8] For example, the questioning of the legitimacy of the death penalty dawned in the context of the Enlightenment at the end of the eighteenth century. See European Commission, 'EU Policy on the Death Penalty', available at www.eurunion.org/legislat/deathpenalty/eumemorandum.htm.

[9] T. Diez, 'Constructing the Self and Changing Others: Reconsidering Normative Power Europe' (2005) 33 *Millennium Journal of International Studies* 613; I. Manners, 'Normative Power Europe: A Contradiction in Terms?' (2002) 40 *Journal of Common Market Studies* 235; T. Forsberg, 'Normative Power Europe, Once Again: A Conceptual Analysis

Clearly, the EU's mission to spread its values is no longer a side-effect of the EU free movement rules in general in terms of EU spill-over into national law, but has evolved into a freestanding desire to promote the Treaty promises of democracy, human rights, equality and sustainable development. Of course, the Council of Europe and the European Convention on Human Rights have largely influenced the EU's commitment to certain values, and have helped the EU shape its human rights agenda.[10]

When trying to pin down what values the EU should safeguard, the starting point is obviously the Treaty itself, the objectives it embodies and the legal definitions provided by it. Article 2 TEU stipulates that the Union is founded on the values of respect for human dignity, freedom, democracy, equality, the rule of law and respect for human rights, including the rights of persons belonging to minorities. In addition, Article 3 TEU makes clear that not only shall the Union aim to promote the well-being of its peoples, but it shall also offer its citizens an area of freedom, security and justice.[11] Of particular importance in understanding how the EU promotes its values is, however, Article 3(5) TEU, which has been dubbed the EU's 'missionary principle', as the article regulates the EU's presence on the global scene and sets the goals of EU relations with the rest of the world.[12] According to this provision, in its relations with the wider world, the Union shall uphold and promote its values and interests and contribute to the protection of its citizens. It also states that the EU shall uphold strict observance and development of international law, including respect for the principles of the United Nations Charter. This promise is reiterated in Article 21(1) TEU that stipulates, inter alia, that the Union's actions on the international scene shall be guided by the principles that have inspired its own creation. However, the EU's mission does not stop there: it also seeks to ensure good global governance, as is clear from Article 21(2)(h) TEU.

of an Ideal Type' (2011) 49 *Journal of Common Market Studies* 1183; M. de Goede, 'The SWIFT Affair and the Global Politics of European Security' (2012) 50 *Journal of Common Market Studies* 214.

[10] On values, see A. Williams, *The Ethos of Europe: Values, Law and Justice in the EU* (Cambridge University Press, 2010). See also C. Calliess, 'The Transnationalization of Values by European Law' (2009) 10 *German Law Journal* 1367.

[11] Moreover, Art. 6 TEU stipulates that the Union recognizes the rights, freedoms and principles set out in the Charter of Fundamental Rights. It is also stated that the Union shall accede to the European Convention on Human Rights (ECHR) (which is under way).

[12] See e.g. M. Broberg, 'What Is the Direction for the EU's Development Cooperation After Lisbon? – A Legal Examination' (2011) 16 *European Foreign Affairs Review* 539.

Notably, Article 21 TEU refers to certain principles of paramount importance to the EU's relationship with the rest of the world, while Articles 2 and 3 TEU simply refer to 'values' that are part of the objectives of the EU. Nonetheless, rather than seeing this dichotomy as an inconsistent use of values and principles, Article 2 and Article 21 TEU should be seen as interchangeable.[13] Moreover, it should perhaps be observed that there is a similar distinction between values in terms of rights and principles in the Charter of Fundamental Rights, which distinguishes between indivisible universal values (human dignity, freedom, equality and solidarity) and, for example, the principles of democracy and the rule of law.[14] After all, both values and principles certainly express and represent a certain normative value or claim which at the EU level means that they serve a function of identification, in terms of 'Member State bonding', through the recognition of shared European norms.[15] And the EU promotes these values and aspirations not only internally but also externally. However, interestingly, although the EU's remit of competence is far more extensive domestically than internationally, the EU and its Member States have been unwilling to treat respect for human rights with the same cross-cutting concern internally as they have in their external policies.[16] In other words, Article 3(5) TEU is broader and bolder compared to the internal competences. Thus the EU seeks to shape the external landscape by drawing up a far-reaching proclamation of human rights as a constitutional compass for its interrelationship with the international legal order.

There is one important exception to the EU's human rights programme generally. The restrictions set by the Charter of Fundamental Rights in Article 51 disappoint those who were hoping for an all-encompassing competence of the EU in these matters. Article 51 of the Charter makes it clear that the document applies to the Member States only when they are

[13] On values in EU Foreign relations law, see M. Cremona, 'Values in EU Foreign Policy', in M. Evans and P. Koutrakos (eds.), *Beyond the Established Legal Orders: Policy Interconnections between the EU and the Rest of the World* (Oxford: Hart Publishing, 2011), p. 275.

[14] The problem is how to identify fully justiciable rights as opposed to partially justiciable principles in Art. 52 of the Charter. P. Craig, *The Lisbon Treaty: Law, Politics and Treaty Reform* (Oxford University Press, 2010), p. 193.

[15] See e.g. Sartor's discussion on Alexy and the notions of principles and values in legal reasoning. G. Sartor, 'A Teleological Approach to Legal Dialogue', in G. Pavlakos (ed.), *Law, Rights and Discourse: The Legal Philosophy of Robert Alexy* (Oxford: Hart Publishing, 2007).

[16] G. de Búrca, 'The Road Not Taken: The EU as a Global Human Rights Actor' (2011) 105 *American Journal of International Law* 649.

implementing EU law. In addition, Article 52(1) of the Charter grants some important exceptions to the application of the Charter as a whole. Subject to the principle of proportionality, limitations may be made if they are necessary and genuinely meet objectives of general interest recognized by the Union or the need to protect the rights and freedoms of others.[17] This severely restricts the reach of the Charter. So while the scope of EU human rights protection internally seems to turn on the meaning of proportionality the story is told otherwise externally.[18]

The picture that emerges at the global level looks different. It is well known that the EU has actively exported its values to candidate countries where human rights have been used as the main driver for institutional reforms.[19] The insistence on human rights has come to represent an important part of the EU's normative powers.[20] The Copenhagen criteria in 1993 emphasized in particular democracy, adequate protection of human rights as well as respect for the concern of minorities as the foremost benchmark for EU membership. In spite of the EU's newly won peace prize, the EU has remaining work to do on the human rights horizon and has been frequently criticized for not doing enough and for largely failing its human rights rhetoric.[21] The question of the function of the EU as a driver for change and a promoter of human rights in candidate countries has had a great impact on the EU law of enlargement.[22] But while the concern for human rights underpins most EU values, it is not the *only* value. Other values (as is evident from Article 2 TEU) are, inter alia, the rule of law, solidarity, justice and tolerance.

[17] The Explanations Relating to the Charter of fundamental rights, OJ (2007) C83/2, see also the discussion in P. Craig, *EU Administrative Law* (Oxford University Press, 2012), p. 473

[18] It is of course true that the Charter refers to the ECHR in Art. 52 (3) in pointing out that the ECHR is always the minimum standard of protection. See E. Herlin-Karnell and M. Fichera, 'The Margin of Appreciation Test and Balancing in the Area of Freedom Security and Justice: A Proportionate Answer for a Europe of Rights?' (2013) 4 *European Public Law* (forthcoming).

[19] M. Cremona, 'Values in EU Foreign Policy'. See also European Commission, 'Europe and the Challenge of Enlargement' (1992) *Bulletin of the European Communities*, supplement 3/92.

[20] G. de Búrca, 'The Road Not Taken: The EU as a Global Human Rights Actor' (2011) 105 *American Journal of International Law* 649.

[21] *Ibid.*

[22] S. Blockmans, *Tough Love: The European Union's Relations with the Western Balkans* (The Hague: Asser Press, 2007). See also D. Kochenov, *EU Enlargement and the Failure of Conditionality: Pre-accession Conditionality in the Fields of Democracy and the Rule of Law* (The Hague: Kluwer Law International, 2008).

In any event, EU values, just like the realm of EU competences in general, are being expanded, with the exception of the occasional touchstone of subsidiarity inspired reasoning in the Court of Justice, and this requires careful consideration from the perspective of the proper monitoring of EU competences. There is a constitutional dimension here anchored in the question of what the EU is empowered to do, and in this regard the reference to 'values' as a means of justification is difficult to monitor. Therefore, it appears as if the debate on the role of the EU as a promoter of values on the global scale is deeply connected to the broader debate on the allocation of competences within Europe.

Furthermore, the Court of Justice has been an active player early on with regard to determining which values the EU should promote.[23] In addition to the more overarching goal of creating an autonomous European legal order which safeguards fundamental rights adequately and granting individuals rights in national courts,[24] the Court has read values into the idea of loyalty as a holistic mechanism for maintaining and establishing continuing European integration. This is particularly the case in the intersection of international law and EU law, where the loyalty principle has played a crucial role in ensuring the survival of the Union project on the margins of Europe by insisting on a united face to the rest of the world.[25]

In somewhat simplified terms, EU internal values operate at a dual level – the EU accepts that some national values are European values, but, as stated in Article 4(2) TEU (the national identity clause), national values can also form part of a national identity and then are no longer 'European' from the perspective of the enforcement of EU law. In addition, national security is a national value in that it remains the sole responsibility of the Member States per Article 4(2) TEU. The mixed compote of supranational values and retained national sovereignty in particular areas and dimensions is highly complex and confirms how difficult it is to superimpose a single

[23] See e.g. Case C-159/90, *Society for the Protection of Unborn Children Ireland Ltd.* v. *Grogan* [1991] ECR 4685; Case C-36/02 *Omega Spielhallen-und Automatenaufstellungs-GmbH* v. *Oberbürgermeisterin der Bundesstadt Bonn* [2004] ECR I-9609; Case C-208/09, *Sayn-Wittgenstein* v. *Von Wien* [2011] ECR I-13693.

[24] Case 6/64 *Costa* v. *ENEL* [1964] ECR 585.

[25] See, generally, P. Eeckhout, *EU External Relations Law* (Oxford University Press, 2011); see Case C-22/70 *Commission of the European Communities* v. *Council of the European Communities* [1971] ECR 263; see also Case C-246/07 *European Commission* v. *Kingdom of Sweden* [2010] ECR I-3317.

definition of values. In any case, it seems quite obvious that the general principles of EU law are manifestations of values. After all, the most fundamental of all EU law principles, the rule of law, is an expression of democratic values.[26] Indeed, it appears as if the rule of law – Article 2 of the TEU – constitutes the main constitutional virtue in EU law when spreading the EU's values. The *Kadi I* case offers a well-known example of where the EU placed EU law values at the centre of the discussion by stressing the importance of the autonomous legal order of the EU.[27] In doing so, the Court emphasized the significance of an EU that not only respects fundamental rights but also actively safeguards them in a legal order based on the rule of law and respect for due process rights.[28]

In any case, it could be argued that the EU would need to model itself on the Utopia that it seeks to project on the rest of the world to ensure greater coherence within the EU itself.[29] It begs the fundamental yet difficult question of what exactly is Europe's *raison d'être*? While this question remains largely unanswered, the commitment to consistency between the EU's pursuit of justice, both within its borders and beyond, is often considered a paramount concern in the European process. Recently, Douglas-Scott argued that the rule of law could be reflected in the justice paradigm in the EU if the meaning of the rule of law is stretched beyond its Treaty-based assertion.[30] The key to understanding justice is to take a holistic view of it which makes it more than an empty notion, and which substantiates the democratic values it embodies.[31] Justice would then form a core part of the rule of law if interpreted as a critical legal concept. As Eleftheriadis observes, the legitimacy of the EU institutions must be vindicated by a theory of international justice and a theory of European law as well, where both theories are capable of accommodating the virtues of institutional fairness and integrity. Therefore, Eleftheriadis argues, the only possible reading of justice in the context of the EU

[26] On the rule of law and the EU, see the chapter by Laurent Pech in this volume. See, also, A. von Bogdandy, 'Founding Principles', in A. von Bogdandy and J. Bast (eds.), *Principles of European Constitutional Law* (Munich: Nomos, 2011), p. 11.

[27] Cases C-402/05 and C-415/05, *Kadi and Al Barakaat* v. *Council* [2008] ECR I-6351.

[28] See e.g. C. Murphy, *EU Counter Terrorism Law* (Oxford: Hart Publishing, 2012), p.224.

[29] K. A. Nicolaïdes and R. L. Howse, 'This Is My EUtopia. . .': Narrative as Power' (2002) 40 *Journal of Common Market Studies* 767.

[30] S. Douglas-Scott, 'The Problem of Justice in the European Union', in J. Dickson and P. Eleftheriadis (eds.), *Philosophical Foundations of EU Law* (Oxford University Press, 2012). For a detailed discussion, see also Laurent Pech's contribution to this volume.

[31] Douglas-Scott, 'The Problem of Justice in the European Union'.

is a political reading of it.[32] This political dimension of the EU's view of justice is crucial for how to understand the EU's communication with the international sphere and the role of values in this dialogue.[33]

According to some scholars, the EU's credibility rests on what it can do unilaterally, by seeking greater consistency between internal practices and proclaimed external objectives, where the need for consistency is coupled with the quest for solidarity.[34] The Lisbon Treaty tries to follow this path by singling out consistency as the guiding principle for EU action abroad and at home. Hence, it should be recalled that Article 7 of the Treaty of the Functioning of the EU (TFEU) stipulates that the EU 'shall ensure consistency between its policies and activities, taking all of its objectives into account and in accordance with the principle of conferral of powers'. In the same vein, Article 13(1) TEU provides that the EU's institutional framework 'shall aim to promote its values, advance its objectives, serve its interests, those of its citizens and those of the Member States, and ensure the consistency, effectiveness and continuity of its policies and actions'. A closer look at Articles 7 TFEU and 13 TEU suggests that not only is consistency an important way of ensuring that the EU is acting *intra vires* but consistency also acts as a significant aid in the drafting and negotiation of EU legislative proposals. Therefore, consistency of EU action is as important internally as externally.

In what follows, the chapter endeavours to map the theoretical framework for how to understand the EU's values in a global context. And yet, the question of whether the EU should 'go global' is obviously more political than legal. Regardless, the normative implications of global EU action have broader consequences for the future, pertaining to questions of legitimacy in the EU and the function of law in this European (global project) process.[35]

[32] P. Eleftheriadis, 'The Moral Distinctiveness of the European Union' (2011) *International Journal of Constitutional Law* 695.

[33] On the difficulties with global justice, see T. Nagel, 'The Problem of Global Justice' (2005) 33 *Philosophy and Public Affairs* 113. On justice in legal theory discourse, see, of course, J. Rawls, *A Theory of Justice* (Cambridge, Mass.: Harvard University Press, 1971), p. 171; see also the chapter by Williams in this volume.

[34] Nicolaïdes and Howse, 'This Is My EUtopia. . .'.

[35] See A. Menon and S. Weatherill, 'Democratic Politics in a Globalising World: Supranationalism and Legitimacy in the European Union', LSE Law, Society and Economy Working Paper 13 (2007), 1, available at http://eprints.lse.ac.uk/24618/1/WPS13-2007 MenonandWeatherill.pdf.

3 Naming problems: identifying the 'right' EU constitutional lens for how to understand values in the international context

Much of EU involvement at the international level is related to the more general aim of ensuring good global governance as stipulated in Article 21 TEU. 'Good governance' in the present contribution is not taken as traditional administrative practice but rather seen as an overarching principle for understanding European governance.[36] As such, it is associated with the rule of law and competence distribution. Still, at the macro level, the discussion also concerns *how* one sees Europe, i.e. the level of supranational features (and intergovernmental aspects) at stake. In MacCormick's terminology, the EU has been described as a commonwealth that marked post-sovereign Europe.[37] Others have described the EU project as 'European Empire'.[38] Without going into the deeper question of the characterization of Europe, it is clear that the discussion takes place 'beyond' the nation state, and it concerns research into the process and actors in post-national society.[39] Therefore, the more general debate on European constitutional law beyond the nation state not only asks some difficult questions of what EU supranationalism or post-national law really means, but also unavoidably prompts the question of the identity of EU law when discussed in the global setting.

The search for the 'right' template of constitutionalism is then linked to the EU as a promoter of values. This is particularly relevant in the international context. Indeed, just as the concept of constitutionalization appears to be a process in the EU integration discourses,[40] so too does the globalization phenomenon in the EU seem to be a process with no clear destination.[41] Already, Pernice's theory of 'multilevel constitutionalism' depicts an ongoing process for the establishment of new

[36] For a recent account on governance, see T. A. Börzel, 'European Governance: Governing With or Without the State?', in P. Dobner and M. Loughlin (eds.), *The Twilight of Constitutionalism*? (Oxford University Press, 2010), p. 73.

[37] N. MacCormick, *Questioning Sovereignty* (Oxford University Press, 1999), p. 155.

[38] J. Zielonka, *Europe as Empire: The Nature of the Enlarged European Union* (Oxford University Press, 2006).

[39] H. Huelss, 'A Force for Good Governance?: The European Union's Normative Power and Standards of Appropriate Governing' (2012) 17 *European Foreign Affairs Review* 93.

[40] A. Somek, 'Constitutionalization and the Common Good', University of Iowa College of Law Paper No. 10-23 (2010).

[41] J. H. H. Weiler, 'Journey to an Unknown Destination: A Retrospective and Prospective of the European Court of Justice in the Arena of Political Integration' (1993) 31 *Journal of Common Market Studies* 417 (437).

structures of governance complementary to, and building upon – while also changing – existing forms of self-organization of people or society.[42] There is a great debate on the different interpretations of constitutionalism and pluralism in contemporary EU law with the latter aiming to address concerns of those who believe that the time is here to recognize diversity without the need of a static, one-size-fits-all model.[43] In this context it is appropriate to mention a further strand of EU constitutionalism somewhat related to pluralism, namely, what has been referred to as 'cosmopolitan law' – inspired by the works of Immanuel Kant.[44] According to the cosmopolitan view advocated by Eleftheriadis, the EU should confine itself to 'eternal peace'.[45] Viewing the EU through this lens would mean that we move as far away from federal models as possible and limit the EU to what Europe needs: maintaining harmony. Other scholars, such as Kumm and Stone-Sweet, argue that there is a lot more to the concept of cosmopolitan law than that of maintaining peace, in that a cosmopolitan legal order presupposes that fundamental rights are respected with regard to every person in a given territory regardless of their nationality or citizenship, and where the 'categorical imperative' becomes the golden thread or norm.[46] Thus, the cosmopolitan notion in the EU context refers to a Europe which struggles morally, politically, economically and historically for reconciliation.[47] While it has been argued that legal cosmopolitanism does not offer ready-made solutions for the structural, constitutional and institutional challenges which the EU currently faces,[48] there may still be merits in applying this concept as a way of rethinking or

[42] I. Pernice, 'Multilevel Constitutionalism in the European Union' (2002) 27 *European Law Review* 511.

[43] Or, as an expression of 'contrapunctual law', aiming for harmony, see M. P. Maduro, 'Contrapunctual Law: Europe's Constitutional Pluralism in Action', in N. Walker (ed.), *Sovereignty in Transition* (Oxford: Hart Publishing, 2003), p. 501.

[44] I. Kant, *Perpetual Peace and Other Essays* (Indiana, Ind.: Hackett Publishing, 1983), p. 117.

[45] See P. Eleftheriadis, 'Cosmopolitan Law' (2003) 9 *European Law Journal* 241.

[46] See F. Amtenbrink, 'The Multidimensional Constitutional Legal Order of the European Union: A Successful Case of Cosmopolitan Constitution-Building?' 39 (2008) *Netherlands Yearbook of International Law* 3–68; A. Stone-Sweet, 'A Cosmopolitan Legal Order: Constitutional Pluralism and Rights Adjudication in Europe' (2012) 1 *Global Constitutionalism* 53; M. Kumm, 'The Cosmopolitan State and Humanity's Law: An Integrative Conception of Global Public Law', The Law and Cosmopolitan Values Lectures, 29 October 2012.

[47] U. Beck and E. Grande, *Cosmopolitan Europe* (Cambridge University Press, 2007), p. 167, cited in A. Williams, *The Ethos of Europe* (Cambridge University Press, 2010), p. 291.

[48] Amtenbrink, 'The Multidimensional Constitutional Legal Order of the European Union'.

contextualizing what is 'at stake'[49] in transnational law. In practical terms, insisting on and applying a universal human rights standard based on the right to justification of decisions and a strict balancing of interest in national courts then helps to achieve a cosmopolitan order. In any case, the popular concept of pluralism also stresses the notion of non-conflict as the key to a successful relationship between different legal orders where the primary notion is finding a balance.[50] Therefore there is a link between cosmopolitan law and pluralism in that it could be argued that both these views are reflected in decentralized approaches – that the EU should not do more than is needed at the supranational level (but at the same time do *enough* to make sure that fundamental rights are protected). Hence, it could be argued that pluralism is also Kantian, just like cosmopolitan law, at least in so far as it accepts that there can be multiple parallel legal worlds. Different courts refer to different jurisdictions and where there is no strict hierarchy in place.[51]

Whichever interpretation is chosen with regard to the conception of EU constitutional dialogue and multi-level Europe,[52] it is instructive in that it tells us that the search for the right constitutional lens is an ongoing development. More crucially, it could help us conceptualize the framework for how to understand the EU from a global perspective. As observed by Zumbansen, 'Constitution', then, becomes an anchoring point and reference perspective for the collision of existing and emerging legal semantics' where global constitutionalism comprises just one layer.[53]

[49] On 'what is at stake' and transnational law, see P. Zumbansen, 'The Ins and Outs of Transnational Private Regulatory Governance: Legitimacy, Accountability, Effectiveness and a New Concept of "Context"' (2012) 13 *German Law Journal* 1269–81; P. Kjaer, 'The Metamorphosis of the Functional Synthesis: A Continental European Perspective on Governance, Law and the Political in the Transnational Space' (2010) 2 *Wisconsin Law Review* 489 (489–533).

[50] See G. Davies, 'Constitutional Disagreement in Europe and the Search for Pluralism', in M. Avbelj and J. Komárek (eds.), *Constitutional Pluralism in the European Union and Beyond* (Oxford: Hart Publishing, 2012), pp. 269–81. For an analysis of pluralism in EU law, see also N. Walker, 'The Idea of Constitutional Pluralism' (2002) 65 *Modern Law Review* 317; M. Maduro, 'Three Claims of Constitutional Pluralism', in Avbelj and Komárek, *Constitutional Pluralism in the European Union and Beyond*, pp. 67–84.

[51] See e.g. P. Kjaer, *Between Governing and Governance* (Oxford: Hart Publishing 2010), pp. 13–34.

[52] See P. Zumbansen, 'Comparative, Global and Transnational Constitutionalism: The Emergence of a Transnational Legal-Pluralist Order' (2012) 1 *Global Constitutionalism* 16

[53] *Ibid*., p. 50.

Moreover, it was recently suggested that constitutionalism, as an idea, sits at the intersection of law and politics, and it is for this reason that when issues emerge at the global level, the notion of 'global constitutionalism' becomes relevant.[54] In the EU context we are therefore confronted with an additional layer of complexity. Not only does it concern the debate on whether the EU should expand its values into the global sphere, but also to what extent the EU internal discourse is readily transferable to the external area. Can we use the EU model with 'global law'[55] – a term that sweeps so broadly that it is difficult to know what it means[56] – or would it be as inappropriate as imposing the state model on the EU when debating the democratic deficit question?[57] While this issue remains largely unanswered, and while this piece can do no more than point at the importance of highlighting these issues, this contribution stresses the need for an awareness of not only the need for improved legitimacy in mainstream EU law but also how to stretch it to the global field. And yet, if EU constitutionalism is in a constant state of flux, and its interaction with the global sphere is a moving target, then, it seems as if the foundational questions to be considered actually arise elsewhere. Arguably, such a debate concerns the legitimacy of EU action in the global arena. After all, it could be said that the different strands of EU constitutionalism all strive to achieve the same result, a proper transnational balance with the aim of ensuring good governance in a broad sense. This, in turn, poses the crucial question: to what extent do we really need the concept of global law at all, and what can it add to the debate on EU values and how they shape the international legal order?

The central issue here is on what grounds could EU action outside Europe's borders be considered a legitimate source of a political power?[58]

[54] See e.g. A. Wiener, et al. 'Global Constitutionalism: Human Rights, Democracy and the Rule of Law' (2010) 1 *Global Constitutionalism* 1.

[55] Along the same lines, regarding the suitability of using state models when debating accountability at the global level, see also N. Krisch, 'Global Administrative Law and the Constitutional Ambition', in P. Dobner and M. Loughlin (eds.), *The Twilight of Constitutionalism*? (Oxford University Press, 2010), p. 245.

[56] A. Somek, 'The Twilight of Constitutional Law', University of Iowa College of Law Legal Studies Research Paper Series No. 09-04 (2009), available at http://papers.ssrn.com/sol3/papers.cfm?abstract_id=1333282.

[57] See e.g. J. Neyer, 'Justice, not Democracy: Legitimacy in the European Union' (2010) 48 *Journal of Common Market Studies* 903.

[58] See P. Eleftheriadis, K. Nicolaïdis and J. H. H. Weiler, 'Foreword: The Changing Landscape of European Constitutionalism' (2011) 9 *International Journal of Constitutional Law* 673.

Any discussions of the constitutional design of the EU – and how the EU projects its values abroad – raises familiar questions regarding the accountability lacuna and the lack of representation in EU decision-making; these questions are central to the debate on the desirability of global law as well as the need for increased legitimacy.[59]

More recently, Teubner stated that a world state as a new constitutional subject is a utopian notion, and a bad one at that.[60] According to Teubner, the notion of global constitutional law functions best not as a unitary mission but as a constitutional theory for conflict of laws.[61] This would then, in short, mimic Davies's view of pluralism: that it is all about finding the right balance as a means of resolving constitutional conflicts.[62] Not only national courts, but also the EU is under an obligation to show mutual respect. Pluralism is part of this exercise in the sense that it insists on mutual understanding rather than advocating for an absolute conflict-solver template. Consequently, if embracing 'global pluralism', it could conceivably be questioned why subsidiarity as a legal concept is needed at all.

In any case, Howse and Nicolaïdis argue that the principle of subsidiarity is less interesting as a legal principle than as a multifaceted notion for rethinking European law in general.[63] Global governance law is seen as part of this process, in finding the right balance between centralization and decentralization. Be that as it may, we are still left without clear guidance on the question of how global law is reconcilable with subsidiarity, and, more crucially, to what extent the different modes of governance and the debate on constitutionalism in contemporary European law and politics are all about ensuring good (global) governance. It is here that subsidiarity could serve

[59] See Krisch, 'Global Administrative Law and the Constitutional Ambition', p. 245 (arguing that accountability rather than legitimacy is the important aspect to debate). I would argue that legitimacy is connected to the rule of law and therefore crucial for the debate on EU action whether within or without the EU borders.

[60] G. Teubner, 'The New Constitutional Question', *Constitutional Fragments: Societal Constitutionalism and Globalization* (Oxford University Press, 2012).

[61] *Ibid.*

[62] Davies, 'Constitutional Disagreement in Europe and the Search for Pluralism', p. 281

[63] R. Howse and K. Nicolaïdis, 'Democracy Without Sovereignty: The Global Vocation of Political Ethics', in Y. Shany and T. Broude (eds.), *The Shifting Allocation of Authority in International Law: Considering Sovereignty, Supremacy, and Subsidiarity* (Oxford: Hart Publishing, 2008), p. 163; P. Schiff Berman, 'Global Legal Pluralism' (2007) 80 *Southern California Law Review* 1155 (1207).

an important function not as a black letter principle but as an overarching notion that helps enhancing the integrity of transnational law by reserving it to the most pressing issues needed to be addressed at the global level and where the national level has failed. The protection of the environment offers an area where the international forum has largely failed to act and where the EU sets out to shape international law by insisting on the value of combating climate change and the virtue of global justice.

4 The EU as norm entrepreneur

In the field of EU climate change, norms deal with environmental problems in general, as well as the manner in which global, common good problems are to be dealt with on the world stage.[64] The EU has often taken the lead in environmental protection measures.[65] Article 11 TFEU makes it clear that environmental protection requirements to promote sustainable development must be integrated into the definition and implementation of EU policies and activities. The use of the precautionary principle is perhaps the most famous example of an EU norm-driven agenda in the environmental sphere. The EU applies this principle to justify action taken with risk, but on a subjective ground where a potential risk is likely and where there is still no clear evidence of the risk at stake.[66] The precautionary principle has also had an impact on the external landscape, as well as the debate on genetically modified organisms (GMOs),[67] where the EU has actively promoted it.[68] While the principle guides EU environmental law, it has also become prominently enshrined in, for example, the Rio Declaration and the United Nations Framework Convention on Climate Change (UNFCCC).[69]

[64] L. van Schaik and S. Schunz, 'Explaining EU Activism and Impact in Global Climate Politics: Is the Union a Norm- or Interest-Driven Actor?' (2012) 50 *Journal of Common Market Studies* 169.

[65] See e.g. C. Burns and N. Carter, 'Environmental Policy', in E. Jones, et al. (eds.), *The Oxford Handbook of the European Union* (Oxford University Press, 2012); J. Scott, 'The Multi-level Governance of Climate Change', in P. Craig and G. de Búrca (eds.), *The Evolution of EU Law*, 2nd edn (Oxford University Press, 2011), p. 805.

[66] See e.g. E. Fisher, *Risk Regulation and Administrative Constitutionalism* (Oxford: Hart Publishing, 2007).

[67] *Ibid.*, p. 207.

[68] See e.g. G. Majone, *Dilemmas of European Integration: The Ambiguities and Pitfalls of Integration by Stealth* (Oxford University Press, 2005).

[69] Ibid.

The ETS ruling[70] offers a powerful test case for the EU as a global agent – or giant – on a green mission in an entrepreneurship spirit.[71] In particular, the ETS ruling serves as a reminder of the Lisbon Treaty's promise that the EU will promote its values abroad – Article 3(5) TEU – and ensure a high level of environmental protection. In its ETS ruling, the Court stated that while matters contributing to the pollution of the air, sea or land territory of the Member States may originate partly outside that territory it is not such as to call into question, in the light of the principles of customary international law, the full applicability of EU Law in that territory.[72] Interestingly, the Court did not refer to the 'full effectiveness' of EU law,[73] as it usually does when stretching EU law into new domains, but simply referred to the 'full applicability' of EU law, which would be hampered if it was denied extraterritorial scope. Therefore, the Court used the environmental provisions to enforce a spill-over of EU law into the external sphere, while still emphasizing that EU law does not regulate externally via the application of the ETS to aviation.[74]

More specifically, the Court held that

> [W]hile the ultimate objective of the allowance trading scheme is the protection of the environment by means of a reduction of greenhouse gas emissions [. . .] The benefit for the environment depends on the stringency of the total quantity of allowances allocated, which represents the overall limit on emissions allowed by the scheme.[75]

According to the Court, for this reason, it made legal sense – given that the international regime had largely failed to act[76] – that the EU anti-pollution legislation governing the ETS was extended to include emissions caused by

[70] See C-366/10, *Air Transport Association of America* v. *Secretary of State for Energy and Climate Change*.

[71] See S. Bogojević, 'Legalising Environmental Leadership: A Comment on the CJEU's Ruling in C-366/10 on the Inclusion of Aviation in the EU Emissions Trading Scheme' (2012) 244 *Journal of Environmental Law* 345.

[72] C-366/10, *Air Transport Association of America* v. *Secretary of State for Energy and Climate Change*, paras. 129–30. The Court moreover held that 'It follows that the European Union had competence, in the light of the principles of customary international law [. . .] to adopt Directive 2008/101, in so far as the latter extends the allowance trading scheme laid down by Directive 2003/87 to all flights which arrive at or depart from an aerodrome situated in the territory of a Member State'.

[73] See e.g. Case C-176/03, *Commission* v. *Council* (2005) ECR I-7879.

[74] Bogojević, 'Legalising Environmental Leadership'.

[75] C-366/10, *Air Transport Association of America* v. *Secretary of State for Energy and Climate Change*.

[76] Bogojević, 'Legalising Environmental Leadership'.

a foreign air carrier. Therefore, EU law applies not only upon European territory, but also upon European airspace.

In any case, the opening lines of the Commission's communication on climate change are instructive in light of what they convey to us about the EU's stance on environmental protection.[77] The Commission states that '[w]hen the EU decided in 2008 to cut its greenhouse gas (GHG) emissions, it showed its commitment to tackling the climate change threat and to lead the world in demonstrating how this could be done'.[78] Therefore, the performance benchmark is not defined exclusively by reference to the regulation of EU destined goods; and the level of the EU's ambition, in terms of its capacity to leverage regulatory change, has been increased by the ETS.[79] Notwithstanding the controversial issues raised by the ETS ruling, there may nonetheless be reasons to favour this kind of contingent unilateralist approach as the EU cannot achieve its climate change goals acting alone.[80] This raises the complex issue of legitimacy and to what extent a certain 'imperialism' is merited in the name of the common good.

In discussing the broader question of what values the EU shall seek to promote with regard to the environment, commentators have referred to 'the climate change regime complex', which is a loosely coupled system of institutions with no clear hierarchy or core, yet with many of its elements linked in complementary ways.[81] Such a regime operates at different levels of governance and in relation to narrowly drawn, discrete, but often overlapping, issue areas. Arguably, on the basis of the regime complex's normative justification there are six criteria for evaluating and assessing it: coherence, accountability, determinacy, sustainability, its epistemic quality, and fairness.[82] These criteria sound increasingly

[77] Communication from the Commission to the European Parliament, the Council, the European Economic and Social Committee and the Committee of the Regions, 'Analysis of Options to Move beyond Greenhouse Gas Emission Reductions and Assessing the Risk of Carbon Leakage', COM (2010) 265 final, 26 May 2010.

[78] *Ibid.*, p. 2.

[79] J. Scott, 'Can the EU Deliver on Citizens Expectations in the Fight against Climate Change?', in M. Dougan, et al. (eds.), *Empowerment and Disempowerment of the European Citizen* (Oxford: Hart Publishing, 2012), p. 189.

[80] *Ibid.*

[81] See R. O. Keohane and D. Victor, 'The Regime Complex for Climate Change', Harvard Project on International Climate Agreements Discussion Paper (2010), pp. 10–33; J. Scott and L. Rajamani, 'EU Climate Change Unilateralism' (2012) 23 *European Journal of International Law* 469.

[82] Keohane and Victor, 'The Regime Complex for Climate Change', p. 3.

similar to the general good-governance vocabulary within the EU.[83] Taken seriously, such an approach would require of the EU to produce a more developed narrative about what it is doing and why as well as explaining the normative basis underpinning its increasingly numerous trade-supported policy demands.[84]

5 Conclusion

This chapter has attempted to conceptualize the question of the EU as a promoter of global values. The chapter further discussed how this aspiration appears to form part of a more general debate on the future of Europe. The question of Europe's *raison d'être* then seems to turn on the EU's ability to uphold its values internally. Yet, if there are difficulties determining exactly what EU constitutionalism means within the EU legal architecture,[85] the debate is bound to become even more challenging on the global stage.

First, the chapter set out to discuss what the EU values are (starting with the Treaty definitions) and secondly, how these values are promoted globally. The intention was to use the recent ETS ruling, where Article 3(5) TEU was deployed as an instrument endowed with freestanding value crucial for the understanding of the relationship between EU law and international law and thereby to discuss the normative framework for the conceptualization of such a relationship. The contribution assessed the EU's function as a promoter of values by looking at the broader normative and constitutional implications of such promotion, while trying to trace it in the context of global constitutionalism. In doing so, the chapter took a step back: while acknowledging the importance of a discussion on the existence of the different strands of EU constitutionalism and why it matters, the author suggested that the focus lies elsewhere, namely, the need for increased legitimacy and accountability, which remains a burning topic in contemporary EU integration of law and policy. Therefore, the contribution cautiously inquired as to what extent the debate is really about ensuring good global governance in

[83] See, of course, European Commission, European Governance, White Paper, COM (2001) 428 final, 25 July 2001, available at http://eur-lex.europa.eu/LexUriServ/site/en/com/2001/com2001_0428en01.pdf

[84] Scott, 'Can the EU Deliver on Citizens' Expectations in the Fight against Climate Change?'.

[85] See e.g. A. von Bogdandy and J. Bast, *Principles of European Constitutional Law* (Oxford: Hart Publishing, 2010).

its widest sense. In addition, the chapter argued that it is exactly in this context that global constitutionalism could make a valid contribution as an aid for visualizing the need for such a discussion. While the search for the meaning and purpose of the EU, and its action on the global scale, is an ongoing process, naming that process and the problems it causes are part of the journey.

Finally, the chapter tentatively looked at the feasibility of the EU becoming a successful actor on the global scene. Specifically it asked to what extent is the EU inactive in safeguarding and promoting its values? Conversely, should the EU safeguard its own integrity with regard to the external sphere? It was argued that the protection of the environment offers an example of a legitimate application of EU externalities as part of the 'common global good'.

While it might not seem to be a daunting conclusion to point out that the protection of the environment is an area that merits EU 'imperialism', since the EU cannot fight global climate change on its own – especially as the international forum has failed to act – other areas may be more complex.[86] The EU's presence on the international scene and its enforcement of values – therefore – is all about contextualization.

[86] E.g. the fight against terrorism and security governance is an area where the EU should consider shielding itself by being firmer in its commitment to legality and the protection of human rights. E Herlin-Karnell, 'The EU as a Promoter of Values and the European Global Project'.

5

Promoting the rule of law abroad: on the EU's limited contribution to the shaping of an international understanding of the rule of law

LAURENT PECH

1 External promotion of the rule of law in the EU's 'Constitution'

In the context of the first-ever high-level meeting on the rule of law at national and international levels organized by the United Nations (UN) General Assembly on 24 September 2012, the European Union (EU) issued a noteworthy statement in which it emphasised that the rule of law 'is of critical importance for the EU's external policy' as respect for this principle is not only 'an essential condition for peace and stability in the consolidation and support of democracy, and in the fight against impunity', but is also 'inextricably linked to the protection of human rights and fundamental freedoms and needs to be pursued both at national and international level'.[1]

This support for the rule of law, however, is not unique. Since the fall of the Berlin Wall, all international organizations and most countries have been keen to articulate their support for this principle. So much so that it has been argued that 'no other single political ideal has ever achieved global endorsement'.[2] In their capacity of *Herren der Verträge*, the EU Member States responded to the increasing emphasis on the rule of law by subjecting the EU's founding Treaties to several important amendments in the 1990s.[3] These successive amendments considerably reinforced the constitutional significance of the rule

[1] EU Delegation to the UN, Statement on the Rule of Law at the National and International Levels, 10 October 2012, UN 6th Committee, EUUN12-091E, available at www.eu-un.europa.eu/articles/fr/article_12682_fr.htm.

[2] B. Tamanaha, *On the Rule of Law* (Cambridge University Press, 2004), pp. 3–4.

[3] For further analysis, see L. Pech, 'A Union Founded on the Rule of Law: Meaning and Reality of the Rule of Law as a Constitutional Principle of EU Law' (2010) 6 *European Constitutional Law Review* 359.

of law in the EU legal order and made clear that this principle had both internal and external dimensions.

As regards the promotion of the rule of law beyond the EU, the Treaties provide that this principle, along with the other foundational values of the EU, constitutes an eligibility condition and accession benchmark, which essentially means that compliance with the rule of law and assimilation of relevant EU standards are, theoretically speaking at least, a prior condition for EU membership.[4] In addition, the EU has committed itself to developing external policies that aim to promote its values. In 1992, the development and consolidation of democracy, the rule of law and respect for human rights were not only identified as the EU's foreign and security policy objectives,[5] but also as one of the general objectives of the (then) European Communities' (EC) policy of development cooperation and of the EC policy in the area of economic, financial and technical cooperation measures with third countries.[6] Following the entry into force of the Lisbon Treaty in December 2009, a new provision – Article 21 of the Treaty on the Functioning of the European Union (TFEU) – has further clarified that all of the EU's external policies must be guided by and seek to promote the principles

> which have inspired its own creation, development and enlargement, and which it seeks to advance in the wider world: democracy, the rule of law, the universality and indivisibility of human rights and fundamental freedoms, respect for human dignity, the principles of equality and solidarity, and respect for the principles of the United Nations Charter and international law.

Beyond this, in common with most national constitutions that make reference to the rule of law,[7] the EU Treaties say very little about what

[4] See Art. 49 TEU: 'any European State which respects the values referred to in Art. 2 and is committed to promoting them may apply to become a member of the Union'. For an exhaustive overview of the role played by the rule of law and democracy in the EU's enlargement process and the argument that measuring compliance with these principles is virtually impossible as they remain contested and open-ended concepts, see D. Kochenov, *EU Enlargement and the Failure of Conditionality* (The Hague: Kluwer Law International, 2008).

[5] Ex Art. 11(1) TEU (now Art. 24 TFEU).

[6] See ex Art. 177(2) TEC (now Art. 208 TFEU) and ex Art. 181(a)(1) TEC (now Art. 212 TFEU), respectively.

[7] With the arguable exception of Spain, as its Constitution includes a rather complete list of the formal components which are at the heart of the *Estado de derecho* (i.e., the principle of legality, the hierarchy of legal provisions, the publicity of legal statutes, the non-retroactivity of punitive provisions, legal security, the accountability of public authorities

this principle entails and how the EU should seek to uphold and promote it beyond its borders. This contribution will therefore first clarify the dominant understanding promoted by the EU in the context of its external action (section 2) before discussing the extent to which the EU may be said to have contributed to the shaping of an international understanding of the rule of law (section 3). It will be argued that notwithstanding the relatively superficial and, at times, fluctuating nature of the definitions one may encounter in EU external instruments and other EU publications, EU institutions tend to promote a broad, substantive and holistic understanding. In other words, the rule of law is generally understood as a principle that includes substantive components (e.g. equality before the law) as well as formal/procedural elements (e.g. legal certainty, judicial review), and which requires a democratic and liberal constitutional order giving full effect to human rights. As regards the shaping of an international understanding, it is submitted that the EU cannot claim much success in terms of norm-building for two main reasons: the EU has accepted the Council of Europe's normative pre-eminence and is promoting an understanding that was initially shaped by other international organizations and which has now become highly consensual on the international plane. Rather than any decisive contribution to the shaping of a new international understanding, the EU may be said to have significantly contributed to the diffusion of a substantive and holistic conception of the rule of law and the progressive solidification of an international consensus regarding its core elements and inextricable links with the principles of democracy and respect for human rights.

2 The EU's external promotion of a substantive and holistic understanding

As this contribution is concerned with the EU's understanding and promotion of the rule of law 'in its relations with the wider world',[8] the

and the prohibition of arbitrary action of public authorities), most national constitutions do not offer comprehensive definitions of the rule of law. This means that it is almost always left to legislators, courts and scholars to flesh the principle out.

8 See Art. 3(5) TEU: 'In its relations with the wider world, the Union shall uphold and promote its values and interests'.

internal functions fulfilled by this principle will only briefly be mentioned here. The EU Treaties first make clear that the rule of law is one of the common foundational principles on which the EU's constitutional order is based.[9] The Treaties also empower the EU to sanction any of its Member States were they found guilty of a serious and persistent breach of these foundational principles.[10] While this latter procedure has never been used, recent episodes indicate the EU institutions' greater willingness to tackle blatant violations of the rule of law by initiating infringement actions against relevant national governments.[11] EU Member States, however, are not subject to a permanent and intrusive monitoring of their adherence to the EU's foundational values contrary to non-EU countries and especially candidate countries.[12]

Another problematic issue, and more directly relevant in the context of this study, is the lack of any comprehensive Treaty definition of these values. This means that the rule of law, as a Treaty principle, does not significantly constrain the EU institutions' freedom of action when, for instance, they act in the international arena, or when they adopt external policies. In other words, it has been essentially left to the EU institutions to clarify through legislation and policy documents what they shall seek to promote abroad under the heading 'rule of law'. That being said, the EU Treaties constantly link the rule of law to the principles of democratic government and human rights protection.[13] It is therefore submitted that EU primary law requires that these principles, albeit left undefined, must not be confused with each other

[9] See Art. 2 TEU. See, generally, A. von Bogdandy, 'Constitutional Principles', in A. von Bogdandy and J. Bast (eds.), *Principles of European Constitutional Law* (Oxford: Hart Publishing, 2006), p. 3.

[10] See Art. 7 TEU. For further analysis, see e.g. W. Sadurski, 'Adding Bite to a Bark: The Story of Article 7, EU Enlargement, and Jörg Haider' (2010) 16 *Columbia Journal of European Law* 385.

[11] See e.g. European Commission, 'Hungary – infringements: Commission takes further legal steps on measures affecting the judiciary and the independence of the data protection authority', MEMO 12/165, 7 March 2012.

[12] For a similar argument regarding the preservation of the fundamental rights *acquis* post EU accession, see Editorial Comments, 'Fundamental Rights and EU Membership: Do as I Say, Not as I Do!' (2012) 49 *Common Market Law Review* 481.

[13] See e.g. Art. 2 TEU and Art. 21 TFEU. While the EU Treaties do mention additional values or principles, democracy, the rule of law and respect for human rights always appear together.

but should rather be understood as *interconnected* and *interdependent* principles. As will be shown below, the EU instruments dedicated to the external promotion of its values[14] are perfectly in line with this view as they constantly link the rule of law with democracy and respect for human rights. And while EU instruments or reports do not always comprehensively specify what the rule of law entails or tend to emphasize variable components of this principle, one may nevertheless contend that the EU generally tends to promote a broad, substantive and holistic understanding of the rule of law whose core elements are as follows: legality, including a democratic process for enacting legal rules; legal certainty; prohibition against arbitrariness; access to independent and impartial courts; respect for human rights and finally, non-discrimination.

2.1 Tour d'horizon *of the main instruments used by the EU to promote the rule of law abroad*

To promote its values abroad, the EU may simultaneously rely on unilateral trade instruments, technical and financial assistance instruments, bilateral 'soft' instruments and bilateral/regional agreements.[15] From a transversal assessment of these instruments, one may draw the conclusion that the rule of law is undoubtedly a value that the EU relentlessly seeks to export 'beyond the borders of the Union by means of persuasion, incentives and negotiation',[16] but other more 'punishing' means have been used and EU cooperation with third countries is also normally conditioned to the respect of the EU's values by these countries.[17] As space constraints preclude a comprehensive examination

[14] See generally the excellent overview provided by M. Cremona, 'Values in EU Foreign Policy', in M. Evans and P. Koutrakos (eds.), *Beyond the Established Legal Orders* (Oxford: Hart Publishing, 2011), p. 292.

[15] See e.g. T. A. Börzel and T. Risse, 'Venus Approaching Mars? The European Union's Approaches to Democracy Promotion in Comparative Perspective', in A. Magen, T. Risse and M. McFaul (eds.), *Promoting Democracy and the Rule of Law: American and European Strategies* (Basingstoke: Palgrave Macmillan, 2009), p. 34.

[16] Opinion of AG Mengozzi in Case C-354/04 *P Gestoras Pro Amnistía and Others* v. *Council* [2007] ECR I-1579, para. 79.

[17] For a recent discussion of the effectiveness and shortcomings of the EU instruments dedicated to the external promotion of its foundational values, see European Parliament resolution of 18 April 2012 on the Annual Report on Human Rights in the World and the

of the relevant EU external instruments, the list below offers an outline of the definitions one may find in these instruments, starting with unilateral financial and technical instruments and ending with bilateral instruments:

European Instrument for Democracy and Human Rights (EIDHR) Regulation
: Actions that participate to the strengthening of the international framework for the protection of human rights, justice, the rule of law and the promotion of democracy may be financed by the EU and the objective of strengthening the rule of law is associated with the objectives of promoting access to justice, the independence of the judiciary, and encouraging and evaluating legal and institutional reforms.[18]

European Neighbourhood and Partnership Instrument (ENPI) Regulation
: The rule of law is linked with the promotion of good governance, and both concepts are said to encompass an effective public administration, an impartial and effective judiciary as well as the fight against corruption and fraud.[19]

Instrument for Pre-Accession Assistance (IPA) Regulation
: The strengthening of the rule of law, including its enforcement, is associated with the strengthening of democratic institutions.[20]

Development Cooperation Instrument (DCI) Regulation
: EU financial assistance is available for actions that seek to consolidate and support democracy, the rule of law, human rights, good governance, gender equality and related instruments of international law. The rule of law is described as one of the key elements that any political environment must guarantee in order to favour long-term development, and its strengthening is linked with improving access to justice and good governance, including actions to combat corruption.[21]

European Union's policy on the matter, including implications for the EU's strategic human rights policy, 2011/2185(INI).

18 Art. 2(1)(a) and (c), Regulation (EC) No1889/2006 of 20 December 2006 on establishing a financing instrument for the promotion of democracy and human rights worldwide, OJ (2006) L 386/1.

19 Art. 2(2)(d), Regulation (EC) No. 1638/2006 of 24 October 2006 laying down general provisions establishing a European Neighbourhood and Partnership Instrument, OJ (2006) L 310/1.

20 Art. 2, Regulation (EC) No. 1085/2006 of 17 July 2006 establishing an Instrument for Pre-Accession Assistance, OJ (2006) L 210/82.

21 Arts. 2(1), 3(3) and 5(2)(f), Regulation (EC) No. 1905/2006 of the European Parliament and of the Council of 18 December 2006 establishing a financing instrument for development cooperation, OJ (2006) L 378/41.

EU's Bilateral Agreements[22]

> The rule of law, along with democracy and respect for human rights, is normally considered an 'essential element' on which these agreements are based but most agreements do not explain what the rule of law stands for with the exception of the Cotonou Agreement which refers to effective and accessible means of legal redress, an independent legal system guaranteeing equality before the law and an executive that is fully subject to the law, as core elements of the rule of law.[23]

When looking at the evolution of all these instruments over the past few years, the most significant change has been the 'legislative mainstreaming' of the EU's key foundational values. To put it differently, the rule of law together with fundamental rights and democratization objectives have been progressively integrated into all aspects of the EU's external policies and actions. This process of legislative mainstreaming is a logical answer to the enshrinement of these foundational values as transversal principles that must constantly guide EU action on the international scene under Article 21 TFEU. The contemplated set of the EU's external instruments for the period 2014–20 further confirms that the EU sees the promotion of these values as a strategic and transversal objective.[24] As regards the definitions contained in the EU external instruments listed above, it will be argued that notwithstanding their relatively diverse and superficial nature,[25] and the regrettable lack of a general and authoritative

[22] European Commission, Inventory of Agreements containing the Human Rights Clause, DG RELEX/B2 Treaties Office, 7 July 2011.

[23] Art. 9(2), Partnership agreement between the members of the African Caribbean and Pacific (ACP) Group of States and the EC and its Member States signed in Cotonou on 23 June 2000, OJ (2000) L 317/3.

[24] See European Commission, Joint Communication to the European Parliament and Council on Global Europe, 'A New Approach to Financing EU External Action', Brussels, 7 December 2011, COM (2011) 865 final. In this Communication, the Commission indicates (pp. 4–6) that it will put human rights, democracy and the rule of law (the concept of good governance is also used and, seemingly, as a synonymous term) at the core of EU external action by redesigning the EU's external instruments so that they will take greater account of these values when it comes to allocating external assistance to partner countries.

[25] For a critical assessment of this lack of uniformity and the argument that three conceptions of the rule of law – the co-operation, development and security and defence models – coexist in EU external relations, see E. Wennerström, *The Rule of Law and the European Union* (Uppsala: Iustus Förlag, 2007). For a broadly similar argument, see also N. Wichmann, 'Promoting the Rule of Law in the European Neighbourhood Policy – Strategic or Normative Power?' (2007) 22.2 *Politique européenne* 81.

conceptual document on the EU rule of law approach,[26] the EU is not 'exporting' a vague or incoherent ideal. Indeed, EU instruments always seek to increase compliance with a number of sub-components of the rule of law, which one may appropriately refer to as its core elements:[27]

(a) legality, including a transparent, accountable and democratic process for enacting law;
(b) legal certainty;
(c) prohibition of arbitrariness;
(d) access to justice before independent and impartial courts, including judicial review of administrative acts;
(e) respect for human rights;
(f) non-discrimination and equality before the law.

It is important to note, however, that these elements may not always be systematically mentioned. In addition, as the primary purpose of the EU external rule of law policies is to improve the situation 'on the ground', i.e. to institutionalize compliance with the rule of law through diverse legal and structural reforms with a view to guaranteeing a 'better functioning' of the executive, legislature and judiciary, it is not unreasonable for the EU to emphasize compliance with different components of the rule of law in order to reflect different priorities and take account of the different geopolitical contexts it may be confronted with. Furthermore, the core elements mentioned above may sometimes be complemented by additional ones depending on the particular problems faced by the recipient of EU assistance. For instance, the EU, not unlike the UN, often links the fight against corruption with the preservation of the rule of law.[28]

26 By contrast, the UN has published a guide on the same; UN Secretary General, Guidance Note on the UN Approach to Rule of Law Assistance, April 2008, available at www.unrol.org/doc.aspx?doc_id=2124. This note offers a clear overview of 'the guiding principles and framework for UN rule of law activities at the national level that apply in all circumstances', with the aims of offering 'a comprehensive and coherent UN approach' derived from UN norms, standards and guidance, and a framework outlining 'the fundamental constituent elements of rule of law efforts'.

27 Council of Europe (Venice Commission), Report on the Rule of Law, Study No. 512/2009, CDL-AD (2011) 003 rev., Strasbourg, 4 April 2011, para. 41.

28 For an example of EU act linking rule of law and fight against corruption, see Commission decision establishing a mechanism for cooperation and verification of progress in

A review of EU actions and policies aimed at specific countries or regions does not invalidate the argument made above whereby the EU generally seeks to export a broad, substantive and holistic understanding. This is not to deny that the EU often fails comprehensively to explain what it means by 'rule of law'. For instance, in the context of the EU's enlargement policy, one may easily find abundant references in Commission reports to the need for candidate countries to make substantial progress as regards the strengthening of the rule of law, and yet find it virtually impossible to come across comprehensive definitions. For instance, in a recent communication, the Commission merely indicated that it 'will further step up its work and intensify the dialogue on the rule of law with candidate countries and potential candidates'.[29] It also is not rare for the EU to advocate specific reforms in the name of the rule of law but without any additional explanation as regards the exact meaning and scope of this principle. For example, the Commission's Opinion on Montenegro's application for EU membership naturally refers to the rule of law but it is merely stated that Montenegro needs to strengthen the rule of law 'in particular through de-politicized and merit-based appointments of members of the judicial and prosecutorial councils and of state prosecutors as well as through reinforcement of the independence, autonomy, efficiency and accountability of judges and prosecutors'.[30] The detailed analysis, on which this opinion is based, is contained in a voluminous, separate 'analytical report', which does not, however, give any meaningful precision on the EU's understanding of the rule of law.[31]

Bulgaria to address specific benchmarks in the areas of judicial reform and the fight against corruption and organised crime, Brussels, 13 December 2006 C (2006) 6570 final. Recital 3 provides that the principle of the rule of law implies 'the existence of an impartial, independent and effective judicial and administrative system properly equipped, *inter alia*, to fight corruption and organised crime'. As regards the UN, see the UN Convention against Corruption, 9–11 December 2003, 2349 UNTS 41. Its Preamble indicates that the States Parties to the Convention share the view that corruption endangers 'sustainable development and the rule of law'.

29 European Commission, 'Enlargement Strategy and Main Challenges 2010–2011', COM (2010) 660, Brussels, 9 November 2010, p. 8.

30 European Commission, 'Opinion on Montenegro's Application for Membership of the European Union', COM (2010) 670, 9 November 2010.

31 European Commission, 'Analytical Report Accompanying the Commission's Opinion on Montenegro's Application for Membership of the European Union', Commission Staff Working Document, COM (2010) 670, SEC (2010) 1334, Brussels, 9 November 2010.

It is nevertheless possible to find communications from the Commission where the meaning of the rule of law is more scrupulously described. For instance, in a communication on the partnership between the EU and the group of African Caribbean and Pacific (ACP) countries, the Commission offered fairly detailed explanations, which are worth reproducing *in extenso*:

> The primacy of the law is a fundamental principle of any democratic system seeking to foster and promote rights, whether civil and political or economic, social and cultural. This entails means of recourse enabling individual citizens to defend their rights. The principle of placing limitations on the power of the state is best served by a representative government drawing its authority from the sovereignty of the people. The principle must shape the structure of the state and the prerogatives of the various powers. It implies, for example:
>
> - a legislature respecting and giving full effect to human rights and fundamental freedoms;
> - an independent judiciary;
> - effective and accessible means of legal recourse;
> - a legal system guaranteeing equality before the law;
> - a prison system respecting the human person;
> - a police force at the service of the law;
> - an effective executive enforcing the law and capable of establishing the social and economic conditions necessary for life in society.[32]

This communication from the Commission offers, therefore, additional evidence that the EU generally tends to promote a substantive and holistic understanding rather than a 'formal' one.

2.2 *The promotion of a substantive and holistic understanding*

From a global and inductive look at the EU external instruments mentioned above, one may draw the conclusion that the EU primarily understands the rule of law as a concept which requires, as previously noted, compliance with a number of core principles in order to guarantee inter alia that governments are subject to the law and, more generally, that national legal systems give full effect to fundamental rights and democratic principles.

[32] European Commission, 'Democratisation, the Rule of Law, Respect for Human Rights and Good Governance: The Challenges of the Partnership between the European Union and the ACP States', COM (1998) 146 final, Brussels, 24 February 1998, p. 4.

Accordingly, the EU can be said to go beyond the formal conception of the rule of law favoured by Raz (to mention but one eminent scholar), according to whom legal norms should possess a number of 'formal' attributes in order to constitute standards capable of providing effective guidance for natural and legal persons: they must be prospective, adequately publicized, clear, relatively stable, and law-making should also be guided by open, stable, clear and general rules.[33] It is important, however, to point out that formal conceptions of the rule of law also often imply compliance with some *institutional* requirements (e.g. the principle of separation of powers) as well as individual *procedural* rights (e.g. the right to be heard), despite Raz's insistence that in his conception the rule of law 'says nothing about fundamental rights'.[34] In any event, the most important point at this stage is that EU external instruments and other EU publications tend to illustrate a 'substantive/thick' rather than a 'formal/thin' understanding of the rule of law.[35] Indeed, the EU promotes an understanding that is not indifferent to the content or the substantive aims of the law and encompasses elements of political morality such as democracy and substantive individual rights. In this author's view, this conception is a logical consequence of a constitutional framework that clearly indicates that the values on which the EU is founded must be viewed as interdependent and mutually reinforcing – a point made previously and which is further confirmed by numerous statements such as this:

> Democracy and human rights are inextricably linked. The fundamental freedoms of expression and association are the preconditions for political pluralism and democratic process, whereas democratic control and separation of powers are essential to sustain an independent judiciary and the rule of law which in turn are required for effective protection of human rights.[36]

33 J. Raz, 'The Rule of Law and its Virtue', *The Authority of Law: Essays on Law and Morality* (Oxford: Clarendon Press 1979), pp. 214–18.

34 *Ibid*., p. 214.

35 Theories emphasizing the formal/procedural aspects of the rule of law are often referred to as 'thin' theories and are opposed to 'thick' conceptions of the rule of law. For further discussion, see e.g. R. Peerenboom, 'Varieties of Rule of Law: An Introduction and Provisional Conclusion', in R. Peerenboom (ed.), *Asian Discourses of Rule of Law* (Abingdon: Routledge, 2004), pp. 2–10. It is nonetheless important not to rigidly oppose these two schools of thought as 'the formal versions have substantive implications and the substantive versions incorporate formal requirements', Tamanaha, *On the Rule of Law*, p. 92.

36 Recital 8 of the Preamble to the EIDHR Regulation. Regulation (EC) No. 1889/2006 of the European Parliament and of the Council of 20 December 2006 on establishing a financing instrument for the promotion of democracy and human rights worldwide, OJ (2006) L 386/1.

To bring this definitional review to a close, notwithstanding the absence of an authoritative reference text setting out what the EU rule of law precisely entails and the *à la carte* application of this principle in some situations,[37] the EU cannot be said to 'export' a vague or incoherent ideal or a narrow conception. And while it is true that EU external policies reflect a very broad understanding of what the rule of law entails (e.g. anti-corruption), the core demands of this principle (e.g. the existence of effective legal remedies to guarantee the protection of fundamental rights) are generally always taken into account. This is not to say that the credibility of EU external action would not benefit from the publication of guidelines comprehensively setting out what its foundational principles entail, the indicators or benchmarks to be used when it comes to assessing a particular country's adherence to them, and the minimum requirements any country is expected to meet. This would help the EU define more effective policies as well as help monitor compliance and progress in a less ad hoc and subjective manner.[38] It may also allow the EU to increase its influence and act more effectively as an international standard setter. However, as will be shown below, it is submitted that there has always been extremely limited room for any decisive EU contribution to the shaping of an international understanding of the rule of law.

3 The EU's limited contribution to the shaping of a substantive and holistic understanding on the international plane

The task of documenting and measuring the EU's contribution to international norm-building is notoriously difficult. Indeed, EU action of this kind is often informal and as a result it is generally difficult to determine 'what influence the EU as such has had on the development of an international norm'.[39] That said, it will be argued that there has always

[37] For the argument that the EU's foundational values can be compared to largely undefined targets whose meaning varies according to the Commission's priorities, see P. Leino and R. Petrov, 'Between "Common Values" and Competing Universals: The Promotion of the EU's Common Values through the European Neighbourhood Policy' (2009) 15 *European Law Journal* 665.

[38] Scholars have rightly noted that non-EU countries, especially candidate countries, have rarely been subject to a consistent, objective and demanding assessment of their compliance with EU's values. See D. Kochenov, *EU Enlargement and the Failure of Conditionality*.

[39] Cremona, 'Values in EU Foreign Policy', p. 307.

been extremely limited room for the EU to play any significant norm-building role with respect to the meaning and scope of the rule of law on the international plane, for two main reasons: first, the EU has agreed to defer to the Council of Europe when it comes to devising policies and standards linked to the rule of law in Europe; second, the EU itself has been influenced by the conceptual work previously undertaken within the confines of other international organizations such as the Council of Europe and the Organization for Security and Co-operation in Europe (OSCE), and has since been promoting an understanding that is consensual at the international level. In these conditions, the conceptual contribution of the EU on the shaping of an international understanding of the rule of law can only but be limited. This is not to say, however, that the EU has not decisively contributed to the international diffusion and progressive predominance of a broad, substantive and holistic understanding through its external policies and actions,[40] and played an important role when it comes to encouraging non-EU countries, especially those wishing to join the EU, to implement rule of law reforms.[41]

3.1 On the EU's recognition of the Council of Europe's normative pre-eminence in Europe

The EU's contribution to the shaping of an original understanding of the rule of law within Europe has been limited if only because the EU's understanding heavily reflects national understandings of this ancient

[40] Regarding the process of diffusion of EU values and norms across Europe and beyond, see e.g. H. Grabbe, 'How Does Europeanization Affect CEE Governance? Conditionality, Diffusion and Diversity' (2001) 8 *Journal of European Public Policy* 1013; T. Börzel and T. Risse, 'The Transformative Power of Europe: The European Union and the Diffusion of Ideas', KFG Working Paper No. 1 (May 2009), available at www.polsoz.fu-berlin.de/en/v/transformeurope/forschung/Trafo_Europ_short.pdf.

[41] This last aspect will not be analysed further as this contribution pursues a more general and conceptual goal and focuses on how the rule of law is understood on the international plane rather than the impact of EU rule of law promotion policies in individual countries. Regarding the effectiveness of these policies in four countries (Romania, Serbia, Turkey and Ukraine), see E. Baracani, 'EU Democratic Rule of Law Promotion', in A. Magen and L. Morlino (eds.), *International Actors, Democratization and the Rule of Law: Anchoring Democracy* (Abingdon: Routledge 2008), p. 54. The author offers the optimistic argument that the EU has been largely successful in terms of removing obstacles to the adoption of democratic rule of law reforms. For further references and a more 'pessimistic' thesis according to which EU democracy promotion and human rights policy have been characterized by low consistency and effectiveness, see F. Schimmelfennig, 'Europeanization beyond Europe', (2012) 7.1 *Living Reviews in European Governance*.

principle.[42] Furthermore, and more recently, the EU has formally recognized the Council of Europe's normative pre-eminence. Indeed, while the memorandum of understanding between these two organizations, adopted on 23 May 2007, sensibly provides that they must 'develop their relationship in all areas of common interest, in particular the promotion and protection of [...] the rule of law',[43] it adds the following and critical caveat: 'The Council of Europe will remain the benchmark for human rights, the rule of law and democracy in Europe'.[44] The advertised ambition to establish common legal standards regarding the rule of law through, inter alia, improved legal cooperation and reciprocal consultations at an early stage in the process of elaborating standards,[45] should therefore be understood in this light. That said, even in the absence of a formal recognition of the Council of Europe's role as the primary standard setter in Europe in the fields mentioned above, there would be little room for normative competition[46] between the EU and the Council of Europe. As a matter of fact, a significant number of common features between the EU and the Council of Europe's conceptions of the rule of law can be highlighted.

Similarly to the EU Treaties, the Council of Europe's most important legal texts lack any precision as regards the meaning and scope of the rule of law. After reviewing provisions such as Article 3 of the Statute of the Council of Europe, which provides that 'every member of the Council of Europe must accept the principles of the rule of law and of the enjoyment by all persons within its jurisdiction of human rights and fundamental freedoms', an official and instructive report rightly noted that 'neither the Statute nor the ECHR elaborate on the concept of the rule of law as such'[47] and that in fact no authoritative definition exists within the Council of

[42] For the argument that, similarly to national legal traditions in Europe the EU rule of law has progressively become a dominant organizational paradigm and a multifaceted legal principle with formal and substantive elements which lacks 'full' justiciability, see L. Pech, 'The Rule of Law as a Constitutional Principle of the European Union', Jean Monnet Working Paper 04/09 (2009).

[43] 'Memorandum of Understanding between the Council of Europe and the European Union, 2007', para. 9, available at www.coe.int/t/der/eu_EN.asp.

[44] *Ibid.*, para. 10. [45] *Ibid.*, paras. 22–5.

[46] On this notion, see e.g. A. Ogus, 'The Economic Approach: Competition between Legal Systems', in D. Nelken and E. Örücü (eds.), *Comparative Law: A Handbook* (Oxford: Hart Publishing, 2007), p. 155.

[47] Council of Europe (Committee of Ministers), *The Council of Europe and the Rule of Law: An Overview*, Committee of Ministers (2008) 170, 21 November 2008, para. 6.

Europe.[48] Unlike the UN or the OSCE,[49] both organizations have also failed to produce a reference text clarifying what the rule of law entails.[50]

From a transversal look at the Council of Europe's legal and policy instruments and the European Court of Human Rights (ECtHR) case law, one may nevertheless conclude that the Council of Europe understands the rule of law in a similar fashion to the EU. First, the EU and the Council of Europe view the upholding and the promotion of the rule of law as one of their *raisons d'être*, and both recognize the rule of law as being one of the 'interrelated trinity of concepts'.[51] To put it differently, the rule of law along with democracy and respect for human rights are understood as *interconnected* and *interdependent* principles as 'there can be no democracy without the rule of law and respect for human rights; there can be no rule of law without democracy and respect for human rights, and no respect for human rights without democracy and the rule of law'.[52] The same report goes on to explain that this might be the reason for the lack of a definition of or even for the necessity of defining the rule of law as the promotion of this principle together with democracy and respect for human rights 'form a single fundamental objective for the Council of Europe'[53] and that it would in fact be risky to disentangle notions 'that are so closely intertwined and mutually supportive'.[54]

Secondly, the EU and the Council of Europe have derived the same core requirements from the principle of the rule of law. Amongst these core requirements, one may refer in particular to the principles of legality, legal certainty, equality of all before the law, access to justice, judicial review and independence of the judiciary.[55] Furthermore, and again similarly to what the EU does, the Council of Europe links the strengthening of the rule of law with efforts to fight phenomena such as corruption, organized crime and money laundering.[56] The existence

[48] *Ibid.*, para. 29. [49] See section 3.2, below.

[50] See, however, the recent 'Checklist for evaluating the state of the rule of law in single states', produced by the Venice Commission and which could usefully serve as a model for the EU when it comes to defining a list of minimum requirements and monitoring progress over time. See European Commission on Democracy through Law (Venice Commission), 'Report on the Rule of Law', Study No. 512/2009, CDL-AD (2011) 003 rev, Strasbourg, 4 April 2011, p. 15.

[51] Council of Europe (Parliamentary Assembly), 'Report of the Committee on Legal Affairs and Human Rights: The Principle of the Rule of Law', Doc. No. 11343, 6 July 2007, para. 5.

[52] Council of Europe (Committee of Ministers), *The Council of Europe and the Rule of Law*, para. 27.

[53] *Ibid.*, para. 28. [54] *Ibid.* [55] *Ibid.*, para. 29.

[56] 'Memorandum of Understanding between the Council of Europe and the European Union', para. 26.

of this high degree of consensus between the EU and the Council of Europe regarding the basic and essential elements of the rule of law makes cooperation between these two organizations unproblematic from a conceptual point of view. And indeed, numerous joint programmes have been devised to promote democracy, respect for human rights and the rule of law within Europe and beyond.[57] It may also be worth noting that the EU regularly requests the assistance of specialized bodies of the Council of Europe such as the Venice Commission to undertake, inter alia, rule of law assessments of controversial national legal developments, and also frequently invites relevant countries to follow the Venice Commission's recommendations.[58] The forthcoming EU accession to the European Convention on Human Rights and other Council of Europe conventions and future EU participation to bodies such as GRECO[59] will further consolidate the partnership between the EU and the Council of Europe and further ensure coherence between EU and Council of Europe norms and standards in the areas of human rights, the rule of law and democracy.[60]

3.2 The EU's understanding in the light of the dominant conception of the rule of law on the international plane

The EU does not only promote an understanding of the rule of law which builds up on the work done by the Council of Europe and is perfectly in

57 Fourteen joint Rule of Law programmes and seven Rule of Law projects were in operation within the period January–December 2011, and cooperation was particularly intensive in such fields as reform of judicial systems and the fight against corruption, money laundering, organized crime and cybercrime. For more information, see Council of Europe, Joint Programmes between the Council of Europe and the European Union in 2011 – Implementation of the Memorandum of Understanding between the Council of Europe and the European Union, ODGProg/Inf (2012) 9, 29 May 2012.

58 European Commission on Democracy through Law (Venice Commission), Annual Report of Activities 2011, August 2012, p. 90, available at www.venice.coe.int/CDL_publications/AR2011ENG.pdf.

59 The Group of States against Corruption (GRECO) was established in 1999 by the Council of Europe to monitor states' compliance with the organization's anti-corruption standards. Council of Europe (Committee of Ministers), Resolution 99(5) of 1 May 1999 establishing the Group of States against Corruption (GRECO).

60 Such is the view expressed by the Committee of Ministers of the Council of Europe; Council of Europe (Committee of Ministers), the impact of the Lisbon Treaty on the Council of Europe, Parliamentary Assembly Recommendation of 30 March 2012, 1982 (2011), CM/AS (2012) Rec 1982 final.

line with the conception of this latter organization, it also promotes, as will be shown below, an understanding which is highly consensual at the international level. Because of this prevalent international consensus regarding the core elements of the rule of law and its close linkage with democracy and respect for human rights, the EU did not have to contribute to the shaping of an original or alternative international understanding. Rather, as a recent statement of the EU Delegation to the UN makes clear,[61] the EU has been anxious effectively to contribute to the concrete strengthening of the rule of law at the national and international levels. Before returning to this statement, the decisive conceptual role played by the OSCE should be briefly mentioned. Indeed, this organization was the first one fully to embrace the promotion of the rule of law in the early 1990s and to define it in a substantive and holistic manner.

Taking note of the new political environment in Europe following the end of the Cold War, members of the OSCE agreed in 1990 to promote state compliance with the rule of law which, decisively, was understood in a 'thick' manner as this short excerpt from the so-called 1990 Copenhagen document shows:

> [The participating States] consider that the rule of law does not mean merely a formal legality [. . .] but justice based on the recognition and full acceptance of the supreme value of the human personality and guaranteed by institutions providing a framework for its fullest expression.[62]

The document further states that 'democracy is an inherent element of the rule of law',[63] and gives a long list of principles to be complied with as they would constitute 'elements of justice which are essential to the full expression of the inherent dignity and of the equal and inalienable rights of all human beings'.[64] Amongst those principles, one may mention the principle of having an executive accountable to the elected legislature, the principle of legality, the principle of separation of powers, the accessibility of the law, the principle of equality of all before the law, effective access to justice, an independent judiciary and compliance with international human rights standards.

[61] EU Delegation to the UN, The Rule of Law at the National and International Levels, UN 6th Committee, EUUN12-091E.

[62] Conference on Security and Cooperation in Europe (CSCE), Document of the Copenhagen Meeting of the Conference on the Human Dimension of the CSCE, Copenhagen, 29 June 1990, para. 2, available at www.osce.org/odihr/elections/14304.

[63] *Ibid.*, para. 3. [64] *Ibid.*, para. 5.

This understanding has also been embraced by the UN, although the UN did not embrace the rule of law as early as the Council of Europe, the OSCE or even the EU, despite the concept being referred to in the preamble to the Universal Declaration of Human Rights adopted by the UN General Assembly in 1948: 'Whereas it is essential, if man is not to be compelled to have recourse, as a last resort, to rebellion against tyranny and oppression, that human rights should be protected by the rule of law'.[65] This early and concise reference nevertheless indicates that the rule of law was initially conceived as sharing a consubstantial link with the protection of human rights. However, it was not until 2004 that the UN Secretary General published a report focusing exclusively and exhaustively on the rule of law and in which the following definition of what is described as 'a concept at the very heart of the Organization's mission'[66] was offered:

> The rule of law [. . .] refers to a principle of governance in which all persons, institutions and entities, public and private, including the State itself, are accountable to laws that are publicly promulgated, equally enforced and independently adjudicated, and which are consistent with international human rights norms and standards. It requires, as well, measures to ensure adherence to the principles of supremacy of law, equality before the law, accountability to the law, fairness in the application of the law, separation of powers, participation in decision-making, legal certainty, avoidance of arbitrariness and procedural and legal transparency.[67]

An important resolution adopted by the UN General Assembly the year following the publication of the Secretary General's report cited above, further demonstrates the continued dominance of an open-ended, substantive and holistic conception similar to the one promoted by the EU and the Council of Europe. Indeed, after recalling that the Heads of State and Government, who gathered at UN Headquarters 14–16 September 2005, 'acknowledge that good governance and the rule of law [. . .] are essential for sustained economic growth, sustainable development and the eradication of poverty and hunger',[68] the 2005 World Summit Outcome resolution stresses that respect for all human

[65] Universal Declaration of Human Rights, UN Doc. A 810 (1948).

[66] UN Security Council, Report of the Secretary-General, 'The Rule of Law and Transitional Justice in Conflict and Post-Conflict Societies', S/2004/616, 23 August 2004.

[67] *Ibid.*, para. 6.

[68] UN General Assembly, Resolution 60/1 on 2005 World Summit Outcome, A/RES/60/1, 24 October 2005, para. 11.

rights, the rule of law and democracy 'are interlinked and mutually reinforcing and that they belong to the universal and indivisible core values and principles of the United Nations'.[69]

This approach is now regularly promoted by the UN Secretary General[70] as well as the UN General Assembly in its resolutions on *The rule of law at the national and international levels*, adopted each year since 2005.[71] In this particular context, the EU's normative influence was at first extremely limited considering that the dialogue initiated by the UN Rule of Law Coordination and Resource Group and the Rule of Law Unit was only supposed to take place with Member States.[72] In 2011, however, the EU gained enhanced participation rights in the work of the UN.[73] But this is unlikely to have a decisive impact of the role of the EU as an aspiring international standard setter considering that the EU does not defend an original or alternative conceptual understanding of the rule of law. This was indeed made clear by the EU Delegation to the UN in a statement issued on 10 October 2012[74] in which the EU welcomes the conception of the rule of law promoted by the UN, as set out in particular in the Declaration of the High-level Meeting of the UN General Assembly on the Rule of Law at the national and international levels,[75] to the extent that it 'affirms linkages with the three main pillars of the United Nations – peace and security, development and human rights – and confirms the importance of equality before the law, the right to access to justice and a full commitment to human rights and

69 *Ibid.*, paras. 11 and 119, respectively.

70 See, in particular, Guidance note of the UN Secretary-General, 'UN Approach to Rule of Law Assistance', April 2008.

71 See S. Barriga and G. Kerschischnig, 'The UN General Assembly Resolution on the Rule of Law: Ambition Meets Pragmatism', (2010) 2 *Hague Journal on the Rule of Law* 253.

72 UN General Assembly, Resolution on the Rule of Law at the National and International Levels, 64th Session of the General Assembly, Agenda item 83, A/RES/64/116, 15 January 2010, para. 7.

73 See J. Wouters, et al., 'The Status of the EU at the UN after the General Assembly Resolution of 3 May 2011', *Global Governance Opinions*, Leuven Centre for Global Governance Studies, July 2011 (authors argue that the resolution is unlikely to improve the EU's capacity decisively to influence the work of the UN Assembly and other relevant UN bodies).

74 UN General Assembly, Resolution on the Rule of Law at the National and International Levels.

75 'Declaration of the High-level Meeting of the General Assembly on the Rule of Law at the National and International Levels', 67th Session of the General Assembly, Agenda item 83, A/67/L.1, 19 September 2012; 'Declaration of the High-level Meeting of the General Assembly on the Rule of Law at the National and International Levels on 24 September 2012', Agenda item 83, A/Res/67/1, 30 November 2012.

fundamental freedoms for all. Perhaps more originally, the EU, along with other participating parties, agreed to make 'substantive pledges' regarding each of the areas covered by the Declaration to show that its support for the rule of law is not simply declaratory.[76] Amongst these pledges, one may note the following:

- Encourage the EU Member States to ratify the 2006 International Convention for the Protection of All Persons from Enforced Disappearance[77] in the name of strengthening the rule of law at the international level;
- Under the heading 'strengthening the rule of law at the national level', the EU committed itself inter alia to conducting a worldwide campaign on justice, focusing on the right to a fair trial; to ensure full coherence and consistency between the EU's internal and external human rights policies; in cooperation with EU Member States, to raise recommendations of the Human Rights Council's Universal Periodic Review in their relations with all third countries;
- Under the heading 'strengthening the nexus between the national and international levels', the EU and its Member States pledged, inter alia, to promote the greatest possible participation in and implementation of the Rome State of the International Criminal Court;[78] to intensify its rule of law dialogue with the countries of the Western Balkans; further to intensify the Rule of Law Initiative for Central Asia[79] and contribute to the implementation of the Council of Europe Neighbourhood Policy for the same region.

To end this overview of how the rule of law is understood at the international level, a brief reference to the World Bank's reliance on the concept is worth making as the World Bank is regularly presented as promoting a 'rather thin conception'[80] in contrast to the one promoted

[76] The EU 'pledge registration form' and other submitted pledges are available at the UN Rule of Law website and repository: www.unrol.org.

[77] International Convention for the Protection of All Persons from Enforced Disappearance, 20 December 2006, in force 23 December 2010, UNGA res 61/177, 12 January 2007.

[78] Rome Statute of the International Criminal Court, Rome, 17 July 1998, 2187 UNTS 90 (entered into force on 1 July 2002).

[79] European Commission, 'Concept Paper: EU Rule of Law Initiative in Central Asia', Concept Paper presented at EU–Central Asia Ministerial Troika in Ashgabat, Turkmenistan, 9–10 April 2008.

[80] The Hague Institute for the Internationalisation of Law (HiiL), Rule of Law Inventory Report: Academic Part, Discussion Paper for the High Level Expert Meeting on the Rule of Law, 20 April 2007, p. 27.

by most organizations such as the OSCE, the UN or the EU. Indeed, according to Ibrahim Shihata, senior vice president of the World Bank from 1983 until 1998, and often presented as the 'architect' of the World Bank's rule of law policies, the rule of law essentially requires foreseeable and binding rules as well as a framework guaranteeing their proper application under the control of an independent judicial branch, and known procedures for eventually amending them.[81] It might be, however, that this conceptual exception to the rule is mainly due to 'the fact that different organizations have different mandates or purposes'.[82] In other words, contrary, for instance, to the EU, the World Bank has a more limited and specialized remit and is furthermore explicitly prohibited from considering political criteria when assessing countries' requests for financial assistance,[83] factors which may explain why the World Bank tends to promote a thin concept of the rule of law.

Save this exception, one may contend that there is now a broad 'consensus on the core meaning of the rule of law and the elements contained within it',[84] and that the EU is not unique when it comes to promoting a broad and substantive understanding and an ideology which views the rule of law, along with democracy and human rights, as one of 'the three pillars'[85] on which any polity must be based. There has been therefore limited room for EU norm-building leadership on the international plane and, indeed, the EU, rather than seeking to shape or defend an original or alternative conception of the rule of law on the international plane, has been more preoccupied with improving individual countries' concrete adherence to the core elements of this principle via its numerous assistance programmes and bilateral agreements.

81 *Ibid.*, p. 28, citing, at n. 96, A. Santos, 'The World Bank's Uses of the "Rule of Law" Promise in Economic Development', in D. Trubek and A. Santos (eds.), *The New Land and Economic Development: A Critical Appraisal* (Cambridge University Press, 2006), p. 270.

82 Rule of Law Inventory Report, p. 28.

83 See e.g. Art. 5(1)(g) of the International Development Association's Articles of Agreement (the IDA is the World Bank's fund for the poorest countries): 'The Association shall make arrangements to ensure that the proceeds of any financing are used only for the purposes for which the financing was provided, with due attention to considerations of economy, efficiency and competitive international trade and without regard to political or other non-economic influences or considerations'.

84 Council of Europe (Venice Commission), Report on the Rule of Law, para. 35.

85 *Ibid.*, para. 1.

4 Conclusion

This contribution first defended the view that the EU is not seeking to 'export' a vague or incoherent conception of the rule of law. Indeed, notwithstanding the absence of a comprehensive definition in the EU Treaties or the multiple and, at times, diverse definitions one may find in EU external instruments and reports, the EU generally emphasizes the decisive importance of a number of sub-components of the rule of law which one may appropriately refer to as its core elements and *conditiones sine quibus* from the point of view of the EU: (i) legality, including a transparent, accountable and democratic process for enacting law; (ii) legal certainty; (iii) prohibition of arbitrariness; (iv) access to justice before independent and impartial courts; (v) respect for human rights; (vi) non-discrimination and equality before the law. It may therefore be concluded that the EU generally promotes an understanding of the rule of law as a principle that includes substantive components as well as formal elements, and which requires a democratic and liberal constitutional order giving full effect to human rights. As regards international norm-building, it is submitted that the EU's contribution to the shaping of an international understanding of the rule of law has been limited if only because the EU's conception is not original on the international plane and actually builds up on the conceptual work first undertaken by other international organizations such as the OSCE. This is not to say, however, that the EU has not significantly contributed, since the early 1990s, to the solidification of an international consensus as regards the core elements of the rule of law and the global diffusion of an ideology that views the rule of law, democracy and human rights as intertwined and mutually supportive principles.

6

EU global peace diplomacy: shaping the law on statehood

STEVEN BLOCKMANS

1 Introduction

This chapter examines the contribution of the European Union to the shaping of the subjects of international law par excellence: states. This is perhaps odd if one considers that recognition of states has traditionally been within the purview of states' foreign policy and that the EU itself is not a state. In fact, the Union's own status as a subject of international law has long been the object of controversy and debate, ever since the Court of Justice focused on the 'autonomy' of the 'new legal order' established by the European Communities.[1] Stressing its autonomy was believed to be necessary to establish an independent identity and could perhaps be seen as a disguised claim to sovereignty, something international organizations – unlike states – have to fight for. The emergence of the EU demonstrates that it is possible for states to transfer the exercise of sovereignty without losing statehood. In fact, all Member States of the EU are internationally recognized states, while the EU has also obtained (international) legal personality of its own.[2] However, this fact does not in any way authorize the Union to legislate or to act beyond the competences conferred upon it by the Member States in the Treaties.[3] Article 4(1) TEU puts beyond doubt that competences not conferred upon the Union in the Treaties remain with the Member States. Moreover, the withdrawal clause of Article 50 TEU offers Member States

The author would like to thank Emilia Nadova for her research assistance.

[1] In particular, of course, in Case C-26/62 *NV Algemene Transport en Expeditie Onderneming Van Gend en Loos* v. *Nederlandse Administratie der Belastingen* [1963] ECR 1, and Case 6/64 *Costa* v. *ENEL* [1964] ECR 585. Later references may be found in Opinion 1/91 (EEA Agreement) [1991] ECR I-6079; Opinion 1/00 (ECAA Agreement) [2002] ECR I-3493; Case C-459/03 *Commission* v. *Ireland* [2006] ECR I-4635 (*Mox Plant*); Joined Cases C-402/05 P and C-415/05 *Kadi and Al Barakaat International Foundation* v. *Council and Commission* [2008] ECR I-6351.

[2] Art. 47 TEU. [3] See Declaration No. 24 attached to the Lisbon Treaty.

the right to negotiate their way out of the Union and resume full responsibility over the exercise of all their sovereign powers.[4] For the purpose of this study it suffices to describe the EU as a Union of democratic states based on the rule of law, which also constitutes a law-based democracy of its own.[5] Thus, it may be concluded that the European Union has outgrown the Westphalian system of international relations. One exponent thereof has been the gradual development of the Union's own external relations and designated institutional architecture, complete with a would-be Minister of Foreign Affairs supported by a diplomatic service. The recognition of third states has become a subject matter apt for coordination at EU level. Nowadays EU partners usually consult each other on this question. They may even act through the EU and adopt a common position underpinned by jointly agreed conditions. It should thus not come as a surprise that the EU contributes its own rules to the definition of the international law on statehood.[6]

[4] See A. Łazowski, 'Withdrawal from the European Union and Alternatives to Membership' (2012) 37 *European Law Review* 523.

[5] See J. Hoeksma, 'The EU as a Democratic Polity in International Law', Centre for the Law of EU External Relations Working Paper 2011/2 (2011). Hoeksma's essay fits in a wider, multidisciplinary setting which deals with the depiction of the EU as a post-national democracy, a new phenomenon in international relations. See the work of Jürgen Habermas, Philippe Schmitter, Andrew Moravcsik, Andreas Føllesdal and others. In the legal realm, see W. van Gerven, *The European Union: A Polity of States and Peoples* (Oxford: Hart Publishing, 2005); B. Jessop, 'The European Union and Recent Transformations in Statehood', in S. Puntscher Riekmann, M. Mokre and M. Latzer (eds.), *The State of Europe: Transformation of Statehood from a European Perspective* (Cambridge University Press 2004), pp. 75–94; E. Stein, 'Democracy beyond Nation-State: On World Trade Organization and European Union (2002) 2 *Georgia Law Occasional Papers Series*; F. Mancini, 'Europe: The Case for Statehood' (1998) 4 *European Law Journal* 29; and D. Curtin, *Postnational Democracy: The European Union in Search of a Political Philosophy* (The Hague: Kluwer Law International, 1997).

[6] The body of knowledge on the issue at hand is surprisingly limited. Most of the legal literature is circumstantial or slightly dated. A section in F. Hoffmeister, 'The Contribution of EU Practice to General International Law', in M. Cremona (ed.), *Developments in EU External Relations Law* (Oxford University Press, 2008), pp. 37–127 presents three major case studies: Cyprus, the former Soviet Union and the former Yugoslavia. Older is J. Frowein's, 'The Contribution of the European Union to Public International Law', in A. von Bogdandy, P. Mavroides and Y. Mény (eds.), *European Integration and International Co-ordination: Studies in Honour of Claus-Dieter Ehlermann* (The Hague: Kluwer Law International, 2002), p. 171. Bruno de Witte's essay deals with the inverse: 'the EU and its Member States as strange subjects' of international law and the potential conflicts arising from their shared, parallel or subsequent interventions at various levels. B. de Witte, 'The Emergence of a European System of Public International Law', in J. Wouters, A. Nollkaemper and E. de Wet (eds.), *The Europeanisation of International Law* (The Hague: TMC Asser Press, 2008), pp. 39–53.

After an anatomy of the international law of statehood (section 2), the chapter will dwell on the European Union's own conditions imposed on entities seeking recognition of their sovereignty and independence under international law (section 3). Three sets of documents are particularly instructive to expose the Union's contribution to the law on statehood. They concern the 1991 'Guidelines on the Recognition of New States in Eastern Europe and in the Soviet Union' and the Badinter Arbitration Commission's subsequent handling of applications for recognition by the EU (section 3.1); the report of the EU's independent fact-finding mission on the status conflicts in Georgia (section 3.2); and the Council conclusions on the two-state solution in the Middle East, which are littered with conditions for the recognition by the EU of Palestine (section 3.3). The conclusion will offer a critical appraisal of the European Union's contribution in shaping the international law on statehood (section 4).

2 The development of international law on statehood

2.1 Factual existence

Before discussing the European Union's contribution to the law on statehood, it is instrumental to map out the current state of that body of international law.[7] The obvious starting point is Article 1 of the Montevideo Convention on the Rights and Duties of States of 1933,[8] which prescribes that '[a] state, as a person of international law should possess the following qualifications: (a) a permanent population; (b) a defined territory;[9] (c) government; and (d) capacity to enter into relations with the other states'. Whereas in practice a lot of emphasis is placed on the last element, the political existence of a state is independent of recognition by the other states. Statehood – as conceived by the

[7] For the ultimate treatise on this issue, see J. Crawford, *The Creation of States in International Law*, 2nd edn (Oxford University Press, 2006).

[8] 165 League of Nations Treaty Series (1936), p. 19.

[9] See ICJ, *Federal Republic of Germany* v. *Denmark*; *Federal Republic of Germany* v. *Netherlands* (North Sea Continental Shelf Case), ICJ Reports 1969, p. 3, in which the Court confirms that statehood requires a defined territory but not necessarily defined or agreed external boundaries: 'The appurtenance of a given area, considered as an entity, in no way governs the precise delimitation of its boundaries, any more than uncertainty as to boundaries can affect territorial rights. There is for instance no rule that the land frontiers of a State must be fully delimited and defined, and often in various places and for long periods they are not'.

Montevideo Convention – is a positive legal theory, to be entirely divorced from the political act of state recognition. Article 3 of the Convention spells out that

> Even before recognition [a] state has the right to defend its integrity and independence, to provide for its conservation and prosperity, and consequently to organize itself as it sees fit, to legislate upon its interests, administer its services, and to define the jurisdiction and competence of its courts. The exercise of these rights has no other limitation than the exercise of the rights of other states according to international law.

The recognition of a state merely signifies that the state which recognizes it accepts the personality of the other with all the rights and duties determined by international law.[10] As such, the Convention codified the declarative theory of statehood as accepted as part of customary international law.[11] The fact that practice and doctrine are both heavily inclined towards the declaratory theory does not mean that recognition is irrelevant to statehood. After all, a state which is not recognized by the international community will experience difficulties concerning its continued existence.[12] However, that primarily concerns the political and

[10] Art. 6: 'Recognition is unconditional and irrevocable'.

[11] See the PCIJ (Permanent Court of International Justice) judgment in *Deutsche Continental Gas-Gesellschaft* v. *Polish State*, 5 Annual Digest (1929–1930) No. 5: 'the recognition of a State is not constitutive but merely declaratory. The State exists by itself (par lui-même) and the recognition is nothing else than a declaration of its existence'. The ICJ also favours the view that statehood exists independently of the will of other states. See *ICJ, Bosnia and Herzegovina* v. *Serbia and Montenegro, Preliminary Objections, Judgment*, ICJ Reports 1996, 595: 'For the purposes of determining its jurisdiction [. . .] the Court has no need to settle the question of what the effects of a situation of non-recognition may be on the contractual ties between the parties to a multilateral treaty'. Thus, the ICJ adheres to the declaratory view, in the sense that the failure to maintain effective control over territory does not extinguish the legal entity in the eyes of the United Nations. However, the Trial Chamber of the International Criminal Tribunal for the former Yugoslavia (ICTY) held that the conflict within the former Yugoslavia was only elevated to the international level after recognition of the independent statehood of Croatia and Bosnia and Herzegovina. See Case IT-96-21-T, *The Prosecutor* v. *Zejnil Delalic, Zdravko Mucic, Hazim Delic and Esad Landzo*, Judgment of 16 November 1998.

[12] As has been pointed out in the literature, the existence of an effective and independent government is the essence of statehood, and, significantly, the recognition of states may take the form of recognition of a government. See S. Talmon, *Recognition of Governments in International Law* (Oxford University Press, 1998). Non-recognition of a government may have two legal facets: that it is not a government in terms of independence and effectiveness (a facet that does not necessarily affect statehood), or that the non-recognizing state is not willing to have normal relations with the state concerned. Non-recognition of governments seems more political than that of states because

practical effects of recognition rather than its legal effects. The point about codification of existing norms is an important one to make: whereas the nineteen states that have signed the Montevideo Convention are limited to the Americas,[13] the Convention does not just apply to the signatories but to all subjects of international law because it merely codified existing legal norms and principles and thus serves as a restatement of customary international law.[14]

2.2 *Legality*

On the basis of the statehood criteria identified above, it was not possible to explain the general rejection of claims to statehood by effective territorial entities which were not established in violation of fundamental norms of public international law. The solution to this dilemma was sought in the development of the law on self-determination during the biggest wave of state creation that the world had ever seen: the decolonization period of the mid-1900s. In its Declaration on the Granting of Independence to Colonial Countries and Peoples of 1960, the UN Security Council placed great emphasis on the respect of the principle of self-determination of peoples:

> All peoples have a right to self-determination; by virtue of that right they may freely determine their political status [. . .] All armed action or repressive measures [. . .] shall cease in order to enable them to exercise peacefully and freely their right to complete independence [. . .] Steps shall be taken [. . .] to transfer all powers of the peoples of those territories [. . .] to enable them to enjoy complete independence and freedom.[15]

The Security Council later refined the principle: if an entity fulfils all the Montevideo criteria but emerged towards statehood in a manner

unwillingness to enter into normal relations is more often expressed by non-recognition of the organs of government. The only precondition for the recognition of a government under international law is its effective exercise of sovereign power (first and foremost, control of a substantial part of the territory and of the apparatus of administration).

13 See also Art. 13 of the 1948 Charter of the Organization of American States (amended 1976).

14 D. Harris (ed.), *Cases and Materials on International Law*, 2nd edn (London: Sweet & Maxwell, 2004), p. 99.

15 UNSC Resolution 1514 (1960). Before that, the norm of external self-determination as conferring rights under international law had been only accepted as applying with regard to mandate and trusteeship territories. See ICJ, International Status of South-West Africa, Advisory Opinion of 11 July 1950.

inconsistent with the principle of self-determination (e.g. by imposing an apartheid regime) then other states are obliged not to recognize the illegitimate government of the new state.[16] As hinted at above, states are under an obligation not to recognize the purported statehood of an effective territorial entity created in violation of a fundamental norm of international law. Such an obligation can derive from a UNSC Resolution or an established rule of international customary law rooted in the maxim *ex injuria jus non oritur*, such as the creation of a state by violating the prohibition of the use of force.[17] Today, it is thus acknowledged that to become a state an entity must, in addition to the traditional criteria, also satisfy modern criteria for statehood which are based on legality.

In 1970 the UN General Assembly elevated the principle of external self-determination to a right, declaring that

> By virtue of the principle of equal rights and self-determination of peoples enshrined in the Charter of the United Nations, all peoples have the right freely to determine, without external interference, their political status and to pursue their economic, social and cultural development, and every State has the duty to respect this right in accordance with the provisions of the Charter. Every State has the duty to promote, through joint and separate action, realisation of the principle of equal rights and self-determination of peoples, in accordance with the provisions of the Charter, and to render assistance to the United Nations in carrying out the responsibilities entrusted to it by the Charter regarding the implementation of the principle. The establishment of a sovereign and independent State, the free association or integration with an independent State or the emergence into any other political status freely determined by a people constitute modes of implementing the right of self-determination by that people.[18]

[16] See UNSC Resolutions 216 and 277 (1965), in which the Security Council condemned the illegal proclamation of republican status of the territory by the illegal regime in Southern Rhodesia and decided that UN members were obliged (i) to refrain from recognizing this regime or from rendering any assistance to it, and (ii) to impose restrictive measures on the regime in accordance with Art. 41 of the Charter. However, as noted above, non-recognition of a new government by other governments does not destroy the de facto status of that government. See in this respect already the judgment in *Great Britain* v. *Costa Rica* (Tinoco Concession Case) 1 RIAA 1923: 'non-recognition for any reason [...] cannot outweigh the evidence [...] as to the de facto character of Tinoco's government, according to the standard set by international law'.

[17] See UNSC Resolutions 541 (1983) and 550 (1984), in which all states were called upon 'not to recognise any Cypriot State other than the Republic of Cyprus', because the Turkish Republic of Northern Cyprus had been created by the unlawful use of force by Turkey.

[18] 'Declaration on Principles of International Law Concerning Friendly Relations and Cooperation among States in Accordance with the Charter of the UN', UNGA Resolution 2625 (XXV) of 24 October 1970.

Self-determination was thus recognized as a positive right against the background of decolonization. Later, it extended beyond decolonization in the form of the right to unilateral secession (and dissolution).[19] Such a right exists in cases where a minority people is exposed to serious harm (e.g., mass and persistent violations of human rights) and when all effective options capable of leading to the realization of the right of self-determination within state boundaries have been exhausted or repudiated by the parent state.

In a pan-European context, the Helsinki Final Act of 1975 unequivocally recognized the right of peoples to internal and external self-determination:

> The participating States will respect the equal rights of peoples and their right to self-determination, acting at all times in conformity with the purposes and principles of the Charter of the United Nations and with the relevant norms of international law, including those relating to territorial integrity of States. By virtue of the principle of equal rights and self-determination of peoples, all peoples always have the right, in full freedom, to determine, when and as they wish, their internal and external political status, without external interference, and to pursue as they wish their political, economic, social and cultural development. The participating States reaffirm the universal significance of respect for and effective exercise of equal rights and self-determination of peoples for the development of friendly relations among themselves as among all States; they also recall the importance of the elimination of any form of violation of this principle.[20]

The Conference on Security and Cooperation in Europe (CSCE) reaffirmed this right in the 1990 Charter of Paris for a New Europe.[21]

The decolonization period spurred another principle, *uti possidetis juris*, modified from its Roman origin to establish the frontiers of newly independent states in Africa and Asia following the withdrawal of European powers. The principle ensured that the frontiers followed the original boundaries of the old colonial territories from which they emerged. In 1964 the Organisation of African Unity passed a resolution stating that the principle of stability of borders – the key principle of *uti possidetis* – would be applied across Africa.[22] Most of Africa was already

[19] See M. Kohen (ed.), *Secession: International Law Perspectives* (Cambridge University Press, 2012).

[20] The Final Act of the Conference on Security and Cooperation in Europe (1975) 14 ILM 1292.

[21] (1991) 30 ILM 193.

[22] See AHG/Res.16(I), 'Border Disputes among African States', in Organization of African Unity, Secretariat, *Addis Ababa*, AHG/Res.1(1)-AHG/Res.24(1), Resolutions adopted by

independent by this time, so the resolution was principally a political directive to settle disputes by treaty based on pre-existing borders rather than by resorting to force. On the other hand, the colonial boundaries often did not follow ethnic lines. This has led to armed conflict amongst differing ethnic groups in many post-colonial countries, including Sudan, the Democratic Republic of the Congo, Angola, Nigeria and Uganda.

Uti possidetis was affirmed as a general principle of international law by the International Court of Justice (ICJ) in its judgment of 22 December 1986 in the *Burkina Faso* v. *Republic of Mali* (Frontier Dispute) case:[23]

> the principle is not a special rule which pertains solely to one specific system of international law. It is a general principle, which is logically connected with the phenomenon of the obtaining of independence, wherever it occurs. Its obvious purpose is to prevent the independence and stability of new States being endangered by fratricidal struggles provoked by the challenging of frontiers following the withdrawal of the administering power. The fact that the new African States have respected the administrative boundaries and frontiers established by the colonial powers must be seen not as a mere practice contributing to the gradual emergence of a principle of customary international law, limited in its impact to the African continent as it had previously been to Spanish America, but as the application in Africa of a rule of general scope. There is no doubt that the obligation to respect pre-existing international frontiers in the event of a State succession derives from a general rule of international law, whether or not the rule is expressed in the formula *uti possidetis*.

The principle of *uti possidetis* was also applied to post-Communist countries, but here too it could not prevent the eruption of inter-ethnic wars (former Yugoslavia, Armenia, Azerbaijan, Georgia, Moldova). The break-up of the Socialist Federal Republic of Yugoslavia (SFRY), the USSR and of Czechoslovakia at the beginning of the 1990s led to the accession (or succession) of Bosnia and Herzegovina, Croatia, Estonia, Slovakia, Slovenia, the former Yugoslav Republic of Macedonia and Ukraine to the 1978 Vienna Convention on Succession of States in Respect of Treaties, which thereby entered into force on 1996.[24] The 1978 Convention did not, however, push the development of the international

the First Session of the Assembly of Heads of State and Government held in Cairo, UAR, from 17 to 21 July 1964.

[23] *Burkina Faso* v. *Republic of Mali* (Frontier Dispute), ICJ Reports 1986, p. 554.

[24] (1978) 17 ILM 1488.

law on statehood forward as its rules about the break-up of states did not reflect state practice of the 1990s.[25]

As an appendix to the most recent episode of state creation on the European continent, the International Court of Justice's Advisory Opinion of 22 July 2010 on the unilateral declaration of independence by Kosovo[26] was equally unhelpful in pushing the development of the international body of law on statehood forward. The ICJ confirmed the legality of the Kosovar unilateral declaration of independence, but stopped short of endorsing a general right for minority groups to secede from their mother states. The Court held that the Kosovar declaration of independence was not prohibited by general international law, or by any other specific sources thereof. However, the ICJ reserved judgment on the more difficult question of whether Kosovar independence was justified based on the principle of remedial self-determination. In fact, the ICJ specifically refused to address the tension between the principles of self-determination (for the Kosovars) and territorial integrity (for Serbia). The Court instead concluded that the authors of the Kosovar declaration of independence were not bound by any specific rules of international law, as they did not act 'in the capacity of an institution created by and empowered to act within [a] legal order' but rather as the 'democratically elected leaders' of Kosovars who 'set out to adopt a measure the significance and effects of which would lie outside that [legal] order'.[27] Thus, in spite of the Court's refusal to admit to any tension between the Kosovar right to self-determination and Serbia's right of territorial integrity, the contours of Serbia as a state changed as a result of the Kosovar exercise of remedial self-determination.[28]

[25] E.g. the Convention distinguishes between 'newly independent states' (euphemism for former colonies) and 'cases of separation of parts of a state' (for all other new states). Art. 16 states that newly independent states receive a 'clean slate', whereas Art. 34(1) prescribes that all other new states remain bound by the treaty obligations of the state from which they separated. Moreover, Art. 17 declares that newly independent states may join multilateral treaties to which their former colonisers were a party without the consent of the other parties in most circumstances, whereas Art. 9 states that all other new states may only join multilateral treaties to which their predecessor states were a part with the consent of the other parties.

[26] ICJ Advisory Opinion, Accordance with International Law of the Unilateral Declaration of Independence in Respect of Kosovo, ICJ Reports 2010.

[27] *Ibid.*, p. 403.

[28] See M. Sterio, 'A Grotian Moment: Changes in the Legal Theory of Statehood' (2011) 39 *Denver Journal of International Law and Policy* 209.

2.3 State of the art?

On the basis of this brief overview of the development of this body of international law, it can be concluded that under the contemporary law of statehood the formation of a state is a matter of fact and law. The entry of the principle of legality and the law of self-determination into the law of statehood has resulted in a more relative role of the principle of effectiveness. As a consequence, not every effective entity satisfying the Montevideo criteria qualifies as a state, and some ineffective entities may acquire statehood. In practice, the fourth Montevideo criterion remains important as it creates a lifeline for would-be states. As mentioned above, recognition constitutes a unilateral declaration of intent. It is entirely at the discretion of any state to decide to recognize another as a subject of international law. The recognition of an entity as a state presupposes that it really exhibits the characteristics of a state within the meaning of international law. According to the prevailing three-element doctrine, this requires territory, a people and a government that is effective and independent both externally and internally, as an expression of state sovereignty. In addition to these three elements, a state or an international organization can also set further conditions for recognition, for example observance of human rights. The recognition of states became less important once decolonization had been completed, but this was reversed in the 1990s – when numerous new states came into being on the territory of the former Soviet Union and the former Socialist Federal Republic of Yugoslavia. It is since then that the European Union has provided its contribution to the development of the international law on statehood.

3 The EU's contribution

Although recognition of states has traditionally been within the purview of every Member State's foreign policy, the subject matter is also suitable for coordination at EU level. The very first product of such coordination was presented on 16 November 1983, in the wake of the proclamation of independence of the Turkish Republic of Northern Cyprus, when ten Member States adopted a declaration under the umbrella of the European Political Cooperation reaffirming the sovereignty of the Republic of Cyprus;[29]

[29] European Council, Declaration of 16 November 1983, *EC Bulletin* 11-1983, point 2.4.1. See, generally, F. Hoffmeister, *Legal Aspects of the Cyprus Problem* (Leiden: Martinus Nijhoff Publishers, 2006).

a declaration which, that same day, was said by the European Commission not to be valid under international law.[30] This was the first instance in which the Community took a position on a recognition issue next to its Member States. Since then, EU Member States have regularly consulted each other on the question whether or not to recognize third states (e.g. East Timor, Kosovo, South Sudan). The cases of succession from the Socialist Federal Republic of Yugoslavia and the Soviet Union stand out for having triggered the most sophisticated European effort in developing conditions and procedures beyond the existing international body of law before deciding on the recognition of de facto states (section 3.1). The EU re-emphasized its conditions in the context of the secessionist activities in Georgia (section 3.2) and refined them in the context of the eternal question of statehood for Palestine (section 3.3).

3.1 Dealing with the succession of states from Yugoslavia and the Soviet Union

3.1.1 Guidelines on recognition of new states in Eastern Europe and the Soviet Union

Before the entry into force of the Treaty on European Union (TEU), European Political Cooperation (EPC) was the principal institutional framework in which the twelve Member States tried to coordinate their positions and actions. Article 30 of the Single European Act had codified the practice of joint diplomatic actions of the Twelve. During the crises over the dissolution of Yugoslavia (1991–2), the EPC produced a considerable number of joint statements (twenty-one statements in 1991 and twenty-four in 1992). Despite all this activity, the positions of the Member States were often different and even opposed. While the majority of Member States favoured a cautious and well-balanced approach, Germany pressed hard in order to satisfy Slovenia's and Croatia's desire to be internationally recognized. These differences are reflected in the changing positions within the EPC during 1991.[31]

[30] Hoffmeister, *Legal Aspects of the Cyprus Problem*, p. 72, with reference to J. Groux and P. Manin, *Die Europäischen Gemeinschaften in der Völkerrechtsordnung* (Luxembourg: Amt für amtliche Veröffentlichungen, 1984), p. 27.

[31] For more details, see M. Weller, 'The International Response to the Dissolution of the Socialist Federal Republic of Yugoslavia' (1992) 86 *American Journal of International Law* 569.

The recognition of the Yugoslav republics was, for the first time, publicly envisaged in a joint statement of the European Community (EC) and its Member States of 6 October 1991, which linked recognition to the end of a negotiating process and to the question of minorities:

> At the meeting of 4 October, it was agreed that a political solution should be sought in the perspective of recognition of the independence of those republics wishing it, at the end of a negotiating process conducted in good faith and involving all parties. The right to self-determination of all the peoples of Yugoslavia cannot be exercised in isolation from the interests and rights of ethnic minorities within the individual republics.[32]

Two and a half months later, the EC and its Member States decided to recognize any Yugoslav republic that requested recognition, after the accomplishment of some preliminary procedures for arbitration. Two declarations adopted on 16 December 1991 – one presenting 'Guidelines on the Recognition of New States in Eastern Europe and in the Soviet Union' and the other 'on Yugoslavia' – were of tremendous importance in this respect.[33] The Guidelines on the Recognition of New States in Eastern Europe and in the Soviet Union stated the following:

> The Community and its Member States confirm their attachment to the principles of the Helsinki Final Act and the Charter of Paris, in particular the principle of self-determination. They affirm their readiness to recognise, subject to the normal standards of international practice and the political realities in each case, those new States which [. . .] have constituted themselves on a democratic basis, have accepted the appropriate international obligations and have committed themselves in good faith to a peaceful process and to negotiations.
>
> Therefore, they adopt a common position on the process of recognition of these new States, which requires:
>
> - respect for the provisions of the Charter of the United Nations and the commitments subscribed to in the Final Act of Helsinki and in the Charter of Paris, especially with regard to the rule of law, democracy and human rights

[32] *EC Bulletin* 10-1991, point 1.4.7.

[33] 'Declaration on the Guidelines on the Recognition of New States in Eastern Europe and in the Soviet Union and Declaration on Yugoslavia, Extraordinary EPC Ministerial Meeting (Brussels)', EPC press releases P. 128/91 and P. 129/91, 16 December 1991; reproduced in *EC Bulletin* 12-1991, points 1.4.5. and 1.4.6; and European Community, Declaration on the Guidelines on the Recognition of New States in Eastern Europe and in the Soviet Union (1992) 31 ILM 1486.

> - guarantees for the rights of ethnic and national groups and minorities in accordance with the commitments subscribed to in the framework of the CSCE
> - respect for the inviolability of all frontiers which can only be changed by peaceful means and by common agreement
> - acceptance of all relevant commitments with regard to disarmament and nuclear non-proliferation as well as to security and regional stability
> - commitment to settle by agreement, including where appropriate by recourse to arbitration, all questions concerning State succession and regional disputes.
>
> The Community and its Member States will not recognise entities which are the result of aggression. They would take account of the effects of recognition on neighbouring States. The commitment to these principles opens the way to recognition by the Community and its Member States and to the establishment of diplomatic relations. It could be laid down in agreements.

From an international point of view, this declaration is remarkable for at least three reasons. First, it departed from the well-established practice that recognition of states is only declaratory of the fact that a certain entity fulfils the objective criteria of statehood. The guidelines prescribed that only states that fulfilled 'the normal standards of international practice' (i.e. the Montevideo criteria) *and* 'the political realities'[34] would be entitled to recognition, if they had: (i) 'constituted themselves on a democratic basis' (i.e. if they had organized referendums on independence); (ii) accepted the appropriate international obligations (e.g. the UN Charter, the Helsinki Final Act and the Charter of Paris); and (iii) 'committed themselves in good faith to a peaceful process and to negotiations'. Thus, the recognition guidelines expressly provided for additional substantive elements relating to the internal system of governance and the effect on the neighbours; they thereby introduced a 'legitimacy' element into the instrument of recognition – subjective and highly euro-centric. Secondly, the guidelines incorporated CSCE documents as reference points, thereby giving those commitments a legal importance that was not foreseen when leaders put their signatures to the Helsinki Final Act and the Charter of Paris. Thirdly, the guidelines went further

[34] Ronald Rich observes that this rider is a stark reminder of Lauterpacht's comment that recognition of states is a matter of policy, but that it has rarely been expressed in such a direct way. See R. Rich, 'Recognition of States: The Collapse of Yugoslavia and the Soviet Union' (1993) 4 *European Journal of International Law* 36; H. Lauterpacht, *Recognition in International Law* (Cambridge University Press, 1947), p. 1.

than the customary rule on non-recognition of territorial acquisition resulting from aggression. While the former would only prohibit annexation of land by an occupying power, the guidelines also impeded the recognition of a new entity (claiming independent statehood) resulting from aggression.

Contrary to the case of the former Soviet Union, there was no internal agreement on the independence of the federal units of the SFRY. As a result, the international community had to deal with the question of recognition in parallel with the armed conflict.[35] The Declaration on Yugoslavia added specific attention to this particular issue:

> The Community and its Member States also require a Yugoslav Republic to commit itself, prior to recognition, to adopt constitutional and political guarantees ensuring that it has no territorial claims towards a neighbouring Community State and that it will conduct no hostile propaganda activities versus a neighbouring Community State, including the use of a denomination which implies territorial claims.

In addition, the Yugoslav republics were to accept the 'draft Convention' under consideration by the Conference on Yugoslavia, and especially the provisions of chapter II on human rights and the rights of national and ethnic groups.[36]

3.1.2 Institutional aspects

In the absence of established mechanisms (ICJ, ECJ and CSCE 'Valetta Mechanism') for dealing with such intra-state conflicts, the EC was compelled to create an ad hoc organ to assess the fulfilment of conditions for statehood.[37] Following a French proposal,[38] an Arbitration Commission was established at the same moment as the EC launched a peace Conference on Yugoslavia in The Hague. An EPC Joint Statement of

[35] On the recognition of states, see e.g. R. Bieber, 'European Community Recognition of Eastern European States: A New Perspective for International Law?' (1992) 86 *Proceedings of the American Society of International Law* 374; R. Rich, 'Recognition of States: The Collapse of Yugoslavia and the Soviet Union'; and C. Warbrick, 'Recognition of States: Part 2' (1993) 42 *International and Comparative Law Quarterly* 433.

[36] *EC Bulletin* 12-1991, point 1.4.6.

[37] See S. Terrett, *The Dissolution of Yugoslavia and the Badinter Arbitration Commission: A Contextual Study of Peace-making Efforts in the Post-Cold War World* (Aldershot: Ashgate, 2000), p. 121.

[38] The idea of creating a 'European Court of Conciliation and Arbitration', in the framework of the CSCE had already been floated by Robert Badinter, President of the French Constitutional Court, in the spring of 1991. See R. Badinter, 'L'Europe du droit' (1993) 4 *European Journal of International Law* 15 (20).

28 August 1991 announced the creation of an Arbitration Commission of five members chosen from the presidents of the constitutional courts of EC Member States.[39] Three members were to be appointed by the European Community and two members were to be appointed unanimously by the Presidency of the SFRY.[40] There was no mention, however, of the law to be applied by the Commission. But in its jurisprudence the 'Badinter Arbitration Commission', as it became known, mentioned the principles of public international law and referred to the peremptory norms of general international law. Thus, the Commission decided that the parties' differences had become international law issues and that this was the applicable law.[41] However, the choice of constitutional experts as members of the Commission indicates the presumption of the EC that the questions to be dealt with would be more of an internal (constitutional) than of an international nature.[42]

The Arbitration Commission never publicly established its rules of procedure. On each 'difference', a *rapporteur* was appointed and the views of the parties were given in written form and collected by fax.[43] There were no hearings, in spite of requests. Decisions could have been taken by a simple majority of the Commission's members, but it seems that all the arbitral opinions were adopted unanimously.[44]

One of the main characteristics of the procedure was its speed. According to the EPC Joint Statement of 28 August 1991, the Arbitration Commission had to give its decision within two months from the start of the procedure. In practice, the opinions were issued even faster: nine days to note that the SFRY was in a process of dissolution; about twenty days,

39 See *EC Bulletin* 7/8-1991, point 1.4.2.1.

40 The Presidency of the SFRY did not appoint any members, so it was the EC that appointed all five members: Robert Badinter (President, French), Aldo Corasaniti (Italian), Roman Herzog (German), Irène Petry (Belgian) and Francisco Tomas y Valiente (Spaniard). For a background to the creation, composition, procedure and jurisdiction of the Badinter Arbitration Commission, see Terrett, *The Dissolution of Yugoslavia and the Badinter Arbitration Commission*, pp. 120–41; and M. Craven, 'The European Community Arbitration Commission on Yugoslavia' (1996) 66 *British Yearbook of International Law* 333.

41 See the introductory note by M. Ragazzi, 'Conference on Yugoslavia Arbitration Commission' (1992) 31 ILM 1488; and A. Pellet, 'Note sur la Commission d'arbitrage de la Conférence européenne pour la Paix en Yougoslavie' (1991) 37 *Annuaire français de droit international* 329.

42 See Terrett, *The Dissolution of Yugoslavia and the Badinter Arbitration Commission*, p. 123.

43 See Pellet, 'Note sur la Commission d'arbitrage de la Conférence européenne pour la Paix en Yougoslavie', p. 332.

44 *Ibid.*

including Christmas holidays, to propose which republics should be recognized; and about a month and a half for the other opinions. While this speed matched the need to find political solutions to an escalating problem quickly, the Arbitration Commission moved extremely fast when compared to the usual length of proceedings in international judicial bodies.

Considering the above, one would be tempted to conclude that, even if the Commission itself ruled otherwise,[45] the Badinter Arbitration Commission neither constituted nor acted as an arbitration body within the meaning of international law.[46] After all, the Commission was not constituted by the parties to the dispute, that is to say, the SFRY and the constituent republics, but by a third party (the EC),[47] and it did not adopt binding awards but issued non-legally binding 'opinions'. It therefore seems more appropriate to conclude that the Commission acted merely as a fact-finding and consultative body of the Conference on Yugoslavia and of the EC, which were given opinions which they chose to follow, or not. In practice, there was a 'complex interaction between the deliberations of the Arbitration Commission and the political decisions of the EC institutions and the Member States'.[48] The deliberations of the Badinter Arbitration Commission were politically influenced and in turn had considerable political effects.[49] It seems that the arbitrators based their opinions on common sense, while taking strongly into consideration the EC's policy aims in the Yugoslav crisis

[45] Arbitration Commission, Interlocutory Decision (1992) 32 ILM 1520, point 2: 'the intention was to create a body capable of resolving, on the basis of law, the differences which were to be submitted to it by the parties, which precisely constitutes the definition of arbitration'. It continued in para. 9, stating that 'the Commission can give a judgment only in law, in the absence of any express authorization to the contrary by the parties, it being specified that in this case it is called upon to express opinions on the legal rules applying'.

[46] See Craven, 'The European Community Arbitration Commission on Yugoslavia', pp. 337–49, who refers, inter alia, to the International Law Commission's 1958 Model Rules on Arbitral Procedure, GA Official Records, 13th Session, Suppl. No. 9, UN Doc. A/3859, pp. 5–8.

[47] However, the SFRY and all the republics implicitly accepted the existence and competences of the Arbitration Commission by participating in the EC Conference on Yugoslavia and, for the first opinions, in the arbitral procedure.

[48] See Ragazzi, 'Conference on Yugoslavia Arbitration Commission', p. 1490.

[49] For example, in Opinion No. 8, the Arbitration Commission quotes the statement of the Council of 27 June 1992 to prove that the SFRY had ceased to exist. Subsequently, in the EPC Joint Statement of 20 July 1992, the EC expressly refers to the Arbitration Commission's conclusions concerning the succession of Yugoslavia.

and in Europe.[50] But even if the Badinter Arbitration Commission cannot be seen as an independent judicial body *stricto sensu*, it was certainly independent of the disputing parties. Also, it attempted to conduct its activities in a broadly judicial manner and it sought to base its opinions on general international law. As such, its opinions may be treated as non-binding but authoritative statements of the relevant bodies of law upon which it touched.[51]

3.1.3 Contribution to the law on statehood

The Badinter Arbitration Commission issued a total of fifteen opinions dealing with a range of issues of international law including questions of statehood, recognition, self-determination and succession. From November 1991 until July 1992, the Commission issued ten opinions, one interlocutory decision and one comment concerning Croatia's constitutional law on minorities.[52] Apart from the speed at which they were delivered, one of the most striking points of the arbitral opinions is their extreme brevity. Both legally and politically complex and difficult questions were dealt with in two to three pages on average, almost without discussion of the contradictory arguments and without motivation or explanation of the reasoning of the Arbitration Commission.

One set of opinions was given at the initiative of Lord Carrington, the chairman of the Conference on Yugoslavia, and includes Opinions Nos. 1 (actual status of the SFRY), 2 (status of the Serbian people in Croatia and Bosnia-Herzegovina), 3 (boundaries), 8 (dissolution of Yugoslavia), 9 (state succession) and 10 (has the SFRY been transformed into the Federal Republic of Yugoslavia (FRY), a state comprising two constituent republics, Serbia and Montenegro?). The questions underlying Opinions Nos. 2 and 3 were first raised by the Republic of Serbia but were redrafted by the chairman. The second group of opinions (Nos. 4 to 7), in which the Arbitration Commission considered the question of recognition of four Yugoslav republics (Slovenia, Croatia, Bosnia-Herzegovina and Macedonia), was delivered in accordance with a mandate given by the EC Council of Ministers on 16 December 1991 in its 'Declaration on the Guidelines on the Recognition of New States in Eastern Europe and in

[50] See D. Lopandić, 'The European Community and the Yugoslav Crisis (1989–1992): Some Issues of International Law' (1994) 41 *Jugoslovenska Revija za Medunarodno Pravo* (1994) 311 (331).

[51] See Craven, 'The European Community Arbitration Commission on Yugoslavia', p. 334.

[52] All texts are published in (1992) 31 ILM 1494 et seq.

the Soviet Union' and its 'Declaration on Yugoslavia'. Following this first batch of opinions, the co-chairmen of the steering committee of the International Conference on Former Yugoslavia submitted a further six questions to the Arbitration Commission on 20 April 1993, concerning succession of state property, archives and debts. These issues were addressed in Opinions 11–15.[53] It is beyond the scope of this study to address all issues raised in all arbitral opinions.[54]

At first sight, one of the most important contributions of the Badinter Arbitration Commission to the development of the international law on statehood was the primacy given to the right of self-determination over the other principles of integrity of the state, non-intervention in internal matters and inviolability of borders. In their Guidelines on the Recognition of New States, the European Community and its Member States declared their readiness to recognize different Yugoslav republics on the basis of unilateral declarations of independence and without consideration of the fact that no agreement had been reached within the Yugoslav federation or between the republics themselves.[55] Interestingly, several provisions of the 1974 Constitution of Yugoslavia expressly proclaimed that the SFRY was based upon and actually constituted an incarnation of the principle of self-determination of peoples, nations and nationalities and also pursued self-determination as an objective of foreign policy.[56] But the 1974 Constitution was amended in 1988 when the right of self-determination was scrapped. Also, the Constitution did not make specific provision for the right of any of the six constituent republics to secede. On the contrary, Article 5(4) stipulated that '[t]he frontiers of the [SFRY] may not be altered without the consent of all Republics and Autonomous Provinces'. The achievement of independence by Slovenia, Croatia, Bosnia-Herzegovina and Macedonia could therefore be seen as a revolutionary process that had taken place beyond the control of the existing rules.[57]

[53] (1993) 32 ILM 1586 et seq.

[54] For further details, see (1993) 32 ILM 1572; Terrett, *The Dissolution of Yugoslavia and the Badinter Arbitration Commission*, pp. 199–253; and Craven, 'The European Community Arbitration Commission on Yugoslavia', pp. 396–409.

[55] For the reaction of the remaining federal bodies of the SFRY, see 32 *Yugoslav Survey* (1991) 4.

[56] The 1974 Constitution is reprinted in S. Trifunovska (ed.), *Yugoslavia Through Documents: From its Creation to its Dissolution* (Dordrecht, Martinus Nijhoff Publishers 1994), pp. 125–34. See e.g. the Preamble ('Introductory Part – Basic Principles'), Principles I, III and VII, as well as Arts. 1 and 2, pp. 244–9.

[57] However, the Yugoslav breakaway republics deemed it fit to hold referendums before declaring their independence. Slovenia: on 23 December 1990, 94.5 per cent voted in

The Badinter Arbitration Commission tackled some general legal problems in its first three opinions. In doing so, the Commission did not directly consider the applicability of the principle of self-determination in relation to the acts of independence of the various republics, but it did stress the importance of the 'rights of peoples and minorities' and even defined the norms that provided for these as being part of *jus cogens*.[58] In the following four opinions, the Commission made pronouncements on the requests for recognition made by four of the six republics. In all four opinions, the Commission ascertained, in particular, whether referendums on independence had been held in each republic and whether each republic had committed itself to respecting the rights of individuals, groups and minorities. Strikingly, whereas in the cases of Croatia, Macedonia and Slovenia it was found that these requirements had been satisfied, in the case of Bosnia-Herzegovina it was emphasized that no referendum had been held involving the *whole* population[59] and therefore that not all criteria for statehood had been fulfilled. The Commission went on to say that this appraisal could be modified if 'safeguards' were established by Bosnia-Herzegovina, 'if necessary by way of a referendum in which all citizens of the Republic were to participate, under international supervision'.[60]

There is little doubt that Opinion No. 1 and the legal reasoning in the other opinions of the Badinter Arbitration Commission, together with the practice of the EC and its Member States (see below), have legally recognized the right of secession of federal units, albeit under the basic condition that a referendum is held in which *all* the citizens of a republic are to participate. The Badinter Arbitration Commission thus elevated

favour of independence; Croatia: on 19 May 1991, 93.2 per cent voted in favour of independence; Macedonia: on 8 September 1991, 95 per cent voted in favour of independence. On 11 April 1991, the presidents of the six republics reached agreement to hold a referendum in each of the republics except for Slovenia (thus including Bosnia-Herzegovina) on the future of the country. However, the referendum proposals ran into problems towards the end of April as divisions occurred on the scheduling of the vote.

58 Opinion No. 1.

59 Instead, a plebiscite had been held on 10 November 1991 by the 'Serbian people of Bosnia-Herzegovina', which had opted for a 'common Yugoslav state'.

60 From 29 February to 1 March 1992, a Bosnian referendum was held. The turnout was 63 per cent. The overwhelming majority of Bosnian Serbs, accounting for 31 per cent of the population, boycotted the vote. Of those voting, 99.4 per cent opted for independence. Subsequently, on 6 April 1992, the EC and the twelve Member States granted their recognition, followed the next day by the US and Croatia. Bosnia-Herzegovina was admitted to the United Nations on 22 May 1992.

the referendum, the 'internal' dimension of self-determination, to the status of a basic requirement to legitimate unilateral secession. Hence, the Yugoslav crisis reveals that, as a consequence of the dissolution of a state, peoples are not legally precluded from exercising a qualified right to unilateral secession, even outside the colonial context.[61] It should be noted that the Badinter Arbitration Commission stopped short of granting all peoples a right to secession, regardless of the circumstances. It made a distinction between two types of situations. On the one hand, the right to external self-determination was granted to peoples inhabiting regional units, the territorial limits of which had previously been defined by an autonomous government and administration *and* which were direct constituent parts of the federation (i.e. 'republics'). Contrary to what was laid down in the 1974 Constitution of the SFRY, the Serbian 'autonomous provinces' of Kosovo and Vojvodina, which were represented at the federal level but which belonged to the Republic of Serbia, were not granted the same right to external self-determination. On the other hand, a special status was granted to persons belonging to groupings (i) that were minorities within republics (e.g. Serbs in Croatia); (ii) that belonged to a majority living in another republic of the SFRY or another state altogether (e.g. Albanians of Kosovo); and (iii) whose territorial limits were not predefined (e.g. Serbs or Croats in Bosnia-Herzegovina). Such minorities were offered legal protection under Article 27 of the 1966 UN Covenant on Civil and Political Rights.[62] In the Yugoslav case, it therefore seems that the Badinter Arbitration Commission, the EC and its Member States linked the granting of the right to external self-determination to territorial units dubbed 'republics' and not directly to the peoples inhabiting them.[63] This is especially clear from Opinions Nos. 2 and 4 concerning the question of the Serbian 'population' in Bosnia-Herzegovina and the recognition of Bosnia-Herzegovina, respectively. In Opinion No. 2, Serbs in Bosnia-Herzegovina were

[61] See Weller, 'The International Response to the Dissolution of the Socialist Federal Republic of Yugoslavia', p. 606; J. Crawford, 'State Practice and International Law in Relation to Secession' 69 (1999) *British Yearbook of International Law* 85–117; and D. Raič, *Statehood and the Law of Self-Determination* (The Hague: Kluwer Law International, 2002), pp. 308–97, in particular pp. 342–66 and 386–94.

[62] For a critical note in this respect, see Craven, 'The European Community Arbitration Commission on Yugoslavia', pp. 390–1.

[63] Contrary to what is laid down in the 1974 Constitution of the SFRY, which speaks in its preamble and Art. 1 of the right to self-determination and secession of the Yugoslav peoples, not of the administrative units.

declared to be a minority, entitled to minority and human rights recognized in international law but not to the right of secession.[64] In Opinion No. 4, as discussed above, the 'citizens' of Bosnia-Herzegovina, without distinction, were recognized as having a unilateral right of self-determination by means of referendum.[65]

The underlying idea for the European stance towards the implementation of the right to self-determination was, of course, to pose certain limits on the disintegration of states in order to safeguard, as far as possible, the principle of inviolability of borders and, thus, to be able to counter claims from existing states to agree to a real territorial autonomy of their minorities abroad.[66] However, it is dubious whether the level of protection of national minorities would have been better if there was a parallel tendency to offer less protection to the stability of the existing republics.[67]

In its Opinion No. 3 of 11 January 1992, the Badinter Arbitration Commission took the view that '[e]xcept where otherwise agreed, the former boundaries become frontiers protected by international law. This conclusion follows from the principle of respect for territorial status quo and, in particular, from the principle of *uti possidetis*, which is today recognized as a general principle'. The Commission's decision generally

[64] The Arbitration Commission, while discussing their rights, did not take into consideration the internal and constitutional aspects of the position of the national communities in Bosnia–Herzegovina and Croatia. Opinion No. 2 was issued several months before Bosnia–Herzegovina was recognized, but the entire opinion was based on principles of international law only. For the Serbian position on the question of self-determination, see the position of the Presidency of the SFRY, published in (1992) 43 *Review of International Affairs* 21.

[65] There was no 'majority' nation/people in Bosnia–Herzegovina. Consequently, 'self-determination' was not based on the right of a 'people' but of all 'citizens'.

[66] As Colin Warbick puts it, 'The idea of self-determination looks to be an inherently destabilizing notion'. C. Warbrick, 'Recognition of States (Current Developments)' (1992) 41 *International and Comparative Law Quarterly* 480.

[67] A good example is the situation in Croatia. The self-determination granted to the Croat people greatly contributed to the disappearance of the SFRY. On the other hand, the Serb community in Croatia was deprived the status of 'equal' and 'constitutive' people of Croatia, granted by the 1974 Constitution of the SFRY. Serbs were promised a 'special status', but Croatia was recognized in spite of the fact that it did not fulfil its obligations concerning this status. Moreover, it is difficult to see how the creation of small 'nation states', in the Balkans, replacing the SFRY, would in any way improve the position of minorities *within* each of those states. As for the protection given by international law, Pellet states: 'A vrai dire, "les droits reconnus aux minorités par les conventions internationales en vigueur" se limitent à peu de choses'. Pellet, 'Note sur la Commission d'arbitrage de la Conférence européenne pour la Paix en Yougoslavie', p. 339.

to apply the principle of *uti possidetis juris* outside the context of decolonization can be seen as the enlargement of the protection of international law to the nascent states on the European continent.[68] As a question of policy, there is a strong case for arguing an expansive view of the principle's field of application. The application of *uti possidetis* in the Yugoslav case was preferable, in the short term at least, to the delimitation of boundaries on the basis of unstable and shifting forces of nationalist sentiment or on the basis of a strict application of the principle of effective control. The escalation of violence, provoked essentially by territorial disputes, prompted the Member States of the EC to take a more defined view and urge Belgrade to commit itself to the 'respect for the integrity of all borders of all republics'.[69] Nevertheless, one may question whether this is a legal technique that will provide a permanent and pacific settlement of the underlying territorial disputes. If *uti possidetis* is to apply to all cases of 'independence', there is nothing to preclude its further application within each of the republics even after their statehood has been established.

Ultimately, two different processes are at work here. First, the identification of presumptive units of statehood, whether it be in virtue of the principle of effective control or self-determination. And secondly, the determination of boundaries within which those entities are to be confined. In its original guise, the principle of *uti possidetis* only serves to address the second question and does not provide a coherent basis for establishing the statehood of the emerging entities. The manner in which the Badinter Arbitration Commission addressed the issue, however, was to use *uti possidetis* as a tool for establishing the presumptive statehood of the entities to emerge from the dismemberment of the SFRY and to deny the autonomous provinces of Kosovo and Vojvodina, as well as the self-proclaimed Serbian republics in Krajina and Bosnia-Herzegovina, the benefit of that presumption. If the Arbitration Commission's first opinions are taken together as a coherent whole – which is not unreasonable given the fact that the first three were handed down on the same day – one is left with the view that, owing to a collapse in central government, the SFRY fell into a process of dismemberment in which, through application of the principle of *uti possidetis*, the succeeding

[68] See Raič, *Statehood and the Law of Self-Determination*, pp. 293–305; and Weller, 'The International Response to the Dissolution of the Socialist Federal Republic of Yugoslavia', p. 589.

[69] EPC Joint Statement of 5 May 1992, *EC Bulletin* 5-1992, point 1.3.4.

entities were presumptively deemed to be the six republics. This being the case, it is clear that the principle of self-determination had little overall influence on territorial settlement. It is also apparent that the principle of effective control played only a subordinate role – it being suggested that in virtue of the internationalization of their borders each of the constituent republics of the former SFRY enjoyed *prima facie* statehood, irrespective of the effectiveness of their government. The principle of *uti possidetis* was employed a priori to protect the integrity of the constitutionally defined territorial units which were then, and only then, able or entitled to exercise some form of external self-determination, whether that be full independence or integration into a confederation of states. In other words, a principle of boundary delimitation was used as the primary determining tool not only for the shape of the new territorial entities but also for their international personality as states.

3.1.4 Outcome

Although the EC and its Member States reiterated, in various ways, their reliance on traditional international legal criteria for recognition, their policy of non-recognition of various states was far from being a consistent application of legal criteria.[70] Thus, Slovenia, which had fulfilled all traditional criteria since July 1991 (Opinion No. 7), remained unrecognized by the EC until mid-January 1992. Macedonia, which also fulfilled all criteria, at least since the end of 1991 (Opinion No. 6), remained unrecognized for a much longer period owing to a dispute over its name.[71] Serbia and Montenegro, as republics with equal standing in law, constituted a new state (the Federal Republic of Yugoslavia) and were recognized as such by the Badinter Arbitration Commission in Opinion No. 8, a decision which was not heeded with serious action by the EC and its Member States. Furthermore, unlike Russia, which was accepted as continuing the international position and obligations of the former Soviet Union, including its status in the United Nations, the FRY was – for political

[70] It is important to note that the Badinter Arbitration Commission itself was accurate and consistent in its Opinions Nos. 4–8.

[71] This problem was eventually spelled out in an EPC Statement of 2 May 1992, *EC Bulletin* 5-1992, in which the EC Member States referred to the former Yugoslav Republic of Macedonia and said that they were 'willing to recognise that state as a sovereign and independent state within its existing borders and under a name that can be accepted by all parties concerned'. See M. Craven, 'What's in a Name? The Former Yugoslav Republic of Macedonia and Issues of Statehood' (1995) 16 *Australian Yearbook of International Law* 199.

reasons – denied the right to continue the status of the former SFRY without a renewed application to the UN.[72] On the other hand, Croatia was recognized even though it had not fully implemented the provisions concerning the 'special status' for the Serb minority (Opinion No. 5), a fact which remained without consequences for months.[73] Bosnia-Herzegovina, which was unable to fulfil the criterion of effective control (a core element of the Montevideo criteria), was recognized in April 1992 after it had organized a referendum, as it had been urged to do by the Badinter Arbitration Commission in its Opinion No. 4.[74]

From the foregoing, it is clear that the legal conditions incorporated in the Guidelines on the Recognition of New States and the Declaration on Yugoslavia, as applied by the Badinter Arbitration Commission in its opinions, were manipulated by the EC and its Member States to influence and direct the behaviour of the recipients.[75] Whereas their premature recognition of some federal units would have amounted to an intervention in the domestic affairs of a state prohibited by Article 2(7) of the UN Charter, the EC and its Member States used the extracurricular mechanism of the two EPC Declarations plus Arbitration Commission to elevate the right of self-determination to a norm of *jus cogens* so as to trump the traditional norm of non-intervention that provided a ruthless 'federal' regime with the cover to smother justified claims of self-determination in a bloodbath.[76]

[72] See Y. Blum, 'UN Membership of the "New" Yugoslavia: Continuity or Break?' (992) 86 *American Journal of International Law* 830; M. Bohte and C. Schmidt, 'Sur quelques questions de succession posées par la dissolution de l'URSS et celle de la Yougoslavie' (1992) 96 *Revue générale de droit international public* II-811; R. Mullerson, 'The Continuity and Succession of States by Reference to the Former USSR and Yugoslavia' (1993) 42 *International and Comparative Law Quarterly* (1993) 473; O. Schachter, et al., 'Symposium: State Succession in the Former Soviet Union and in Eastern Europe' (1993) 33 *Virginia Journal of International Law* 253; and M. Scharf, 'Musical Chairs: The Dissolution of States and Membership in the United Nations' (1995) 28 *Cornell International Law Journal* 29.

[73] See the Badinter Arbitration Commission's comments on Croatia's Constitutional Law of 4 December 1991, as amended on 8 May 1992 (1992) 31 ILM 1505.

[74] See, further, D. Türk, 'Recognition of States: A Comment' (1993) 4 *European Journal of International Law* 66 (69).

[75] See J. Charpentier, 'Les Declarations des Douze sur la reconnaissance des nouveaux états' (1992) 96 *Revue générale de droit international public* I-353; and S. Oeter, 'Selbstbestimmungsrecht im Wandel: Űberlegungen zur Debatte um Selbstbestimmung, Sezessionsrecht und "vorzeitige" Anerkennung' (1992) 52 *ZaöRV* 741.

[76] In fact, even heavier duties rest upon the shoulders of the international community of states to make sure that human rights and fundamental freedoms – of a *jus cogens* nature – are not grossly and persistently violated. On the (conditional) duty to intervene

As such, the EC and its Member States supplanted the previous practice on the recognition of states, which was largely based on meeting the Montevideo criteria for statehood, with a raft of new requirements based on legitimacy.[77]

3.2 *Dealing with the breakaway regions in Georgia*

The European Union's neighbourhood is littered with potential and actual flash points for conflict.[78] The judgments about the EU's reaction to the flare-up of armed hostilities over the breakaway regions of South Ossetia and Abkhazia in August 2008, Russia's incursion into Georgia, and its unilateral recognition of the two de facto states, have varied – from the illustration of EU leaders held together in a wobbly red jelly on the cover of *The Economist* of 6 September 2008 to the assessment that '[w]ithout the European Union's intervention and rapid reaction on the part of the French president the Russians would already have made Tbilisi theirs'.[79] The reference here is to the diplomatic initiative of Nicolas Sarkozy, who – as holder of the EU's Presidency in the second half of 2008 – visited Moscow and Tbilisi, brokered a six-point agreement on 12 August 2008, and then pushed hard for both signatories to follow the terms of the ceasefire agreement. In a rare display of unity, the EU Member States at their emergency European Council summit on

(if need be militarily) in a state's internal affairs on humanitarian grounds, see e.g. M. Sornarajah, 'Internal Colonialism and Humanitarian Intervention' (1981) 11 *Georgia Journal of International and Comparative Law* 75; H. G. Schermers, 'The Obligation to Intervene in the Domestic Affairs of States', in A. Delissen and G. Tanja (eds.), *Humanitarian Law of Armed Conflict – Challenges Ahead: Essays in Honour of Frits Kalshoven* (Dordrecht: Martinus Nijhoff Publishers 1991), pp. 583–93; A. Cassese, 'Ex Iniuria Ius Oritur: Are We Moving towards International Legitimation of Forcible Humanitarian Countermeasures in the World Community?, (1999) 10 *European Journal of International Law* 23; and S. Blockmans, 'Moving into UNchartered Waters: An Emerging Right of Unilateral Humanitarian Intervention? (1999) 12 *Leiden Journal of International Law* 759.

77 For an analysis of the European Communities' strategic logic of conditional recognition, see R. Caplan, *Europe and the Recognition of New States in Yugoslavia* (Cambridge University Press, 2005), pp. 49–72.

78 See S. Blockmans and R. A. Wessel, 'The European Union and Peaceful Settlement of Disputes in its Neighbourhood: The Emergence of A New Regional Security Actor?', in A. Antoniadis, R. Schütze and E. Spaventa (eds.), *The European Union and Global Emergencies: Law and Policy Aspects* (Oxford: Hart Publishing, 2011), pp. 73–103.

79 See J.-D. Giuliani, 'Editorial: Europe and Russia', *Robert Schuman Foundation Newsletter*, 24 August 2008.

1 September – only the third in its history – stuck together in an unprecedented condemnation of Russian 'aggression'.[80]

However, with the sense of urgency over the Georgian crisis dissipating, unity between the Member States slowly eroded. High-level EU diplomacy has since been replaced by attempts to mitigate the consequences of the war on the ground. The Foreign Affairs Council authorized a European Union Monitoring Mission (EUMM) in Georgia to replace Russian troops in the buffer-zone and monitor compliance by all sides with the EU-brokered Six-Point Agreement and the Agreement on Implementing Measures of 8 September 2008.[81] The EU has also pledged millions of euros for the reconstruction of the devastated Georgian economy.[82] On the ground, however, the inaptly named 'frozen conflicts' have been resolved, not in a peaceful manner by the EU but by force by Russia.[83] Moscow was quick to recognize both South Ossetia and Abkhazia as sovereign and independent states.[84] Both entities are heavily dependent on trade with Russia.

Given the volatile situation and the involvement of its biggest geographical neighbour, the EU proceeded cautiously. In December 2008 the Council created, for the first time in its history, an Independent – International (i.e. not EU) – Fact-finding Mission to investigate the origins and the course of the conflict in Georgia, 'including with regard to international law (including the Helsinki Final Act), humanitarian law and human rights, and the accusations made in that context (including

80 Presidency Conclusions, Extraordinary European Council, Brussels, 1 September 2008, Doc. 12594/08, p. 11. See also N. N. Petro, 'The Legal Case for Russian Intervention in Georgia' (2008) 32 *Fordham International Law Journal* 1524.

81 Council Joint Action 2008/736/CFSP of 15 September 2008 on the European Union Monitoring Mission in Georgia, EUMM Georgia, OJ (2008) L 248/26 (as amended).

82 See, further, M. Merlingen and R. Ostrauskaitė, 'EU Peacebuilding in Georgia: Limits and Achievements', in S. Blockmans, J. Wouters and T. Ruys (eds.), *The European Union and Peacebuilding: Policy and Legal Aspects* (The Hague: TMC Asser Press, 2010), pp. 269–93.

83 In the aftermath of the August 2008 Russo-Georgian war, President Medvedev laid down five principles that would guide Russian foreign policy: The primacy of international law; the quest for a multi-polar world; no isolation of Russia; the protection of its citizens; and – last but not least – spheres of influence: 'Russia, just like other countries in the world, has regions where it has its privileged interests'.When asked what these priority regions were, he replied: 'Certainly the regions bordering [on Russia], but not only them'. See P. Reynolds, 'New Russian World Order: The Five Principles', *BBC News*, 1 September 2008.

84 Statement by President of Russia Dmitry Medvedev, 26 August 2008, available at www.kremlin.ru/eng/speeches/2008/08/26/1543_type82912_205752.shtml.

allegations of war crimes)'.[85] The geographical scope and time span of the investigation was to be sufficiently broad to determine all the possible causes of the conflict. The composition of the Fact-finding Mission was decided by Ambassador Heidi Tagliavini, the head of mission, and comprised of some twenty recognized experts, in particular lawyers, historians, military staff and human rights experts, all Europeans.[86] Additionally a Senior Advisory Board was set up, in order to review the Mission's work and to provide it with counsel and guidance. This board included four former Ministers of Foreign Affairs or of Defence, a former long-time President of the International Committee of the Red Cross and a former UN Under-Secretary-General and Head of the Department of Peacekeeping Operations, again all Europeans. The Fact-finding Mission was all, but in name, European. Its report may therefore be perceived as a European perspective – at least as far as the legal aspects are concerned.

On 30 September 2009 the Mission formally presented the results of its investigation in the form of a Report to the Council of the EU, the OSCE and the UN, as well as to the parties of the conflict.[87] The report seems to accept the view – clearly predominant in state practice and literature – that recognition is not a constitutive element of statehood. The report argues that 'there is no authoritative definition of the relevant criteria'. It lists three 'minimal preconditions' for statehood (defined territory, permanent population, and effective government),[88] but continues to state that 'these objective criteria for determining statehood are very general and flexible, and [that] their application to concrete cases always remains a question of appreciation'.[89] This is especially true for the 'effectiveness' of government condition: 'The emergence of a new state,

[85] See Art. 1(2) of Council Decision 2008/901/CFSP of 2 December 2008 concerning an independent international fact-finding mission on the conflict in Georgia, OJ (2008) L 323/66.

[86] See the Acknowledgements of the report for the complete list. Report prepared by the Independent International Fact-Finding Mission on the Conflict in Georgia, vols. 1–3 (hereinafter the 'Report'), available at www.ceiig.ch/Report.html.

[87] *Ibid.*

[88] *Ibid.*, vol. 2, p. 127. See K. Doehring, 'State', in R. Bernhard (ed.), *Encyclopedia of Public International Law*, vol. 4 (Amsterdam: North Holland and Elsevier Science, 2000), p. 601; G. Dahm, J. Delbrück and R. Wolfrum, *Völkerrecht*, vol. 1.1 (Berlin: De Gruyter, 1988), p. 131; A. Cassese, *Public International Law* (Oxford University Press, 2001), p. 48; I. Brownlie, *Principles of International Law*, 7th edn (Oxford University Press, 2008), pp. 71–2. Cf. also Opinion No. 1 of the European Conference on Yugoslavia : 'the state is commonly defined as a community which consists of a territory and a population subject to an organized political authority', reprinted in (1992) 3 ILM 1494.

[89] Report, vol. 2, p. 128.

especially as a result of secession from an existing state, is usually a process extended through time. Throughout this process, independence can decrease or increase, depending on a number of factors'. The report then refers to the respect of legal principles of international law, notably self-determination and the prohibition on the use of force, as accepted 'additional standards' for the qualification of an entity as a state.[90] Whereas the Fact-finding Mission is unclear whether the 1991 Guidelines elaborated by the EU foreign ministers, in particular the respect for basic international obligations, especially in the field of human and minority rights, were applied as legal conditions or as a matter of political discretion, the report states that 'these normative considerations can work in the same direction as the principle of effectiveness and underscore an entity's claim to statehood'.[91] One may thus have the impression that an entity must satisfy cumulatively the 'minimal preconditions' and 'additional standards' before it can expect to see its statehood recognized. Indeed, the 'assessment of statehood in international law and in international politics overlaps, but differs. The political practice of recognition of states, as a rule, starts out from the objective criteria identified in international law, but may be guided by additional considerations. It is very possible that an entity short of statehood is recognized as a state by another state or states for particular political motives'.[92]

The report then goes on to apply the 'minimal pre-conditions' to South Ossetia and Abkhazia and finds that both entities satisfy the criteria of defined territory and permanent population. With regard to the criterion of effective government, the Fact-finding Mission seems to concede that the government of South Ossetia is effective by using a reference to the 'jurisdiction of South Ossetia' and the qualification of the military operations carried out by South Ossetia forces in Georgia as 'equivalent to an armed attack to the territory of another State'.[93] However, according to the report, the South Ossetia government fails the independence test due to the systematic and permanent influence exercised by the Russian Federation and therefore is treated as an entity short of statehood. Abkhazia, on the contrary, is considered as a state-like entity, its government being both sufficiently effective and independent. Nonetheless, the report recommends not to recognize Abkhazia, as the state-building process is not legitimate because the entity never had

[90] *Ibid.* See also Crawford, 'State Practice', at 128–31; and M. N. Shaw, *International Law*, 6th edn (Cambridge University Press, 2008), p. 206.

[91] Shaw, *International Law*, p. 206. [92] *Ibid.* [93] Report, vol. 2, p. 244.

the right to secede (in fact, there is no 'right to secession' under international law)[94] and does not meet the basic requirements concerning human and minorities rights. In sum, the report manages to uphold the principle of effectiveness which pervasively underpins the international legal order.[95]

The EU welcomed the presentation of the report and took note of its content. Underlining the independent nature of the report, the EU expressed the hope that its findings can contribute towards a better understanding of the origins and the course of the 2008 conflict and, 'in a broader perspective, serve as an input to future international efforts in the field of preventive diplomacy'.[96] As co-Chair of the Geneva talks, where vital security and humanitarian issues arising from the conflict are substantially addressed, the EU continues to play a leading role, together with the UN and the OSCE, in the search for a peaceful settlement of the disputes. In practice, the recommendations of the report which it commissioned have been followed by EU Member States, as indeed the majority of states around the world. Abkhazia and South Ossetia have been recognized by just six and five UN members, respectively.[97]

3.3 Council conclusions on Palestine

Resolution of the Arab/Israeli conflict is a strategic priority for the EU.[98] The EU and its Member States have historically recognized Israel's right to statehood, living in peace with its neighbours within secure and internationally recognized boundaries. The Union's position towards the Palestinians, however, has been defined progressively over the

[94] See G. Abi-Saab, 'Conclusions', in M. Kohen (ed.), *Secession: International Law Perspectives* (Cambridge University Press, 2006), p. 474.

[95] See T. Gazzini, 'Criteria for Statehood as Applied by the EU's Independent Fact-Finding Mission on the Conflict in Georgia', *European Journal of International Law: Talk!*, 8 December 2009, available at www.ejiltalk.org/criteria-for-statehood-as-applied-by-the-eus-independent-fact-finding-mission-on-the-conflict-in-georgia/.

[96] EU Council, Presentation of the Report of the Independent International Fact-Finding Mission on the Conflict in Georgia, press release 13875/09 (Presse 278), Brussels, 30 September 2009.

[97] Abkhazia has been recognized by Russia, Nicaragua, Venezuela, Nauru, Vanuatu and Tuvalu. South Ossetia has been recognized by the same UN members, except for Vanuatu. Abkhazia and South Ossetia also recognize each other, and have been recognized by other non-UN Member States (Transnistria and Nagorno-Karabakh).

[98] 'A Secure Europe in a Better World', *European Security Strategy*, Brussels, 12 December 2003, p. 8.

decades: from open-ended support of Palestinian self-determination in the 1980 Venice Declaration to implicit support for a democratic, viable and peaceful sovereign Palestinian state in the 1999 Berlin European Council.[99] After the eruption of the second Intifada in 2000, the EU further articulated its vision for a peaceful Middle East through the creation of two states, Israel and Palestine, living in peace and security within internationally recognized borders.[100] The state of Palestine would be viable, independent, sovereign and democratic, and it would be established along the 1967 borders, with minor and mutually agreed adjustments if necessary. Already in its 2003 European Security Strategy, the EU declared the two-state solution, 'which Europe has long supported', as being 'widely accepted': 'Implementing it will require a united and cooperative effort by the European Union, the United States, the United Nations and Russia [the "Quartet"], and the countries of the region, but above all by the Israelis and the Palestinians themselves'.[101]

In order to see progress – 'not just process' – the EU has for a number of years undertaken a wide range of activities, both political and practical, to try and peacefully resolve the decades-old conflict. Since the 1993 Oslo Accords, the EU has taken numerous initiatives on the ground and adopted a comprehensive strategy by funding projects on governance, security and development. The EU plays a distinctive role in Palestinian state-building efforts. It is the largest international donor and it uses capacity-building and democracy promotion as a conflict resolution tool. According to the 2005 EU–Palestinian Territories ENP Action Plan,

> [a]chieving Palestinian statehood requires full implementation of the Quartet Roadmap and an end to violence in order to reach a fair and lasting peace in the Middle East, on the basis of the relevant UN Security Council Resolutions, and allowing for the establishment of an independent, viable, sovereign and contiguous Palestinian state, living side by side with the state of Israel in peace and security.[102]

[99] Compare European Council, Declaration on the Situation in the Middle East by the European Council in Venice, 12–13 June 1980, point 7; and European Council, Presidency Conclusions, Berlin, 24–25 March 1999.

[100] See European Council, Presidency Conclusions, Annex III, 'Declaration on the Situation in the Middle East, Laeken, 14–15 December'. See also the Presidency Conclusions from the European Council in Seville on 25 June 2002.

[101] 'A Secure Europe in a Better World', *European Security Strategy*, Brussels, 12 December 2003, p. 8.

[102] Available at www.enpi-info.eu/library/content/eu-palestinian-territories-enp-action-plan.

The reference here is to the 2003 Roadmap for Peace,[103] which requires the Palestinian Authority to make democratic reforms and abandon the use of violence in exchange for statehood. Israel, for its part, must support and accept the emergence of a reformed Palestinian government and end Israeli settlements of the Gaza Strip and West Bank as Palestinian terrorism is removed. The EU has supported the Palestinian National Authority in an effort to meeting its Roadmap obligations by deploying two Common Security and Defence Policy (CSDP) missions (European Union Co-ordinating Office for Palestinian Police Support (EUPOL COPPS) and European Union Border Assistance Mission at the Rafah Crossing Point (EUBAM Rafah)) and it is also involved in judiciary sector reform.[104] The EU has also tried to wield negative conditionality on the Palestinian side in order to influence conflict resolution, but without any success.[105] Similarly, the EU has repeatedly voiced its strong opposition to continuing Israeli settlement construction in the Occupied Palestinian Territories (OPT), including in and around East Jerusalem, and has urged Israel on numerous occasions immediately to end these and other illegal activities under international law, but to no avail.[106] Neither peace nor a Palestinian state has been built and in the meantime the dangerous stalemate has continued.

It is the combination of the fundamental changes that have swept across the Arab world since the beginning of 2011, the May 2011 Cairo reconciliation agreement bringing hopes of reuniting the Fatah-ruled Palestinian National Authority (PA) and the Hamas Government in Gaza, that have tested the EU's, as indeed the international community's, resolve when dealing with a Palestinian push for recognition of

[103] Roadmap for Peace in the Middle East: Israeli/Palestinian Reciprocal Action, Quartet Support, US Department of State, Bureau of Public Affairs, 16 July 2003, available at http://2001-2009.state.gov/r/pa/ei/rls/22520.htm.

[104] More information is available at the EEAS website http://eeas.europa.eu/mepp/index_en.htm.

[105] For example, the EU chose to ban the Hamas-led government in Gaza and legitimize the Fatah movement of President Abbas in the West Bank in order to weaken Hamas politically and financially. This, however, proved to be a fatal mistake for EU mediation efforts in the aftermath of the 2008 Israeli war in Gaza, which led to a rise in Palestinian popularity of Hamas leaders in government and the unpopularity of Fatah.

[106] See e.g. Council Conclusions on the Middle East Peace Process, Brussels, 10 December 2012, point 3. Since July 2007, however, the construction of the Wall has disappeared from Council's language and has not been mentioned in its Conclusions ever again, in spite of the ICJ's Advisory Opinion in the *Wall Case*. ICJ Advisory Opinion, Legal Consequences of the Construction of a Wall in the Occupied Palestinian Territory, ICJ Reports 2004, p. 136.

statehood.[107] In the lead up to a crucial vote in the UN General Assembly, EU Member States exchanged views on the Middle East Peace Process and in May 2011 adopted the following conclusions which spell out a number of conditions for recognition of Palestinian statehood:

> 2 [...] Our goal remains a just and lasting resolution to the Israeli–Palestinian conflict, with the State of Israel and an independent, democratic, contiguous, sovereign and viable State of Palestine, living side by side in peace and security and mutual recognition. A way must be found through negotiations to resolve the status of Jerusalem as the future capital of two States. Recalling the Berlin Declaration, the EU reiterates its readiness to recognize a Palestinian State when appropriate.
>
> [...]
>
> 6. The EU has consistently called for intra-Palestinian reconciliation behind President Mahmoud Abbas as an important element for the unity of a future Palestinian state and for reaching a two state solution. Reconciliation should also be in the long term interest of Israel by helping to engage all parties in a process leading to a sustainable peace agreement. The EU welcomes that Palestinian reconciliation has led to the cessation of rocket attacks from the Gaza Strip and insists on the need for a permanent truce. In this regard, the EU reiterates its call for the lifting of Gaza closure.
>
> [...]
>
> 10. The EU looks forward to continuing its support [...] for a new Palestinian government [...] [which] should uphold the principle of non-violence, and remain committed to achieving a two-state solution and to a negotiated peaceful settlement of the Israeli-Palestinian conflict accepting previous agreements and obligations, including Israel's legitimate right to exist. The EU's ongoing engagement with a new Palestinian government will be based on its adherence to these policies and commitments. The EU calls on the international community, Israel, and regional partners to work with the government on this basis. The EU also looks forward to the holding of elections.
>
> [...]
>
> 12. The EU calls on the future Palestinian government to continue the PA's institution-building efforts and to uphold current standards in terms of transparent and efficient public finance management, as consistently commended by the UN, the IMF and the World Bank [...] The EU welcomes the outcome of the reports which state that the PA is above

[107] Before the crucial November 2012 vote in the UN General Assembly, the right of the Palestinian people to a state was recognized by approximately 100 countries. See Institute for Middle East Understanding, 'How Many Countries Recognize Palestine as a State?' (2008), available at http://imeu.net/news/article0065.shtml.

> the threshold for a functioning state in the key sectors studied. In this regard the EU expresses its full appreciation of the current Government's success in implementing the state building plan.[108]

In short, the EU's conditionality on Palestinian statehood is premised on its (i) unity of government, (ii) viability of the state's institutions and the delivery of public services, (iii) democratic credentials, (iv) good neighbourliness and (v) a negotiated settlement on the status of Jerusalem.

The first two conditions are aspects of the 'effective government' criterion of Montevideo, with the 'unity of government' requirement (at central level) being quite a straightforward one. The 'viability' criterion, however, goes much further than what classic international law on statehood prescribes. It measures the capacities of the state's institutions, the state's ability to deliver public services, and its ability to uphold standards in terms of transparent and efficient public finance management. The EU hereby relies on reports from other international organizations.[109] In September 2010, the World Bank reported to the Ad Hoc Liaison Committee (AHLC)[110] that 'if the PA maintains its performance in institution-building and delivery of public services, it is well-positioned for the establishment of a state at any point in the near future'.[111]

108 Foreign Affairs Council Conclusions, Doc. 10440/11 (Presse 143), 23–24 May 2011, pp. 14–16.

109 See Chair's summary of the meeting of the Ad Hoc Liaison Committee, Brussels, 13 April 2011, available at www.europarl.europa.eu/meetdocs/2009_2014/documents/wgme/dv/201/201106/20110608_6_meetingahlc_en.pdf. See also Office of the United Nations Special Coordinator for the Middle East Peace Process, 'Palestinian Statebuilding: An Achievement at Increased Risk', Ad Hoc Liaison Committee Meeting, Brussels, 21 March 2012, available at http://unispal.un.org/UNISPAL.NSF/0/336CBEA9224C9080852579C6006AC079.

110 The AHLC is a fifteen-member committee that serves as the principal policy-level coordination mechanism for development assistance to the Palestinian people. The AHLC is chaired by Norway and co-sponsored by the EU and US. In addition, the UN participates together with the World Bank and the IMF. The AHLC seeks to promote dialogue between donors, the PA and the government of Israel. The AHLC was established on 1 October 1993 by the Multilateral Steering Group of the multilateral talks on Middle East peace in the context of the Washington Conference.

111 World Bank, 'The Underpinnings of the Future Palestinian State: Sustainable Growth and Institutions', Economic Monitoring Report to the Ad Hoc Liaison Committee, 21 September 2010, available at http://siteresources.worldbank.org/INTWESTBANKGAZA/Resources/WorldBankSep2010AHLCReport.pdf. In the World Bank's assessment, the PA's achievements in key state functions posited by the Organisation for Economic Co-operation and Development (OECD) as strategically important for state-building bode well for the future. This resonates with the PA's performance indicators in six areas where the UN is most engaged.

This chimes with the criteria assessed by the IMF, which considered that the PA is 'able to conduct the sound economic policies expected of a future well-functioning Palestinian state, given its solid record of accomplishment in reforms and institution-building in the public finance and financial areas'.[112] Arguably, putting the economic and financial criteria to the test would disqualify many a middle-income country around the world, perhaps even some EU Member States. Whereas these performance indicators may serve a proper interest in their own right (i.e. to assess the necessity of economic and financial reform in return for emergency funding), they are hardly model conditions for the recognition of statehood; nor are these conditions typically 'European' – their status has merely been elevated by the European Union.

The requirement that the composition of the government reflects the democratic will of the people is a legitimacy criterion which the EU has consistently called for since its 1991 Guidelines for the Recognition of States. The 'good neighbourliness' condition rests on Palestinian respect for the three principles adopted by the Quartet: commitment to non-violence; recognition of Israel; and acceptance of previous agreements and obligations, in particular the Oslo Accords.[113] The requirement that the status of Jerusalem, as the capital of two states, is settled through negotiations flows from the last. Good neighbourliness has thus been given an international content particular to the Israeli–Palestinian conflict,[114] much like it was 'Europeanized' in the early 1990s in the context of the recognition of the successor states of the former Yugoslavia.

[112] IMF, 'Macroeconomic and Operational Challenges in Countries in Fragile Situations', 15 June 2011, available at www.imf.org/external/np/pp/eng/2011/061511a.pdf. See, in particular, point 130: 'These reforms have enabled the PA to tightly control expenditures, apply rigorous budget preparation and execution practices, and establish fiscal transparency and accountability in line with international standards. The Palestine Monetary Authority is able to fulfill the core functions of a central bank'.

[113] Israel, on the other hand, has never been asked to comply with these principles as a precondition for negotiations. Arguably it would fail the test of compliance with equivalent principles. Israel's acceptance of the right of Palestinians to self-determination is at best questionable and Israel's actions on the ground are directly undermining this right. Moreover, Israel continues unlawfully to use violence as a means to its ends, and has been found to violate international human rights law and international humanitarian law in the Palestinian territories. See e.g. the so-called 'Goldstone Report': 'Human Rights in Palestine and other Occupied Arab Territories', Report of the United Nations Fact Finding Mission on the Gaza Conflict, A/HRC/12/48, 15 September 2009.

[114] See, in general, J. Quigley, *The Statehood of Palestine: International Law in the Middle East Conflict* (Cambridge University Press, 2010).

Sophisticated as they may have been in their development, the EU's extra conditions for the recognition of statehood of Palestine were never officially 'codified', nor did the criteria withstand the test of time and politics. In the Palestinian push for international recognition through a UN General Assembly resolution according it 'Non-Member Observer State' status in the United Nations (unsuccessfully in September 2011, successfully on 29 November 2012),[115] the Member States of the EU split up in their appreciation of Palestinian statehood.[116] As such, the majority of EU Member States negated the Quartet's (and thus its own) requirement that a two-state solution be the outcome of a negotiated settlement.

4 Concluding remarks

The search for the answer to the question central to this contribution – 'what is the contribution of the European Union to the development of the international law on statehood?' – unravels a string of recent debates within the Council of the EU about whether or not to recognize entities positioning themselves as independent and sovereign states. Driven by a sense of moral superiority about their own democratic values and respect for human rights and fundamental freedoms,[117] the Member States acted through 'their' Union – a secondary subject under international law – to develop conditions and procedures for the recognition of aspirant states as primary subjects of international law which go beyond the traditional criteria set out by the 1933 Montevideo Convention.

[115] Resolution adopted by the General Assembly on the status of Palestine in the United Nations, A/RES/67/19, published 4 December 2012.

[116] The EU fell apart in three groups: fourteen EU Member States voted in favour (Austria, Belgium, Denmark, Cyprus, Finland, France, Greece, Ireland, Italy, Luxembourg, Malta, Portugal, Spain, Sweden), twelve abstained (Bulgaria, Estonia, Germany, Hungary, Latvia, Lithuania, the Netherlands, Poland, Romania, Slovakia, Slovenia and the United Kingdom), and only the Czech Republic joined the US and Israel in opposing the move. Not only are EU Member States split over the issue of recognition of statehood and legitimate government, also the High Representative for Foreign Affairs and Security Policy has taken a separate stance from that of Ministers of Foreign Affairs. This has led to questions of 'competence creep' of the High Representative/Vice President and the EEAS.

[117] The European Council of 9–10 December 1991, which drafted the Maastricht Treaty, introduced the value-based fundaments upon which the future EU would rest.

From an international point of view, the 1991 'Guidelines on the Recognition of New States in Eastern Europe and in the Soviet Union', which were adopted a week after the European Council summit at Maastricht, present the most remarkable 'Europeanization' of the law on statehood, for at least three reasons. First, the guidelines departed from the well-established practice that recognition of states is only declaratory of the fact that a certain entity fulfils the objective criteria of statehood. The guidelines prescribed that only states that fulfilled the Montevideo criteria *and* 'political realities' would be entitled to recognition, if they had (i) constituted themselves on a democratic basis (i.e. if they had organized referendums on independence); (ii) accepted the appropriate international obligations (e.g. the UN Charter, the Helsinki Final Act and the Charter of Paris); and (iii) committed themselves in good faith to a peaceful process and to negotiations. Thus, the Union's cosmopolitan worldview[118] led it to develop additional substantive elements relating to the internal system of governance and the principle of good neighbourliness to *legitimate* the political recognition of state-like entities. These extra criteria were subjective and highly euro-centric. Secondly, the guidelines incorporated CSCE documents as reference points, thereby giving those commitments a legal importance that was not foreseen when leaders put their signatures to the Helsinki Final Act and the Charter of Paris. Thirdly, the guidelines went further than the customary rule on non-recognition of territorial acquisition resulting from aggression. While the former would only prohibit annexation of land by an occupying power, the guidelines also impeded the recognition of a new entity (claiming independent statehood) resulting from aggression.

An additional reason which made the 1991 guidelines so unique was the process through which they were applied. The Badinter Arbitration Commission itself made an important contribution to the development of the law on statehood by giving primacy to the right of self-determination over the other principles of integrity of the state, non-intervention in internal matters and inviolability of borders. It stressed the importance of the 'rights of peoples and minorities' and even defined the norms that provided for these (e.g. Article 27 of the 1966 UN Covenant on Civil and Political Rights) as being part of *jus cogens*. There

[118] Later codified in Arts. 3(5) and 21 TEU, which form the starting point for contributions to B. Van Vooren, S. Blockmans and J. Wouters (eds.), *The EU's Role in Global Governance: The Legal Dimension* (Oxford University Press, 2013).

is little doubt that *opinio juris* of the Badinter Arbitration Commission, together with the practice of the EC and its Member States, have contributed to the legitimation of secession of regional units, the territorial limits of which had previously been defined by an autonomous government and administration and which were direct constituent parts of the federation, albeit under the basic condition that a referendum is held in which all the citizens of the unit are to participate. The EU thus elevated the referendum, the 'internal' dimension of self-determination, to the status of a basic requirement to legitimate unilateral secession.

The underlying idea for the European stance towards the implementation of the right to self-determination was, of course, to pose certain limits on the disintegration of states in order to safeguard, as far as possible, the principle of inviolability of borders and, thus, to be able to counter claims from existing states to agree to a real territorial autonomy of their minorities abroad. Whereas the premature recognition of some regional units would have amounted to an intervention in the domestic affairs of a state prohibited by Article 2(7) of the UN Charter, the EU elevated the right of self-determination to a norm of *jus cogens* so as to trump the claim based on the principle of non–intervention that would otherwise have provided a ruthless 'federal' regime with the cover to smother justified claims of self-determination in a bloodbath. The Badinter Arbitration Commission's decision to apply the 'general principle' of *uti possidetis* outside the context of decolonization can be seen as the enlargement of the protection of international law to the nascent states on the European continent. In fact, the EU supplanted the previous practice on the recognition of states, which was largely based on meeting the 'effectiveness' of Montevideo, with a raft of new requirements based on 'legitimacy', as understood in the European context.

The EU's acceptance of the 2009 report of the independent international, yet exclusively European, Fact-finding Mission for the conflicts in Georgia resonates this finding. The report lists the three Montevideo criteria as 'minimal preconditions' for statehood but considers them 'very' (i.e. too) 'general and flexible', especially the 'effectiveness' of government condition. The report therefore refers to the respect of principles of international law, notably self-determination and the prohibition on the use of force, as accepted 'additional standards' for the qualification of an entity as a state which 'can work in the same direction as the principle of effectiveness and underscore an entity's claim to statehood'. An entity must thus satisfy cumulatively the minimal preconditions *and* the additional standards before it can expect to see its statehood recognized by the EU.

The 2011 Council conclusions on the EU's conditionality for Palestinian statehood confirm this finding. In short, EU recognition of a Palestinian state is premised on the latter's (i) unity of government, (ii) viability of state institutions and the delivery of public services, (iii) democratic credentials, (iv) good neighbourliness and (v) a negotiated settlement on the status of Jerusalem. The first two conditions are aspects of the 'effective government' criterion of Montevideo, spelling out the obvious – but in the Palestinian case rather elusive – 'unity of [central] government' requirement. The 'viability' criterion, however, goes much further than what classic international law on statehood prescribes. It measures the capacities of the state's institutions, its ability to deliver public services, and its ability to uphold standards in terms of transparent and efficient public finance management. The EU hereby relies on criteria from other international organizations, e.g. performance in institution-building and delivery of public services, as set forth by the World Bank, and the ability to conduct sound economic and financial policies, assessed by the IMF. Whereas these sophisticated performance indicators may serve a proper interest in their own right (i.e. to assess the necessity of economic and financial reform in return for emergency funding), they are hardly model conditions for the recognition of statehood.[119] Putting these economic and financial criteria to the test would no doubt disqualify many a middle-income country around the world, perhaps even some EU Member States, but it would not rob them of their statehood.

The latter begs the question with which authority the EU can make such claims. Cosmopolitan treaty objectives aside, will any future entities seeking recognition of statehood be able to comply with the Union's laundry list of 'Montevideo Plus' conditions? Arguably, a reality check is called for. A sober assessment can only lead to the conclusion that the EU's extra conditions for the recognition of statehood were never 'codified' and did not withstand the test of time. Instead, political expediency has dictated the adoption of different sets of rules and led to inconsistencies in implementation. As a 'realist' power, the EU has moulded the international law on statehood as an instrument to serve its political aims, for instance to regulate a conflict which was – at the

[119] Nor are these conditions typically 'European' – their status has merely been elevated by the EU.

outset – an internal one. Only the rules which matched these objectives were applied. As such, the EU has contributed valuable ideas which may well serve the future development of the international law pertaining to the creation of states or, at the very least, the assessment of the traditional criteria on statehood. But in order to forge the kind of coherent, consistent and effective EU external action that the Treaty on European Union calls for, the EU would be better advised to limit the 'Montevideo Plus' to the respect for the right of self-determination and the prohibition of the use of force.

7

Shaping the WTO's institutional evolution: the EU as a strategic litigant in the WTO

TILMAN KRÜGER

1 Introduction

When becoming operational as a fully fledged international organization in 1995, the World Trade Organization (WTO) succeeded a regime that had existed under the General Agreement on Tariffs and Trade (GATT) for more than four decades. An important institutional innovation was a dispute settlement system with compulsory jurisdiction and a considerable amount of judicial independence to ensure the enforceability of the negotiated commitments.[1] Over the years, the increasing heterogeneity of the membership led to collective action problems amongst the membership in the WTO.[2] At the same time, authoritative decisions on important aspects of the organization's institutional evolution were taken by the WTO's Appellate Body and a substantial amount of regulatory authority in the WTO has moved from the political to the judicial sphere.[3] This judicialization of WTO governance is usually explained with the Appellate Body's handling of an increasing caseload in light of a largely dysfunctional legislative branch: acting as a quasi-constitutional court rather than a mere

I would like to thank the editors for very helpful comments. Funding by the German Research Foundation is gratefully acknowledged.

1 M. Matsushita, 'The Dispute Settlement Mechanism at the WTO: The Appellate Body – Assessment and Problems', in A. Narlikar, et al. (eds.), *The Oxford Handbook on The World Trade Organization* (Oxford University Press, 2012), p. 510.

2 C. D. Ehlermann and L. Ehring, 'Decision-making in the World Trade Organization: Is the Consensus Practice of the World Trade Organization Adequate for Making, Revising and Implementing Rules on International Trade?' (2005) 8 *Journal of International Economic Law* 51 (69).

3 J. L. Goldstein and R. H. Steinberg, 'Regulatory Shift: The Rise of Judicial Liberalization at the WTO', in W. Mattli and N. Woods (eds.), *The Politics of Global Regulation* (Princeton, NJ: Princeton University Press, 2009), p. 211.

arbitrator,[4] the Appellate Body is viewed as dominating the WTO's institutional evolution.[5] While 'strategic behaviour'[6] of litigants is generally acknowledged, their role beyond the mere provision of cases usually remains unclear. As will be shown in this chapter, this approach cannot be entirely maintained.

More than any other WTO member, the European Union (EU) has embraced the WTO's institutional evolution towards greater judicialization. The EU supports the current role of judicial decision-making[7] and has proposed reforms further to increase judicial power in the organization, e.g. by creating a permanent and more professional panel system.[8] To promote its vision, the EU does not only take action in the

[4] S. Cho, 'Of the World Trade Court's Burden' (2009) 20 *European Journal of International Law* 675 (677). Other explanations, which invoke judicial activism on the part of the Appellate Body, have also been put forward, e.g. C. E. Barfield, *Free Trade, Sovereignty, Democracy: The Future of the World Trade Organization* (Washington, DC: AEI Press, 2001). These explanations are usually refuted, however, with reference to the Appellate Body's case law: P. Van den Bossche, 'From Afterthought to Centrepiece: The WTO Appellate Body and its Rise to Prominence in the World Trading System', in G. Sacerdoti, et al. (eds.), *The WTO at Ten: The Contribution of the Dispute Settlement System* (Cambridge University Press, 2006), p. 315.

[5] A. Stone Sweet, 'Judicialization and the Construction of Governance' (1999) 32 *Comparative Political Studies* 147 (179–80). For a recent application, see A. Stone Sweet and T. L. Brunell, 'The Politics of Majoritarian Activism in the European Convention on Human Rights, the European Union, and the World Trade Organization' (2013) 1 *Journal of Law and Courts* 61. The theoretical and empirical foundations of this explanation have been developed primarily in the context of research on judicial politics and the role of the Court of Justice of the European Union (ECJ) in EU integration processes: A. Stone Sweet, *The Judicial Construction of Europe* (Oxford University Press, 2004); K. J. Alter, *The European Court's Political Power: Selected Essays* (Oxford University Press 2009).

[6] Stone Sweet (1999), 'Judicialization and the Construction of Governance', p. 179.

[7] The EU has made this clear on various occasions and in various forms and forums. The essence of the EU's position can be found on the website of the European Commission's Directorate-General for Trade, which is responsible for implementing the EU's common trade policy: 'The [WTO dispute settlement] system has, so far, worked well to solve very important disputes and avoiding "trade wars". For this reason, the EU considers that, overall, the system is functioning well and has helped to ensure real market-opening. Moreover, it compares extremely well with other international dispute settlement systems in terms of speed and efficiency [. . .] The EU is fully committed to making the system even more effective, predictable and transparent'; European Commission, 'Tackling Unfair Trade: Dispute Settlement'; available at http://ec.europa.eu/trade/policy/accessing-markets/dispute-settlement/index_en.htm.

[8] For a detailed overview of the DSU reform negotiations, see T. A. Zimmermann, *Negotiating the Review of the WTO Dispute Settlement Understanding* (London: Cameron May, 2006). For the EU's proposals, see WTO, Contribution of the European Communities and its Member States to the improvement and clarification of the WTO Dispute Settlement Understanding, TN/DS/W/38, 23 January 2003.

WTO's negotiating forums but acts strategically also *as a litigant* in WTO dispute settlement proceedings towards a further judicialization of WTO governance. The EU's litigation strategies add further support to the validity of the hypothesis of the EU shaping the international legal order proposed by the editors in the introduction. Examples of EU litigation behaviour discussed below suggest that the EU does indeed pursue 'milieu goals' that aim at long-term 'shaping' of the WTO system; the incidents also suggest that the EU's approach towards litigation in the WTO differs from the approaches of other WTO members due to specificities of EU trade policy-making.

Following this introduction, a brief overview of the EU's changing role in international trade governance and its stance towards the WTO will be provided. Next, two examples of EU efforts to shape the WTO's institutional evolution through litigation will be discussed. Two further sections will elaborate on implications of these examples for the WTO and the EU. Although the cases do not allow for broad generalizations, they offer room for observations on dynamics underlying institutional evolution in the WTO and on peculiarities of EU trade policy-making, as well as for concluding remarks on the links of this chapter's findings to the active paradigm of the EU's engagement with the international legal order.[9]

2 The EU's changing role in the WTO: from reluctance to active leadership

The beginnings of a common European commercial policy date back to 1957, when the Treaty Establishing the European Economic Community harmonized external European tariffs, following the gradual reduction of tariffs that had already begun within the European Coal and Steel Community (ECSC).[10] To a certain extent, European commercial policy was modelled on and in accordance with GATT rules, which had been put in place in 1947.[11] Only because of GATT Article XXVI(5), for

[9] See the introduction to this volume.

[10] J. L. Mortensen, 'The World Trade Organization and the European Union', in K. E. Jørgensen (ed.), *The European Union and International Organizations* (Abingdon: Routledge 2009), p. 83.

[11] This is clearly reflected by a number of provisions in the Treaty of Rome; see G. de Búrca and J. Scott, 'The Impact of the WTO on EU Decision-making', in G. de Búrca and J. Scott (eds.), *The EU and the WTO: Legal and Constitutional Issues* (Oxford: Hart Publishing, 2003), p. 2.

instance, which states that 'the provisions of this Agreement shall not prevent [. . .] the formation of a customs union or of a free-trade area', could the Treaty of Rome come into force. The GATT thus 'enabled'[12] the formation of the European Economic Community (EEC); at the same time, the GATT 'itself was moulded to the requirements of one of its most important participants'.[13] During that time, the Member States of the ECSC retained tight control over trade policy-making[14] and the domestic priorities of the individual Member States continued to dominate the European role in the GATT: accounting only for around 17 per cent of the global gross domestic product (GDP), the EEC was in a relatively weak position compared to the then-omnipotent US.[15] The EEC also lacked sufficient institutional authority and capacities to represent a unified position in the GATT.[16] Even in the rare situations in which it managed to coordinate successfully at the European level, the bloc remained a reactive and defensive player in international trade governance,[17] fending off demands for market liberalization rather than agreeing on a proactive European trade agenda.[18]

The situation changed during the early 1980s, when exporters in Europe increasingly sought to exploit the advantages of international trade liberalization. Right before the Uruguay Round of negotiations commenced in 1986,[19] the EU and the US dominated the shaping of the global trading system together.[20] The creation of the WTO

[12] Mortensen, 'The World Trade Organization and the European Union', p. 83.

[13] C. Bretherton and J. Vogler, *The European Union as a Global Actor* (Abingdon: Routledge, 1999), p. 55.

[14] Art. 113(2) of the EEC Treaty granted exclusive competencies to the Council of the European Union as the ultimate decision-maker and the European Commission was put in charge of the day-to-day work. The EEC Treaty stated: 'The Commission shall submit proposals to the Council for implementing the common commercial policy'. Following the coming into force of the Treaty of Lisbon, Art. 207 of the Treaty on the Functioning of the European Union (TFEU) now contains a similar clause, which was modified to account for the new role of the European Parliament in the EU's policy process.

[15] R. H. Steinberg, 'The Transformation of European Trading States', in Jonah D. Levy (ed.), *The State After Statism: New State Activities in the Age of Liberalization* (Cambridge, Mass.: Harvard University Press, 2006), p. 344.

[16] *Ibid.*, pp. 348–52. [17] *Ibid.*

[18] Mortensen, 'The World Trade Organization and the European Union', p. 84.

[19] Multilateral trade negotiations took place in the context of so-called 'rounds' already during the GATT, and continue to do so today. The first of these rounds commenced in Geneva in 1947; for an overview, see www.wto.org/english/thewto_e/whatis_e/tif_e/fact4_e.htm#rounds.

[20] Member States' proportion of the global GDP provides the best approximation to their power during the GATT and within the WTO. US market power has declined since 1947,

manifested this dominance and reflected in large parts a bargain between the US, the EU and other developed countries such as Canada and Japan.[21] After the first years of the WTO's existence, during which much of the work within the organization circled around 'leftovers'[22] from the old GATT regime, the EU strongly advocated a new round of negotiations in the late 1990s. Specifically, it pushed towards deeper multilateral rules on issues such as labour and environmental standards, competition or public procurement.[23] Most other WTO members opposed the EU's broad agenda, especially emerging economies and developing countries but, to a certain extent, also the US.[24]

The disagreement over a new trade agenda was only one sign for the lack of progress in the WTO's political decision-making bodies, which quickly cooled off the euphoria that had accompanied the WTO's inception. Neither the negotiations in ministerial conferences nor those in the WTO's technical committees led to the successful conclusion of new agreements or the revision of existing – and often outdated – trade rules.[25] In light of growing frustrations, WTO Member States

while that of Europe has risen: in 1948, US GDP accounted for around 65 per cent of all GATT Member States; in 1970, the US share had already fallen to 46 per cent, and in the early 1990s, the US accounted for 'only' 33 per cent of WTO Member States' total GDP. The European Communities' share was only around 14 per cent in 1970 but accounted for about 31 per cent right before the installation of the WTO. The reasons for this development are manifold, of course, but include a decline of US private sector productivity, profitability and competitiveness, the enlargement of the EC/EU, and the rising shares of emerging economies, such as China: Steinberg, 'The Transformation of European Trading States', p. 346; John H. Barton, et al., *The Evolution of the Trade Regime: Politics, Law, and Economics of the GATT and the WTO* (Princeton, NJ: Princeton University Press, 2006), pp. 4–10.

21 Steinberg, 'The Transformation of European Trading States', p. 346.

22 C. D. Ehlermann, 'Tensions between the Dispute Settlement Process and the Diplomatic and Treaty-Making Activities of the WTO' (2002) 1 *World Trade Review* 301 (302).

23 A. R. Young, 'Trade Politics Ain't What it Used to Be: The European Union in the Doha Round' (2007) 45 *Journal of Common Market Studies* 789 (797–811).

24 S. J. Evenett, 'Five Hypotheses Concerning the Fate of the Singapore Issues in the Doha Round' (2007) 23 *Oxford Review of Economic Policy* 392 (402).

25 Ehlermann and Ehring, 'Decision-making in the World Trade Organization', p. 53. The continuing failure (and likely death) of the negotiations conducted in the context of the Doha Development Agenda is only the most recent evidence for the all-encompassing political gridlock in the WTO. The Doha Development Agenda represents the central objective of the current negotiating round amongst the WTO membership, the 'Doha Round', which aims at improving the trading prospects of developing countries. A closely related aim of the negotiations is to adjust the international trading system to today's demands and challenges more broadly by, inter alia, revising the rules governing the trade relations amongst the WTO's Member States. The negotiations, which cover about twenty areas of trade, were

then assessed other options. In 2006, the European Commission released its Global Europe strategy[26] with the aim of adjusting EU trade policy more thoroughly to the needs of European producers, exporters and investors. While it stated a continued *general* support of the EU for multilateral liberalization efforts, the strategy envisaged a much more aggressive pursuance of bilateral and regional free trade and investment agreements with countries in Latin America, Asia and elsewhere. To a considerable extent, this strategy stood in contrast to the EU's pre-2006 approach, which had clearly privileged multilateral over bilateral or regional efforts with the WTO as the central site for international economic governance.[27]

However, and important as it was, the Global Europe strategy did not mean a complete turnaround for EU trade policy. The EU remained (and remains) committed to a rules-based, legalized orientation of international trade governance, embracing procedural justice and advocating a further judicialization at the international level.[28] Several of the EU's external activities provide evidence for this, e.g. in the areas of financial regulation,[29] monetary policy[30] and consumer protection.[31] In the WTO, the EU has come all the way to being a proactive leader.[32] While it laments the lack of political progress,[33] the EU shows itself deeply satisfied with the institutional evolution of the WTO towards a stronger

officially launched in 2001 in Doha, Qatar. For more information, working documents and current developments, see www.wto.org/english/tratop_e/dda_e/dda_e.htm.

26 Directorate-General for External Trade, European Commission, 'Global Europe – Competing in the World: A Contribution to the EU's Jobs and Growth Strategy' (2006), available at http://trade.ec.europa.eu/doclib/docs/2006/october/tradoc_130376.pdf.

27 The strategic adjustment had become necessary as soon as the US private sector started to benefit from efforts of the US executive to conclude bilateral free-trade and investment agreements. A. M. Sbragia, 'The EU, the US, and Trade Policy: Competitive Interdependence in the Management of Globalization' (2010) 17 *Journal of European Public Policy* 368 (369–70).

28 W. Jacoby and S. Meunier, 'Europe and the Management of Globalization' (2010) 17 *Journal of European Public Policy* 299–300.

29 E. Posner and N. Véron, 'The EU and Financial Regulation: Power without Purpose?' (2010) 17 *Journal of European Public Policy* 400.

30 N. Jabko, 'The Hidden Face of the Euro' (2010) 17 *Journal of European Public Policy* 318.

31 R. Daniel Kelemen, 'Globalizing European Union Environmental Policy' (2010) 17 *Journal of European Public Policy* 335 (347).

32 Mortensen, 'The World Trade Organization and the European Union', p. 83.

33 In a speech delivered in 2001, the European Commissioner for Trade said: 'The situation is serious [. . .] There is a real risk that without genuine progress the WTO will be sidelined in the future'. K. de Gucht, European Commissioner for Trade, 'The Need to Preserve the Multilateral Trade System', speech at the Plenary Session of the 8th WTO's

judicial branch in the WTO.[34] Across its activities, the EU advocates further increasing its judicial decision-making power and puts great emphasis on the WTO's 'rules-based orientation'.[35]

3 Rule development in the WTO through litigation

The EU's negotiating position in the context of the Doha Round and on the reform of the WTO's Dispute Settlement Understanding (DSU), which is the legal text governing the settlement of disputes in the WTO, clearly show that the EU supports steps towards even greater judicialization in the WTO.[36] Owing to the crisis of political decision-making in the WTO, however, these efforts have so far led nowhere.[37] But negotiating proposals do not capture the entirety of EU activities towards changing the status quo in the WTO: the EU actively contributes to rule development in the WTO also as a litigant in the context of WTO dispute settlement and in addition to its immediate, case-specific interests. Two examples for such behaviour will now be illustrated.

3.1 *Establishing precedent in the WTO*

Stare decisis[38] does not exist *de jure* in the WTO or in international law in general[39] and the findings of WTO panels and the Appellate Body

Ministerial Conference, Geneva, 15 December 2011, available at http://trade.ec.europa.eu/doclib/docs/2011/december/tradoc_148468.pdf.

34 Various EU proposals towards a further strengthening of WTO dispute settlement referred to later in this chapter clearly support such an assessment. Through its proposals, the EU generally tries to reinforce the 'rules-based nature of the WTO'; WTO, Minutes of the Dispute Settlement Body Meeting on 20 May 2008, WT/DSB/M/250, 1 July 2008, para. 57.

35 Zimmermann, *Negotiating the Review of the WTO Dispute Settlement Understanding*, p. 204. This orientation contrasts an orientation towards power-based forms of decision-making, which is supported by the US: J. H. H. Weiler, 'The Rule of Lawyers and the Ethos of Diplomats: Reflections on the Internal and External Legitimacy of WTO Dispute Settlement', Jean Monnet Working Paper 09/00 (2000).

36 WTO, Contributions of the European Communities and its Member States to the Improvement of the WTO Dispute Settlement Understanding, TN/DS/W/1, 13 March 2002; WTO, TN/DS/W/38.

37 Zimmermann, Negotiating the Review of the WTO Dispute Settlement Understanding, p. 91.

38 *Stare decisis* originates from the Latin phrase *stare decisis et non quieta movere*, which translates as 'to stand by decisions and not disturb the undisturbed': G. Adeleye, et al., *World Dictionary of Foreign Expressions: A Resource for Readers and Writers* (London: Bolchazy-Carducci Publishers, 1999), p. 371.

39 R. Bhala, 'The Myth about Stare Decisis and International Trade Law (Part One of a Trilogy)' (1999) 14 *American University International Law Review* 845 (847–9).

have usually been considered to have no binding effects other than for the parties involved in the dispute.[40] At the same time, and over the years of the WTO's existence, panels, the Appellate Body and litigants have continuously referred to earlier judicial reports; these references have raised questions as to whether precedent – which forms one element of *stare decisis* – exists in the WTO.[41] Specifically, different views exist on the issue of how binding earlier Appellate Body reports are vertically, i.e. for the WTO's ad hoc panels, which are the lower instances in the WTO's dispute settlement system. In an early report in *Japan – Alcoholic Beverages II*, the Appellate Body stressed the non-binding character of adopted panel and Appellate Body reports. Referring to common practice under the GATT regime as well as to Article IX:2 WTO Agreement,[42] the Appellate Body stated that conclusions and recommendations in adopted panel reports created 'legitimate expectations among WTO Members' but were 'not binding, except with respect to resolving the particular dispute between the parties to that dispute'.[43] Subsequent panels acted accordingly and the Appellate Body, in its Article 21.5 report in *US – Shrimp*, extended the same reasoning to adopted Appellate Body reports.[44]

In 2004, the Appellate Body changed its approach, stating that 'following the Appellate Body's conclusions in earlier disputes is not only appropriate, but is what would be expected from panels, especially where the issues are the same'.[45] Four years later, in *US – Stainless Steel (Mexico)*, the Appellate Body went even further: showing itself deeply concerned about a decision by a panel to depart from Appellate Body jurisprudence, the Appellate Body demanded that

[40] R. Bhala, 'The Precedent Setters: De Facto Stare Decisis in WTO Adjudication (Part Two of a Trilogy)' (1999) 9 *Journal of Transnational Law and Policy* 1 (3).

[41] In such an understanding, the other parts are consistency, certainty, rationality and the giving of defensible reasons: A. Scully-Hill and H. Mahncke, 'The Emergence of the Doctrine of Stare Decisis in the World Trade Organization Dispute Settlement System' (2009) 36 *Legal Issues of Economic Integration* 133 (134).

[42] Art. IX: 2 WTO Agreement provides that the Ministerial Conference and the General Council have the exclusive authority to adopt interpretations of the WTO agreements.

[43] WTO, Japan – Taxes on Alcoholic Beverages – Report of the Appellate Body, WT/DS8, 10, 11/AB/R, 4 October 1996, pp. 13–14.

[44] WTO, United States – Import Prohibition of Certain Shrimp and Shrimp Products – Recourse to Article 21.5 of the DSU by Malaysia – Report of the Appellate Body, WT/DS58/AB/RW, 22 October 2001, para. 109.

[45] WTO, United States – Sunset Reviews of Anti-Dumping Measures on Oil Country Tubular Goods from Argentina – Report of the Appellate Body, WT/DS268/AB/R, 29 November 2004, para. 188.

panels follow its jurisprudence on identical legal issues 'absent cogent reasons' to do otherwise.[46] The Appellate Body was also explicit on how it interpreted its own role and the role of panels in the WTO system by referring to the 'hierarchical structure contemplated in the DSU'.[47] According to the Appellate Body, the DSU foresees 'distinct roles' for the organs at different levels of decision-making, including a hierarchically superior position of the Appellate Body vis-à-vis the ad hoc panels.[48]

The Appellate Body's interpretation resonated very differently across the WTO's membership. The US strongly opposed it, blaming the Appellate Body for having 'significantly departed from the established understanding of the relationship between panel and Appellate Body reports and the role of the Appellate Body and that of Members'.[49] According to the US, the Appellate Body had 'misperceived the WTO Agreement and this Member-driven organization' and 'purported to create a new legal effect for Appellate Body reports, one that would appear to grant to the Appellate Body the very authority to issue authoritative interpretations of the covered agreements'.[50] Referring to the same report, the EU very much 'welcomed the clarifications from the Appellate Body' that, '[w]hilst self-evident [...] confirmed the rules-based nature of the WTO, and the multilateral aspects of dispute settlement'.[51]

Apart from these concerns regarding the general orientation of the WTO,[52] the diverging US and EU reactions were driven also by the case-specific interests of the two. At issue was the practice of zeroing, which describes, in essence, a calculation methodology that leads to an artificial inflation of dumping margins.[53] Because of this inflation, other WTO members are more often found to dump their export products.

46 WTO, United States – Final Anti-dumping Measures on Stainless Steel from Mexico – Report of the Appellate Body, WT/DS344/AB/R, 30 April 2008, para. 160.

47 *Ibid.*, para. 161. 48 *Ibid.*

49 WTO, Minutes of the Dispute Settlement Body Meeting on 20 May 2008, WT/DSB/M/250, 1 July 2008, para. 48.

50 *Ibid.*, para. 52. 51 *Ibid.*, para. 57.

52 The rules-based and power-based orientations of decision-making in the WTO have been discussed earlier in the chapter. See Zimmermann, *Negotiating the Review of the WTO Dispute Settlement Understanding*; Weiler, 'The Rule of Lawyers and the Ethos of Diplomats'.

53 WTO, United States – Final Dumping Determination on Softwood Lumber from Canada – Recourse to Article 21.5 of the DSU by Canada – Report of the Appellate Body, WT/DS264/AB/RW, 15 August 2006, para. 142.

And because such a finding usually leads to the imposition of anti-dumping duties, the home country of the product has a strong interest against zeroing.[54] Before the WTO was established, zeroing was commonly applied, including in Europe and the US; while the practice had been challenged already under the GATT, it had not been found inconsistent with the GATT's provisions.[55] Also, the new WTO rules did not explicitly prohibit dumping or zeroing; rather, a so-called anti-dumping agreement was put in place to govern the application of anti-dumping measures by WTO members.[56]

The first dispute in the context of WTO dispute settlement, *EC – Bed Linen*, was brought against the EU. The EU defended itself with reference to Article 2 of the anti-dumping agreement, which, in its view, did not prevent the EU from adopting zeroing.[57] However, the Appellate Body rejected the EU's position, striking down the zeroing practice for the first time. Following this report, a whole series of disputes ensued, which were now brought frequently by the EU and which aimed at taking zeroing away from the US as well. The results of these proceedings left the US increasingly isolated for its failure to comply with WTO law after a series of adverse Appellate Body rulings. Clearly then the US had reasons to discard the strong precedential force of earlier Appellate Body reports that had found zeroing to be inconsistent with WTO law. At the same time, the EU fought to eliminate US zeroing ever since its own use of the method had been put to an end following the Appellate Body's *EC – Bed Linen* report.

But there was more to the different positions on precedent than these immediate interests on zeroing. It is important to note that precedent helps to ensure the consistency of judicial findings and increases, especially in its vertical form, the authority of decisions in a hierarchic court system.[58] Apart from their interests on zeroing, the US and the

[54] There are many facets to zeroing, which need not (and cannot) be dealt with here: E. A. Vermulst and F. Graafsma, *WTO Dispute Settlement: Anti-Dumping, Countervailing Duties and Safeguards* (London: Cameron May, 2005).

[55] For instance, a GATT panel had rejected a complaint by Japan in the *EC – Audio Cassettes* case in 1995: S. Cho, 'Global Constitutional Lawmaking' (2010) 31 *University of Pennsylvania Journal of International Law* 621 (634).

[56] The official name of the agreement is Agreement on Implementation of Article VI of the General Agreement on Tariffs and Trade 1994.

[57] WTO, European Communities – Anti-Dumping Duties on Imports of Cotton-Type Bed Linen from India – Report of the Appellate Body, WT/DS141/AB/R (1 March 2001), paras. 81.

[58] Stone Sweet, *The Judicial Construction of Europe*, p. 10.

EU thus argued also in light of their diverging views on judicialization: the EU promoted the view that the Appellate Body's reports amount to 'authoritative pronouncements on the law'[59] and that 'decisions of the hierarchical higher body are followed by the hierarchical lower body'.[60] After the Appellate Body had issued its report, the EU 'particularly welcomed the clarifications [. . .] to the effect that "absent cogent reasons, an adjudicatory body would resolve the same legal question in the same way in a subsequent case"'.[61] The EU took these views not only as a disputant but also as third party, and 'not only because of [a] trade interest in the particular case, but also because of a wider systemic interest'.[62] Whereas the US rejected precedent in light of its preferences towards a more power-based orientation of the WTO, the EU supported precedent as an important contribution to the rules-based orientation of the WTO.[63]

Over the years, the Appellate Body incrementally expanded its jurisprudence on zeroing in subsequent reports and struck down different types of zeroing that were challenged before it.[64] While it was consistent in its references to earlier case law, the Appellate Body used different approaches to discard zeroing, including rare teleological interpretations of WTO law.[65] When it was confronted with the panel decision that disobeyed existing Appellate Body jurisprudence in *US – Stainless Steel (Mexico)*, the Appellate Body confidently reversed the

[59] *US – Stainless Steel (Mexico)*, Third Party Submission by the European Communities, para. 164.

[60] *Ibid.*, para. 131.

[61] WTO, Minutes of the Dispute Settlement Body Meeting on 20 May 2008, WT/DSB/M/250, 1 July 2008, para. 57.

[62] J. Flett, 'From the Green Room to the Court Room (And Back): Judicial Clarification of Ambiguity in WTO Law and the Effects on Subsequent Negotiations' (2011) 1 *Oñati Socio-Legal Series* 1 (35).

[63] This is interesting in light of the fact that precedent plays an important role in the US common law system, which would suggest that the US promoted the establishment of precedent also internationally: Sara McLaughlin Mitchell and E. J. Powell, *Domestic Law Goes Global: Legal Traditions and International Courts* (Cambridge University Press, 2011).

[64] Examples include the disputes European Communities – Anti-Dumping Duties on Malleable Cast Iron Tube or Pipe Fittings from Brazil (DS219), United States – Laws, Regulations and Methodology for Calculating Dumping Margins (Zeroing) (DS294) and United States – Continued Existence and Application of Zeroing Methodology (DS350); a list of WTO disputes involving zeroing can be accessed at www.wto.org/english/tratop_e/dispu_e/dispu_subjects_index_e.htm?id=G132#selected_subject.

[65] For a detailed discussion, see Cho, 'Global Constitutional Lawmaking', pp. 633–41.

panel's findings on zeroing. Although initiated by its goal to eliminate zeroing, the EU's strategic targeting of US dumping calculations as claimant and as third party, and its continued insistence on the precedential effects of the Appellate Body's case law motivated the Appellate Body to assume a stronger role for itself. Together with US non-compliance, this provoked a showdown situation between a panel and the Appellate Body – over the legality of zeroing as well as over the status of adopted Appellate Body reports in the WTO's legal system. With the adoption of the Appellate Body's report in *US – Stainless Steel (Mexico)*, the EU could then claim a double win with reference to both, its immediate, case-specific interests on zeroing as well as its long-term, systemic interests on the establishment of a stronger court system in the WTO.

3.2 Opening Appellate Body hearings to the public

Increasing the transparency of WTO dispute settlement is high on the agenda of a number of developed country WTO members. US representatives insist that transparency is important to satisfy domestic demands and to counter allegations of WTO critics that 'faceless, unelected, unaccountable bureaucrats in Geneva have usurped US sovereignty by writing rules for Americans that should be determined only by Americans'.[66] The EU demands greater transparency as well, stressing the fundamental function of public scrutiny in judicial systems as a means 'to secure continued public support and confidence in the WTO system'.[67] Developing country members of the WTO have continuously opposed calls for greater transparency in the WTO's judicial proceedings.[68] Their core argument has remained identical since the Appellate Body adopted a

[66] J. Hippler Bello, 'Editorial Comment. The WTO Dispute Settlement Understanding: Less Is More' (1996) 90 *American Journal of International Law* 416.

[67] European Commission, 'Tackling Unfair Trade: Dispute Settlement', available at http://ec.europa.eu/trade/tackling-unfair-trade/dispute-settlement/. See also L. Ehring, 'Public Access to Dispute Settlement Hearings in the World Trade Organization' (2008) 11 *Journal of International Economic Law* 1021 (1023).

[68] J. P. Trachtman and P. M. Moremen, 'Costs and Benefits of Private Participation in WTO Dispute Settlement: Whose Right Is It Anyway?' (2003) 44 *Harvard International Law Journal* 221 (227). See also, for instance, the statements made by Kenya representing a group of African countries during the DSU negotiations; *Proposal by the African Group*, WTO Doc. TN/DS/W/15, 25, September 2002; or the *Poposals made by Cuba, Honduras, India, Malaysia Pakistan, Sri Lanka, Tanzania and Zimbabwe*, WTO Doc. TN/DS/W/18, 7 October 2002.

procedure to accept unsolicited *amicus curiae* briefs for consideration.[69] The main fear was and remains that non-state actors from developed countries – well organized and resourceful business associations or civil society organizations – will use greater transparency to judicial decision-making in the WTO to advance their own specific interests to the detriment of developing countries.[70] Although some developing countries such as Colombia, Ecuador, Nicaragua and Panama have partly lessened their previously harsh opposition to public hearings before panels and the Appellate Body,[71] economically and politically powerful countries such as Brazil, China, India and Mexico continue to reject proposals to open dispute settlement hearings to the public, which have been made in the context of the DSU reform negotiations.[72]

To move ahead nonetheless, the EU, the US and Canada jointly requested that a panel opened its hearings to the public. They succeeded in 2005, when the panel in *US/Canada – Continued Suspension of Obligations*[73] accepted the joint request to open the panel's hearings for public observation.[74] Even though Article 14.1 DSU stipulates that 'Panel deliberations shall be confidential', the panellists interpreted the term deliberations so as to cover the panel's internal considerations and not the disputants' exchange of arguments before it.[75] Following this initial success, the same parties continued to push for public hearings during subsequent disputes in which they appeared as litigants. Later panels followed the example of the interpretation in *US/Canada – Continued*

[69] In *European Communities – Measures Affecting Asbestos and Products Containing Asbestos* (DS135), the Appellate Body had decided to open WTO dispute-settlement proceedings for unsolicited amicus curiae briefs; it did so despite and against the stern opposition of a vast majority of Member States: S. Charnovitz, 'Judicial Independence in the World Trade Organization', in L. Boisson de Chazournes, et al. (eds.), *International Organizations and International Dispute Settlement: Trends and Prospects* (New York: Transnational Publishers, 2002), p. 219.

[70] Barton, *The Evolution of the Trade Regime. Politics, Law, and Economics of the GATT and the WTO*, p. 25; Trachtman and Moremen, 'Costs and Benefits of Private Participation in WTO Dispute Settlement, p. 227.

[71] Alberto Alvarez-Jiménez, 'Public Hearings at the WTO Appellate Body: The Next Step' (2010) 59 *International and Comparative Law Quarterly* 1079 (1086).

[72] Ehring, 'Public Access to Dispute Settlement Hearings in the World Trade Organization', p. 1032.

[73] Both panels were identically composed and the panels' (as well as the later Appellate Body) reports in the two disputes were circulated in parallel.

[74] WTO, United States – Continued Suspension of Obligations in the EC – Hormones Dispute, Report of the Panel, WT/DS320/R, 31 March 2008, para. 7.40.

[75] *Ibid.*, para. 7.49.

Suspension of Obligations;[76] opponents of open hearings continued to reject such interpretations with reference to the confidentiality requirement enshrined in the DSU.[77]

The issue of public hearings gained new momentum with the involvement of the Appellate Body, again in the *US/Canada – Continued Suspension of Obligations* disputes. The Appellate Body sided with the disputants and supporting third parties in a special procedural ruling, and authorized the public observation of oral hearings before it, subject to specific terms and procedures.[78] In support of this decision, the Appellate Body linked Article 17.10 DSU, which stipulates that the 'proceedings of the Appellate Body shall be confidential', closely to Article 18.2 DSU, which provides that '[n]othing in this Understanding shall preclude a party to a dispute from disclosing statements of its own positions to the public'. Accordingly, the Appellate Body found that the confidentiality requirement in Article 17.10 DSU cannot be absolute but had to be 'relative and time-bound' and 'more properly understood as operating in a relational manner'.[79] Since July 2008, the practice has been slowly consolidated and a couple of appellate hearings were open to the public.[80]

While Member States' criticism was less severe after the Appellate Body's authorization of public hearings than after its single-handed decision to accept unsolicited amicus curiae briefs,[81] the changes that occurred through the interpretations in *US/Canada – Continued Suspension of Obligations* must not be underestimated. Even proponents of opening the WTO's judicial hearings to the public believed that the necessary changes to the DSU had to result from political agreement: besides the confidentiality requirement enshrined in Article 17.10 DSU, most believed that the Appellate Body's ability to amend the rules

[76] Ehring, 'Public Access to Dispute Settlement Hearings in the World Trade Organization', p. 1026.

[77] Alvarez-Jiménez, 'Public Hearings at the WTO Appellate Body', p. 1084.

[78] WTO, United States – Continued Suspension of Obligations in the EC – Hormones Dispute – Report of the Appellate Body, WT/DS320/AB/R (16 October 2008), Annex IV, para. 11.

[79] *Ibid*., paras. 5–6.

[80] For an overview, see Alvarez-Jiménez, 'Public Hearings at the WTO Appellate Body', pp. 1083–98. A recent public hearing before the Appellate Body took place in the context of the United States – Measures Affecting Trade in Large Civil Aircraft – Second Complaint (DS353) dispute.

[81] WTO, United States – Continued Suspension of Obligations in the EC, WT/DS320/AB/R, para. 11.

and procedures for hearings before it was strongly constrained by the scope of its mandate and the authorization granted to it by the WTO's Member States.[82] The Appellate Body thus needed to provide for a creative, teleological reading of Articles 17.10 and 18.2 DSU and the confidentiality requirement contained therein, and to depart from its usually firm adherence to a textual reading of WTO law.

For the litigants, the lesson learnt from the Appellate Body decisions on public hearings was that what could not be done via negotiations – i.e. changing the dominant interpretation and thus meaning of the DSU – could be done through litigation. The Appellate Body knowingly upset a numerical majority of WTO members, including those that had been so opposed to its handling of unsolicited amicus curiae briefs a few years earlier. However, the Appellate Body did not – like on precedent – invent its interpretation but relied on arguments made by litigants and previous panels. The litigants succeeded because they appealed to the Appellate Body's 'judicial self-image' as a strong court and invoked the need to increase the 'legitimacy of the Appellate Body'.[83]

4 Implications of the EU's litigation behaviour for institutional evolution in the WTO and in the EU

The two examples discussed show how the EU could contribute to the institutional evolution of the WTO; although still contested, precedent and open panel and appellate hearings are today recurring features of WTO dispute settlement proceedings. In both cases, political agreement was lacking and judicial law-making proved to be the only way to allow for the evolution of WTO law. As litigant, the EU selected its arguments not only on the basis of its immediate, case-specific interests in the particular dispute at hand but also on the basis of its long-term, 'overall perspective on what the rules *should* be',[84] across several disputes; it used a variety of forums, including panel and appellate proceedings and repeat appearances as a third party, in order to

[82] Victoria Donaldson and Alan Yanovich, 'The Appellate Body's Working Procedures for Appellate Review', in Sacerdoti, *The WTO at Ten*, p. 413.

[83] Ehring, 'Public Access to Dispute Settlement Hearings in the World Trade Organization', p. 1029.

[84] Trachtman and Moremen, 'Costs and Benefits of Private Participation in WTO Dispute Settlement, p. 223.

promote and lock-in its preferred interpretations. The EU's success begs, in turn, the question as to the implications of the findings for governance in the WTO and for the EU's internal processes of trade policy-making.

4.1 Implications for governance in the WTO

The changes to WTO governance stimulated through the EU's (and other members') litigation behaviour are by no means trivial, particularly because of the severity of the WTO members' collective action problems. For once, the members' continued clinging to consensual decision-making in the WTO prevents the adoption of almost any piece of legislative guidance for panels and the Appellate Body. The membership is also unable to control the panels' and especially the Appellate Body's decisions politically. Judicial reports can only be blocked if there is a consensus amongst WTO Member States in favour of such a decision – so far, this has never happened. The membership's capacity to counterbalance judicial decisions is thus hampered by very demanding decision-making rules *ex ante* and *ex post*, which affords especially the Appellate Body leeway to fill lacunae in WTO treaty texts.[85]

In this regard, it is important to note that the changes discussed above – establishing precedent, opening Appellate Body hearings to the public – could not be achieved via legislation through political agreement amongst the WTO's members. At least to a certain extent, the results contradicted previously held convictions about the text and meaning of the DSU: before it decided otherwise, the Appellate Body's reports exerted no binding effects other than to the parties in a dispute; likewise, public hearings before the Appellate Body were deemed impossible without textual changes to the DSU that could only be introduced by political agreement. Also, the changes occurred in light of persistent and forceful objection by many WTO members.

The examples discussed above show in detail that, and how, the EU could stimulate changes to WTO governance through litigation. Because the Appellate Body puts great emphasis on a coherent and consistent application of the legal provisions before it, the Appellate Body had to be convinced to be bold, depart from its usual approach and engage in constitutional adjudication rather than in arbitrational dispute

[85] R. H. Steinberg, 'Judicial Lawmaking at the WTO: Discursive, Constitutional, and Political Constraints' (2004) 98 *American Journal of International Law* 247, p. 249.

resolution.[86] The EU supported such a role for the Appellate Body more than any other WTO member. The similarities in the language used by the EU and the Appellate Body reflect shared preferences between the two that go beyond mere semantics; the EU's third-party submission in *US – Stainless Steel (Mexico)* and the Appellate Body's later finding are remarkable examples here.[87] The key to the EU's relative success as a litigant, it appears, is to promote changes that are in line with the Appellate Body's own preferences. The EU's advocacy for a strong judiciary in the WTO helps to ensure the Appellate Body's responsiveness even against the strong opposition of many or economically very powerful and thus important Member States.[88]

The findings above support a widely held suspicion about WTO dispute settlement, namely that WTO Member States with greater material and staff resources may be better able to utilize the system for their own endeavours than others.[89] They do so, however, from a different angle: the EU may be better able to shape WTO governance as a litigant because it is able to formulate a vision in the first place and then translate this vision into a litigation strategy. Also, it is interesting to note that the position of the Appellate Body as advocated by the EU is in many ways similar to the position of the ECJ within the EU; the reasoning of those representing the EU before the Appellate Body – i.e. the European Commission's Legal Service – reflects the Commission's internal approach to judicial power and to the role of the ECJ within the EU.[90] Compared to developing countries' and

[86] Cho, 'Global Constitutional Lawmaking', p. 641.

[87] WTO, United States – Final Anti-dumping Measures on Stainless Steel from Mexico – Report of the Appellate Body, WT/DS344/AB/R, 30 April 2008, para. 160 and Third Party Submission by the European Communities, para. 169. The US maintained that the Appellate Body 'approach towards precedent would transform the WTO dispute settlement system into a common law system [. . .] that was nowhere agreed among Members', WT/DSB/M/250, para. 53.

[88] Not surprisingly, advocates of greater transparency in the WTO have already begun to envision the consolidation of the openness of WTO appeal hearings: Alvarez-Jiménez, 'Public Hearings at the WTO Appellate Body', p. 1079; Ehring, 'Public Access to Dispute Settlement Hearings in the World Trade Organization', p. 1030.

[89] C. P. Bown, Self-Enforcing Trade: Developing Countries and WTO Dispute Settlement (Washington, DC: Brookings Institution Press, 2009); G. C. Shaffer, Defending Interests: Public-Private Partnerships in WTO Litigation (Washington, DC: Brookings Institution Press, 2003).

[90] K. J. Alter, 'Who Are the "Masters of the Treaty"?: European Governments and the European Court of Justice' (1998) 52 *International Organization* 121 (129).

emerging economies' intentional use of strategies, the EU appears better equipped to ensure the responsiveness of the Appellate Body.[91]

4.2 *Implications for EU trade policy-making*

The EU's ability to attain the Appellate Body's responsiveness stems from a degree of convergence of preferences between the two. This convergence becomes even more obvious if one considers the dynamics, actors and interests involved in the formulation of the EU's preferences towards the WTO legal order. As early as in the 1960s, the constantly growing number and heterogeneity of the European Member States had made it increasingly difficult for the Commission to advance European interests internationally.[92] Following US–EU negotiations on agriculture during the Kennedy Round negotiations (1964–7), many in Europe became convinced that increasingly complex trade negotiations called for a more effective and competent representation of the EU as a whole.[93] After several adjustments to the set-up of EU trade policy-making, the Uruguay Round negotiations (1986–93) were conducted by a much stronger European Commission to allow for EU representation with one strong voice.[94] Within the Commission, the Directorate-General for External Trade (DG Trade) and the Commission's Legal Service took the lead on matters of trade negotiations and litigation. Over time, greater resources and institutional innovations have enabled the Commission to gain unique expertise and knowledge on trade matters, acting as *the* focal point for EU Member States, the private sector, civil society

[91] Obviously, far-reaching conclusions can hardly be drawn from the above examples alone. However, research conducted elsewhere shows that the EU has been able to formulate and advance arguments in line with the preferences of the Appellate Body also in other cases, e.g. in the area of safeguard measures: T. Krüger, 'The Judicialization of Governance in the WTO: "Strategic Litigation" as an Explanatory Factor?', Paper presented at the Third Biennial Global Conference of the Society of International Economic Law, Singapore, 13 July 2012, available at http://papers.ssrn.com/sol3/papers.cfm?abstract_id=2097816.

[92] Steinberg, 'The Transformation of European Trading States', p. 349; Mortensen, 'The World Trade Organization and the European Union', pp. 83–4.

[93] During the negotiations, the Commission could not agree to anything more than the lowest common denominator position within the Council, which was rejected by the US: Steinberg, 'The Transformation of European Trading States', p. 364.

[94] S. Meunier, *Trading Voices: The European Union in International Commercial Negotiations* (Princeton, NJ: Princeton University Press, 2005), p. 102.

and other domestic actors;[95] today, the Commission is the single most influential actor in EU trade policy.[96]

Research on international trade negotiations convincingly argues that domestic dynamics of trade policy formulation have to be taken into account to explain international outcomes.[97] In the EU, the relative autonomy of the Commission has been found to be a particularly important factor.[98] The EU's overall objectives are critically shaped by the Commission, either in the form of managed globalization, which has been the product of DG Trade headed by Pascal Lamy (Trade Commissioner from 1999 to 2004), or in the form of Global Europe, which strongly reflected the leadership of Lamy's successor, Peter Mandelson.[99] While the two strategies focused on different venues for EU action on trade matters – multilateralism under managed globalization, bilateralism and regionalism under Global Europe – they both cemented the Commission's lead role to choose the EU's preferred venues, define overall goals and select strategies. The EU's changing role in the WTO was thus due not only to the exogenous developments referred to earlier in this chapter but also to dynamics from within. The Commission is not an unbiased agent but adds its own preferences into that what becomes the EU's position on matters related to trade.[100]

There can be no doubt that domestic factors play an important role also regarding the EU's actions in WTO litigation proceedings.[101] Over time, the strengthening of the Commission's role has been accompanied

[95] G. C. Shaffer, 'What's New in EU Trade Dispute Settlement? Judicialization, Public–Private Networks and the WTO Legal Order' (2006) 13 *Journal of European Public Policy* 832 (837).

[96] M. Knodt, 'Common Commercial Policy', in Hubert Heinelt and Michèle Knodt (eds.), *Policies within the EU Multi-Level System* (Baden-Baden: Nomos, 2011), p. 77.

[97] R. D. Putnam, 'Diplomacy and Domestic Politics: The Logic of Two-Level Games' (1988) 42 *International Organization* 427 (433); Meunier, *Trading Voices: The European Union in International Commercial Negotiations*, p. 1.

[98] T. Delreux and B. Kerremans, 'How Agents Weaken their Principals' Incentives to Control: The Case of EU Negotiators and EU Member States in Multilateral Negotiations' (2010) 32 *Journal of European Integration* 357.

[99] M. Elsig, 'The EU's Choice of Regulatory Venues for Trade Negotiations: A Tale of Agency Power?' (2007) 45 *Journal of Common Market Studies* 927 (935).

[100] Meunier, *Trading Voices. The European Union in International Commercial Negotiations*, p. 58.

[101] In fact, a growing literature shows how states use international adjudication to manage conflicting demands from multiple actors including, importantly, different domestic interests; see e.g. C. L. Davis, *Why Adjudicate? Enforcing Trade Rules in the WTO* (Princeton, NJ: Princeton University Press 2012).

by an increasingly active use of WTO dispute settlement – to open up foreign markets and, as could be illustrated above, to strengthen the rule of law in and institutional evolution of the WTO. This emphasis on rules and legal and judicial institutions reflects the Commission's own preferences: the large amount of legal and technical expertise needed for the conduct of WTO dispute settlement proceedings puts the Commission in an advantageous position as it is the only actor that possesses such expertise. Within the Commission, DG Trade and the Legal Service benefit from the exact same advantages vis-à-vis other Directorates. Where these voice concerns and try negatively to affect the interests of DG Trade and its constituents (e.g. the business community and trade ministries in EU Member States) in response to their own sector-specific demands (e.g. strong environmental concerns), DG Trade can use its lead role on trade matters to steer intra-Commission coordination in its preferred direction.[102]

Like in trade negotiations, the EU influences the world trading system 'by providing appropriate tools [. . .] that it has had to conceive when it had to address its own processes of internal liberalization'.[103] The incident relating to precedent in the WTO is a case in point: considering the positive experiences European lawyers have made with precedent-based judicial decision-making in the judicial construction of Europe, the Legal Service's advocacy for vertical precedent in the WTO serves the purpose 'to reassert the underlying stability and permanence of the law, and therefore the legitimacy of courts, with reference to precedent and settled canons of interpretation and reasoning'.[104] Precedent-based decision-making creates argumentation frameworks, within which litigants and judges operate. Repeat litigation, 'sustained by a mix of analogic reasoning and the self-interest of legal actors, that is, potential litigants and judges',[105] further cements these frameworks. Knowing about the opportunities such a system offers for skilled litigants from the history of EU integration, the motivation of the Commission's Legal Service also to implement precedent in the WTO becomes obvious.

102 Delreux and Kerremans, 'How Agents Weaken their Principals' Incentives to Control', pp. 364 ff.
103 P. A. Messerlin, 'The Influence of the EU in the World Trade System', in Narlikar, *The Oxford Handbook on The World Trade Organization*, p. 232.
104 Stone Sweet, *The Judicial Construction of Europe*, p. 10.
105 *Ibid.*, pp. 32, 41.

The EU's success is thus tied, at least partly, to the strong role of the Commission. After formulating its strategies, for which it did not need a consensus amongst EU Member States, the Commission could position the EU as a proactive leader within the WTO. Due also to the Commission's successes in the WTO, the EU Member States have come generally to embrace this vision and support the parallel promotion of trade liberalization and the international rule of law. However, more recent events show the fragility of this set-up, as the recent economic turmoil in the EU and beyond may contribute to a new popularity of measures that have been rejected as unduly protectionist for some time. Also, the coming into force of the Treaty of Lisbon has elevated the role of the European Parliament, which is now more actively involved in EU trade policy-making. While the full implications of these changes are still to be seen, the European Parliament's own interests in EU policy formulation and its responsiveness to actors and interests that lack access to the Commission mean that this new role for the Parliament could be a real game changer.[106]

5 Conclusions

Although limited in number and scope, the above illustrations are a case in point that the EU shapes the international legal order in ways that are often overlooked by existing assessments of the bloc's role as an international actor. Contributing to institutional evolution in the WTO also as a litigant in dispute settlement proceedings, the EU adheres to the active paradigm of shaping the international legal order: the EU's strategic choices as a litigant towards the WTO's institutional evolution promote goals clearly related to a long-term vision of the international legal order and not only to the immediate interests in a particular trade dispute. Although results can only be achieved slowly, the real value of the EU's strategic litigation approach becomes clear in light of the difficulties of WTO members to change the WTO's institutional set-up through negotiations: where political decision-making is in constant gridlock, the judicial arena provides a real option to induce change.

Assessing its ethical dimension, the EU's record appears more ambiguous. The EU's approach to international relations has strong normative

[106] The recent rejection of the proposed Anti-Counterfeiting Trade Agreement (ACTA) exemplifies the potential consequences of this new role for the Parliament in EU trade policy-making.

implications at different levels even though it does not necessarily guarantee 'fair outcomes'. In the WTO, the EU's efforts appear to have increased the equality before the law by helping to increase the transparency of judicial decision-making. Yet, they were not the result of EU attempts to promote a just vision of international (trade) governance per se. Rather, the EU primarily tried to ensure its own vision of, and advantages within, the international legal order. Contrary to what has been proposed by Andrew Williams earlier in this volume, the EU does not follow imperatives that could satisfy *moral* demands such as the alleviation of poverty through its foreign and development policies and practice.[107]

Within Europe, the EU's efforts as a strategic litigant in the WTO have ethically ambiguous consequences as well. From an output-oriented[108] perspective of legitimacy, one is tempted to praise the Union's internal set-up for its enabling of successful EU representation in the WTO: the Commission's autonomy in EU trade policy has made it a successful player in the WTO. However, the same amount of Commission autonomy may mean, of course, that not all those affected by EU trade policy decisions have similar chances to participate in the relevant formulation processes.[109]

[107] See Andrew Williams's contribution to this volume.

[108] Fritz W. Scharpf, *Governing in Europe: Effective and Democratic?* (Oxford University Press, 1999), p. 3.

[109] *Ibid.*, pp. 7–10.

8

EU climate change policy: can the Union be just (and) green?

CHRISTINA ECKES

1 Introduction

The European Union actively shapes its environment. Climate change policy is a particularly illustrative example of the Union applying an active paradigm to protect the global environment through both internal and external actions. The Union's position and ability to shape its environment are influenced by several interconnected factors: first, certain environmental issues, such as climate change, concern 'global public goods' and therefore entail a presumption that they can only be effectively addressed on a global scale in a collective, if not concerted, effort. Secondly, the EU is explicitly mandated by the EU Treaties to pursue environmental protection beyond its own borders and has exclusive competence for the related field of external trade. Further, in the particular context of shared EU competences for environmental matters, the perceived need for concerted action leads to an inherent presumption that the EU can better deal with environmental concerns with *transnational* effects (than its Member States) and that hence the requirement of subsidiarity is met.[1] Thirdly, in the past fifteen years environmental law has increasingly been constructed through detailed international rule-making, rather than only insulated national action. Fourthly, recent environmental legal regimes largely provide for the possibility of EU participation.[2]

I would like to thank Dennis van Berkel, Anatole Boute and the two editors for their insightful comments on an earlier draft. All remaining errors are of course my own.

[1] See, for more detail, C. Eckes, 'Environmental Policy "Outside-In": How the EU's Engagement with International Environmental Law Curtails National Autonomy' (2012) 13 *German Law Journal* 1151.

[2] Prominent examples are: Kyoto Protocol on the United Nations Framework Convention on Climate Change (UNFCCC), Kyoto, Japan, 11 December 1997, (1998) 37 ILM 22; Convention on Access to Information, Public Participation in Decision-Making and Access to Justice in Environmental Matters, Aarhus, Denmark, 25 June 1998, 2161 UNTS 447;

As part of this volume's inquiry into 'the EU's shaping of the international legal order', this chapter examines the EU's attempts to globalize its climate change policies.[3] One aim is to identify evidence for the fact that under specific circumstances it can take a leading role in shaping the international legal order. Further, the chapter addresses normative questions surrounding the Union as a climate change actor capable of producing just outcomes[4] and whether and in what way climate change action could contribute to finding a way out of the Union's current *Sinnkrise*.[5]

Section 2 demonstrates that the Union has a strong mandate under the EU Treaties to reach out and pursue the Union objective of environmental protection beyond the boundaries of its own legal order. It is further institutionally well equipped to do so. Section 3 analyses the EU's participation in the international climate change regime. It discusses how the Kyoto Protocol mirrors the Union's practice of governing through targets, timetables and action plans. Furthermore, it turns to the more recent developments under the international climate change regime, including the rather inconclusive negotiations at Copenhagen (2009) and Cancun (2010) and the limited success at Durban (2011).[6] Section 4 turns to the European Union Emissions Trading Scheme (EU ETS) as a means to attain the Union's Kyoto targets but also as a unilateral means of promoting climate change mitigation internally as well as externally. Section 5 discusses a number of questions surrounding the Union's motivation to pursue external environmental policy-making. Is the Union's environmental action built on a European value system? Is it rooted in a theory of justice? Is climate change an example of the Union's *raison d'être* as a political construction that empowers citizens in times of globalization? The final section concludes that the Union makes a true commitment to climate change mitigation, as well as climate

Stockholm Convention on Persistent Organic Pollutants, Stockholm, Sweden, 22 May 2001, 2256 UNTS 119; Convention on Biological Diversity, Rio de Janeiro, Brazil, 5 June 1992, 1760 UNTS 79, with the Cartagena Protocol on Biosafety, Montreal, Canada, 29 January 2000, 2226 UNTS 20; and most recently Nagoya Protocol on Access to Genetic Resources, Nagoya, Japan, 29 October 2010, COP 10 Decision X/1.

3 For the related issue of the Union's external energy policy, see the chapters by Anatole Boute and Peter Van Elsuwege in this volume.

4 See chapter by Andrew Williams in this volume.

5 *Sinnkrise* is best translated as 'existential crisis' or 'crisis of meaning'.

6 At the time of writing this chapter, the latest United Nations Climate Change Conference at Doha, Qatar, 26 November–12 December 2012 had not yet commenced.

justice – formally, rhetorically and in practice. It pursues both a multilateral and a unilateral approach to reduce emissions and to make other states commit to do the same. While other factors play a role, such as the Union's ambitions as an international player and its integrationist agenda, justice considerations are also central to the Union's climate actions. However, whether and to what extent just climate action can serve as an example for EU leadership and contribute to addressing the Union's *Sinnkrise* is doubtful. A 'just green' agenda is worth pursuing but only as part of a broader functional, rather than philosophical, *raison d'être*.

2 The Union and the environment: codification of the EU's outreach

The Union is a complex and compound political entity with a multipolar power structure. Member States and the Union strive for influence and visibility, including on the international plane. Part of complexity of the Union's power structure is the principle of conferral.[7] The Union is empowered to act within its competences and mandate under the EU Treaties. It is therefore central for any analysis of Union policy-making to identify the scope of its mandate under the Treaties.

The Union's commitment to environmental protection, including in its external relations, is rooted in but also fragmented and qualified by the EU Treaties. The EU's aims as defined by Article 3 of the Treaty on European Union (TEU) include, in paragraph 3, sustainable development and a high level of protection of and improvement in the quality of the environment.[8] Yet, the environment is not listed as a separate aim but presented as part of the economic logic of the internal market. Similarly, the environment is given particular but auxiliary importance by the integration principle in Article 11 of the Treaty on the Functioning of the European Union (TFEU), which makes the comprehensive claim that '[e]nvironmental protection requirements must be integrated into the definition and implementation of the Union's policies and activities, in particular with a view to promoting sustainable development'.[9] This principle is a specific expression of coherency concerns that run through the (post-Lisbon) EU Treaties.

[7] Art. 5(1) TEU. [8] See also the Preamble of the TEU.

[9] See also the link between the internal market and environmental matters in Art. 3(3) TEU and Art. 114(3)(4) and (5) TFEU.

The EU's environmental objectives are encompassing and allow for a broad range of measures, including extraterritorial environmental objectives.[10] Nothing in Article 191 TFEU limits 'Union policy on the environment' to internal objectives or to the Union's territory. At the same time, Member States remain competent to adopt more stringent national measures.[11] Environmental protection is a competence shared between the EU and its Member States (Article 4(2)(e) TFEU). Articles 191, 192 and 193 TFEU set out the details of the Union's competence. Articles 191(1) and (4) TFEU address the Union's competence to take external actions to protect the environment. Article 191(2) TFEU identifies the precautionary principle and the 'polluter pays' principle as basic considerations that should guide environmental regulation, including regulation with external effects and external action, as is the case in relation to the ETS discussed in the following section.

Already prior to Lisbon, the Treaties stated that the EU can promote environmental protection in the international context. The Treaty of Lisbon per Article 191(1) TFEU adds the particular focus on combating climate change. Article 21 TEU further interlinks international law and environmental matters. It requires the EU to consider environmental preservation as part of its external objectives. More specifically, Articles 21(2)(d) and 21(2)(f) TEU declare that the EU should 'foster the sustainable economic, social and environmental development of developing countries, with the primary aim of eradicating poverty' and 'help develop international measures to preserve and improve the quality of the environment and the sustainable management of global natural resources, in order to ensure sustainable development'. Article 191(4) TFEU sets out the rules on how the Union and the Member States '[w]ithin their respective spheres of competence' shall cooperate with third countries and with the competent international organizations. It also expresses the specific concern of the Member States that the EU might pre-empt them bit by bit from being able to participate in the international environmental debate. This becomes apparent in its second subparagraph, which states that the exercise of this external power 'shall be without prejudice to Member States' competence to negotiate in international bodies and to conclude international agreements'. The Union has hence been equipped by the EU

[10] J. H. Jans and H. H. B. Vedder, *European Environmental Law: After Lisbon* (Groningen: Europa Law Publishing, 2012), p. 38.

[11] Art. 193 TFEU.

Treaties with a strong mandate to pursue climate change mitigation policy, including through external action, while at the same time Member States attempted to avoid a competence creep of the Union in the area of the environment.

Institutionally, the Union is exceptionally well equipped to pursue climate change mitigation. The Commission's Directorate General (DG) for environment is responsible for a broad range of environmental matters, such as air and water pollution and waste management. However, the Union's institutional set up isolates other environmentally relevant areas by attributing them to other DGs. Examples are fisheries conservation, control of pesticides, forestry, and organic farming, as well as energy security.[12] In February 2010, a new DG for climate change was created ('DG Clima'), which is responsible for a range of issues that were previously covered by other DGs.[13] The creation of the new DG highlights the great priority given to climate change, not only in the letter of the EU Treaties but also in institutional practice. Yet, the institutional structure reflects not only the importance but also the fragmentation of environmental protection under the EU Treaties.

3 EU external environmental agenda in action: United Nations Framework Convention on Climate Change, Kyoto Protocol and Durban Platform for Enhanced Action

The creation of the international greenhouse gas (GHG) reduction regime is a particularly interesting example of the Union's ability to shape international law. Furthermore, climate change is one of the most topical and relevant issues of global justice[14] of which the Union has taken ownership. Between the 1992 UN Conference on Environment and Development[15]

[12] See for the latter the paper from the High Representative and the European Commission to the European Council, Climate Change and International Security, S113/08, 14 March 2008.

[13] See the description provided on the 'What We Do' section of the DG Clima website, available at http://ec.europa.eu/dgs/clima/mission/index_en.htm; DG Clima has 160 Commission officials and external staff.

[14] Fundamentally: D. Miller, *National Responsibility and Global Justice* (Oxford University Press, 2007); specifically on the global injustice of climate change: J. T. Roberts and B. C. Parks, *A Climate of Injustice Global Inequality, North-South Politics, and Climate Policy* (Cambridge, Mass.: MIT Press, 2007).

[15] United Nations Conference on Environment and Development, Rio de Janerio, Brazil, 3–14 June 1992.

and the 1997 Kyoto Protocol Amendment[16] to the United Nations Framework Convention on Climate Change (UNFCCC),[17] the EU positioned itself as a leading player in the global debate on curbing greenhouse gas emissions. It participates as a Regional Economic Integration Organisation (REIO) under the UNFCCC – a category created specifically for the EU and used in other environmental agreements,[18] which, however, does not give it voting rights. EU Member States continue to hold these rights individually, but the Union can also cast their twenty-seven votes for them. The Kyoto Protocol aims to 'achieve [. . .] stabilization of greenhouse gas concentrations in the atmosphere at a level that would prevent dangerous anthropogenic interference with the climate system'.[19] The most controversial point in the negotiations surrounding the greenhouse gas reduction regime remains the question of differentiation.[20] The Kyoto Protocol crucially applies the principle of Common but Differentiated Responsibilities and Respective Capabilities (CDRRC) set out in Article 3 UNFCCC,[21] which aims at a differential treatment in favour of developing countries amongst others by imposing emissions reduction commitments only on industrialized countries and countries with economies in transition. At the same time, it does not address the historical contributions of industrialized countries, by relating industrialized countries' emissions reduction commitments to their 1990 emissions levels. This way 'the Protocol effectively grandfathered earlier emissions'.[22] A central question remains: what is a just and workable differentiation of mitigation commitments?

[16] Kyoto Protocol to the United Nations Framework Convention on Climate Change, 10 December 1997, FCCC/CP/1997/L.7/Add. 1, reprinted in (1998) 37 ILM 22.

[17] United Nations Framework Convention on Climate Change, 29 May 1992, A/AC.237/18 (Part II)/Add. 1, reprinted in (1992) 31 ILM 849

[18] The first such agreement was the 1979 Geneva Convention on Long-Range Transboundary Air Pollution, 13 November 1979, 13 UNTS 10541, reprinted in (1979) 18 ILM 1442.

[19] Art. 2 Kyoto Protcol.

[20] Durban opted for the compromise of only indirectly mentioning the principle of CDRRC (see below).

[21] Art. 3 UNFCCC states that 'parties should protect the climate system for the benefit of future and present generations of human kind on the basis of equity and in accordance with their common but differentiated responsibility and respective capabilities. Accordingly, developed countries should take the lead in combating climate change and the adverse effects thereof'. The provision does not mention the word 'principle'.

[22] J. Brunnee, 'Climate Change, Global Environmental Justice and International Environmental Law', in J. Ebbesson and P. Okowa, *Environmental Law and Justice in Context* (Cambridge University Press, 2009), p. 327.

The EU has had a great input in setting up the Kyoto Protocol, which relies on methods with which the EU has been very successful: governing through technocratic market regulation. The Union took the emerging scientific evidence seriously (acceptance of the 2° Celsius limit in contrast with other Annex I parties), led by example, offered carrots and threatened the stick to convince other countries to follow.[23] Yet, even though 'without the EU's determined leadership in the 1990s there would not have been a Kyoto Protocol',[24] the development of the climate change regime demonstrates that leadership is not an isolated phenomenon: it requires recognition and acceptance by those who are led. Already when negotiating the Kyoto Protocol the Union managed to ensure relatively ambitious targets in line with the precautionary principle, but had to give up most of the other elements of its position, including a strict command-and-control approach with policies and measures.[25] Instead, Kyoto is based on more cost-effective flexible mechanism. At the same time, elements of Kyoto mirror the Union's internal mode of governance through targets, timetables and action plans. It is based on a differentiated target-setting mechanism identifying ceilings on the emissions of greenhouse gases and dates by which these ceilings must be met. The UNFCCC obliges parties to report annually their greenhouse gas inventories and to report on their implementation progress every four years. Similar structured reporting procedures[26] are known under EU law, with its strong institutionalized compliance assessment mechanisms.[27] Self-reporting on implementation progress is a commonly used tool for enhancing compliance with EU directives, including under environmental legislation.[28] The Union also supports its Member

[23] See the following section on the EU Emissions Trading Scheme (ETS) for a specific example of the 'carrot and stick' policy.

[24] R. Wurzel and J. Connelly, 'The European Union as a Leader in International Climate Change Politics', in Rüdiger Wurzel and James Connelly (eds.), *The European Union as a Leader in International Climate Change Politics* (Abingdon: Routledge, 2011), p. 272. See also H. Compston and I. Bailey (eds.), *Turning Down the Heat* (Basingstoke: Palgrave Macmillan, 2008).

[25] L. van Schaik and S. Schunz, 'Explaining EU Activism and Impact in Global Climate Politics: Is the Union a Norm- or Interest-Driven Actor?' (2012) 50 *Journal of Common Market Studies* 169 (179–80).

[26] Art. 7(4) Kyoto Protocol.

[27] Analysing the EU's combination of enforcement and management approaches: Jonas Tallberg, 'Paths to Compliance: Enforcement, Management, and the European Union' (2002) 56 *International Organization* 609.

[28] Art. 17 Habitats Directive requires Member States to report every six years about the progress made with its implementation. Council Directive 92/43/EEC of 21 May 1992 on

States in their international reporting obligations.[29] The UNFCCC and the Kyoto Protocol are examples of international institution-building for a specific substantive purpose. The market-based mechanisms included in the Kyoto Protocol that provide schemes of joint implementation amongst developed countries and between developed and developing countries require a comprehensive and quite laborious administrative apparatus to function smoothly. Under international law the Kyoto Protocol remains one of the exceptions that provide for an enforcement mechanism that can invoke sanctions. The enforcement branch of the Kyoto Compliance Committee is responsible for determining whether a Party included in Annex I (Annex I Party) is not in compliance with its emissions targets, the methodological and reporting requirements for greenhouse gas inventories, and the eligibility requirements under the mechanisms.[30] It can make a declaration of non-compliance, require the party to submit a compliance action plan, suspending a party's eligibility to use the Kyoto trade mechanisms, and deduct excess emissions during the first commitment period (times 1.3) from the assigned amount of emissions in the second commitment period.[31]

The EU made a great contribution to the creation and internal set-up of the Kyoto Protocol; yet the substantive success of the Kyoto Protocol in terms of real greenhouse gas reduction remains limited, and some go as far as criticizing it for standing in the way of progress to international climate change mitigation.[32] The Kyoto Protocol enforcement mechanism[33] might be a lesser problem than the lack of a broader

the conservation of natural habitats and of wild fauna and flora. EU waste legislation also imposes various reporting obligations on Member States. See http://ec.europa.eu/environment/waste/legislation/d.htm.

[29] The European Environmental Agency, for instance, runs a Reporting Obligations Database (ROD), available at http://rod.eionet.europa.eu/.

[30] See Art. 18 Kyoto Protocol and for meetings and documents of the enforcement branch, available at http://unfccc.int/kyoto_protocol/compliance/enforcement_branch/items/3785.php. See also Xueman Wang and Glenn Wiser, 'The Implementation and Compliance Regimes under the Climate Change Convention and its Kyoto Protocol' (2002) 11.2 *Review of European Community and International Environmental Law* 181.

[31] Annex to Decision 27/CMP.1 on Procedures and Mechanisms Relating to Compliance under the Kyoto Protocol, 92, FCCC/KP/CMP/2005/8/Add. 3, 30 March 2006 (hereinafter 'Compliance Procedures'), Part XV, Consequences Applied by the Enforcement Branch, p. 75.

[32] See e.g. www.guardian.co.uk/commentisfree/2011/dec/08/kyoto-fail-durban-climate-conference. Accessed on 20 November 2012.

[33] Critical: Jon Hovi, et al., 'A Credible Compliance Enforcement System for the Climate Regime' (2012) 12 *Climate Policy* 741.

political will to make commitments that can be enforced. The two greatest polluters, the US and China, have not committed to emissions reduction obligations under the Kyoto Protocol.[34] For about three-quarters of total global emissions no binding reduction commitment has been made.[35] Furthermore, it was doubtful for a long time whether a second commitment period would follow. In 2009, the Copenhagen Accord failed to include any binding targets.[36] This was due to a range of factors, including lack of unity of the Member States,[37] and led immediately to questions regarding the Union's ability to take international leadership.[38] One year later, the Cancun Agreements (2010)[39] adopted the 2° Celsius target as a benchmark but equally failed to include legally binding commitments. In 2011 the Durban Platform[40] advanced the climate change agenda in several aspects. It implemented the Cancun commitments, extended the Kyoto Protocol for a second commitment period and initiated a process to negotiate a post-2020 climate regime. However, several important issues are left to the negotiations in Qatar in 2012, such as the length of the commitment period post-2020 and the ambition of individual countries to limit emissions. The ongoing international debate concerns in particular the issue of 'differentiation'. By contrast with the UNFCCC and the Kyoto Protocol, the Durban Platform does not specifically mention the CDRRC principle. This leaves

34 The US signed but did not ratify. China is a non-Annex I country and hence not bound by emissions reduction obligations.

35 World Resources Institute, Climate Analysis Indicators Tool (CAIT), available at http://cait.wri.org.

36 Dec. 2/CP.15, FCCC/CP/2009/11/Add. 1 (30 March 2010). See also European Parliament Resolution of 10 February 2010 on the outcome of the Copenhagen Conference on Climate Change (COP 15), P7_TA(2010)0019, available at www.europarl.europa.eu/sides/getDoc.do?type=TA&reference=P7-TA-2010-0019&language=EN.

37 European Parliament Resolution on the Copenhagen Conference, para. 5. A specific example of how the lack of unity hampered the Union's negotiation position is the delay of the financial deal that it offered to developing countries; similarly, see van Schaik and Schunz, 'Explaining EU Activism', p. 182.

38 J.-P. Lehmann, 'Fallout from Copenhagen: Has the EU Lost its Global Relevance?', *YaleGlobal*, 5 January 2010, available at http://yaleglobal.yale.edu/content/fallout-copenhagen-has-eu-lost-its-global-relevance.

39 Dec. 1/CP.16, FCCC/CP/2010/7/Add. 1 (15 March 2011) and Dec. 1/CMP.6, FCCC/KP/CMP/2010/12/Add. 1 (15 March 2011).

40 Dec. 1/CP.17, FCCC/CP/2011/9/Add. 1 (15 March 2012); for information about the COP and related documents, see http://unfccc.int/meetings/durban_nov_2011/meeting/6245.php; see for an analysis: L. Rajamani, 'The Durban Platform for Enhanced Action and the Future of the Climate Regime' (2012) 61.2 *International and Comparative Law Quarterly* 501.

room for debate. One can argue on the one hand that it contains a reference to the UNFCCC as a whole (which sets out the CDRRC) and to the right of developing countries to emit to develop. On the other hand, it envisages an 'agreed outcome with legal force' 'applicable to all countries', which is widely understood to mean that developing countries should in future take on obligations of emissions reduction. The considerable difference in aggregated effect of current mitigation pledges between countries persists. What do we do with this 'ambition gap', which above all reflects a fundamental difference in attitude? Climate change mitigation, by definition, lacks direct reciprocity. The reduction of emissions by one state benefits all. This requires states to make commitments to the public good without being able to avoid free-riding. All states are part of a broader game that is characterized by strong interdependency, in which developed countries depend on developing countries to choose a low-carbon development path,[41] while (at least some) developing countries will shoulder particularly high costs of climate changes directly related to disproportionately high emissions of developed countries.[42] The (perceived) lack of reciprocity was also the core reason why the US withdrew from the Kyoto Protocol, because China – since 2008 the greatest emitter in absolute terms[43] – did not enter into the mutual exchange of obligations. In the Durban negotiations, the US insisted on 'symmetry' of obligations between developed and developing countries. The debate demonstrates a deeper chasm of attitude. While both the US and China hold back on their commitments and favour a long timeline for reduction commitments to start, the EU and those countries particularly affected by climate change argued in favour of short timelines at Durban and refused to allow the work plan for enhancing mitigation ambition to vanish from the agenda.[44] Furthermore, for internal political reasons it is impossible to move binding multilateral (environmental) treaties through the US Congress[45] – this

[41] J. Goodman, 'Climate Change and Global Development: Towards a Post-Kyoto Paradigm?' (2012) 23.1 *Economic and Labour Relations Review* 107 (109).

[42] See Potsdam Institute for Climate Impact Research and Analytics, 'Turning Down the Heat: Why a 4°C Warmer World Must Be Avoided', *World Bank* Report, 18 November 2012, available at http://climatechange.worldbank.org/sites/default/files/Turn_Down_the_heat_Why_a_4_degree_centrigrade_warmer_world_must_be_avoided.pdf.

[43] World Resources Institute, Climate Analysis Indicators Tool, n. 35.

[44] Durban Platform, para. 7.

[45] G. Banga, J. Hovi and D. Sprinz, 'US Presidents and the Failure to Ratify Multilateral Environmental Agreements' (2012) 6:1 *Climate Policy* 755; T. Skodvin and S. Andresen,

problem is not new nor does it appear that it will change any time soon.[46] Considerations of reciprocity played a broader role. The remaining, fully committed Kyoto Annex I Parties (EU, Australia, New Zealand, Norway and Switzerland) agreed to a second commitment period *conditional* on the agreement of a roadmap towards legally binding commitments from all parties.[47]

The creation and development of the international greenhouse gas reduction regime has proven a cumbersome task. The Union has applied its strength in setting up a regulatory regime but it has only partially been successful in convincing other great emitters to commit under this regime. One suggested method of enhancing the overall commitment to greenhouse gas reduction is empowering lower-scale action[48] rather than international rule-making. However, where such local or even regional climate change policy has external consequences, one open question remains: who should determine policies aimed at preserving a global public good and with what legitimation?

4 European Union Emissions Trading Scheme: is there a unilateralist way towards multilateralism?

Internally, the EU has pursued a model of differentiated climate governance by allocating different targets to reduce greenhouse gases to each of the Member States, including in the areas of transport, agriculture and waste.[49] Starting from a model of interstate negotiation in the context of the Kyoto Protocol it has moved to establishing national

'An Agenda for Change in US Climate Policies? Presidential Ambitions and Congressional Powers' (2009) 9:3 *International Environmental Agreements: Politics, Law and Economics* 263.

[46] The most frustrating historical example is perhaps President Woodrow Wilson's failure to have the Senate ratify the treaty establishing the League of Nations.

[47] Canada, Japan and Russia received an effective relaxation of their emissions targets.

[48] Prominently, E. Ostrom, 'Nested Externalities and Polycentric Institutions: Must We Wait for Global Solutions to Climate Change before Taking Actions at Other Scales?' (2010) 49 *Econ Theory* 353. An example of lower-scale governance is California's emissions cap-and-trade-scheme, which was introduced after cap-and-trade failed nationally.

[49] See the 'Effort-sharing Decision' 406/2009/EC of 23 April 2009 on the effort of Member States to reduce their greenhouse gas emissions to meet the Community's greenhouse gas emissions reduction commitments up to 2020, OJ 2009 L 140/136, in particular Art. 8. See also C. Haug and A. Jordan, 'Burden Sharing: Distributing Burdens or Sharing Efforts?', in A. Jordan, et al. (eds.), *Climate Change Policy in the European Union: Confronting the Dilemmas of Mitigation and Adaptation*? (Cambridge University Press, 2010), p. 83.

targets, including in legislation such as the Renewable Energy Directive of 2009.[50] The flagship of European climate policy, the EU ETS,[51] was met with sharp international criticism when it was extended to cover emissions attributable to aviation.[52] It included emissions of third-country carriers on flights in and out of Europe in order to improve its environmental effectiveness and to ensure a level playing field by avoiding distortions of competition between European and third-country carriers.[53] It obliges operators to surrender each year a number of allowances equal to their *actual* emissions (rather than only those produced within the Union) and threatens considerable penalties in the case of non-compliance.[54] Internationally, the inclusion of aviation in the ETS was called everything from 'discriminatory' and a 'violation of international law'[55] to 'an attack on other countries' sovereignty.'[56] More analytical critics questioned whether the ETS gives adequate weight to the above-mentioned CDRRC principle.[57] 'Driven by competitiveness concerns' the Union required compliance with the ETS by all businesses active in the EU market irrespective of their origin.[58] The ETS has also been challenged before the Court of Justice of the European Union (ECJ).

[50] Directive 2009/28/EC of 23 April 2009 on the promotion of the use of energy from renewable sources and amending and subsequently repealing Directives 2001/77/EC and 2003/30/EC, OJ (2009) L 140/16.

[51] Directive 2008/101/EC of the European Parliament and of the Council of 19 November 2008 amending Directive 2003/87/EC so as to include aviation activities in the scheme for greenhouse gas emissions allowance trading within the Community, OJ (2008) L 8/3. The ETS is charged to account for about 40 per cent of the Kyoto reduction commitments. C. Damro and D. MacKenzie, 'The European Union and the Politics of Multi-Level Climate Governance', in Compston and Bailey (eds.), *Turning Down the Heat*, p. 65.

[52] In November 2012, the implementation of the extension to foreign carriers was delayed by one year as a result of the international resistance and with the hope to reach an international agreement. See J. Chaffin and A. Parker, 'EU Freezes Foreign Airline Carbon Charge', *Financial Times*, 12 November 2012, available at www.ft.com/intl/cms/s/0/52716c10-2cc8-11e2-9211-00144feabdc0.html#axzz2CgbeoKpN. Days later, the US House passed a bill barring US airlines from paying penalties under the ETS.

[53] Recital 16 of the Preamble to Directive 2008/101/EC.

[54] Penalty of €100 per tonne CO_2. Art. 16(3), Directive 2008/101/EC.

[55] C. Voigt, 'Up in the Air: Aviation in the EU Emission Trading Scheme and the Question of Sovereignty', Presentation at the Centre for European Legal Studies, University of Cambridge, 15 February 2012, citing S. N. A. Zaidi, Civil Aviation Secretary of India at the Durban negotiations.

[56] *Ibid.*, citing the joined Statement by China and Russia, 27 September 2011.

[57] J. Scott and L. Rajamani, 'EU Climate Change Unilateralism' (2012) 23 *European Journal of International Law* 469.

[58] *Ibid.*, p. 481.

The case brought by a group of US airlines and their trade association challenged the validity of the Aviation Directive[59] in light of international agreements and customary law in so far as that Directive extends the ETS to the part of flights that takes place outside the airspace of EU Member States. On 21 December 2011 the Court upheld the inclusion of aviation within the ETS,[60] pointing out that the extension of the ETS to aviation did not infringe principles of customary international law, such as the principle that each state has complete and exclusive sovereignty over its airspace, that aircraft overflying the high seas are subject to the exclusive jurisdiction of the country in which they are registered, and the freedom to fly over the high seas. Neither Advocate General Kokott nor the ECJ saw difficulties with external effects of the Union's unilateral approach to climate change. Indeed, both specifically pointed out the necessity of an inclusive approach to greenhouse gas emissions with global consequences.[61] The Court further pointed to the precautionary and the 'polluter pays' principle in Article 191(2) TFEU and emphasized the territorial link that the ETS concerned businesses active on EU territory.[62] The ETS consists of domestic measures that use market mechanisms to hold external emitters of greenhouse gases financially responsible. At the same time, the Union continues the international debate on emissions trading systems. The ETS is explicitly aiming to become part of a future 'global network of emission[s] trading systems'[63] and in August 2012 Australia and the Union agreed, despite the considerable technical challenges,[64] on a pathway towards fully linking their emissions trading systems

59 Directive 2008/101/EC.

60 Case C-366/10, *Air Transport Association of America and Others* v. *Secretary of State for Energy and Climate Change* (ATAA case) 2011 ECR I-0000.

61 *Ibid.*, para. 129. Opinion of Advocate General Kokott of 6 October 2011 in Case C-366/10, ATAA case, para. 154.

62 Case C-366/10, ATAA case, para. 128.

63 Art. 25, Directive 2009/29/EC of the European Parliament and of the Council of 23 April 2009 on amending Directive 2003/87/EC so as to improve and extend the greenhouse gas emissions allowance trading scheme of the Community OJ L 140/63; see also, Commission, 'Questions and Answers on the Commission's Proposal to Revise the ETS', MEMO/08/35 of 23 January 2008, available at http://europa.eu/rapid/pressReleasesAction.do?reference=MEMO/08/35; European Parliament, 'Climate Change and the Environment', available at http://circa.europa.eu/irc/opoce/fact_sheets/info/data/policies/environment/article_7298_en.htm.

64 G. Metcalf and D. Weisbachy, 'Linking Policies When Tastes Differ: Global Climate Policy in a Heterogeneous World', Harvard Project on International Climate Agreements Discussion Paper 2010-38, July 2010, Belfer Center for Science and International Affairs,

in practice.[65] It was only after sharp international criticism and the International Civil Aviation Organization agreeing to establish a high-level group to develop a global system to tackle airlines' carbon emissions by the time of its next general assembly in September 2013 that the EU delayed implementation of the ETS extension to foreign carriers.[66]

The ETS is to some extent the answer to the question: What will the Union do if it has reached the end of the multilateral governance road? The ETS is an example of where the Union reached the limits of participation in international negotiations and turned towards unilateral action. It unilaterally pursued the substantive objective of protecting the environment, with the continuous secondary motive to lead by example.[67] The great uncertainties on the international plane have led to the acceptance that potentially a choice has to be made between measures pursuing the objective of climate change mitigation and the broader goal of promoting effective multilateralism, which has been a longstanding commitment of the EU and is explicitly enshrined in the EU Treaties.[68] This is not to say that the ETS was designed with a blind eye towards international developments. On the contrary, the EU has also increasingly made climate change a subject in its bilateral relations,[69] the Commission monitors internal measures in light of the outcome of international negotiations,[70] and the ETS was created with the intention of joining it with the emerging carbon market in the US and elsewhere, eventually to create a global carbon market.[71] In short,

Harvard Kennedy School, available at http://belfercenter.ksg.harvard.edu/publication/20264/linking_policies_when_tastes_differ.html.

65 European Commission and Australian Minister Combet, joint press release, 'Australia and European Commission Agree on Pathway Towards Fully Linking Emissions Trading Systems', IP/12/916, Brussels, 28 August 2012, available at http://europa.eu/rapid/press-release_IP-12-916_en.htm.

66 See n. 52.

67 K. Kulovesi, 'Climate Change in EU External Relations: Please Follow My Example (Or I Might Force You To)', in E. Morgera, *The External Environmental Policy of the European Union: EU and International Law Perspectives* (Cambridge University Press, 2012), p. 115.

68 Art. 21(1) TEU. European Union, 'The Enlarging European Union at the United Nations: Making Multilateralism Matter', April 2004, available at http://eeas.europa.eu/organisations/un/docs/eu-un_en.pdf.

69 E. Morgera, 'Relevance beyond Borders: Recent Developments in the EU' (2010) 40 *Environmental Policy and Law* 234.

70 European Commission, 'Analysis of Options to Move beyond 20% Greenhouse Gas Emission Reductions and Assessing the Risk of Carbon Leakage', 26 May 2010, COM (2010) 265 final. See also, Art. 28 (1), Directive 2009/29/EC, n. 63.

71 European Parliament Resolution on the Copenhagen Conference, para. 13.

the Union pursues a multilateral governance mode in its external environmental policy; however, where this governance mode fails to deliver an acceptable outcome it is willing to prioritize substance over structural and relationship considerations and move to unilateral action.

It is likely that other unilateral measures of the Union will be criticized, such as banning certain credits under the Clean Development Mechanism as of May 2013, e.g. the destruction of certain greenhouse gases, which will produce large amounts of cheap credits and lead to distortion and perverse incentives.[72] The unilateral ban on these credits under the ETS was indeed a direct reaction to the stalled negotiations under the Kyoto Protocol, where this issue was equally brought up. In 2007, the EU offered an unconditional '20–20 by 2020' in which it offered a 20 per cent reduction target and 20 per cent target for the use of renewable energy. Beyond this, as a 'carrot', it offered a 30 per cent reduction target if other developed countries committed to comparable actions.[73] At the same time, the Union threatened the stick of border tax adjustments to avoid greenhouse gas emissions 'leaking' from the EU without the intended overall reduction and the entailed economic damage to the EU.

Stalled negotiations similarly fuelled plans for requiring EU importers of energy-intensive products to purchase emissions allowances equivalent to the greenhouse gas emissions caused by the manufacturing of these products. However, the latter seem to be off the table for the moment.[74] Furthermore, there are several other EU environmental measures that attempt to strike a balance between effective multilateralism in order to reach an international solution and necessary unilateralism aimed at ensuring substantive progress of environmental protection.[75]

5 Motivated by a 'European' value system?

The Union has a clear formal and practical commitment to climate change mitigation. Is this commitment grounded in and motivated by

[72] See e.g. Directorate-General for Climate Action, 'Commission Adopts Ban on Industrial Gas Credits', 8 June 2011, available at http://ec.europa.eu/clima/news/articles/news_2011060801_en.htm.

[73] European Council, Presidency Conclusions, 8–9 March 2007, p. 31.

[74] See http://ec.europa.eu/clima/policies/ets/cap/leakage/index_en.htm.

[75] See e.g. Directive 2009/31/EC of 23 April 2009 on the geological storage of carbon dioxide, OJ (2009) L 140/114, which is aimed to bring an inspiring example of domestic legislation to the negotiation under the UNFCCC and the Kyoto Protocol.

a European value system? Is it an ethical commitment in that it is based on a theory of justice?

5.1 *Climate justice*

The Union emphasizes two reoccurring normative points in its climate change discourse: first, that it 'leads by example', and second, that it is willing to take an approach of 'differentiated responsibilities' because it is 'particularly concerned about the additional challenges that developing countries face'.[76] Commission President Barosso identified 'climate change justice' as a core policy priority of the Union and argued that this should be reflected in the budget.[77] Margot Wallström called climate justice 'our moral obligation' in the prelude to the Copenhagen Climate Conference in December 2009, and argued that 'Copenhagen must deliver a global agreement based on social and development needs, burden sharing and the "polluter pays principle"',[78] pointing out that '[d]eveloping countries will need substantial financial and technological assistance from the industrialised world'.[79] The European Parliament specifically '[c]all[ed] on the EU and its Member States to enforce the principle of "climate justice" in the long-term perspective 2050 and beyond'.[80] Hence, beyond and besides economic or other *interests*, the European climate debate also expresses normative standpoints or *values*. Union officials cannot be accused of shying away from making ethical considerations explicit.

The Union has been criticized for approaching the environment through an economic lens, using 'the exigencies of the market as a sort

[76] See e.g. http://ec.europa.eu/clima/publications/docs/supporting_a_climate_for_change_en.pdf. For a discourse analysis of the EU's climate change policy, see e.g. S. Scheipers and D. Sicurelli, 'Normative Power Europe: A Credible Utopia?' (2007) 45.2 *Journal of Common Market Studies* 435; S. Baker, 'Environmental Values and Climate Change Policy: Contrasting the European Union and the United States', in S. Lucarelli and I. Manners (eds.), *Values and Principles in European Union Foreign Policy* (Abingdon: Routledge, 2006).

[77] Statement of President Barroso on the budget review, 19 October 2010, available at http://ec.europa.eu/commission_2010-2014/president/pdf/statement_en.pdf.

[78] M. Wallström (Vice President of the European Commission), 'The Low-Carbon Economy: A Necessity and an Opportunity', Presidency Conference on Climate and Jobs: The EU's Global Agenda, 9 September 2009, Palais des Beaux-Arts, Brussels, available at http://europa.eu/rapid/press-release_SPEECH-09-377_en.htm?locale=en.

[79] *Ibid.*

[80] European Parliament Resolution on the Copenhagen Conference.

of value surrogacy'.[81] Broader EU environmental policy may to some extent be a spill-over from the Union's primary concern of trade liberalization both within the single market and outside.[82] This goes to the heart of the broader criticism of how the Union manages market and non-market values.[83] However, the ETS is different from production requirements, such as, for instance, the safe use of certain chemicals. The latter largely have effects for the immediate surroundings of the production area. The main argument in favour of emissions trading is that pollution reduction takes place where the costs of reduction are the lowest. Economists regard cap-and-trade schemes as the most cost-efficient way of reaching pollution reductions.[84] Furthermore, Union policy-making on the environment has been stirred by both idealistic and economic factors. On the one hand, a few environmentally minded Member States pushed forward;[85] on the other, the desire to harmonize regulations inside the single market was a major driving force. Domestic politics and the green agenda of a few 'pioneer states' like Germany, Austria and Sweden, coupled with the pressure exerted by some domestic constituencies that wanted to ensure that the other Member States adapted to their 'higher' standards, and not vice-versa (a form of regulatory competition), was central to the development of EU climate policy.[86] As in other policy areas, internal political and economic considerations play an important role.[87] Intergovernmentalist theories

[81] A. Williams, 'Promoting Justice after Lisbon: Groundwork for a New Philosophy of EU Law' (2010) 30 *Oxford Journal of Legal Studies* 663.

[82] See Art. 3(3) TEU; J. McCormick, *Environmental Policy in the European Union* (Basingstoke: Palgrave Macmillan, 2001) 18; C. Bretherton and J. Vogler, *The European Union as a Global Actor* (Abingdon: Routledge, 1999), p. 85.

[83] See e.g. M. Rhodes, 'The Social Dimension of the Single European Market: National versus Transnational Regulation' (1991) 19 *European Journal of Political Research* 245. F. Scharpf, 'The European Social Model' (2002) 40 *Journal of Common Market Studies* 645.

[84] This is well explained by J. Peace and R. N. Stavins: 'In Brief. Meaningful and Cost Effective Climate Policy: The Case for Cap and Trade', Pew Center on Global Climate Change, June 2010, available at www.c2es.org/publications/meaningful-and-cost-effective-climate-policy-case-cap-and-trade.

[85] Part III of Wurzel and Connelly, *The European Union as a Leader* analyses in detail the positions of UK, France, Germany, Netherlands, Poland and Spain. National positions are nuanced. Germany, for example, protected its heavy industry under risk from international competition by negotiating free emissions rights.

[86] See on the power increase of 'green political parties', in the EU: L. Röpke, et al., 'Kurz zum Klima: Europas grüne (R)Evolution' (2012) 65 *ifo Schnelldienst* 51–2.

[87] See for the case of GMOs, R. Falkner, 'The European Union as a "Green Normative Power"? EU Leadership in International Biotechnology Regulation' (2007) 14 *Journal of European Public Policy* 507.

demonstrate that the growing importance of the environmental policy, while reflecting a growing internal value system, is also directly linked to the intricacies of the Union's policy-making process, i.e. that the EU's leadership (ambitions) in climate policy-making is a 'dynamic process of competitive multi-level reinforcement among the different EU political poles within a context of decentralized governance'.[88] The EU's inner multipolar rather than hierarchical organization has been one factor in the EU's external climate change policy-making. However, justice has actually been given a prominent role in the climate change debate – more so than economic interests, such as the interests of resource-rich countries and the fossil-fuel interests in US politics.[89] Supported by a value-guided language in Article 37 of the Charter of Fundamental Rights and in the EU Treaties the Union has been successful in phrasing climate change as an issue of human rights and of justice.[90] Justice might not be enough to guide the Union's decision-making in all respects but it has supported a strong normative argument that it is unjust to prosper at the cost of public good and ultimately at the cost of those who are geographically or economically less well placed to adapt to the changing climate.

However, what should be the Union's position when an ethical standpoint stands in the way of political effectiveness considerations? The two questions of 'what is just?' and 'what is best for the environment?' do not necessarily lead to the same answer. Even if the EU Member States agreed on an approach to climate change mitigation that is supported by a theory of justice and aimed to promote it this way, their approach would not necessarily be the best way to achieve the greatest positive outcome for the environment. A finely balanced compromise that convinces more states that represent the greatest share of emissions to enter into a legally binding commitment to reduce emissions and comply with them is better for the environment than a just (and hence high) commitment

[88] M. A. Schreurs and Y. Tiberghien, 'Multi-Level Reinforcement: Explaining European Union Leadership in Climate Change Mitigation' (2007) 7.4 *Global Environmental Politics* 19. See for a critique: A. Jordan, H. van Asselt, F. Berkhout, D. Huitema and T. Rayne, 'Understanding the Paradoxes of Multilevel Governing: Climate Change Policy in the European Union' (2012) 12 *Global Environmental Politics* 43

[89] A. Bowen, '"Globalisation in an Age of Crisis", Remarks on "Facing the Climate Change Challenge in a Global Economy" by L. Branstetter and W. Pizer', NBER Conference, Bank of England, 15 September 2011.

[90] E.g. State of the Union 2012, p. 16, available at http://ec.europa.eu/soteu2012/files/soeu_web.pdf; see also specifically focused on climate change and development: http://ec.europa.eu/clima/publications/docs/supporting_a_climate_for_change_en.pdf.

to mitigation by a group of states that only represent about a quarter of all emissions. The justice argument simply is not accepted by some of the greatest emitters[91] and it might ultimately prove counterproductive to the objective of effective climate change mitigation. This tension between the ethically right position and the most effective strategy to achieve the greatest possible effect on the preservation of a public good goes to the heart of the discussion on the Union's debate about its *raison d'être*. Does the Union need to develop a more value-informed ethical understanding of its role and added value, or does it need to take a functional approach and contribute to solving pressing problems in a governance mode?

5.2 Values: constructing identity and serving interests

Marise Cremona interestingly distinguished between a 'constitutive' and 'instrumentalist' dimension of Union values.[92] The first refers to values as a 'characteristic of the Union's identity' and the second to values as the key to achieving specific Union objectives. It is argued here that value questions are central to climate change mitigation, which aims to preserve a public good for the long-term and potentially requires sacrificing certain national, often economic, interests in the short term. The value discourse underlying the Union's climate change policies serves both the 'instrumentalist' and the 'constitutive' dimension of values.

As regards the first 'instrumentalist' dimension, the value of environmental protection has served as justification for 'European integration' in the form of harmonization of product requirements as well as other forms of market integration and trade simplification.[93] Global environmental concerns come with a presumption that action at a bigger scale, i.e. measures covering a greater percentage of the world population or a greater share of the territory where emissions are produced or consumed, is more effective and will therefore relatively easily satisfy the subsidiarity requirement. In this light, Member States' attempts in the EU Treaties to protect their competences from the pre-emptive effect

[91] For US views, see the following section, below.

[92] M. Cremona, 'Values in the EU Constitution: The External Dimension', in M. Millns and S. Aziz (eds.), *Values in the Constitution of Europe* (Dartmouth: Ashgate, 2004).

[93] For the Commission's policy on regulation of the internal market and the environment, see http://ec.europa.eu/enterprise/policies/single-market-goods/internal-market-for-products/index_en.htm and http://ec.europa.eu/environment/integration/internal_market_en.htm.

of Union exercise of external environmental powers is understandable, even though unsuccessful.[94]

As to the 'constitutive' dimension, the Union's surprisingly united position on the necessity to mitigate climate change cannot be seen in isolation. Climate change is an issue to which the US and other powerful nations take a far more nationalistic or inward-looking approach[95] that is blocking advances in international cooperation. Hence, the Union's position has found a clear opponent in the US and a number of other states. Just as in the International Criminal Court (ICC), climate change is an example of the EU uniting in the face of opposition. Indeed, the US has a fundamentally different understanding of global environmental responsibility or 'climate justice'. Even in the Obama administration, which accepts the scientific evidence of escalating anthropogenic climate change, the basic ethical understanding of 'do no harm', i.e. no nation has the right to harm the global public good for its own benefit,[96] is not widely accepted, while 'do no harm' is the ethical core of the 'precautionary principle' under EU law.[97] It is politically impossible to take into account effects of domestic emissions that occur outside of the US in impact assessments of US legislation. This difference becomes further apparent in an article on climate justice co-authored by Cass Sunstein,[98] which discusses climate change in terms of corrective and distributive justice (rather than a question of 'do no harm') and compares climate change mitigation with development aid.[99]

The contrast between the EU and the US discourse is what helped in forming a relatively strong EU position. By being on one side of the scale

[94] Art. 191(4) TFEU; see also Eckes, 'Environmental Policy "Outside-In"'.

[95] Climate change is not a widespread concern or an issue in the broader public debate. It was not mentioned at any point in the three presidential debates in October 2012. President Obama, however, did refer to climate change in his victory speech on 6 November 2012.

[96] See specifically on why 'the world beyond a country's borders cannot but come into the assessment of justice in a country': A. Sen, *The Idea of Justice* (Cambridge, Mass.: Harvard University Press, 2009), pp. 71–2.

[97] S. Gardiner, 'Ethics and Global Climate Change', 114 *Ethics* (April 2004) 555 (576).

[98] From September 2009 to August 2012, Sunstein was the head of the Office of Information and Regulatory Affairs (OIRA), a unit of the White House Office of Management and Budget that reviews every regulation proposed by an executive branch agency. The importance of Cass Sunstein in the Obama administrations is illustrated by the fact that he was called 'Regulatory Tsar'. For a critical account, see J. M. Broder, 'Powerful Shaper of US Rules Quits with Critics in Wake', *New York Times*, 3 August 2012, available at www.nytimes.com/2012/08/04/science/earth/cass-sunstein-to-leave-top-regulatory-post.html?_r=0.

[99] E. A. Posner and C. R. Sunstein, 'Climate Change Justice' (2008) 96 *Georgetown Law Journal* 1566.

of possible approaches to climate change mitigation, smaller differences within the EU became less important in comparison to the group that was blocking progress on the international plane. The EU assumed a leading role, which became part of its (self-created) image as successful international player, acting for a green and just cause. Identity theories confirm the relevance of opposition for the creation of a 'self'. Identity expresses the 'self' as distinguished from 'others'.[100] The details of how national (here European) identity is shaped are contentious, but the core of identity remains *distinction over time*.[101] Identity emerges by contrast to the 'foreign'.[102] Climate change policy is a good example of how a sense of opposition to the US contributes to constructing an external identity of the Union. This of course raises the question of whether the EU can only successfully take leadership when it is acting in opposition.

Scholars, philosophers and policy-makers have suggested that empowering Europeans in the age of globalization could become the *raison d'être* of the Union.[103] Yet, is the Union the natural response to globalization challenges? Does it offer a better response because of size? What is needed to convince citizens of the value and need for Union, particularly at a time of economic crisis where citizens are asked to make sacrifices for its continued existence? Originally, the Union (the EEC) was founded to address the most pressing problems of the European continent at the time: peace and economic recovery. Since then it has

[100] E. T. Olson, 'Personal Identity', in Edward N. Zalta (ed.), *The Stanford Encyclopedia of Philosophy* (2002), available at http://plato.stanford.edu/archives/fall2002/entries/identity-personal.

[101] D. Miller, *Citizenship and National Identity* (Oxford: John Wiley and Sons, 2000); David Miller, *On Nationality* (Oxford University Press, 1995); A. D. Smith, *National Identity* (Harmondsworth: Penguin Books, 1991); William Bloom, *Personal Identity, National Identity and International Relations* (New York: Cambridge University Press, 1990); P. Boerner (ed.), *Concepts of National Identity: An Interdisciplinary Dialogue – Interdisziplinäre Betrachtungen zur Frage der nationalen Identität* (Baden-Baden: Nomos Verlagsgesellschaft, 1986).

[102] Smith, *National Identity*, p. 8.

[103] U. Beck, 'Europa als Antwort auf die Globalisierung', in H.-U. Joerges (ed.), *Der Kampf um den Euro: Wie riskant ist die Waehrungsunion*? (Hamburg: Hoffmann and Campe, 1998), p. 19; P. Bofinger, J. Habermas and J. Nida-Rümelin, 'Einspruch gegen die Fassadendemokratie', *Frankfurter Allgemeinen Zeitung*, 3 August 2012, available at www.faz.net/aktuell/feuilleton/kurswechsel-fuer-europa-einspruch-gegen-die-fassadendemokratie-11842820.html; J. Habermas, *Zur Verfassung Europas – Ein Essay* (Berlin: Suhrkamp, 2011); J. M. Barroso, 'Political Guidelines for the Next Commission', 3 August 2009, available at http://ec.europa.eu/commission_2010-2014/president/pdf/press_20090903_en.pdf.

grown into a comprehensive and powerful economic and political entity far beyond the limited framework of other international organizations. A *raison d'être* today would first have to address current pressing (economic) problems in which the populations of all Member States are interested. Beyond this, it would have to justify a political construction as comprehensive and powerful as the Union. A unified external environmental agenda as such does not meet either of these two requirements – despite certain synergies between climate change policy and energy security and the economic advantages of climate change policy, such as the export of energy-efficient products.[104] At the same time, an environmental policy with climate change at its core could make a substantive contribution the Union's identity as a political entity that empowers EU citizens in a globalized world.[105] Arguably, it might have even greater identity appeal if it is formulated as part of a comprehensive value system and built on a theory of justice. Yet, a philosophically convincing theory of justice or a compelling system of values that is not translatable in real life successes towards the solution of existing problems will not satisfy the Union's critics. The Union's climate change mitigation efforts demonstrate this. Ultimately, this brings us to the rather uninspiring conclusion that functionality (output legitimacy)[106] must be part of any *raison d'être* of the Union. This was also the tone of the most recent 'New Vision of Europe'.[107]

6 Conclusion

The Union takes the role of an independent player alongside the Member States in the area of environmental policy. The Kyoto Protocol and the

[104] L. M. Brown, A. Hanafi and A. Petsonk, 'The EU Emissions Trading System – Results and Lessons Learned', Environmental Defense Fund Report, 2012, available at www.edf.org/sites/default/files/EU_ETS_Lessons_Learned_Report_EDF.pdf.

[105] See on this point J. Habermas, *Zur Verfassung Europas*, in particular the final chapter.

[106] 'Output legitimacy' relates to the effectiveness and efficiency of policy-making, i.e. the performance of the political entity. In the context of the EU, the concept has received much attention in the democratic deficit and identity debates. See e.g. F. Scharpf, *Governing in Europe: Effective and Democratic*? (Oxford University Press, 1999).

[107] 'Final Report of the Future of Europe Group', 17 September 2012, available at www.cer.org.uk/sites/default/files/westerwelle_report_sept12.pdf, specifically mentioning 'climate negotiations'; see also R. Sikorski and G. Westerwelle, 'A New Vision of Europe', *New York Times*, 17 September 2012, available at www.nytimes.com/2012/09/18/opinion/a-new-vision-of-europe.html?_r=1&adxnnl=1&adxnnlx=1351180827-i8Ajl2P9kMwr30U2Kkybxw.

more recent climate negotiations are examples of the Union's attempts to rope other international players into an institutional governance model. While the Union has promoted regulatory mechanisms that closely combine environmental concerns with economic interests, it has equally attempted to contribute to a broader debate on climate justice. Yet, the Union is not only an active driver of multilateral governance, but also subjected to an international landscape of intertwining and interlocking jurisdictions and economies. It does not only stir this process in which public power is exercised outside the domestic framework. It is also exposed to these trends and has to adapt to them to be an effective international actor. Differentiated multilateral and unilateral structures might be the only way forward for any form of greenhouse gas reduction.

The Union has demonstrated in the international negotiations of the climate change mitigation regime that its technical bureaucratic governance model can have some success. At the same time, the regime has not delivered what it promised at the outset. Yet the Union project might be able to offer inspiration not only for the governance model but also in accepting, forming and administering a multi-speed approach of differentiated geometries that are intended eventually to lead to a broader-based collective action over time. Amongst EU Member States, international cooperation between some, such as Schengen or the Euro Stability Mechanism, are deliberately constructed in an inclusive manner, and so is the ETS.

The Union's actions are driven by a multitude of motivations. This gives ammunition to the critics questioning the Union's normative leadership in human rights protection and in other environmental matters.[108] One motivation is its aspiration to become a world player. Climate justice and preserving climate as a public good are core elements of the Union's climate change mitigation policy. Exporting both governing structures and values contributes to one's own importance on the international plane, but only as long as these structures work and are supported by other international players. A philosophical fundament might be part of what the Union is missing in its identity creation; it should underpin efficiency and functionality, which are central to the Union's *raison d'être* – but it cannot replace them.

[108] R. Youngs 'Normative Dynamics and Strategic Interests in the EU's External Identity' (2004) 42.2 *Journal of Common Market Studies* 415; Falkner, 'The European Union as a "Green Normative Power"?', p. 507.

The Union is in a period of crisis in which it is pushed to justify its added value. A way of addressing climate change mitigation more effectively than states is one of the (many) successes of the Union. By offering the better solution the Union also competes for citizens' support and potentially ownership. The Union remains one possible reply to the globalization disconnect between those affected and those taking the decisions – one possible way to mitigate the consequences of global interdependence by coordinating a response at the supranational level. While the existence of states is not generally called into question, the Union's existence or at least legitimacy is, particularly in light of its recent streak of perceived or real failures, of which the Copenhagen negotiations is only one example. The Union's output legitimacy is shaken. The Union's ETS is one way in which the EU continues to pursue its environmental agenda in face of the difficulties of the climate change mitigation negotiations on the international plane. An alternative geopolitical model in opposition to the US is in itself attractive for EU citizens. However, the Union needs a deeper *raison d'être* to justify its existence and satisfy those who question its legitimacy. At the same time, the meta-debate about justice, responsibilities and values is important but cannot replace the tangible effects of real practical measures.

9

The EU's governance of external energy relations: the challenges of a 'rule-based market approach'

PETER VAN ELSUWEGE

1 Introduction

With the Lisbon Treaty, the legal framework for the development of an 'Energy Policy for Europe' was significantly strengthened.[1] For the first time, a specific title and provision is devoted to energy.[2] Even though Article 194 TFEU makes no explicit reference to the external dimension of the European energy policy, the well-known implied-powers doctrine – codified in Article 3(2) TFEU – provides the authority to adopt international measures that are necessary to achieve the EU's internal objectives.[3] Moreover, the principles and objectives of the EU's external action, including inter alia the promotion of 'an international system based on stronger multilateral cooperation and good global governance'[4] also apply to the external aspects of the EU's internal policies. Hence, the political ambition to play a more active role in the development of an international, or at least pan-European, legal energy framework has a sound foundation in the EU Treaties.

The aim of this chapter is first to clarify the building blocks of the EU's external energy policy based upon an analysis of relevant policy documents and instruments. It is argued that the EU's strategy can best be defined as the promotion of a 'rule-based market approach', which is inspired by the EU's own mechanisms and procedures. Secondly, the legal challenges surrounding the implementation of this approach are

[1] The ambition to establish a comprehensive Energy Policy for Europe (EPE) was agreed at the March 2006 European Council. See Brussels European Council, Presidency Conclusions, 23–24 March 2006, 775/1/06.

[2] Title XX and Art. 194 TFEU. For an analysis, see L. Hancher and F. Maria Solerno, 'Energy Policy after Lisbon', in A. Biondi, P. Eeckhout and S. Ripley (eds.), *EU Law after Lisbon* (Oxford University Press, 2012), pp. 367–402.

[3] Case 22/70 *Commission* v. *Council* (ERTA) 1971 ECR 263.

[4] Art. 23(3) TEU.

addressed. Specific attention is devoted to the relationship between EU law and international investment law, the uniform application of EU law principles in international contexts and the peculiar energy partnership with Russia. Last, but not least, the governance of the EU's external energy policy is confronted with the ethical dimension of the EU's external action.

2 The gradual development of an EU external energy policy: from a plethora of initiatives to a strategic approach

Energy occupies a special place within the process of European integration.[5] On the one hand, strengthening cooperation on the primary sources of energy such as coal and nuclear power has been a driving force behind the establishment of the European Communities.[6] On the other hand, the development of a supranational European energy policy aiming at the liberalization of electricity and gas markets is a relatively new phenomenon.[7] For a long time, the Member States jealously defended their sovereign powers in the interest of national energy companies. This, however, did not imply that energy remained out of the Community's activities.[8] In the mid-1990s, the European Commission developed several initiatives in order to consolidate the internal energy market.[9] At the external level, the end of the Cold War and the disintegration of the Soviet Union triggered a more active role for the EU.[10]

On the occasion of the June 1990 Dublin European Council, Ruud Lubbers, at that time Prime Minister of the Netherlands, proposed intensifying energy cooperation with the former Communist countries aiming at the modernization of energy sectors in these countries on the

[5] A. Belyi, 'EU External Energy Policies: A Paradox of Integration', in J. Orbie (ed.), *Europe's Global Role: External Policies of the European Union* (Abingdon: Routledge, 2008), p. 203.

[6] Treaty Establishing the European Coal and Steel Community (ECSC), Paris, April 1951; Treaty Establishing the Atomic Energy Community (EURATOM), Rome, March 1957.

[7] D. Geradin (ed.), *The Liberalization of Electricity and Natural Gas in the European Union* (The Hague: Kluwer, 2001).

[8] In the absence of an explicit legal basis on energy in the pre-Lisbon context, energy-related measures were adopted on the basis of Community competences in the fields of the internal market, competition, common commercial policy, environment and transport.

[9] European Commission, 'An Energy Policy for the European Union', White Paper, COM (1995) 682 final, 13 December 1995.

[10] See S. Haghighi, Energy Security: The External Legal Relations of the European Union with Major Oil and Gas Supplying Countries (Oxford: Hart Publishing, 2007).

basis of market-oriented reforms.[11] Supported by the other Member States, the European Commission developed the idea of a European Energy Charter including a list of principles and objectives for East–West energy cooperation in the post-Cold War period.[12] After an international conference held in The Hague, organized under the auspices of the Government of the Netherlands acting as the President-in-Office of the Council of the European Communities, the representatives of fifty countries and the European Communities signed the European Energy Charter.[13] In line with the Commission's initial proposals, the Charter is nothing more than a political declaration, a 'code of conduct [. . .] to be implemented by a series of specific agreements or protocols imposing binding obligations on the signatories'.[14] After intensive negotiations, the Energy Charter Treaty (ECT) and the Protocol on Energy Efficiency and Related Environmental Aspects (PEEREA) were signed in December 1994 and entered into force in April 1998. In contrast to the Charter, the ECT and PEEREA are legally binding multilateral instruments strengthening the rule of (international) law on energy issues.[15] The ECT is essentially based on three major sources: bilateral investment treaties (BITs), EU directives on the liberalization of energy markets and the General Agreement on Tariffs and Trade (GATT).[16] Until today, it is the only comprehensive, multilateral international legal regime for the protection and promotion of investments and trade in the energy sector.

The EU and its Member States are not only amongst the founding fathers of the Energy Charter process, they also actively promote respect for the principles of international energy law in the context of their external relations. For instance, all Partnership and Cooperation Agreements (PCAs) concluded with the former Soviet Republics provide

[11] Energy Charter Secretariat, The Energy Charter Treaty and Related Documents, available at www.encharter.org/fileadmin/user_upload/document/EN.pdf#page=211.

[12] European Commission 'European Energy Charter', COM (1991) 36 final, 14 February 1991.

[13] Significantly, as well as all western and eastern European countries, Australia, Canada and the US took part in the Hague Conference and signed the European Energy Charter. With Indonesia becoming the – so far – latest signatory in May 2009, the Energy Charter has now been signed by fifty-eight countries. For more information, see www.encharter.org.

[14] European Commission, European Energy Charter, COM (1991) 36 final, pp. 3–4.

[15] However, many of the provisions related to energy efficiency are formulated in general terms so that their direct legal implications are limited. See the chapter by A. Boute in this volume.

[16] A. Konoplyanik and T. Wälde, 'Energy Charter Treaty and its Role in International Energy', 24 (2006) *Journal of Energy and Natural Resources Law* 528.

that bilateral cooperation 'shall take place within the principles of the market economy and the European Energy Charter'.[17] Moreover, in so far as the ECT and its Protocols also cover matters covered by the PCAs, the former shall apply.[18] Whereas the Euro-Mediterranean Association Agreements (EMAAs) do not include similar explicit references to the ECT, because the Mediterranean partners are not parties to this multilateral framework,[19] it is noteworthy that the Barcelona Declaration launching the Euro-Mediterranean Partnership (EMP) in 1995 nevertheless referred to 'the association of Mediterranean countries with the Treaty on the European Energy Charter' as an objective of this new policy.[20] Hence, the promotion and effective implementation of the ECT may be regarded as the first emanation of an embryonic external energy policy of the EU in the 1990s.

The limits of this approach became obvious in the EU's relations with Russia. Despite Russia's signature of the ECT in 1994, the agreement has never been ratified in the State Duma. In 2009 the Russian government even decided to terminate its provisional application of the ECT. Even though the provisions on investment protection and arbitration remain valid until 2029,[21] this reduces the significance of the ECT as the key legal reference point for EU–Russia energy relations. The inability to agree on an important Transit Protocol further illustrates the problems in developing the ECT as the key legal instrument for a pan-European energy community.[22]

Arguably, the EU's external energy policy increasingly focuses on the export of the EU's own rules and procedures, in particular in relation to its neighbouring countries. With regard to the EU's southern neighbours, a Euro-Mediterranean Energy Forum was set up in the wake of the Barcelona Declaration. In this context, the EU and its Member States stressed the priority character of legislative and regulatory reforms of the Mediterranean partners' energy sectors. Significantly, the

[17] See e.g. Art. 61 of the PCA with Ukraine, OJ (1998) L 49/18.

[18] See e.g. Art. 100 of the PCA with Ukraine, OJ (1998) L 49/26.

[19] Some Mediterranean countries are observers to the ECT. See www.encharter.org/index.php?id=61.

[20] For the text of the Barcelona Declaration, see www.eeas.europa.eu/euromed/docs/bd_en.pdf.

[21] This follows from Art. 45(3)(b) ECT. *Yukos Universal* v. *The Russian Federation* PCA Case No. AA 227, Interim Award on Jurisdiction and Admissibility, 30 November 2009, para. 339.

[22] Belyi, 'EU External Energy Policies', p. 213.

principles underlying the EU's internal liberalization process such as the establishment of independent regulatory authorities, the unbundling of production, transport, distribution and sales activities and the progressive introduction of competition in the production and distribution process, constitute the key reference points for the Mediterranean countries.[23] At the 2003 Euro-Mediterranean Conference on energy, the ministerial representatives of the EMP countries agreed on the establishment of the Rome Euro-Mediterranean Energy Platform (REMEP) in order to support the approximation of the laws and regulations of the Mediterranean partner countries (in the first place, Morocco, Tunisia and Algeria) with those of the EU.[24]

A similar approach has been developed vis-à-vis the Union's Eastern neighbours. In 1995 the EU initiated the Interstate Oil and Gas Transportation to Europe (INOGATE) programme with Armenia, Azerbaijan, Belarus, Georgia, Kazakhstan, Kirgizstan, Moldova, Tajikistan, Turkmenistan, Ukraine and Uzbekistan. A key objective of this programme is to converge the energy markets 'on the basis of the EU internal market principles'.[25] At their ministerial conferences in Baku (2004) and Astana (2006), the partner states confirmed the priority status of the regulatory convergence objective and adopted a road map to strengthen their cooperation in this field.[26]

The launch of a formal European Neighbourhood Policy (ENP) confirmed and strengthened the EU's ambition to extend the internal energy market regulation to its direct neighbours.[27] All ENP Action Plans include provisions on the gradual integration of the partners' energy markets into that of the EU. Not surprisingly, the 2008–13 Action Plan of the Euro-Mediterranean Energy Partnership identified 'the further harmonization of energy policies and regulatory frameworks between the Euro-Mediterranean Partner countries towards the longer-term goal

[23] European Commission, Enhancing Euro-Mediterranean Cooperation on Transport and Energy, COM (2001) 126 final, pp. 11–12.

[24] Council of the EU, 'Ministerial Declaration of the Euro-Mediterranean Conference on Energy, 15767/03, Rome, 1–2 December 2003'.

[25] 'About Inogate', available at www.inogate.org/.

[26] 'Ministerial Declaration on Enhanced Energy Cooperation between the EU, the Littoral States of the Black and Caspian Seas and their Neighbouring Countries, Astana, 30 November 2006', available at http://ec.europa.eu/dgs/energy_transport/international/regional/caspian/doc/2006_11_30_astana_conclusions.pdf.

[27] European Commission, European Neighbourhood Policy, Strategy Paper, COM (2004) 373 final, 12 May 2004, p. 17.

of creating a common Euro-Mediterranean energy market' as a key priority.[28] With regard to the Eastern neighbours, the Eastern Partnership launched in 2008 aims at the political association and economic integration of six former Soviet Republics (Ukraine, Moldova, Belarus, Armenia, Azerbaijan, Georgia) on the basis of legal approximation and convergence to EU standards and norms.[29] Not surprisingly, specific attention is devoted to the energy *acquis*. One of the Eastern Partnership's thematic platforms is devoted to energy security, and the integration of regional energy markets and energy efficiency programmes is a so-called 'flagship initiative' of the Eastern Partnership.[30]

The projection of the EU's own regulatory framework to its direct neighbours is most explicit and far-reaching in the context of the European Energy Community Treaty (EnCT).[31] This multilateral agreement, initially concluded between the European Community and the countries of the Western Balkans (Croatia, Serbia, Bosnia and Herzegovina, Montenegro, Former Yugoslav Republic of Macedonia, Kosovo and Albania), and later extended to Moldova and Ukraine, essentially provides for the extension of the EU's legislation on energy, environment and competition to non-EU countries. In contrast to voluntary approximation clauses or traditional soft law instruments such as Action Plans or Memorandums of Understanding,[32] the EnCT is a binding legal instrument providing for the actual implementation of EU legislation in non-EU Member States. The Energy Community has its own institutional framework, legal instruments and decision-making procedure.[33]

In its 2011 Communication, 'On Security of Energy Supply and International Cooperation – The EU Energy Policy: Engaging with Partners beyond our Borders', the Commission for the first time tried to translate its gradually developed external energy policy into a strategic

[28] Annex 1 to the 'Ministerial Declaration on the Euro-Mediterranean Energy Partnership, 18 December 2007', 16707/07.

[29] E. Lannon and P. Van Elsuwege, 'The Eastern Partnership: Prospects of a New Regional Dimension within the European Neighbourhood Policy', in E. Lannon (ed.), *The European Neighbourhood Policy's Challenges* (Brussels: Peter Lang, 2012), pp. 285–322.

[30] See http://eeas.europa.eu/eastern/initiatives/index_en.htm.

[31] The Energy Community Treaty, OJ (2006) L 198/18.

[32] B. Van Vooren, 'A Case Study of Soft Law in EU External Relations: The European Neighbourhood Policy', 34 (2009) *European Law Review* 696.

[33] R. Karova, 'Energy Community for South East Europe: Rationale Behind and Implementation to Date', European University Institute Working Paper 2009/12 (2009).

approach for the Union.[34] More than ever, it appears that the EU's external energy policy is characterized by '*a rule-based market approach*' developed on the basis of a multilayered strategy.[35]

In the Union's direct neighbourhood, the aim is to create a pan-European energy community with countries acting on the ground of shared rules and principles derived from EU internal market legislation. The key instrument to achieve this objective is the further expansion of the EnCT to relevant neighbouring countries.[36] Hence, the Energy Community is gradually developing from a pre-accession instrument into a tool for 'integration without membership'. It is an interesting test case of 'legally binding sectoral multilateralism' as a model to achieve the EU's external action objectives, in particular in the EU's neighbourhood.[37]

At the global stage, the ambition is to integrate the EU's energy objectives as much as possible into multilateral instruments. This implies, amongst other things, the defence of EU interests in the context of multilateral forums such as the WTO, the G8, the International Energy Agency and the International Energy Forum and in bilateral energy dialogues with key energy suppliers and transit countries.[38] Significantly, the EU also actively supports the reinforcement of the ECT. According to the November 2011 Council conclusions on strengthening the external dimension of the EU energy policy, the ECT 'might become a global instrument, recognized as the basis for international energy regulation'.[39]

In other words, the EU's external energy policy aims at the development of a legally binding framework for energy based on the extension of its own internal market model, on the one hand, and on the elaboration

[34] European Commission, Communication from the Commission to the European Parliament, the Council, the European Social and Economic Committee and the Committee of the Regions on Security of Energy Supply and International Cooperation, 'The EU Energy Policy: Engaging with Partners beyond our Borders', COM (2011) 539 final.

[35] Council of the EU, On Strengthening the External Dimension of the EU Energy Policy, 3127th Transport, Telecommunications and Energy Council Meeting, 25 November 2011, 17615/11, p. 2.

[36] To date, Norway, Turkey and Georgia have observer status. With Turkey, negotiations for accession to the EnCT were opened in 2009, Georgia is envisaging an application for membership and Armenia has requested to become an observer. European Commission, 'Report from the Commission to the European Parliament and Council under Art. 7 of Decision 2006/500/EC (Energy Community Treaty)', COM (2011) 105 final.

[37] S. Blockmans and B. Van Vooren, 'Revitalising the European "Neigbourhood Economic Community": The Case for Legally Binding Sectoral Multilateralism', 17 *European Foreign Affairs Review* (2012) 577.

[38] Council of the EU, 'On Strengthening the External Dimension of the EU Energy Policy', p. 4.

[39] *Ibid.*, p. 6.

of the Energy Charter process, on the other hand. The question is, of course, to what extent those two pillars of the EU's approach are mutually compatible and what challenges have to be overcome to achieve the EU's rather ambitious objectives.

3 Legal challenges to the EU's external energy policy

Three issues deserve particular attention: (i) the relationship between international investment law and EU law; (ii) the uniform application of the EU energy *acquis* within the European Energy Community; and (iii) the development of a legal framework for energy relations with the Russian Federation.

3.1 Investment protection and the requirements of EU law

Even though the EU considers the promotion of the ECT as a key objective of its external energy policy, the full application of this international legal regime creates a number of challenges from the perspective of EU law. A particular problem exists with regard to investment protection, which forms a substantive part of the ECT. In the recent past, questions about the compatibility between the protection offered under BITs or the ECT and EU law, in particular regarding competition and state aid, have been raised before arbitration courts and the Court of Justice of the EU (ECJ). Good illustrations of this controversy are the arbitration cases initiated against Hungary by Electrabel, AES and EDF respectively.[40] Those companies had signed long-term Power Purchase Agreements (PPAs) with the Republic of Hungary in the mid-1990s. The PPAs contained provisions regarding pricing and market privileges in return for investment in the electricity infrastructure. After Hungary's accession to the EU in 2004, the European Commission considered the benefits awarded to certain electricity producers through PPAs to be incompatible with the EU rules on state aid.[41] After Hungary had adopted new energy legislation, which put an end to the preferential regime under the PPAs, the companies involved claimed a

[40] *AES Summit Generation Ltd.* v. *Hungary*, ICSID No. ARB/01/04 (ECT); *Electrabel SA* v. *Hungary*, ICSID Case No. ARB/07/19; *EDF International* v. *Hungary*, PCA Case No. 2009-13.

[41] European Commission, Prior notification of a concentration (Case COMP/M.6642 – Eaton Corporation/Cooper Industries), OJ (2005) C 324/12, leading to Commission Decision of 4 June 2008 on the state aid C 41/05 awarded by Hungary through Power Purchase Agreements, OJ (2009) L 225/53.

violation of Hungary's obligations of investment protection under the ECT[42] and started arbitration proceedings based on the International Convention for the Settlement of Investment Disputes (ICSID).[43] Notwithstanding the Tribunal's observation that Hungary's motivations were unrelated to its EU law obligations – a controversial conclusion criticized by Arbitrator Stern[44] – it determined that the introduction of new price regulations was not an arbitrary or unreasonable measure and did not, therefore, infringe the relevant ECT provisions and legitimate expectations of the claimants.[45] Accordingly, a potential stalemate for Hungary where it could have been confronted with either an infringement of its EU law obligations or its international obligations under the ECT has been avoided.

Another relevant case to illustrate the potential frictions between a Member State's EU law requirements, on the one hand, and the rules of international investment law, on the other hand, is the judgment of the ECJ in *Commission* v. *Slovakia*.[46] In this case, the Commission argued that the preferential market access granted to the Swiss energy company ATEL in Slovakia violated the principle of non-discriminatory third-party access to the transmission system as laid down in Article 20 of Directive 2003/54/EC concerning common rules for the internal market in electricity. According to the Slovak Republic, the contract with ATEL was in essence an 'investment' within the meaning of the applicable BIT. Forcing ATEL to renounce its priority access right would, from this perspective, amount to an expropriation at odds with the ECT and the provisions of a Swiss–Slovak BIT. Significantly, in his Opinion to this case, Advocate General Jääskinen confirmed that secondary EU legislation should be interpreted in accordance with the ECT, which is a binding international agreement from the perspective of EU law.[47] Without entering into a detailed analysis, he quickly concluded that

[42] In particular, they claimed a violation of Arts. 10(1), 10(7) and 13 ECT.

[43] *AES Summit Generation Ltd.* v. *Hungary* ICSID Case No. ARB/01/04. It is also noteworthy that Budapesti Erőmű Zrt., a Hungarian subsidiary of Electricité de France International SA unsuccessfully launched an application for an annulment of the Commission decisions on state aid awarded by Hungary through PPAs, Joint Cases T-80/06 and T-182/09, *Budapesti Erőmű Zrt* v. *Commission* [2012], nyr.

[44] *AES Summit Generation Ltd. and AES-Tisza Erömü Kft.* v. *Hungary* ICSID Case No. ARB/07/22, point 10.3.19.

[45] See A. Boute, 'Challenging the Re-Regulation of Liberalized Electricity Prices under Investment Arbitration', (2011) 32.2 *Energy Law Journal* 511.

[46] Case C-264/09, *Commission* v. *Slovakia* [2012], nyr.

[47] Opinion of AG Jääskinen to Case C-264/09, *Commission* v. *Slovakia*, para. 60.

'EU energy law as it stands under Directive 2003/54 and Regulation No. 1228/2003 cannot be considered as failing to achieve the standards required by the Energy Charter Treaty'.[48] The Court, for its part, did not even consider a potential violation of the ECT and only examined the compatibility of the third-party access requirement under Directive 2003/54 with the Swiss–Slovak BIT 'since the latter agreement relates directly to investment protection'.[49] This argument is disputable because the ECT also explicitly deals with investment protection and many of the investment standards invoked under the BIT are largely similar to the protection offered under the ECT.[50] It is, therefore, surprising that both the Advocate General and the Court came to the conclusion that a full application of EU energy law in this case would breach the BIT but ignored the implications with regard to the ECT. The assumption that EU legislation is in line with the ECT is probably inspired by the fact that the EU is a contracting party and one of the driving forces behind the ECT but, as follows from the outcome of this case, contradictions between the requirements under EU law and the investment protection regime under the ECT cannot be excluded.

In *Commission* v. *Slovakia*, this contradiction was solved by reference to Article 307(1) EC (now Article 351(1) TFEU), which exempts Member States from their EU law obligations for agreements concluded before their accession to the Union. Whereas this solution illustrates the EU's respect for the international legal order, it also presents a danger for the effective implementation of EU law. The claims of investors against the application of EU law requirements on the basis of international investment agreements – be it at the bilateral or multilateral level – potentially compromises the completion of the EU internal energy market.[51] A crucial problem for the Union is the risk of misinterpretation of EU law by arbitral tribunals.[52] Taking into account that such tribunals derive their authority from an international treaty, they are not bound by EU law. Moreover, an arbitration tribunal is not a 'court or tribunal of a Member State' within the meaning of Article 267 TFEU and can, therefore, not seek preliminary rulings under the

[48] *Ibid.*, para. 63.
[49] Case C-264/09, *Commission* v. *Slovakia*, para. 30.
[50] A. Boute, 'Comment on Case C-264/09' (2012) 49 *Common Market Law Review* 1188.
[51] *Ibid.*, p. 1196.
[52] This does not exclude the fact that the opposite situation may also be problematic, as argued by A. Boute in his comment on *Commission* v. *Slovakia*: A. Boute, 'Comment on Case C-264/09'.

TFEU.[53] Hence, there is a risk that arbitration leads to the unequal treatment of investors amongst EU Member States and undermines the autonomy of the EU legal order.[54] The latter is a constitutional cornerstone of the EU and basically implies that questions of interpretation and application of EU law cannot be settled according to procedures outside the EU, but only according to the rules of settlement, which the Union itself has instituted. This principle is derived from the combined reading of Article 19 TEU, according to which the ECJ ensures that in the interpretation and application of the EU Treaties the law is observed, and Article 344 TFEU, which lays down that the Member States undertake not to submit a dispute concerning the interpretation or application of the Treaties to any other mode of settlement than those provided by those Treaties.[55] Safeguarding the autonomy of the EU legal order, thus, implies that the ECJ is the final arbiter when it comes to the interpretation and application of Union law, a task that cannot be attributed to other courts or tribunals.[56]

In principle, the Commission has no problems with third-party arbitration mechanisms set up in agreements with third countries. This openness towards the international legal order was perhaps most clearly expelled in *Opinion 1/91*, where the ECJ observed that an international agreement providing for its own system of courts, including a court with jurisdiction to settle disputes between the contracting parties, 'is in principle compatible with Community law'.[57] The fact that the EU has accepted investment arbitration through its ratification of the ECT can be regarded as an illustration of this openness. Only when the court or tribunal established by an international agreement potentially affects the ECJ's role as the final arbiter on the interpretation or application of EU law provisions is the question of autonomy at stake.

[53] Case 102/81, *Nordsee* [1982] ECR 1095, paras. 10–12; Case C-126/97, *Eco Swiss China Time Ltd.* v. *Benetton International NV* [1999] ECR I-3055, para. 34, Case C-125/04, *Denuit and Cordenier* v. *Transorient* [2005] ECR I-923, para. 13.

[54] This risk has been highlighted in a Note prepared by the European Commission services in November 2006. See H. Wehland, 'Intra-EU Investment Agreements and Arbitration: Is European Community Law an Obstacle?' (2009) 58 *International Comparative Law Quarterly* 309.

[55] I. Govaere, 'Beware of the Trojan Horse: Dispute Settlement in (Mixed) Agreements and the Autonomy of the EU Legal Order', in C. Hillion and P. Koutrakos (eds.), *Mixed Agreements Revisited* (Oxford: Hart Publishing, 2010), p. 188.

[56] Case C-459/03, *Commission* v. *Ireland* [2006] ECR I-4635, para. 154.

[57] Opinion 1/91 [1991] ECR I-6079, para. 40.

In order to avoid problems resulting from the interaction between EU law and international commitments of Member States, the European Parliament and the Council recently adopted an 'information exchange mechanism' requiring the Member States to inform the Commission about their intergovernmental agreements with third countries having an impact on the internal energy market or on the security of energy supply in the Union.[58] Accordingly, the Commission can assess the compatibility of those agreements with the EU law requirements of the Member States and, if necessary, provide advice on how to solve the identified problems. This mechanism may be regarded as a preventive instrument aiming to avoid conflicts between EU and international law and is certainly a welcome development. However, it does not necessarily solve all issues. For instance, the information requirement only concerns 'legally binding agreements' and it is for the Member States themselves to decide whether or not an intergovernmental agreement with a third country has an impact on the EU's energy market.[59] Hence, Member States can relatively easily escape the compatibility assessment with all the consequences it entails in terms of potential litigation before international arbitration tribunals and/or the ECJ.[60]

3.2 The Energy Community Treaty and the uniform application of EU law

The protection of the EU's autonomous legal order and the uniform application of EU rules are also of particular significance with regard to the Treaty establishing the Energy Community. In contrast to the ECT, which is essentially based on the application of international trade rules

[58] Decision No. 994/2012/EU of 25 October 2012, OJ (2012) L 299/13. It is noteworthy that this Decision only covers agreements concluded with third countries. A more specific problem is that the agreements concluded between EU Member States, often related to investment protection ('intra-BITS'). According to the European Commission, such agreements constitute an 'anomaly within the internal market' and should be terminated. See *Eureko* v. *Slovakia*, PCA Case No. 2008-13, para. 180; J. Kleinheisterkamp, 'Investment Protection and EU Law: The Intra- and Extra-EU Dimension of the Energy Charter Treaty' (2012) 15 *Journal of International Environmental Law* 100.

[59] B. Van Vooren, 'Europe Unplugged: Progress, Potential and Limitations of EU External Energy Policy Three Years Post-Lisbon', SIEPS Report 2012/5, pp. 69–72.

[60] The preamble of Decision 994/2012/EU explicitly provides that 'the information exchange mechanism, including assessments to be made by Member States in implementing it, is without prejudice to the application of the Union rules on infringements, State aid and competition'.

to the field of energy, the EnCT explicitly deals with the export of EU legislation to non-EU Member States.[61] In such a situation, only the ECJ can ultimately decide on the interpretation of the relevant legislation. This is reflected in Article 94 of the EnCT, which provides that

> The institutions shall interpret any term or other concept used in this Treaty that is derived from European Community law in conformity with the case law of the Court of Justice or the Court of First Instance of the European Communities. Where no interpretation from those Courts is available, the Ministerial Council shall give guidance in interpreting this Treaty. It may delegate that task to the Permanent High Level Group. Such guidance shall not prejudge any interpretation of the *acquis communautaire* by the Court of Justice or the Court of First Instance at a later stage.

Significantly, there is no judicial authority within the Energy Community to ensure the homogenous interpretation of the EU's energy *acquis*. This is a crucial difference with the European Economic Area (EEA), which also provides for the application of EU legislation in non-EU Member States. Under the terms of the EEA Surveillance Agreement, the European Free Trade Association (EFTA) Surveillance Authority and the EFTA Court are competent to deal with infringement procedures and requests for advisory opinions on behalf of the national courts of EFTA countries.[62] Within the Energy Community, the Ministerial Council – consisting of one representative of each contracting party and two representatives of the EU – has the prime responsibility for the interpretation of the Treaty and can determine a breach of obligations by one of the parties.[63] In case of a 'serious and persistent' breach of the obligations, the Ministerial Council may unanimously decide to suspend certain rights stemming from the EnCT.[64]

It is questionable whether this rudimentary dispute settlement procedure sufficiently guarantees the effectiveness, efficiency and enforcement of the *acquis communautaire* in the EU's relations with third countries.[65]

[61] M. Hunt and R. Karova, 'The Energy Acquis under the Energy Community Treaty and the Integration of South East European Electricity Markets: An Uneasy Relationship?', in B. Delvaux, M. Hunt and K. Talus (eds.), *EU Energy Law and Policy Issues* (Cambridge: Intersentia, 2011), pp. 51–86.

[62] Arts. 34–6 of the EEA Surveillance Agreement, OJ (1994) L 344/3.

[63] Arts. 47, 48, 91 and 94 EnCT.

[64] Art. 92 refers to the suspension of voting rights and exclusion from meetings or mechanisms established under the Community Treaty as potential sanctions.

[65] A. Łazowski, 'Enhanced Multilateralism and Enhanced Bilateralism: Integration without Membership in the European Union' (2008) *Common Market Law Review* 1433.

Article 6 EnCT almost verbatim reflects the principle of loyal cooperation enshrined in Article 4(3) TEU but without the possibility to initiate judicial proceedings against the contracting parties this might remain nothing more than a declaration of intent without practical consequences. For (potential) EU candidate countries, the mechanism of pre-accession conditionality may be instrumental to ensure the effective implementation of the EU's legislation.[66] The adaptation costs for countries without such a clear perspective are much bigger and it remains to be seen whether the incentives offered within the context of the ENP will be sufficient to ensure the achievement of the EU's ambitious objectives.[67]

3.3 Respect for the rule of law in the EU's energy relations with Russia

Taking into account that more than 30 per cent of all EU energy imports come from Russia and that the Union is by far Russia's most important trading partner in energy goods, the development of 'a new and strong legal base' for energy cooperation with the Russian Federation is a crucial challenge for the success of the EU's external energy policy.[68] The existing legal framework is considered to be insufficient and out of date. For instance, Article 65 of the PCA provides that '[c]ooperation shall take place within the principles of the market economy and the European Energy Charter, against a background of the progressive integration of the energy markets in Europe'. Owing to Russia's refusal to ratify the ECT, and its decision to terminate the provisional application of this multilateral agreement, EU–Russia energy cooperation is essentially based on non-legally binding dialogues and commitments. Most important is the EU–Russia energy dialogue,

[66] European Commission, 'Report from the Commission to the European Parliament and Council under Art. 7 of Decision 2006/500/EC (Energy Community Treaty)', COM (2011) 105 final, p. 8.

[67] R. Petrov, 'Energy Community as a Promoter of the European Union's "Energy *acquis*" to its Neighbourhood' (2012) 38 *Legal Issues of Economic Integration* 331; H. Prange-Gstöhl, 'Enlarging the EU's Internal Energy Market: Why Would Third Countries Accept EU Rule Export?' (2009) 39 *Energy Policy* 5296.

[68] European Commission, Communication from the Commission to the European Parliament, the Council, the European Social and Economic Committee and the Committee of the Regions on Security of Energy Supply and International Cooperation, 'The EU Energy Policy: Engaging with Partners beyond our Borders', COM (2011) 539 final, p. 8.

which was established at the EU–Russia Paris summit in 2000 and aims to create trust and transparency in EU–Russia energy relations through the organization of regular meetings at different political levels. This dialogue inter alia resulted in the establishment of an early-warning mechanism for preventing and overcoming emergency situations in the energy sector[69] and a common understanding on the preparation of a road map for EU–Russia energy cooperation until 2050.[70] Both instruments are at best described as 'soft law' mechanisms, which certainly have their merits but cannot conceal the lack of legally binding norms regarding investment protection, transit or dispute resolution. As a result, investment issues are often to be solved in the context of BITs concluded between Russia and individual Member States.[71]

Despite the obvious mutual interdependence, both the EU and Russia have different strategic interests leading to opposing views on the preferred legal framework. For Russia, 'security of demand' is crucial.[72] Therefore, a market structure with vertically integrated gas companies operating on the basis of long-term contracts and delivering gas through their own pipelines with no freedom of access to other suppliers is in Russia's interest. For the EU, however, 'security of supply' is a key concern and for this reason a diversification of suppliers within a flexible energy market is essential.[73]

It is no secret that Russia is not very happy with the EU's Third Energy Package, which requires the effective separation between the operation of electricity and gas transmission networks from supply and production activities of vertically integrated energy companies.[74] Significantly,

[69] This early warning mechanism was established in 2009 in the wake of the Russia–Ukraine gas crisis and has been updated in 2011. See http://ec.europa.eu/energy/international/russia/doc/20110224_memorandum.pdf.

[70] http://ec.europa.eu/energy/international/russia/doc/20110224_understanding_roadmap_2050.pdf.

[71] N. Rubins and A. Nazarov, 'Investment Treaties and the Russian Federation: Baiting the Bear?' (2008) 9 *Business Law International* 100.

[72] S. Seliverstov, 'Energy Security of Russia in the EU: Current Legal Problems' (2009) *Note de l'Ifri*, L'Institut français des relations internationals, available at http://ifri.org/downloads/noteseliverstovenergysecurity.pdf.

[73] European Commission, Communication from the Commission to the European Parliament, the Council, the European Social and Economic Committee and the Committee of the Regions on Security of Energy Supply and International Cooperation, 'The EU Energy Policy: Engaging with Partners beyond our Borders', COM (2011) 539 final.

[74] 'Medvedev Criticises the EU's Third Energy Package', *Voice of Russia*, 3 November 2011.

undertakings from third countries, which intend to acquire control over an electricity or gas network, need to comply with the same unbundling requirements as EU undertakings. If they do not comply with these requirements, they should be refused the certification that is required for distribution system operators.[75] This, of course, has significant implications for *Gazprom*, which faces a legal obligation to 'unbundle' the ownership and operation of its gas pipelines on EU territory and to allow access to these pipelines to other energy companies.[76] Vladimir Putin described this requirement as 'robbery' and 'confiscation of Russian property' and announced that Russia would take the necessary steps to challenge the validity of the EU energy legislation.[77]

In the view of the Russian government, the Third Energy Package is contrary to Article 34(1) PCA, which spells out that the parties shall use their best endeavours to prevent a deterioration of the market conditions under which their respective companies operate.[78] In addition, the Russian government announced it would raise the issue in the WTO.[79] The '*Gazprom* clause' raises questions of compatibility with different provisions of the General Agreement on Trade in Services (GATS) such as the most-favoured-nation principle (Art. II GATS), the prohibition of market access barriers (Art. XVI GATS) and the national treatment obligation (Art. XVII GATS).[80] Finally, Russia may invoke investment protection clauses

[75] This follows from Art. 11 (also known as the '*Gazprom clause*') of Directive 2009/73 of 13 July 2009 concerning common rules for the internal market in natural gas, OJ (2009) L 211/94; a similar clause is included in Directive 2009/72 regarding the internal market in electricity, OJ (2009) L 211/54.

[76] In response to the Third Energy Package, *Gazprom* plans to reform its European assets, including the creation of two subsidiaries for selling and transporting natural gas, respectively. 'Gazprom Plans Reform of Assets to Avoid EU Probe – Report', *Russia Today*, 20 September 2012, available at http://rt.com/business/news/gazprom-eu-probe-gas-anti-trust-610/.

[77] A. Rettman 'Putin and Barroso in Public Scrap on EU Energy Law', *EUobserver.com*, 24 February 2011, available at http://euobserver.com/24/31869.

[78] Transcript of Press Conference between Vladimir Putin and José Manuel Barroso in February 2011, available at http://web.archive.org/web/20120520173631/http://premier.gov.ru/eng/events/pressconferences/14257/.

[79] See 'Russia May Contest EU Energy Rules in WTO', *PeakOil*, 16 November 2011, available at http://peakoil.com/publicpolicy/russia-may-contest-eu-energy-rules-in-wto-source/.

[80] For an analysis, see V. Van Hoorn, 'Unbundling, Reciprocity and the European Internal Energy Markets: WTO Consistency and Broader Implications for Europe' (2009) 1 *European Energy and Environmental Law Review* 51; T. Cottier, S. Matteotti-Bertukova and O. Nartova, 'Third Country Relations in EU Unbundling of Natural Gas Markets: The "Gazprom Clause" of Directive 2009/97 EC and WTO Law', NCCR Trade Regulation

included in BITs concluded with certain EU Member States. Particularly for the new Member States, those agreements have been concluded before their accession to the Union and, therefore, potentially escape the application of EU law in accordance with Article 351 (1) TFEU, as illustrated in the *Commission* v. *Slovakia* case.[81] An interesting test case is the pending arbitration procedure launched by *Gazprom* against the Lithuanian government under the United Nations Convention on International Trade Law (UNCITRAL) arbitration rules.[82] According to *Gazprom*, Lithuania's legislation requiring the unbundling of *Lietuvos Dujos*, in which it holds a 37 per cent stake, violates the investment protection clauses of a 1999 BIT between Russia and Lithuania.[83] The Lithuanian government, for its part, filed a lawsuit against *Gazprom* at the Stockholm arbitration tribunal relating to overcharged gas prices for about 5 billion litas (€1.4 billion) in the period 2004–12.[84] This initiative was influenced by the European Commission's decision to investigate *Gazprom*'s allegedly unfair price policy in several Central and East European countries.[85] Taking into account the high stakes, in terms of both financial and strategic interests, the importance of this energy battle can hardly be underestimated. As Katinka Barysch observed, the energy dispute 'is likely to keep EU judges and competition officials busy for years to come'.[86]

Whatever the outcome of the announced procedures may be, and notwithstanding the unavoidable political battering, it appears that the EU's 'rule-based market approach' triggers the increased use of legal arguments on behalf of the Union's partners. Of particular significance is certainly Russia's initiative to present a 'Draft Convention on Ensuring International Energy Security' on the occasion of the 2010 EU–Russia

Working Paper No. 2010/06 (2010), available at www.nccr-trade.org/publication/third-country-relations-in-eu-unbundling-of-natural-gas-markets-the-gazprom-clause-of-directi/.

[81] Case C-264/09, *Commission* v. *Slovakia*.

[82] At the time of writing, the case was still pending before the Permanent Court of Arbitration. See www.pca-cpa.org/.

[83] '*Gazprom* Seeks International Arbitration against Lithuanian Government', *Gazprom News*, 1 March 2012, available at www.gazprom.com/press/news/2012/march/article130681/.

[84] 'Lithuania files lawsuit against *Gazprom*', *Baltic Times*, 3 October 2012.

[85] N. Nielsen, 'Lithuania Suing Russian Energy Giant Gazprom', *EUObserver.com*, 4 October 2012.

[86] K. Barysch, 'The EU and Russia: All Smiles and No Action?', policy brief, Centre for European Reform, 18 April 2011, available at www.cer.org.uk/sites/default/files/publications/attachments/pdf/2011/pb_russia_april11-157.pdf.

energy dialogue.[87] This document reflects the Russian vision on how to deal with energy issues, including a strong focus on national sovereignty regarding energy sources and security of demand.[88] On several points the Russian proposal differs fundamentally from how the EU interprets fair competition and national sovereignty in the ECT. For instance, the Draft Convention recognizes the legitimacy of dual energy pricing and provides that diversification of energy production and transportation should not hinder existing contractual relations.[89] This approach is at odds with the EU's conception of a competitive energy market.[90] It is, therefore, no surprise that the draft Convention received a lukewarm approach within the EU. The recent Commission and Council documents on the EU's external energy strategy ignore the idea of a new global legal instrument for energy security but rather regard the integration of a substantial energy chapter in a new EU–Russia framework agreement as the preferred option.[91]

4 External energy policy and the ethical dimension of the EU's external action

Apart from the identified legal challenges, the successful implementation of the EU's external energy policy also presents important political dilemmas. Most obvious is the difficulty of reconciling the promotion of the EU's values with the reality that important energy partners are not

[87] Draft Convention on Ensuring International Energy Security, *Anniversary Conference of the EU–Russia Energy Dialogue*, December 2010, available at http://ua-energy.org/upload/files/Convention-engl1.pdf.

[88] K. Westphal, 'The Energy Charter Revisited: The Russian Proposal for an International Energy Convention and the Energy Charter Treaty', *SWP Comments*, Stiftung Wissenschaft und Politik, 8 March 2011.

[89] Art. IV.3.5 and Art. II.2(c) of the Draft Convention on Ensuring International Energy Security.

[90] A. Belyi, S. Nappert and V. Pogoretskyy, 'Modernizing the Energy Charter Process? The Energy Charter Conference Road Map and the Russian Draft Convention on Energy Security' (2011) 5 *Oil, Gas and Energy Law Intelligence* 78.

[91] European Commission, Communication from the Commission to the European Parliament, the Council, the European Social and Economic Committee and the Committee of the Regions on Security of Energy Supply and International Cooperation, 'The EU Energy Policy: Engaging with Partners beyond our Borders', COM (2011) 539 final; Council of the EU, On Strengthening the External Dimension of the EU energy policy, 3127th Transport, Telecommunications and Energy Council Meeting, 25 November 2011, 17615/11.

always the best pupils when it comes to respect for human rights, democracy and the rule of law.

Given the importance attached to the export of EU values in the Treaty of Lisbon,[92] it is impossible to escape this issue in the context of the EU's external energy policy. Recent statements by European Council President Herman Van Rompuy and High Representative Catherine Ashton about the state of the rule of law and judiciary in Russia illustrate that the EU does not shy away from openly criticizing its most important energy partner.[93] However, the 'ethical dimension' of the EU's external action faces its limits when this risks undermining the vital interests of the Union. A good demonstration is the EU's reaction to the outbreak of violence between Russia and Georgia in August 2008. In an extraordinary European Council meeting, the EU Heads of State or Government decided to suspend the ongoing negotiations on a new framework agreement with Russia.[94] Shortly afterwards, the European Commission proposed to renounce this position because it would undermine the EU's own strategic interests.[95] This suggestion was followed by the Council with the caveat that the decision to restart negotiations in no way legitimized the status quo in Georgia or Russian action contrary to the EU's values and principles.[96]

The tension between values and interests is most obvious in the Union's relations with the countries of Central Asia. As energy producers and transit countries they occupy a strategic position.[97] However, their track record in terms of human rights protection is not always very positive.[98] This often puts the EU in a difficult position when crucial energy deals have to be signed with autocratic leaders. In January 2011,

[92] See the chapter by Ester Herlin-Karnell in this volume.

[93] A. Rettman, 'EU President: Magnitsky Case "Emblematic" for Russia', *EUobserver.com*, 20 April 2012, at http://euobserver.com/24/115968 and 'Statement by EU High Representative Catherine Ashton on the sentencing of "Pussy Riot" punk band members in Russia', 17 August 2012, press release A310/12.

[94] Council of the European Union, Presidency Conclusions: Extraordinary European Council, 1 September 2008, 12594/2/08 Rev. I.2.11.

[95] European Commission, Review of EU–Russia Relations, COM (2008) 740 final, 5 November 2008, p. 5.

[96] Extract from the press release of the 2903rd meeting of the External Relations Council, Brussels, 10 and 11 November 2008.

[97] S. de Jong and J. Wouters, 'Central Asia and the EU's Drive towards Energy Diversification', Leuven Centre for Global Governance Studies Working Paper 64 (June 2011).

[98] A. Warkotsch, 'Human Rights, Democratisation and Good Governance', in A. Warkotsch (ed.), *The European Union and Central Asia* (Abingdon: Routledge, 2011), p. 102.

for instance, a memorandum of understanding on cooperation in the energy field was signed in Brussels in the presence of Commission President Barosso and Uzbek President Karimov. The latter has reigned since 1990 with an iron hand over the former Soviet Republic. He is held responsible for the 2005 Andijan massacre and persistent human rights violations in the country.[99] Engaging in formal contacts with such a figure naturally leads to allegations of double standards in the EU's human rights policies.[100] With Turkmenistan, too, another country with an authoritarian presidential regime, the conclusion of an energy partnership raised similar concerns.[101]

In an attempt to counter criticisms about the EU's lenient approach vis-à-vis the Central Asian regimes, the Union attaches great importance to the installation of structured bilateral human rights dialogues.[102] Notwithstanding the political significance of this instrument, its practical impact on the domestic situation in the respective countries appears to be rather limited.[103] According to the European Parliament, 'the existence of the human rights dialogues should not be used as an excuse for excluding human-rights-related questions arising in other fields of cooperation or for not engaging in further actions'.[104] Hence, there is a constant pressure both from within (European Parliament) and outside (NGOs) the EU to respect the ethical dimension of the EU's external action in the context of its external energy policy. However, the realist argument that if the Union is too tough on human rights conditionality this will hamper its long-term interests also plays a crucial role in the discussions.[105] The result is an almost constant struggle to reconcile

[99] On the worrying state of affairs in Uzbekistan, see Human Rights Watch Report 2012, available at www.hrw.org/sites/default/files/related_material/uzbekistan_2012.pdf.

[100] S. Tisdall, 'Why Does the EU Give Credibility to Such Dictators as Islam Karimov?', *Guardian*, 26 January 2011.

[101] J. Boonstra, 'The EU–Turkmenistan Energy Relationship: Difficulty or Opportunity?, available at www.edc2020.eu/fileadmin/publications/Pbrief_No_5_Oct_2010_The_EU_Turkmenistan_energy_relationship_difficulty_or_opportunity.pdf.

[102] General Secretariat of the Council of the EU, 'The European Union and Central Asia: The New Partnership in Action', at http://eeas.europa.eu/central_asia/docs/2010_strategy_eu_centralasia_en.pdf (p. 16).

[103] V. Axyonova, 'The EU–Central Asia Human Rights Dialogues: Making a Difference?' *EUCAM Policy Brief*, Centre for European Policy Sudies, available at www.ceps.eu/book/eu-central-asia-human-rights-dialogues-making-difference.

[104] European Parliament, Resolution of on the State of Implementation of the EU Strategy for Central Asia, P7-TA (2011) 0588, 15 December 2011, para. 12.

[105] De Jong and Wouters, 'Central Asia and the EU's Drive towards Energy Diversification', p. 38.

the human rights and (energy) security concerns of the EU and its Member States.

Arguably, the choice of instruments for the implementation of the EU's external energy policy may have an impact on the balancing act between values and interests. For instance, the conclusion of binding international agreements requires the consent of the European Parliament.[106] Given the Parliament's sensitivity to the promotion of values in the EU's external energy cooperation,[107] one may expect a stronger focus on ethical issues in comparison to tools, which are situated entirely in the executive sphere. An example of the latter is the frequent practice of signing non-legally binding memorandums of understanding (MoUs). For instance, the two MoUs establishing and updating an early-warning mechanism with Russia explicitly mention that '[t]his Memorandum does not constitute an international agreement or other legally binding document and does not establish rights and obligations governed by international law'.[108] The numerous MoUs on energy cooperation with third countries also include the standard clause that '[t]he present document records political intent alone and provides for no legal commitment'.[109] As a result, the involvement of the European Parliament is not required.[110]

Whereas the use of soft law instruments has the advantage of flexibility, it appears somewhat contrary to the EU's preference for a 'rule-based approach' in its external energy relations. The Commission, for instance, recently declared that '[w]ork urgently needs to be stepped up on *a comprehensive and coherent legal environment* for EU energy relations

[106] This follows from a combined reading of Art. 194(2) and Art. 218(6)(a)(v) TFEU.

[107] European Parliament Resolution on engaging in energy policy cooperation with partners beyond our borders: a strategic approach to secure, sustainable and competitive energy supply, P7-TA (2012) 0238, 12 June 2012, point 106.

[108] Section 13 of the 2009 Memorandum. Memorandum on an Early Warning Mechanism in the Energy Sector within the Framework of the EU–Russia Energy Dialogue, 16 November 2009, available at http://ec.europa.eu/energy/international/russia/doc/reports/2009_11_16_ewm_signed_en.pdf; section 14 of the 2011 Memorandum. Memorandum on a Mechanism for Preventing and Overcoming Emergency Situations in the Energy Sector within the Framework of the EU–Russia Energy Dialogue, 24 February 2011, available at http://ec.europa.eu/energy/international/russia/doc/20110224_memorandum.pdf.

[109] See, for instance, the MoUs signed with the countries of Central Asia, available at http://ec.europa.eu/energy/international/caucasus_central_asia_en.htm.

[110] A MoU is usually signed by the Commissioner for Energy (sometimes together with the High Representative and the Minister of the country holding the Presidency of the Union). For comments on this practice, see Van Vooren, 'Europe Unplugged', pp. 40–2.

with key suppliers and transit countries'.[111] It is questionable whether a network of MoUs is sufficient to guarantee the level of legal certainty the EU is aiming for. In this respect, it is noteworthy that the Commission proposed to 'negotiate EU-level agreements with third countries where necessary to achieve the EU core objectives'.[112] A first concrete example is the negotiation of an agreement with Azerbaijan and Turkmenistan on a legal framework for a Trans-Caspian (natural gas) pipeline system.[113] In this case, the formal procedure of Article 218 TFEU will have to be followed and one may expect that the European Parliament will keep a close eye on the balance between values and interests.[114]

5 Conclusions

The EU's governance of external energy relations provides a perfect example of how the Union aims to achieve its external action objectives. In the absence of a comprehensive international legal framework on energy issues, the EU actively promotes the export of its own values and norms on the basis of what has been identified as a 'rule-based market approach'. The clear ambition is to create a legally binding framework regulating relations with key energy partners and transit countries. Apart from the initiation of numerous policy initiatives and energy dialogues, two legal instruments merit specific attention. On the one hand, this is the ECT as the only multilateral legal instrument dealing with energy-related questions of transit and investment protection. On the other hand, this is the EnCT providing for the extension of the EU's internal market to its neighbouring countries. Both instruments are part of a comprehensive, multilayered strategy to promote the rule of law in international energy relations.

Despite the Union's general openness to international law, potential conflicts between the requirements of EU law and the protection offered under international legal regimes cannot be excluded. In particular, rules

[111] European Commission, Communication from the Commission to the European Parliament, the Council, the European Social and Economic Committee and the Committee of the Regions on security of energy supply and international cooperation, 'The EU Energy Policy: Engaging with Partners beyond our Borders', COM (2011) 539 final, p. 13.

[112] *Ibid.*, p. 5.

[113] Council of the European Union, 'The Council Gives Go-ahead for Negotiations on Trans-Caspian Pipeline', 14095/11 (Presse 307), Brussels, 12 September 2011.

[114] De Jong and Wouters, 'Central Asia and the EU's Drive towards Energy Diversification', p. 38.

on investment protection under the ECT or BITs may conflict with the EU’s energy and competition legislation. A key concern for the Union is to avoid undermining the autonomy of the EU legal order and the uniform application of EU legislation as a result of investment arbitration procedures. A related issue is to guarantee the correct and comprehensive application of the EU’s energy rules in the framework of the EnCT. It is questionable whether the existing dispute settlement procedure provides sufficient guarantees in this respect.

The tensions between the application of EU law and the elaboration of an international legal regime for energy issues are well illustrated in the context of EU–Russia energy relations. The Union’s ‘rule-based market approach’ appears to be at odds with Russia’s interests in a stable energy market based on vertically integrated energy companies working with long-term energy contracts. It is hard to see how both visions can easily be reconciled. As a result, the EU may be tempted to use more unilateral initiatives such as the inclusion of a ‘*Gazprom* clause’ in the Third Energy Package or the launch of investigation measures against *Gazprom* under EU competition rules. Arguably, this assertive attitude of the European Commission reveals a belief that the objectives of the external energy policy can only be achieved when the principles underlying the Union’s internal energy policy (diversification of supply, unbundling, free and fair competition, etc.) are fully respected in the relations with third countries. Together with the constant struggle to find a balance between values and interests, this ambition to project the internal rules and principles to the outside world is an essential feature of the EU’s governance mode of external energy relations.

10

The EU's shaping of international law on energy efficiency

ANATOLE BOUTE

1 Introduction

This chapter aims to examine the EU's contribution to the creation of international law on energy efficiency. To achieve the policy objectives of climate change mitigation and energy security, the EU has played an active role on the international diplomatic scene and contributed to the creation of different international legal acts in this field. The EU was a crucial actor in the negotiation, adoption and entry into force of the Kyoto Protocol.[1] The Energy Charter Treaty and its Protocol on Energy Efficiency and Related Environmental Aspects[2] also resulted from an EU initiative aimed at stimulating energy investments, including in the field of energy efficiency, in the former Soviet Union following its disintegration.[3] More recently, the EU initiated, in the context of the G8, what became the International Partnership for Energy Efficiency Cooperation.[4] However, the potential value of these initiatives was consistently watered down by the refusal of large developing and other developed states to commit to binding international obligations that would interfere with their energy system – a sector of high strategic importance – and

The author is grateful to Neale Tosh for excellent research assistance, and to Nathaniel Jezzi and Elisa Morgera for most interesting comments on a previous draft of this chapter.

[1] Kyoto Protocol to the United Nations Framework Convention on Climate Change (1998) 37 ILM 22 (hereinafter 'Kyoto Protocol'). R. Wurzel and J. Connelly, 'Introduction: European Union Political Leadership in International Climate Change Politics', in R. Wurzel and J. Connelly (eds.), *The European Union as a Leader in International Climate Change Politics* (Abingdon: Routledge, 2011), paras. 3–20; M. Scheurs and Y. Tiberghien, 'Multi-level Reinforcement: Explaining European Union Leadership in Climate Change Mitigation' (2007) 7 *Global Environmental Politics* 19.

[2] (1995) 34 ILM 373.

[3] See R. Lubbers, 'Foreword', in T. W. Wälde (ed.), *The Energy Charter Treaty: An East–West Gateway for Investment and Trade* (The Hague: Kluwer, 1996), p. xiv.

[4] European Commission, 'An Action Plan for Energy Efficiency', COM (2006) 545 final, p. 19.

that could limit their economic development and industrialization. States have generally proved to be reluctant to transfer part of their sovereignty to reduce their carbon intensity and energy intensity. In this context, the EU has developed an innovative mode of external governance that consists of promoting the adoption of EU energy efficiency regulation by other countries in the context of partnership agreements. In line with the subject matter of this book, the first objective of this chapter is to analyse the specific external energy efficiency governance mode that the EU has developed in reaction to states' reluctance to commit to binding international energy and climate obligations.

The external EU energy efficiency policy must be placed in the context of the tremendous economic growth and associated increases in energy consumption and greenhouse gas emissions in the developing world. The EU increasingly competes for energy resources with emerging economies and energy producers themselves.[5] Moreover, the bulk of future greenhouse gas emissions increases will come from emerging and transition economies. The relevance of Europe's energy security and climate change mitigation policy therefore depends, to a very large extent, on reductions in the energy intensity and carbon intensity of non-EU countries. EU Member States – as developed economies – have a historic responsibility related to the amount of greenhouse gases that they emitted in the process of their industrialization and which have accumulated in the atmosphere. Moreover, the EU is one of the largest energy consumers and importers and accordingly plays a central role in achieving global energy security. There are therefore strong moral reasons for the EU to help insulate developing countries from energy shocks and to assist them in reducing their future greenhouse gas emissions. It is against this background that the EU external energy efficiency policy is characterized by strategic (geopolitical) interests and, at the same time, touches upon moral issues that go to the heart of the difficult equity question[6] that underlies contemporary international climate change and energy security politics. Following the analytical

[5] European Commission, 'Energy Efficiency or Doing More with Less', Green Paper, COM (2005) 265 final, pp. 28 and 38; European Commission, Communication on Security of Energy Supply and International Cooperation: 'The EU Energy Policy: Engaging with Partners beyond our Borders', COM (2011) 539 final, p. 2.

[6] C. Fischer and R. Morgenstern, 'Metrics for Evaluating Policy Commitments in a Fragmented World: The Challenges of Equity and Integrity', in J. Aldy and R. Stavins (eds.), *Post-Kyoto International Climate Policy: Implementing Architectures for Agreement* (Cambridge University Press, 2010), pp. 300–42 (p. 324).

approach of this book, the second objective of this chapter is to examine the policy objectives of the EU external energy efficiency strategy by identifying and discussing the strategic interests, moral values and goals which are at stake.

The structure of the argument is as follows. The first part of the chapter questions the moral justification underlying the EU external energy efficiency policy. The analysis focuses on the climate change dimension of this external policy before turning to its energy security dimension. The second part of the chapter examines the policy instruments that the EU developed to achieve the external energy efficiency policy objectives. It looks at the EU's influence of the international climate change regime – in particular, the Kyoto Protocol – and the international energy regime – the Energy Charter Treaty – before examining regulatory convergence towards the energy efficiency *acquis communautaire* in the context of bilateral partnerships and the European Neighbourhood Policy.

This chapter argues that the innovative approach to engaging with the international legal order in the context of EU external energy efficiency has merits given the current deadlock in the negotiation of an international climate change and energy architecture. However, the current implementation of this policy is unlikely to be efficient in helping non-EU countries to generate energy efficiency improvements: promoting convergence towards the *acquis communautaire* suffers from the strategic agenda that is pursued by this policy. The EU aims to exercise influence on energy trade to secure energy supply and uses the EU regulatory model as a tool to achieve this geopolitical objective. This affects the moral goal of assisting developing and transition economies into becoming more energy and carbon efficient.

2 External energy efficiency policy goals: moral engagement or strategic interest?

Energy efficiency has long been a cornerstone of the EU internal energy policy. It lies at the heart of the EU strategy to tackle the dual energy-related challenges of climate change and security of supply.[7] Indeed, according to the European Commission, energy efficiency improvements

[7] European Commission, 'European Strategy for Sustainable, Competitive and Secure Energy', Green Paper, COM (2006) 105 final.

constitute 'without doubt the quickest, most effective and most cost-effective manner for reducing greenhouse gas emissions'.[8] Moreover, energy savings contribute to reducing EU dependency on energy imports and to maintaining the energy supply/demand balance in a climate-friendly way.[9] The International Energy Agency confirms that 'the most important contribution to reaching energy security and climate goals comes from the energy that we do not consume'.[10]

Based on similar considerations of energy security and climate change mitigation, the EU has extended the energy efficiency policy to the realm of external relations. According to the European Commission, '[i]t is at least as important to achieve improved energy efficiency in other industrialized countries and emerging economies as in Europe'.[11] The analysis hereunder first examines the climate change component of the external EU energy efficiency policy, before turning to the energy security objectives of this approach.

2.1 The climate change dimension

Climate change has become a priority in EU external relations[12] and energy efficiency plays an increasingly important role in this external climate policy. This policy is based on the recognition that greenhouse gas emissions growth will, following the shift in global energy demand patterns, be largely driven by non-OECD countries.[13] Measures need to be taken drastically to improve energy efficiency in emerging and transition economies in order to ensure that emissions remain at levels where the risk of dangerous anthropogenic interference with the

8 European Commission, 'Energy Efficiency or Doing More with Less', p. 4.

9 Directorate-General Energy and Transport, 'Measures to Secure Electricity Supply', Note by Directorate-General Energy and Transport Directives 2003/54/EC and 2003/55/EC on the internal market in electricity and natural gas, 16 January 2004; available at http://ec.europa.eu/energy/electricity/legislation/doc/notes_for_implementation_2004/security_of_gas_supply_en.pdf.

10 International Energy Agency, *World Energy Outlook 2011* (Paris: OECD, 2011), p. 40.

11 European Commission, Communication on the Second Strategic Energy Review: 'An EU Energy Security and Solidarity Action Plan', COM (2008) 781 final, p. 13.

12 European Council, 'Council Conclusions on EU Climate Diplomacy', 3106th Foreign Affairs Council Meeting, Brussels, 18 July 2011, available at www.eu-un.europa.eu/articles/en/article_11220_en.htm; European External Action Service and European Commission, 'Towards a Renewed and Strengthened EU Climate Diplomacy', Joint Reflection Paper, 9 July 2011, available at http://eeas.europa.eu/environment/.

13 European Commission, 'Key Facts and Figures on the External Dimension of the EU Energy Policy', Staff Working Paper, SEC (2011) 1022 final.

climate system is avoided.[14] The EU external energy efficiency policy aims to address this concern by promoting the use of energy-efficient technologies in non-EU countries so that these countries can contribute to the efforts being made to reduce global greenhouse gas emissions. According to the European Commission, stimulating energy efficiency improvements abroad is 'called for in the light of our shared commitment with our neighbouring countries to combat climate change'.[15] The scope of the external EU energy efficiency policy is not limited to neighbouring countries and developing countries, but encompasses cooperation with the large energy consuming countries (e.g. China, India, the US, Canada and Japan) 'with the objective of encouraging the rational use of energy worldwide'[16] and thus stabilizing global greenhouse gas emissions. The EU's moral engagement in this field is linked to the general EU sustainable development agenda.[17]

Moral considerations relating to Europe's 'shared commitment to combat climate change' (i.e. pure environmental motives)[18] are, however, not the central driving force to – and certainly not the only reason underlying – the climate change dimension of the EU external energy policy.[19] The EU is not acting 'selflessly', with the sole objective of avoiding the global climate change disaster. According to the European Commission, '[t]he principal reasons for strengthening energy efficiency cooperation with third countries are closely linked to the geopolitical and strategic interests of the EU and the business opportunities arising from the EU's leading role in this area'.[20] The geopolitical and strategic objectives primarily concern the energy security benefits of external

[14] International Energy Agency, *World Energy Outlook 2011*, p. 40.

[15] European Commission, Communication on the Development of Energy Policy for the Enlarged European Union, its Neighbours and Partner Countries, COM (2003) 262 final, p. 29; see also Parliament Resolution of 3 February 2009 on the Second Strategic Energy Review [2009] OJ C67 E/16, para. 62.

[16] European Commission, 'European Strategy for Sustainable, Competitive and Secure Energy', p. 17.

[17] L. van Schaik and S. Schunz, 'Explaining EU Activism and Impact in Global Climate Politics: Is the Union a Norm- or Interest-Driven Actor?' (2012) 50 *Journal of Common Market Studies* 169 (174).

[18] It must be noted that merely aiming to avoid climate disasters itself does not necessary make an act moral. Climate change disasters will generate huge costs for the EU and the consideration that such financial costs introduce is more prudential than moral.

[19] Van Schaik and Schunz argue that, although interests certainly played a role, the EU's external climate policies were predominantly driven by norms rather than interests. Van Schaik and Schunz, 'Explaining EU Activism and Impact in Global Climate Politics', p. 183.

[20] European Commission, 'Energy Efficiency or Doing More with Less', p. 33.

energy savings that will be discussed below. In addition, these strategic objectives relate to the diplomatic efforts made by the EU to show leadership in international climate negotiations and increase its influence on the international scene.[21] The business opportunities refer to the opening of new export markets for EU energy efficiency products which would contribute to consolidating the strategic position that the EU manufacturing industry occupies in this field.[22] This external commercial policy objective is based on the consideration that, following energy efficiency efforts in the aftermath of the 1970s energy crises, EU companies are at the forefront regarding energy efficiency and renewable energy technology.[23]

The fact that the EU is not acting in a purely selfless (i.e. benevolent) way but has mixed motives does not per se affect the moral value of its external energy efficiency policy. However, as will be argued below, strategic, geopolitical and commercial considerations become problematic if they lead to a reduced effectiveness of the moral agenda.

Despite the focus of the European Commission on strategic, geopolitical and commercial interests to justify its external energy efficiency policy, compelling ethical reasons can be found to legitimize EU engagement in the promotion of energy savings and greenhouse gas emissions reductions abroad. First, EU Member States – as developed and industrialized economies – are responsible for 'the largest share of historical and current global emissions of greenhouse gases',[24] and therefore have a historic 'carbon debt' towards the developing world.[25] International climate agreements recognize that the share of emissions originating in developing countries will grow to meet their social and development needs.[26] To stabilize the carbon stock in the atmosphere, the EU must,

[21] Wurzel and Connelly, 'Introduction', in *The European Union as a Leader in International Climate Change Politics*, p. 14. See also the chapter by Christina Eckes in this volume.

[22] European Commission, 'Energy Efficiency or Doing More with Less', p. 34.

[23] *Ibid*. Agreeing with van Schaik and Schunz, it must be noted that the economic benefits of this approach are affected by a high degree of uncertainty. Van Schaik and Schunz, 'Explaining EU Activism and Impact in Global Climate Politics', p. 176.

[24] Preamble of United Nations Framework Convention on Climate Change (1992) 31 ILM 849.

[25] R. Agarwala, 'Toward a Global Compact for Managing Climate Change', in Aldy and Stavins, *Post-Kyoto International Climate Policy*, pp. 179–200 (182).

[26] See e.g. 'Outcome of the Work of the Ad Hoc Working Group on Long-term Cooperative Action under the Convention', Decision 1/CP.16 adopted by the Conference of the Parties of the United Nations Framework on Climate Change, Sixteenth Session, Cancun,

given its historical carbon responsibility as an industrialized economy, take the lead in combating climate change and assisting emerging economies in their transition towards a low-carbon economy.[27] This moral obligation to act is reinforced by the fact that climate change will most severely affect the least developed countries.[28]

Furthermore, the EU external energy efficiency policy can be justified by the necessity to develop climate policy alternatives given the current deadlock in the negotiation of an international climate change regime. The EU cannot directly and solely be held responsible for the slow progress made on the conclusion of a post-2012 international climate architecture. However, the EU carbon debt provides a strong moral impetus for the EU actively to engage with the design of climate change mitigation approaches that would be acceptable to the developing world. The promotion of energy efficiency improvements is an alternative – or complement – to the current top-down approach[29] of the Kyoto Protocol that consists in setting absolute caps on the amount of greenhouse gases that states can emit. Improving energy efficiency – or reducing energy intensity – is a policy that fits well with the Chinese and Indian approaches to climate change mitigation. China and India consistently refuse to be bound by absolute emissions reduction targets[30] but, within the framework of the Copenhagen Accord,[31] these countries announced reductions in the carbon intensity of their economies.[32] With that in mind, an international energy efficiency policy could be an innovative

Mexico, UN Doc. FCCC/CP/2010/7/Add. 1, 15 March 2011 (hereinafter 'the Cancun Agreements'), items 6 and 47.

[27] Item 35 of the Cancun Agreements.

[28] R. Keohane and K. Raustiala, 'Toward a Post-Kyoto Climate Change Architecture: A Political Analysis', in Aldy and Stavins, *Post-Kyoto International Climate Policy*, p. 372; European Commission, 'Towards a Global Partnership for Sustainable Development', COM (2002) 82 final, p. 12.

[29] D. Bodansky, 'W[h]ither the Kyoto Protocol? Durban and beyond', Policy Brief, Harvard Project on Climate Agreements: Viewpoints, August 2011, available at http://belfercenter.ksg.harvard.edu/publication/21314/whither_the_kyoto_protocol_durban_and_beyond.html.

[30] See e.g. R. C. Schmidt and R. Marschinski, 'Can China Benefit from Adopting a Binding Emissions Target?' (2010) 38 *Energy Policy* 3763.

[31] Decision 2/CP.15 adopted by the Conference of the Parties of the United Nations Framework on Climate Change, Fifteenth Session, Copenhagen, Demark, UN Doc. FCCC/CP/2009/11/Add. 1, 30 March 2010 (hereinafter 'the Copenhagen Accord').

[32] See the Copenhagen Accord, Appendix II. See also S. Kypreos, 'From the Copenhagen Accord to Efficient Technology Protocols' (2012) 44 *Energy Policy* 341.

way to overcome the gap that currently separates developed countries from their developing counterparts in international climate change negotiations. This approach could stimulate the participation of large emerging economies in international efforts to mitigate climate change.

Another important ethical reason for the EU to stimulate energy efficiency improvements in non-EU countries relates to the phenomenon of carbon leakage. The implementation of climate policies in the EU can act as an incentive for energy-intensive companies to relocate their production facilities to countries that do not impose a price on carbon emissions.[33] An increasingly large part of China's greenhouse gas emissions result from the production of goods destined for export to and use in the developed world.[34] Independent of the impact that carbon leakage can have on the competitiveness of the EU domestic industries and on the effectiveness of EU climate policies, it is undeniable that the importers of goods produced in a carbon-intensive way hold a certain responsibility for the emissions associated with the manufacturing process and transport of these goods to the EU.[35] Influencing the energy and thus carbon intensity of the production process abroad can be seen as a way for the EU to address the carbon impact of its consumption patterns. It provides a more consensual alternative – or complement – to border tax adjustments and other trade restricting measures.

A related issue is the carbon cost of securing Europe's external energy supply, particularly in respect of natural gas imports from Russia. To increase the amount of natural gas available for export, Russia is stimulating the use of coal for electricity production.[36] Freeing up gas for export by replacing it with coal – one of the most carbon-intensive

[33] K. Neuhoff, *Climate Policy after Copenhagen: The Role of Carbon Pricing* (Cambridge University Press, 2011), p. 13.

[34] X. Dai and Z. Diao, 'Towards a New World Order for Climate Change: China and the European Union's Leadership Ambition', in Wurzel and Connelly, *The European Union as a Leader in International Climate Change Politics*, p. 253; Y. Zheng, J. Qi and X. Chen, 'The Effect of Increasing Exports on Industrial Energy Intensity in China' (2011) 39 *Energy Policy* 2688.

[35] On the Chinese position, see Dai and Diao, 'Towards a New World Order for Climate Change', p. 255.

[36] See Government of the Russian Federation, Resolution No. 1715-r of 13 November 2009 on Russia's Energy Strategy until 2030, Rasporiazhenie Pravitel'stva RF 'Ob Energeticheskoi strategii Rossii na period do 2030 goda' *Sobranie Zakonodatel'stva Rossiiskoi Federatsii* (SZ RF), 30 November 2009, No. 48, item 5836.

primary energy sources – in the domestic fuel mix will affect Russia's greenhouse gas emissions. The emissions associated with the increased use of coal, in a certain sense, represent the impact on climate change of Europe's energy security.[37] It could therefore be said that the EU has a moral responsibility to integrate the climate costs of its external energy supply by promoting efficiency improvements in the Russian energy infrastructure.[38] Saving energy in Russia through energy efficiency investments could free gas for export in a more climate-friendly way than replacing gas with coal for electricity production.[39]

In addition, the EU has a moral responsibility to improve energy efficiency in non-EU countries because of the perverse effect that the Clean Development Mechanism (CDM) of the Kyoto Protocol has on the implementation of energy efficiency policies in developing countries.[40] In accordance with the additionality criterion of the Kyoto Protocol, greenhouse gas emissions reduction projects are only eligible for support under the CDM if investors can prove that these projects would not have been financially viable in the absence of this additional support.[41] Developing countries therefore have an incentive to delay domestic energy efficiency policies that would positively influence the financial viability of emissions reduction projects.[42] Developed countries benefit from these delays as they stimulate the availability of relatively cheap emissions credits (Certified Emissions Reductions) to help them meet their international emissions reduction obligations.

[37] See K. Rosner, 'Dirty Hands: Russian Coal, GHG Emissions and European Gas Demand', *Journal of Energy Security*, August 27, 2009, available at www.ensec.org/index.php?option=com_content&view=article&id=207:dirty-hands-russia-coal-ghg-emissions-aamp-european-gas-demand&catid=98:issuecontent0809&Itemid=349.

[38] Jefferson Institute, 'Improving Energy Relations with Russia: The Roles of Energy Efficiency and Alternative Energy' (2009), pp. 3–5, available at www.isn.ethz.ch/isn/Digital-Library/Publications/Detail/?ots591=0c54e3b3-1e9c-be1e-2c24-a6a8c7060233&lng=en&id=99690.

[39] A. Goldthau, 'Improving Russian Energy Efficiency: Next Steps' (2008) 46 *Russian Analytical Digest* 9; International Energy Agency, *Optimizing Russian Natural Gas* (Paris: OECD, 2006).

[40] See Neuhoff, *Climate Policy after Copenhagen*, p. 224; H. van Asselt and J. Gupta, 'Stretching Too Far? Developing Countries and the Rule of Flexibility Mechanisms beyond Kyoto' (2009) 28 *Stanford Environmental Law Journal* 311 (347).

[41] Modalities and procedures for a clean development mechanism as defined in Art. 12 of the Kyoto Protocol, Decision 3/CMP.1 adopted by the Conference of the Parties to the Kyoto Protocol, FCCC/KP/CMP/2005/8/Add. 1, 30 March 2006, para. 43.

[42] Neuhoff, *Climate Policy after Copenhagen*, p. 224.

2.2 *The energy security dimension*

The traditional approach to external energy security primarily focuses on access to and protection of upstream energy investments (i.e. investments in the exploitation of oil and gas reserves), transport and transit of energy resources and international energy trade.[43] The EU external energy efficiency policy complements this approach: by promoting energy savings abroad, the EU aims positively to influence the future availability of energy sources.[44] This policy results from the impact on international energy markets of the rapid growth in energy consumption in emerging economies.[45] It is based on the reasoning that energy savings in non-EU countries would 'free up resources' that could be exported to the EU.[46] Such cooperation is of particular importance for the relationship between the EU and non-EU energy-producing countries. The promotion of energy efficiency in Russia, for instance, would 'increase the [European] security of energy supply because [. . .] energy savings in Russia would contribute to the availability of a higher level of Russian energy supply for export to the EU'.[47] The main reasons for energy efficiency cooperation with non-EU countries are thus primarily related to the 'geopolitical and strategic interests of the EU' (i.e. guaranteeing the future availability of energy sources to supply Europe).[48] Moreover, although not explicitly acknowledged by the EU, cooperation in the field of energy efficiency with energy producers is of strategic importance because of the opportunity this offers to work together on less strategically sensitive issues than traditional upstream energy projects.

43 See S. Haghighi, *Energy Security: The External Legal Relations of the European Union with Major Oil and Gas Supplying Countries* (Oxford: Hart Publishing, 2007).

44 European Commission, 'European Strategy for Sustainable, Competitive and Secure Energy', p. 17; 'Energy Policy for Europe (EPE)', Annex III to the Brussels European Council of 23/24 March 2006, Presidency Conclusions 7775/1/06 REV 1, 18 May 2006, p. 34; European Council, 'Transport, Telecommunications and Energy', press release, 2924th Council Meeting: Energy, 6670/09 (Presse 43), Brussels, 19 February 2009; European Parliament, Resolution on Security of Energy Supply in the European Union, P6_TA (2006) 0110, Brussels, 23 March 2006.

45 European Commission, 'Energy Efficiency or Doing More with Less', p. 33.

46 European Commission, 'The Development of Energy Policy for the Enlarged European Union', p. 29.

47 See Thematic Group on Energy Efficiency of the EU–Russian Energy Dialogue, Terms of Reference, 27 September 2007, Annex 2, available at http://ec.europa.eu/energy/international/bilateral_cooperation/russia/thematic_groups__en.htm.

48 European Commission, 'Energy Efficiency or Doing More with Less', p. 33; European Commission, 'An Energy Policy for Europe', COM (2007) 1 final, Annex 1.

Such cooperation would contribute towards improving the mutual trust and understanding between the EU and its energy suppliers.[49]

The integration of energy efficiency in the external energy security policy must be placed in the context of the historically limited legal competences of the EU in the energy field. The EC Treaty did not contain an energy title. Article 194 of the Treaty on the Functioning of the European Union (TFEU) introduces specific energy policy objectives and competences – including security of energy supply – but does not refer to external EU action to achieve these objectives. In contrast, the EC Treaty (by Article 174(1)) provided a strong legal basis for external relations in the field of environmental protection.[50] The TFEU added an explicit reference to external climate change action. It provides that 'Union policy on the environment shall contribute to [. . .] promoting measures at [the] international level to deal with regional or worldwide environmental problems, and in particular combating climate change'.[51] Because energy efficiency is a key part of EU climate policy, external action in this field can be based on the external environmental competences of the EU. Integrating energy efficiency in the external energy policy can thus be a way for the EU to overcome the limited legal basis upon which it can act in respect of external energy security by making use of the broader EU external environmental competences. In addition, the deployment of energy efficiency as an instrument of external energy security can be supported by the extensive *acquis communautaire* in this field. In connection with the implied external power doctrine, the energy efficiency *acquis* gives authority to the EU to develop international measures that are necessary to achieve the objective pursued with these measures, e.g. energy security.[52]

The energy security dimension of the EU external energy efficiency policy does not only pursue strategic objectives. It is also based on ethical

[49] With regard to Russia, see e.g. S. Handke and J. J. de Jong, *Energy as a Bond: Relations with Russia in the European and Dutch Context* (The Hague: Clingendael International Energy Programme, 2007), p. 60: www.clingendael.nl/publications/2007/20070900_ciep_energy_handke.pdf.

[50] According to Durán and Morgera, 'it is almost impossible to clearly define the substantive boundaries of EU environmental policy'. G. M. Durán and E. Morgera, *Environmental Integration in the EU's External Relations* (Oxford: Hart Publishing, 2012), p. 13.

[51] Art 191 (1) TFEU [2010] OJ C83/47. See also Art 21(2)(d) and (f), Consolidated Version of the Treaty on European Union [2008] OJ C115/13 EU. On the Treaty basis for external environmental action, see the contribution of Christina Eckes in this book.

[52] Case 22/70 *Commission* v. *Council* (ERTA) 1971 ECR 263.

considerations. According to the European Commission, 'the EU needs to take a strong, effective and *equitable* position on the international stage to secure the energy it needs'.[53] External energy efficiency is part of the EU development policy that aims to eradicate poverty in the context of the Millennium Development Goals.[54] Indeed, by improving the efficiency of the energy system in developing countries, the EU aims to minimize the impact of energy shocks (e.g. price volatility or energy scarcity) on these countries.[55]

Although the European Commission does not elaborate in detail on the ethical foundation of its external energy security policy, one could easily advance compelling moral reasons to justify this action. The EU has a moral responsibility to help insulate developing countries from energy shocks because of the EU's role as an important energy consumer and importer. The large amounts of energy that the EU Member States purchase on the international markets influence world energy prices, stoke price fluctuations and thus affect other countries, particularly those with more vulnerable economies. Energy consumers (e.g. industry) in the EU are ready to pay higher prices for their energy than consumers in developing countries, thereby limiting the availability of energy for competing consumers in poorer parts of the world. Moreover, the EU promotes energy efficiency improvements and the use of renewable energy sources in developing countries as a way to facilitate access to 'secure, affordable, clean and sustainable energy services'.[56] The European Commission considers access to energy 'a key ingredient to poverty eradication'.[57] Many regions in the developing world are characterized by the limited extent of their centralized electricity supply.

[53] European Commission, 'Security of Energy Supply and International Cooperation', p. 2 (emphasis added).

[54] European Commission, 'Increasing the Impact of EU Development Policy: An Agenda for Change', COM (2011) 637 final, p. 8.

[55] *Ibid.*

[56] *Ibid.*, p. 9. See also European Commission, 'Towards a Global Partnership for Sustainable Development', COM (2002) 82 final, p. 13; Council and Parliament Regulation (EC) Establishing a Financing Instrument for Development Cooperation 1905/2006 of 18 December 2006 [2006] OJ L378/41.

[57] European Commission, 'Rio+20: Towards the Green Economy and Better Governance', COM (2011) 363 final, p. 6. Importantly for an assessment of EU influence on the international scene, the outcome document of the Rio+20 UN Conference recognizes the importance of access to sustainable energy services for poverty eradication, including the more efficient use of energy. 'The Future We Want', Report of the UN Conference on Sustainable Development, A/CONF.216/16, Rio de Janeiro, Brazil, 20–22 June 2012.

Decentralized electricity production from renewable energy sources can often provide a cost-efficient alternative to extensions of the electricity grid.[58] In addition, by reducing the cost of future energy supply and by stimulating innovation and modernization of the infrastructure, assistance given to developing countries towards improving their energy efficiency can, at the same time, make a contribution to their economic and social development.[59] Nevertheless, in a similar way to the climate change dimension of the EU external energy efficiency policy, it could be argued that the policy objective of poverty eradication through access to energy is not only supported by moral considerations but also by commercial interests. The promotion of energy efficiency policies in the developing world, together with technology transfers and development funding, could be seen as a way to stimulate the export of the products of the EU energy efficiency manufacturing industry.[60]

3 External energy efficiency policy instruments: regulatory convergence based on partnership agreements

Partnerships and the promotion of regulatory convergence towards EU energy market rules are central elements of the EU external energy efficiency policy.[61] In its recent Communication on Security of Energy Supply, the European Commission proposes to develop the EU external energy policy by '[b]uilding up the external dimension of our internal energy market; [s]trengthening partnerships for secure, safe, sustainable and competitive energy; [i]mproving access to sustainable energy for developing countries; and [b]etter promoting EU policies beyond its borders'.[62] The European Commission highlights the 'need for new initiatives to develop mutually beneficial energy partnerships with key players'.[63] These partnerships should address 'all subjects of

[58] European Commission, 'Rio+20: Towards the Green Economy and Better Governance'.
[59] European Commission, 'Energy Efficiency or Doing More with Less', p. 33; European Commission, 'Security of Energy Supply and International Cooperation', p. 3.
[60] See European Commission, 'Increasing the Impact of EU Development Policy', p. 9.
[61] See the chapter by Peter Van Elsuwege in this book. Interestingly, the Rio+20 outcome document 'The Future We Want' highlights the importance of 'toolboxes', 'best practices', 'good examples' and 'models', in applying policies on green economy.
[62] European Commission, 'Security of Energy Supply and International Cooperation', pp. 3–4.
[63] *Ibid.*, p. 3.

common interests', including energy efficiency, energy security and low-carbon technologies.[64]

The promotion of regulatory convergence on the basis of partnerships must be placed in the context of the international opposition to EU initiatives directed at the creation of binding international agreements on energy efficiency. It provides an alternative approach to 'top-down' carbon and energy efficiency obligations which emerging economies, together with some large developed countries, tend to resist. Hereafter the EU initiatives to create a binding international energy efficiency regime are briefly examined, followed by an assessment of whether regulatory convergence – as a new energy efficiency governance mode – could be effective in generating energy savings in emerging economies.

3.1 *Multilateral agreements on energy security and climate change*

The EU was one of the driving forces behind the adoption and entry into force of the Kyoto Protocol – the cornerstone, together with the United Nations Framework Convention on Climate Change (UNFCCC), of international efforts to combat climate change.[65] The success of the Kyoto Protocol has, however, been undermined by the lack of binding commitments given by developing countries to limit their greenhouse gas emissions and the subsequent refusal of the US to ratify the Protocol.[66] International negotiations on a post-2012 international climate architecture face a similar challenge: states are reluctant to transfer sovereignty in respect of control over their greenhouse gas emissions (including the monitoring of these emissions) to the international community.

The Energy Charter Treaty, in particular its Protocol on Energy Efficiency and Related Environmental Aspects, is another EU-sponsored multilateral framework that, amongst other things, aims to stimulate energy efficiency improvements based on cooperation between the

[64] *Ibid.* [65] See the chapter by Christina Eckes in this book.

[66] It must be noted that, based on equity considerations (cf. the principle of 'common but differentiated responsibility'), the EU supported the claim of developing countries that, in a first phase, they should be allowed to develop without being bound by emissions reduction obligations – a position strongly opposed by the US and that eventually resulted in the refusal by the US to ratify the Protocol. See van Schaik and Schunz, 'Explaining EU Activism and Impact in Global Climate Politics', p. 180.

contracting parties.[67] However, the added value of the Energy Charter Treaty for energy efficiency improvements is limited by the fact that the energy efficiency obligations it imposes on contracting parties 'are no more than hortatory'.[68] The relevant provisions of the Treaty and the Protocol are vague, largely non-binding and limited by their subordination to economic considerations. According to Bradbrook, these provisions 'effectively give each country *carte blanche* to do as much or as little in relation to energy efficiency as it might wish at any given time. [They] effectively make each country the sole arbiter of what is appropriate action'.[69]

More recently, the EU has initiated a framework for cooperation on energy efficiency in the context of the G8.[70] The initial idea advocated by the European Commission was to create an International Agreement on Energy Efficiency involving both developed and developing countries, including Brazil, China, India, Japan, Russia and the US. The European Commission also sought to provide binding energy saving targets and standards, such as minimum performance requirements for goods and services, labelling and certification.[71] However, following the opposition of the US and of the emerging economies participating in this initiative, the EU proposal was 'watered down to a voluntary "partnership"'.[72] The G8+5 (including China, India and Korea) International Partnership for Energy Efficiency Cooperation (IPEEC)[73] aims to support energy efficiency policies of the participants by, for instance, compiling best practices, exchanging information, enabling joint research and developing public–private partnerships. The IPEEC is thus another declaration of the need to cooperate in the field of energy efficiency where the actions by states are purely discretionary.

[67] See Art. 3(1) of the Protocol on Energy Efficiency. See also A. Bradbrook, 'Significance of the Energy Charter Treaty' (1999) 64 *Applied Energy* 251.

[68] *Ibid.*, p. 254. [69] *Ibid.*, p. 256. Brackets added.

[70] European Commission, 'An Action Plan for Energy Efficiency', p. 19.

[71] See International Energy Agency, 'IEA Ministerial Meeting: Andris Piebalgs Calls for an International Agreement on Energy Efficiency', press release, 15 May 2007, IP/07/671, available at http://europa.eu/rapid/pressReleasesAction.do?reference=IP/07/671 &type=HTML; European Parliament, 'Security of Energy Supply in the European Union', item 10. See also D. Lesage, T. Van de Graaf and K. Westphal, 'G8+5 Collaboration on Energy Efficiency and IPEEC: Shortcut to a Sustainable Future?' (2010) *Energy Policy* 6419 (6424).

[72] *Ibid.*

[73] See 'Joint Statement by G8 Energy Ministers: Aomori, Japan on 8 June 2008', available at www.g8.utoronto.ca/energy/.

3.2 *Bilateral partnerships and the European Neighbourhood Policy*

Energy efficiency is a central element of the European Neighbourhood Policy (ENP).[74] According to the European Commission, energy cooperation in the context of the Neighbourhood Policy will be stepped up through 'the development of new partnerships on renewable energy sources and energy efficiency'.[75] The Energy Community Treaty[76] provides a framework for cooperation based on the integration of the energy *acquis communautaire*.[77] Moreover, energy efficiency is a key aspect of the so-called Interstate Oil and Gas Transportation to Europe (INOGATE) programme,[78] the Eastern Partnership[79] and the Black Sea Synergy initiative.[80]

In the context of these initiatives, the EU has often included energy efficiency in the Partnership and Cooperation Agreements and ENP Action Plans that it has signed with partner countries.[81] The energy

[74] European Commission and High Representative of the EU for Foreign Affairs and Security Policy, 'Eastern Partnership Roadmap 2012–13: The Bilateral Dimension', Joint Staff Working Document, SWD (2012) 109 final, p. 31.

[75] European Commission and High Representative of the EU for Foreign Affairs and Security Policy, 'A New Response to a Changing Neighbourhood', Joint Communication, COM (2011) 303, p. 10.

[76] [2006] OJ L198/18.

[77] See the chapter by Peter Van Elsuwege in this volume. It must be noted that Art. 35 of the Energy Community Treaty only provides that the Energy Community 'may adopt measures', in the field of energy efficiency.

[78] See Ministerial Declaration on Enhanced Energy Cooperation between the EU, the Littoral States of the Black and Caspian Seas and their Neighbouring Countries, Astana, 30 November 2006, available at http://ec.europa.eu/dgs/energy_transport/international/regional/caspian/doc/2006_11_30_astana_conclusions.pdf; 'Conclusions of the Ministerial Conference on Energy Cooperation between the EU, the Caspian Littoral States and their Neighbouring Countries, Baku, 13 November 2004', available at http://ec.europa.eu/dgs/energy_transport/international/regional/caspian/doc/final_energy_conclusions_en.pdf.

[79] European Commission and High Representative of the EU for Foreign Affairs and Security Policy, 'Eastern Partnership Roadmap 2012–13', Joint Staff Working Document, SWD (2012) 109 final; European Commission, 'EU–Eastern Europe: Towards a Partnership in Energy Efficiency', press release, Brussels, 25 November 2009, IP/09/1818, available at http://europa.eu/rapid/pressReleasesAction.do?reference=IP/09/1818&format=HTML.

[80] European Commission The Black Sea Synergy: A New Regional Cooperation Initiative, COM (2007) 160 final.

[81] See e.g. 'EU/Armenia Action Plan Priority Area 6', available at http://ec.europa.eu/world/enp/pdf/action_plans/armenia_enp_ap_final_en.pdf; 'EU/Georgia Action Plan', item 4.6.2, available at http://ec.europa.eu/world/enp/pdf/action_plans/georgia_enp_ap_final_en.pdf; 'EU/Moldova Action Plan', item 66, available at http://ec.europa.eu/world/enp/pdf/action_plans/moldova_enp_ap_final_en.pdf.

efficiency component is of particular relevance in the context of the external relations of the EU with energy producing (e.g. Azerbaijan)[82] and transit (e.g. Ukraine)[83] countries. Outside the Neighbourhood Policy, energy efficiency is considered a 'key area of common interest and cooperation' in the EU–Russian Energy Dialogue.[84] It is also central to the EU–China Dialogue on Energy and Transport Strategies[85] and the EU–US Energy Council.[86] Moreover, the access to energy agenda of the EU external energy efficiency policy is pursued in the context of the Joint EU–Africa Energy Partnership and the EU–Africa Partnership on Infrastructure.[87]

3.3 *Regulatory convergence towards the energy efficiency* acquis

Within the framework of partnership agreements, third countries are encouraged to approximate their energy and environment regulation to EU legal principles.[88] In contrast to the harmonization of national regulations within the EU, partner countries do not participate in the creation of these principles, but are invited unilaterally to integrate ready-made rules into their legal systems on a voluntary basis and without real

[82] 'Partnership and Cooperation Agreement between the EU, its Member States and Azerbaijan of 22 April 1996', 2104 UNTS 31 (2000); 'Memorandum of Understanding on a Strategic Partnership between the EU and Azerbaijan in the Field of Energy of 7 November 2006', available at http://ec.europa.eu/dgs/energy_transport/international/regional/caucasus_central_asia/memorandum/doc/mou_azerbaijan_en.pdf; 'EU/Azerbaijan Action Plan', item 4.6.2, available at http://ec.europa.eu/world/enp/pdf/action_ plans/azerbaijan_enp_ap_final_en.pdf.

[83] 'EU/Ukraine Action Plan', item 56, available at http://ec.europa.eu/world/enp/pdf/action_plans/ukraine_enp_ap_final_en.pdf.

[84] E.g. EU–Russia Energy Dialogue, 'Joint Report EU–Russia Energy Dialogue 2000–2010: Opportunities for our Future Energy Partnership', p. 10, available at http://ec.europa.eu/energy/international/russia/doc/reports/2010-11-report-10thtanniversaryfinal.pdf.

[85] EU–China Dialogue on Energy and Transport Strategies, 'EU–China Dialogue on Energy and Transport Strategies: Memorandum of Understanding', item 3.1, available at http://ec.europa.eu/energy/international/bilateral_cooperation/china/doc/dialogue/2005_mou_eu_china_energy_transport_strategies.pdf.

[86] EU–US Energy Council, Press Statement, Lisbon, 19 November 2010, 16724/1 (Presse 314), available at www.consilium.europa.eu/uedocs/cms_data/docs/pressdata/EN/foraff/117862.pdf.

[87] European Commission and Parliament, Interconnecting Africa: The EU–Africa Partnership on Infrastructure, COM (2006) 376 final, p. 7.

[88] European Commission, Security of Energy Supply and International Cooperation, p. 6; Durán and Morgera, *Environmental Integration in the EU's External Relations*, p. 135. See also the chapter by Peter Van Elsuwege in this volume.

enforcement procedures.[89] It thus involves 'one-side[d] alignment by third countries that are excluded from the Union's rule-making institutions'.[90]

The *acquis* in the field of energy efficiency consists of a considerable number of documents.[91] Directive 2006/32/EC of 5 April 2006 on Energy End-Use Efficiency and Energy Services,[92] applicable until 5 June 2014,[93] provides a general framework to enhance the cost-effective improvement of energy efficiency in the Member States. It aims to remove the existing bottlenecks impeding the efficient use of energy and to create a market for energy services and other energy efficiency improvement measures.[94] Directive 2006/32/EC establishes a general, indicative energy savings target of 9 per cent to be attained by the Member States within nine years.[95] Moreover, it requires Member States to publish so-called Energy Efficiency Action Plans (EEAPs) describing the measures taken to achieve the target, such as market-based support schemes for energy efficiency improvements ('white certificates') and the conclusion of voluntary agreements and informative mechanisms (e.g. energy audits). The EU institutions have recently agreed to replace Directive 2006/32/EC with a new directive – Directive 2012/27/EU on Energy Efficiency.[96]

[89] R. Petrov, 'Exporting the *Acquis Communautaire* into the Legal Systems of Third Countries' (2008) 13 *European Foreign Affairs Review* 33 (46); R. Dragneva and K. Wolczuk, 'EU Law Export to the Eastern Neighbourhood', in P. J. Cardwell (ed.), *EU External Relations Law and Policy in the Post-Lisbon Era* (The Hague: TMC Asser Press, 2012), pp. 217–27; A. Albi, 'The EU's "External Governance" and Legislative Approximation by Neighbours: Challenges for the Classic Constitutional Templates' (2009) 14 *European Foreign Affairs Review* 209 (215).

[90] A. Magen, 'The Shadow of Enlargement: Can the European Neighbourhood Policy Achieve Compliance?' (2003) 12 *Columbia Journal of European Law* 384 (386).

[91] See e.g. A. Boute, 'Energy Efficiency in the European Union: The Policy Framework', in M. M. Roggenkamp and U. Hammer (eds.), *European Energy Law Report VII* (Cambridge: Intersentia, 2007), p. 135.

[92] Parliament and Council Directive 2006/32/EC of 5 April 2006 on energy end-use efficiency and energy services and repealing Council Directive 93/76/EEC (2006) OJ L114/64.

[93] See Parliament and Council Directive 2012/27/EU of 25 October 2012 on energy efficiency, amending Directives 2009/125/EC and 2010/30/EU and repealing Directives 2004/8/EC and 2006/32/EC [2012] OJ L315/1.

[94] Art. 1, Parliament and Council Directive 2006/32/EC of 5 April 2006 on energy end-use efficiency and energy services and repealing Council Directive 93/76/EEC [2006] OJ L114/64.

[95] Art. 4, Parliament and Council Directive 2006/32/EC of 5 April 2006.

[96] Parliament and Council Directive 2012/27/EU of 25 October 2012 on energy efficiency, amending Directives 2009/125/EC and 2010/30/EU and repealing Directives 2004/8/EC and 2006/32/EC [2012] OJ L315/1.

Directive 2012/27/EU enlarges the scope of binding measures, e.g. by introducing energy efficiency obligation schemes that require energy suppliers to generate yearly energy savings of 1.5 per cent of their energy sales.[97] However, it maintains indicative national energy savings targets – not binding targets.

A second document of considerable relevance to energy efficiency improvements in the EU is Directive 2003/87/EC of 13 October 2003 establishing a scheme for greenhouse gas emissions allowance trading within the Community,[98] as modified by Directive 2009/29/EC.[99] The operators of the installations that fall within the scope of application of this Directive are required to cover their greenhouse gas emissions with a corresponding amount of emissions rights (allowances). In theory, scarcity of allowances is supposed to incentivize emissions reductions and thus stimulate energy efficiency improvements. The European Union Emissions Trading Scheme (EU ETS) is the pillar of the EU decarbonization policy in the energy sector and, in particular, the electricity production sector. Following the amendments that Directive 2009/29/EC introduced to the scheme, full auctioning of these allowances will be the rule from 2013 onwards: the operators of power plants will have to purchase all their allowances at market prices. Importantly, energy efficiency is also part of the EU energy liberalization agenda. Directive 2009/72/EC of 13 July 2009 concerning common rules for the internal market in electricity aims to create a free market that would send the right signals to potential investors in energy savings and renewable energy.[100] Following the regulatory convergence approach of the EU external energy efficiency policy, partner countries would have to integrate these legislative documents into their own internal legal order.

The European Commission justifies the legitimacy of its regulatory convergence approach by pointing out the quality of EU energy and environmental law. It has stated that '[t]he EU has some of the world's highest standards of market transparency and regulation [. . .] Through international cooperation the EU can help other countries raise their

[97] Art. 7, Parliament and Council Directive 2012/27/EU of 25 October 2012.

[98] [2003] OJ L275/32.

[99] Parliament and Council Directive 2009/29/EC of 23 April 2009 amending Directive 2003/87/EC so as to improve and extend the greenhouse gas emissions allowance trading scheme of the Community [2009] OJ L140/63.

[100] Parliament and Council Directive 2009/72/EC of 13 July 2009 concerning common rules for the internal market in electricity and repealing Directive 2003/54/EC [2009] OJ L211/5 recital 6.

standards'.[101] By promoting the integration of the *acquis* in partner countries, the EU would thus be able to assist these countries with the creation of a 'best practice' regulatory framework that would be conducive to energy efficiency improvements and renewable energy investments.[102] Given that the quality of EU norms is the EU's main argument in support of the assertion that its exercise of normative power towards partner countries is legitimate, it is important to assess whether the energy efficiency *acquis* provides an adequate regulatory model to generate energy savings abroad.

Energy experts often identify the declarative nature and the lack of enforcement of energy efficiency regulations, together with the absence of appropriate financing mechanisms and regulatory instability, as the main obstacles to the realization of energy savings in developing and transition economies.[103] To what extent do EU energy efficiency rules present an adequate template to overcome these barriers? Directive 2006/32/EC on Energy End-Use Efficiency has been heavily criticized for its largely declarative nature and in particular for the absence of mandatory energy efficiency improvement targets.[104] It only provides for indicative targets. In addition, many of the provisions of this Directive are characterized by non-binding language.[105] The *acquis* in the field of energy efficiency thus appears – at least until the entry into force of the new Directive on Energy Efficiency – to suffer from similar deficiencies in energy efficiency regulation found in many developing and transition economies, in as much as it is also characterized by non-binding

[101] European Commission, Security of Energy Supply and International Cooperation, p. 9.

[102] See Art. 13, para. 2 (e), Council and Parliament, Regulation (EC) 1905/2006 of 18 December 2006 establishing a financing instrument for development cooperation [2006] OJ L378/41.

[103] Energy Charter Secretariat, *Investing in Energy Efficiency: Removing the Barriers* (Energy Charter Secretariat, 2004), p. 42, available at www.encharter.org/fileadmin/user_upload/document/Energy_Efficiency_-_Removing_the_Barriers_to_Investment_-_2004_-_ENG.pdf; A. Sarkar and J. Singh, 'Financing Energy Efficiency in Developing Countries: Lessons Learned and Remaining Challenges' (2010) 38 *Energy Policy* 5560; World Bank, *Clean Energy and Development: Towards an Investment Framework* (Washington, DC: World Bank, 2006). With regard to Russia, see e.g. P. Opitz, 'Energy Savings in Russia: Political Challenges and Economic Potential' (2007) *Russian Analytical Digest* 5; International Finance Corporation, *Energy Efficiency in Russia: Untapped Reserves* (Washington, DC: World Bank Group, 2008).

[104] On this criticism, see A. Boute and A. De Geeter, 'Directive 2006/32/EC on Energy End-Use Efficiency and Energy Services: Realising the Transition to Sustainable Energy Markets?' (2006) *Journal of European Environment and Planning Law* 414.

[105] Or 'discretionary requirements'. *Ibid.*, p. 421.

language. 'Exporting' this part of the *acquis* abroad[106] is thus unlikely to address the barrier presented by the non-binding nature and lack of enforcement of energy efficiency regulation in emerging economies.[107] Paradoxically, the European Commission explicitly recognizes this deficiency and has therefore proposed binding energy saving targets and other mandatory mechanisms (e.g. related to heat generation and renovation of buildings) in its proposal for a new Energy Efficiency Directive.[108] This, however, has not prevented the EU from continuing to advocate the existing *acquis* as model to be followed by its partner countries. By the same token, the European Commission has acknowledged that regulatory deficiencies undermine the effectiveness of the EU ETS in incentivizing the decarbonization of energy supply.[109] Regulatory unpredictability and oversupply of allowances jeopardize the ability of this scheme to attract energy-efficient and low-carbon investments.[110] Nevertheless, the EU continues to encourage partner countries, where relevant, to implement carbon pricing based on the EU regulatory model.[111]

Instead of highlighting the limits of its regulatory approach and proposing possible solutions to overcome it, the EU advocates its regulation as model. By silencing the regulatory deficiencies that affect the *acquis* in the energy efficiency field, the EU undermines its legitimacy to influence the legislation of its partners. This approach could be understood in the light of the geopolitical interests at stake. Exporting

[106] According to Durán and Morgera, approximation 'build[s] upon the EU's own successes in environmental protection, as well as replicate its shortcomings'. Durán and Morgera, *Environmental Integration in the EU's External Relations*, p. 135.

[107] Scholars point out the risk that the outcome of regulatory convergence, as advocated by the European institutions, is likely to remain 'laws in books'. See A. Buzogány and O. Costa, 'Greening the Neighbourhood? The Environmental Dimension of the ENP in Morocco and Ukraine' (2009) 14 *European Foreign Affairs Review* 525 (537).

[108] European Commission, Proposal for a Directive on Energy Efficiency and Repealing Directives 2004/8/EC and 2006/32/EC, COM (2011) 370 final. This proposal resulted in the recently adopted Directive 2012/27/EU.

[109] European Commission, Proposal for a Directive amending Directive 2003/87/EC so as to improve and extend the greenhouse gas emissions allowance trading system of the Community, COM (2008) 16 final.

[110] Institutional Investor Group on Climate Change, 'Shifting Private Capital to Low Carbon Investment: An IIGC Position Paper on EU Climate and Energy Policy', pp. 6–11, available at www.iigcc.org/__data/assets/pdf_file/0016/12247/IIGCC-Position-Paper-on-EU-Climate-and-Energy-Policy.pdf.

[111] European Commission, Security of Energy Supply and International Cooperation, p. 6. See also 'Ministerial Declaration on Enhanced Energy Cooperation'.

the EU internal energy market model – including energy efficiency – is a way of influencing the rules of energy trade so as to further the interests of the EU in neighbouring energy producing and transit countries and more generally on the international energy markets.[112] In relation to the EU's Eastern neighbourhood and its interaction with Russia, it could be seen as a way to 'keep a regional hegemon at distance'.[113] To understand the strategic component of regulatory convergence towards the internal energy market model, it is interesting to highlight Russia's increasing criticism of this EU external normative approach in the former Soviet Union.[114]

4 Conclusion

The EU has contributed to the creation of an international law on energy efficiency by influencing the adoption and entry into force of the Kyoto Protocol, the Energy Charter Treaty and its Protocol on Energy Efficiency, and the G8+5 International Partnership for Energy Efficiency Cooperation. Moreover, the EU aims to generate energy savings abroad by exporting the energy efficiency *acquis* in the context of partnership agreements, in particular with neighbouring and developing countries.

The EU's engagement with energy efficiency improvements in developing and transition economies can be justified on moral grounds. From a climate change perspective, the EU has a historic responsibility, through its carbon debt, to assist emerging economies in limiting the tremendous greenhouse gas emissions growth that is expected to result from their industrialization and economic development. From an energy security perspective, the EU – as one of the largest energy consumers and importers in the world – has a moral responsibility to help shield developing countries from energy price shocks and scarcity. There are, at the same time, geopolitical and strategic interests that play a central role in the EU external energy efficiency policy. Generating energy

[112] See C. van der Linde, 'Juridisch Imperialisme', *Energie Nederland*, 13 June 2006, available at http://web.archive.org/web/20070221071456/http://www.clingendael.nl/publications/2006/20060613_ciep_col_vanderlinde.pdf.

[113] H. Prange-Gstöhl, 'Enlarging the EU's Internal Energy Market: Why Would Third Countries Accept EU Rule Export?' (2009) 37 *Energy Policy* 5296.

[114] Cambridge Energy Research Associates, *Securing the Future: Making Gas Interdependence Work* (Cambridge Energy Research Associates, 2007). See also D. Averre, 'Competing Rationalities: Russia, the EU and the "Shared Neighbourhood"' (2009) 61 *Europe-Asia Studies* 1689.

savings abroad, particularly in energy-producing and transit countries, increases the availability of energy available for export to the EU. Moreover, the promotion of energy efficiency policies reinforces the competitive advantage of the EU energy efficiency manufacturing industry and opens new markets for exports.

The EU external energy efficiency policy is also of strategic interest from an internal EU policy perspective. It enables the EU to circumvent the limited legal basis for external legal relations in the field of energy security by making use of the broader external competences for environmental protection and, in particular, climate change mitigation. In addition, the implied power doctrine legitimizes an external energy policy in this field given the extensive energy efficiency *acquis*.

Moral considerations officially underlie the regulatory convergence policy of the EU: by exporting the *acquis*, the EU would promote 'some of the world's highest standards' in the sector and would therefore contribute to the creation of a regulatory framework that will generate energy efficiency improvements. Importantly, in this context, strategic and geopolitical considerations are also key. 'As a major energy consumer, importer and technology provider, the EU has an interest in the energy policy developments of its partners across the globe'[115] and promoting the *acquis* as a model is a means of influencing these policy and regulatory developments to the benefit of the EU.

The key role of strategic interests in the EU external energy efficiency policy, besides moral goals, is as such perfectly justifiable. However, the focus on these strategic considerations at the expense of the moral goals of this external policy considerably reduces the legitimacy of the EU's exercise of its normative power in relation to its partners. It also affects the effectiveness of this innovative external governance approach to generate the ultimate objective of energy savings abroad. By promoting the *acquis* as model, and silencing its deficiencies, the EU misses a chance to share the negative lessons that it learned from its regulatory experience and that its partners should try to avoid in the creation of a functioning framework for energy efficiency improvements.

[115] European Commission, Security of Energy Supply and International, p. 9.

11

The EU: shaping migration patterns in its neighbourhood and beyond

LAURE DELCOUR

1 Introduction

Over the past two decades, migration issues have become increasingly important on the EU's agenda. Even though fragmented and strongly constrained by Member States' determination to retain their sovereignty,[1] a legal and policy framework for the EU's migration policy was laid down in the Treaty on the European Union and gradually expanded in the Treaty of Amsterdam, the Tampere, the Hague and the Stockholm Programmes. This framework was primarily meant to address the growing sense of urgency and public fears that developed around the control of migration flows into the European Union in the 1990s,[2] at a time when a borderless area emerged on the continent after the entry into force of the Convention implementing the Schengen agreement. Irregular migration, in particular, was increasingly presented as a threat in EU Member States' policy discourses on migration.[3] This perception, also fuelled by European media, gave an impetus to the coordination between EU Member States' policies and to an increased European-level involvement in migration-related policy areas. Immigration and asylum, which emerged as matters of common interest under the Treaty of Maastricht, became a full Community responsibility with the Treaty of Amsterdam. This Treaty also paved the way for the development of an external dimension for the EU's migration policy by calling upon the establishment of an 'area of freedom, security and justice in which the free

[1] A. Weinar, 'EU Cooperation Challenges in External Migration Policy', Research Report, EU–US Immigration Systems 2011/02 (2011), Robert Schuman Centre for Advanced Studies, San Domenico di Fiesole (FI): European University Institute, p. 6.

[2] H. de Haas, 'The Myth of Invasion: The Inconvenient Realities of African Migration to Europe' (2008) 29 *Third World Quarterly* 1309.

[3] B. A. Vollmer, 'Policy Discourses on Irregular Migration in the EU: "Number Games" and "Political Games"' (2011) 13 *European Journal of Migration and Law* 317–39.

movement of persons is ensured in conjunction with appropriate measures with respect to external border controls, asylum, immigration'.[4] This entailed creating effective common instruments on immigration, asylum and external borders.[5]

In line with the objectives set in the Treaty of Amsterdam, since the beginning of the last decade the Union has more and more sought to pursue its migration policy externally, especially at its periphery. In the EU's discourse, the new borders resulting from its last waves of enlargement indeed confront the Union with new risks related to migration:

> Neighbours who are engaged in violent conflict, weak states where organised crime flourishes, dysfunctional societies or exploding population growth on its borders all pose problems for Europe.[6]

Migration issues are thus salient under the European Neighbourhood Policy (ENP)[7] created in 2004. Neighbours play a key role in migration flows to the EU, either as countries of origin or transit countries. As a consequence, while the EU pursues its migration policy worldwide, it places a particular emphasis on its neighbourhood.[8] The EU has developed a wide array of migration tools under the ENP, including migration dialogues, visa facilitation and readmission agreements, visa liberalization dialogues and mobility partnerships. Most of these instruments have been designed specifically for neighbouring countries, with which the European Union intends to build a 'special'[9] relationship, based upon '"deep" forms of cooperation'.[10]

While the migration toolbox used under the ENP was conceived for a specific external policy targeting bordering countries, this chapter

[4] Art. 2, Treaty on the European Union OJ (1997) C224.

[5] Title IV, Arts. 61–3, Treaty on the European Union.

[6] Council of the European Union, A Secure Europe in a Better World, European Security Strategy (2003).

[7] ENP countries include the Southern Mediterranean partners (Algeria, Morocco, Tunisia, Libya, Egypt, Jordan, Lebanon, Israel, the Palestinian Authority, Syria) and six former Soviet Republics participating in the EU's Eastern Partnership (Armenia, Azerbaijan, Belarus, Georgia, Moldova and Ukraine).

[8] B. Ferrero-Waldner, 'Migration, External Relations and the European neighbourhood Policy' (Europa 2006) available at www.eu-un.europa.eu/articles/fr/article_5767_fr.htm.

[9] Art. 8 TEU.

[10] D. Hanf, 'The ENP in the Light of the New "Neighbourhood Clause" (Article 8 TEU)', College of Europe Research Papers in Law No. 2/2011, available at http://www.coleurope.eu/content/studyprogrammes/law/studyprog/pdf/ResearchPaper_2_2011_Hanf.pdf.

maintains that its impact is not circumscribed to the EU's fringes. The ENP migration toolbox indeed provides the Union with a *leverage affecting migration patterns beyond the EU's Southern and Eastern peripheries*. By shaping ENP partner countries' response to international migration, the EU influences migration flows and governance not only in the neighbourhood but also in adjacent regions. This is tightly connected to the specific features of the migration policy area which, as underlined by Kunz, Lavenex and Panisson, 'is not a stronghold of global governance'.[11] In a policy area characterized by both interdependence of states' migration policies and the lack of an international migration regime,[12] the *neighbourhood* thus plays a pivotal role in the EU's approach to migration[13] *worldwide* and in the EU's influence on *global* migration patterns.

In order to understand the connections between various levels of migration governance (bilateral, regional, inter-regional and international) better, this chapter relies upon the concept of *trans-regionalism*, defined by Alexander Betts as 'sets of formal and informal institutions [and, one may add, norms] that cut across and connect different geographical regions, constituting or constraining the behaviour of states and non-state actors in a given policy field'.[14] Migration cooperation under the ENP is analysed as an illustration of *trans-regional governance*, which, by creating intersections between different regions, contributes to shaping global migration governance in the absence of a formal multilateral institutional framework.

The chapter looks specifically (although not exclusively) at the EU's approach and policy toolbox designed to combat irregular migration under the European Neighbourhood Policy. As pointed out by Düvell, there are a number of pathways to irregular migration, e.g. irregularity by birth, visa overstay or non-return of refused

[11] R. Kunz, S. Lavenex and M. Panisson, 'Governance through Partnership in International Migrations', in Kunz, Lavenex and Panisson (eds.), *Multi-Layered Migration Governance: The Promise of Partnership* (London: Routledge, 2011), p. 23.

[12] A. Betts, 'The Global Governance of Migration and the Role of Transregionalism', *ibid.*

[13] European Council, 15–16 December 2005, Presidency Conclusions 15914/1/05, IV, 8 (2006). Neighbours' centrality in the EU's migration policy is also confirmed by the fact that the EU's Global Approach to Migration was revised in the wake of 2011 upheavals in the Southern Mediterranean. European Commission, Communication to the Council, the European Parliament, the European Economic and Social Committee and the Committee of the Regions on the Global Approach to Migration and Mobility, COM (2011) 743 final, Brussels, 18 November 2011.

[14] Betts, 'The Global Governance of Migration and the Role of Transregionalism'.

asylum-seekers.[15] This contribution focuses on a pathway which is particularly salient in EU–ENP countries relations, i.e. clandestine entry from a neighbouring country into EU territory. Dramatic attempts by groups of sub-Saharan migrants to climb over the border fences of the two Spanish enclaves Ceuta and Melilla in 2005, boats full of Tunisian refugees arriving at the tiny Italian island of Lampedusa in 2011 are only two among the many examples that have fed EU policy concerns on neighbours' capacities effectively to manage migration and control their borders.

In assessing the EU's influence on the control of irregular migration flows, the chapter attempts to gauge whether the EU is effective in promoting the values entrenched in its constitutional framework when implementing its external migration policy in the neighbourhood, or whether it rather pursues self-centred policies that are not ethically justifiable. It asks whether EU policies rely upon the human rights-based approach that the Union claims to diffuse in its external action, or whether they rather reflect an interest-based approach.

The chapter starts with an analysis of the migration policy toolbox developed by the European Union in its neighbourhood and examines the actual implementation of EU-induced agreements and norms by Southern and Eastern neighbours. It sheds light on ethical tensions that stem from the externalization of EU migration policies to the neighbourhood. The analysis then moves to the effects of EU policies on migration patterns involving the 'neighbours of neighbours' and other countries. It points to the disruptive and even harmful implications that EU-induced restrictive migration policies adopted by neighbouring countries have on adjacent regions.

2 The externalization of EU migration policies to the neighbourhood: emerging migration governance and ethical ambiguities around the EU's buffer zone

The limitation of immigration and refugee flows, as well as the control and restriction of illegal entries, have emerged as the overarching objectives pursued by the Union and its Member States in migration and asylum policies.[16] Yet, the gradual harmonization of migration

[15] F. Düvell, 'The Pathways in and out of Irregular Migration in the EU: A Comparative Analysis' (2011) 13 *European Journal of Migration and Law* 247.

[16] C. Boswell, 'The External Dimension of EU Immigration and Asylum Policy' (2003) 79 *International Affairs* 619.

and asylum policies engaged in the 1990s proved insufficient effectively to control migration flows and prompted the EU to look for alternatives.[17] While in the 1990s EU immigration and asylum policy and external relations developed in parallel,[18] at the end of the decade a consensus developed around the idea that 'the EU's external relations should be used to attain the EU's security objectives'.[19] Ever since it was launched, the European Neighbourhood Policy has been a major policy framework for 'integrating migration concerns into external policy'.[20] However, in essence the externalization of EU migration policy is embedded in (implicit) policy assumptions that raise fundamental ethical challenges.

The EU's key concern in migration cooperation with third countries is to 'protect [its] internal security from outside threats'.[21] The EU's external migration policy, particularly in the neighbourhood, 'has emphasized migration control measures despite attempts to stress preventive elements in the EU's global approach to migration'.[22] The ENP's priorities in this respect include improved 'border management, including short seacrossings [...] cooperation in the fight against illegal immigration, and management of legal migration and implementation of migration plans (for example with the three central Maghreb countries, Libya and Egypt) [...] cooperation between neighbouring countries in the effective control of borders by specialised and trained

[17] *Ibid.*; A. Bilgic, 'Is the EU Offloading Future Migration Issues to the "Southern Neighbourhood"?: Thinking Environmental Migration in Relation to Externalisation' (2011) Review as part of Foresight Project, Migration and Global Environmental Change, UK Government Office for Science, available at www.bis.gov.uk/assets/foresight/docs/migration/case-studies/11-1160-cs8-eu-offloading-future-migration-issues.pdf, p. 3.

[18] For instance, migration control was not included amongst the key political objectives of the Euro-Mediterranean Partnership launched in 1995. Bilgic, 'Is the EU Offloading Future Migration Issues to the "Southern Neighbourhood"?', p. 4.

[19] S. Wolff, G. Mounier and N. Wichmann, 'The External Dimension of Justice and Home Affairs: A Different Security Agenda for the EU?', p. 13.

[20] C. Boswell, 'Evasion, Reinterpretation and Decoupling: European Commission Responses to the External Dimension' of Immigration and Asylum' (2008) 3 *West European Politics* 498.

[21] S. Wolff, G. Mounier and N. Wichmann, 'The External Dimension of Justice and Home Affairs: A Different Security Agenda for the EU? (2009) 31 *Journal for European Integration* 12.

[22] D. Wunderlich, 'The Limits of External Governance: Implementing EU External Migration Policy' (2012) 9 *Journal of European Public Policy* 1421; European Commission, Communication to the Council, the European Parliament, the European Economic and Social Committee and the Committee of the Regions on the Global Approach to Migration and Mobility, COM (2011) 743 final, 18 November 2011.

personnel'.[23] EU migration policies, then, aim at tackling potential threats in the neighbourhood in order not to import them to the EU. To achieve these priorities and combat illegal migration, the EU has primarily sought to export its own policy norms and templates with a view to 'normalising the behaviour of target partners'.[24]

The neighbourhood (understood here in a broad sense, i.e. not only ENP partner countries but all countries sharing a border with the EU, including the Russian Federation, Turkey and the Western Balkans) has clearly emerged as a buffer zone playing a crucial role in keeping illegal migrants outside the EU's borders. The provisions related to migration under EU neighbour agreements and policy documents 'externalize migration control functions' and reflect 'an extension of the EU migration regime outside of the Union'.[25] According to Bilgic, the buffer zone resulting from such externalization performs three functions in the EU's migration policy: neighbouring countries act as migrant filters, exercise selection of migrants and also serve as a 'dumping ground' of unwanted migrants expelled from the EU.[26] These functions are discussed in detail below.

2.1 Neighbouring countries as filters

First, the role of *filter*: cooperation between the EU and neighbouring countries permits stopping migrants either before their attempts to enter the EU's territory or during their entry to the Union.[27] The EU has sought to securitize legal migration flows to its neighbourhood by exporting a series of conditions on migration management in exchange for increased mobility of neighbours' citizens to the EU. For instance, it has required from Western Balkans and from countries under the Eastern Partnership[28] the application of a mechanism for the monitoring of migration flows, the establishment of bodies responsible for collection

[23] European Commission, Communication to the Council and the European Parliament: 'Strategy Paper on European Neighbourhood Policy (EC)', COM (2004) 373 final, p. 23.

[24] T. Balzacq, 'The Frontiers of Governance: The External Dimension of EU Justice and Home Affairs', in T. Balzacq (ed.), *The External Dimension of EU Justice and Home Affairs: Governance, Neighbours, Security* (London: Palgrave, 2009), p.19.

[25] S. Lavenex and E. Uçarer, *Migration and the Externalities of European Integration* (Oxford: Lexington Books, 2002), p. 216.

[26] Bilgic, 'Is the EU Offloading Future Migration Issues'?, p. 8. [27] *Ibid*., p. 9.

[28] These requirements are formulated for those Eastern Partners having concluded a Visa Liberalisation Action Plan, e.g. Georgia, Moldova and Ukraine.

and analysis of data on migration stocks and flows, and the definition of an updated migration profile including data on both legal and illegal migration.[29] The EU also requires from those countries the implementation of a law on foreigners governing the admission and stay of third-country nationals that would define rights and obligations for the persons concerned (including family members of third-country nationals). Finally, it expects from partner countries clear-cut visa categories. Such requirements have undoubtedly contributed to introducing more restrictive migration policies in the Balkans and in some of the countries included in the Eastern Partnership. The Georgian example shows how the EU has affected migration management with the view to enabling the country effectively to fulfil its role as a filter. The EU's influence, however, is at the cost of the liberal approach to migration developed by Georgian authorities. Migrants who enter Georgia legally are so far not required to obtain any permit to work. In addition, the country does not require any visa for citizens from a number of countries worldwide and it has set up a bilateral visa-free regime with a series of countries as well.[30] Finally, Georgia has developed a very liberal approach with respect to the delivery of residence permits (up to one year). Such an open-door approach to migration is considered a pillar of the government of Georgia's economic strategy,[31] which primarily seeks to attract foreign investment and to create a favourable business environment.[32] In this context, EU norms on the admission and stay of third countries' nationals have a low resonance in Georgia. To some extent, the country is ready to revise its legal framework, to regulate residence permits more strictly and to introduce different visa categories. Such reforms are envisioned as a trade-off between the degree of security requested by the EU and the degree of flexibility necessary to pursue an open-door policy, which Georgia is not ready to abandon.[33] Georgian officials view the reinforcement of control over migration as a

[29] Government of Montenegro, 'Roadmap: Visa Liberalisation with Montenegro', 5 May 2008, p. 5.

[30] Ministry of Foreign Affairs of Georgia 2012: www.mfa.gov.ge/index.php?sec_id=96&lang_id=ENG.

[31] Interview conducted with the Head of International Relations Department, the Civil Registry Agency Tbilisi, November 2011.

[32] *Ibid.*

[33] Georgia's approach may nonetheless evolve as a result of a rising number of migrants and asylum requests, which has sparked debate within the government on the relevance of the country's migration policy. Interview conducted with a Civil Rights Agency official, Tbilisi, March 2013.

strategy to meet EU concerns while also enabling the country to safeguard its core norms and values. Yet, given the EU's strong reliance on conditionality under the visa liberalization process, it seems unlikely that the country will be able to maintain its liberal approach if it wants to proceed further toward a visa-free regime with the EU. As illustrated by the case of Georgia, the diffusion of EU security concerns to the neighbourhood can therefore harm partner countries' own approaches to migration.

Besides migration management, border management tools are prominent instruments to stop migrants on their way to the EU. They include 'the rules, techniques and procedures regulating activities and traffic across defined border areas or zones'.[34] As pointed out by Wolff, the EU has increasingly sought 'joint ventures' with neighbours (primarily South Mediterranean partners) in patrolling maritime borders.[35] It has also institutionalized border management as part of its cooperation with Russia and ENP partners, even though some countries were initially reluctant to cooperate. For instance, the EU had strived to launch border management cooperation with Morocco since 1998 but it had to wait until 2005, when the country became increasingly concerned by unregulated migration flows and first agreed to establish cooperation with Spain.[36] Yet, EU–Moroccan cooperation on border management remained to a significant extent shaped by Moroccan priorities, e.g. over the disputed Western Sahara Territory, while the Commission was apparently unable to monitor the use of the money allocated to Morocco for border management.[37] The EU's capacity to influence migration and border management processes in the neighbourhood thus appears constrained by two factors: the importance of neighbours as countries of transit or origin in migration flows to the EU (which provides them with a leverage in interacting with the Union), and the neighbours' expectations on their future relations with the EU (those Eastern partners willing to join the Union have a more limited capacity to negotiate EU norms and policies).

Besides the EU's actual capacity to shape migration developments, the role of 'filter' devoted to neighbours raises ethical questions since

[34] A. Hills, 'Towards a Rationality of Democratic Border Management', in M. Caparini and O. Marenin (eds.), *Borders and Security Governance: Managing Borders in a Globalised World* (Geneva: Geneva Centre for the Democratic Control of Armed Forces, 2006), p. 33.

[35] S. Wolff, 'Border Management in the Mediterranean: Internal, External and Ethical Challenges' (2008) 21 *Cambridge Review of International Affairs* 261.

[36] D. Wunderlich, 'The Limits of External Governance: Implementing EU External Migration Policy', p. 1422.

[37] *Ibid.*, p. 1425.

it involves exporting surveillance and identification technologies to countries lacking vibrant civil societies, democratic structures and oversight.[38] This, in turn, constitutes a challenge to the EU's foreign policy in so far as it potentially contradicts its ethical dimension, especially under the neighbourhood policy which intends to develop 'a privileged relationship [...] build[ing] on mutual commitment to common values principally within the fields of the rule of law, good governance, the respect for human rights'.[39]

2.2 Neighbouring countries and externalization of asylum claims

Secondly, neighbours have a *selection function* for asylum-seekers who may, based upon their selection, either be returned or ultimately reach the EU. The building of asylum systems in the EU's periphery as part of EU neighbours cooperation indeed suggests that Member States 'offload asylum responsibility'[40] to the neighbourhood. Neighbours are given a crucial role in identifying 'genuine refugees *outside* the EU borders'.[41] This role rests upon the underlying assumption that neighbours 'offer sufficient protection' for those seeking international protection.[42] Yet, this assumption comes up against neighbours' views on asylum, their practices and the overall weakness of asylum systems (or lack thereof) in the EU's periphery. For instance, the fact that Moroccan authorities do not engage with migrants transiting through their territory hampers the EU's approach to asylum. As indicated by Wunderlich, the Moroccan Ministry of Interior views asylum 'as an illegitimate way of economic immigration'[43] and therefore decided to dismantle the Moroccan asylum service. This, in turn, raises questions as to the human rights protection offered to asylum-seekers.[44] Such questions are particularly salient in the case of

[38] S. Wolff, 'Border Management in the Mediterranean: Internal, External and Ethical Challenges', p. 266.

[39] European Commission, European Neighbourhood Policy Strategy Paper, COM (373) final (2004), p. 3. The ENP's value-based dimension has been strengthened under the renewed approach adopted in 2011. Joint Communication by the High Representative of the Union For Foreign Affairs and Security Policy and the European Commission, Joint Communication to the European Parliament, the Council, the European Social and Economic Committee and Committee of the Regions on a New Response to a Changing Neighbourhood: 'A Review of European Neighbourhood Policy', COM (2011) 303, Brussels, 5 May 2011.

[40] Bilgic, 'Is the EU Offloading Future Migration Issues'?, p. 8. [41] *Ibid.* [42] *Ibid.*

[43] D. Wunderlich, 'The Limits of External Governance: Implementing EU External Migration Policy', p. 1423.

[44] *Ibid.*, p. 1425.

Libya. The European Parliament recently expressed concern over the detention of persons (including women and children) in extreme conditions (including frequent threats and abuses) and called the EU and Member States to take these concerns into account when negotiating migration control agreements with Libya.[45]

2.3 Neighbouring countries as a 'dumping ground'

Thirdly, the neighbourhood appears as '*a dumping area of the EU*',[46] or a region to which Member States extradite illegal migrants who have crossed the EU's borders. This function is underpinned by readmission agreements, which are part of the EU's policy to return illegal migrants. They have emerged as the key EU policy tool to curb irregular migration originating from, or transiting through, partner countries.[47] Initially used by EU Member States, readmission agreements appeared as the first instrument for common action under EC law after the entry into force of the Treaty of Amsterdam.[48] While the Treaty of Lisbon introduces an express European Union competence over readmissions under Article 79(3) TFEU, this competence is shared with Member States which continue to retain their rights to conclude bilateral readmission agreements with third countries.[49] As noted by Cassarino, readmission agreements concluded by the EU constitute only a tiny share of the overall number of readmission agreements, and the system of readmission remains predominantly bilateral with most Member States being involved in such agreements.[50] So far fourteen EU agreements have been reached out of the twenty-one mandates given by the Council to negotiate with third

[45] European Parliament, Plenary Session, press release, 'Human Rights: Migrants' Security in Libya, Executions in Iran, Violence in Burma', 2012, available at www.europarl.europa.eu/news/en/pressroom/content/20121116IPR55721/html/Human-rights-migrants%27-security-in-Libya-executions-in-Iran-violence-in-Burma.

[46] Bilgic, 'Is the EU Offloading Future Migration Issues'?, p. 9.

[47] F. Trauner and I. Kruse, 'EC Visa Facilitation and Readmission Agreements: Implementing a New EU Security Approach in the Neighbourhood' (2008) CEPS Working Document No.290.

[48] C. Billet, 'EC Readmission Agreements. A Prime Instrument of the External Dimension of the EU's Fight against Irregular Immigration: An Assessment after Ten Years of Practice' (2010) 12 *European Journal of Migration and Law* 47.

[49] *Ibid.*, p. 9.

[50] J.-P. Cassarino, 'Readmission Policy in the European Union' (2010) Study by Directorate-General for Internal Policies, European Parliament Policy Department, p. 9.

countries.[51] Agreements are in force mostly with the EU's geographical neighbours, i.e. countries included under the ENP (Ukraine, Georgia, Moldova and soon Armenia), the Russian Federation, the Western Balkans (Albania, Bosnia and Herzegovina, Former Yugoslav Republic of Macedonia, Montenegro, Serbia) and Turkey.[52] This is a clear indication of both the importance of these countries in terms of migration flows to the EU[53] and their role in the EU's migration policy.

Readmission agreements set out clear obligations and procedures for the authorities of partner countries as to when and how to take back people who are illegally residing on EU territory. While the EU has concluded only a few readmission agreements, these agreements are a powerful instrument for the Union to engage neighbouring countries in combating irregular migration. This is because of two factors. First, the scope of these agreements is very broad since neighbouring countries commit themselves to readmit not only their own nationals but also third-country nationals and stateless persons who transited through their territory to enter the EU illegally. Such a broad scope has proved problematic in engaging South Mediterranean partners in readmission, even though provisions on cooperation in readmission were included in the Association agreements signed, e.g. with Tunisia and Jordan.[54] While the Council issued a mandate over a decade ago to negotiate readmission agreements with two South Mediterranean partners, no agreement has been reached either with Morocco (Council mandate issued in September 2000) or with Algeria (Council mandate issued in November 2002).[55] In essence, South Mediterranean countries are reluctant to conclude readmission agreements with the EU[56] because of their

[51] Calculated based upon Billet, 'EC Readmission Agreements', p. 51; and J.-P. Cassarino, 'Readmission Policy in the European Union', p. 14. Author updates, based upon data obtained from European Commission Directorate-General Home, available at http://ec.europa.eu/dgs/home-affairs/what-we-do/policies/pdf/eu_readmission_agreements_en.pdf.

[52] The readmission agreement negotiated with Turkey was initialed in June 2012. See Statement by EU Commissioner Cecilia Malmström on the initialling of the EU–Turkey Readmission Agreement, MEMO/12/477, Brussels, 21 June 2012, available at http://europa.eu/rapid/press-release_MEMO-12-477_en.htm?locale=en.

[53] Countries with which readmission agreements are signed are selected 'using certain criteria such as the migratory patterns from or via the country concerned, together with the number of persons awaiting return, the proximity to the EU's external borders, or the value added to bilateral negotiations led by Member States'. Billet, 'EC Readmission Agreements', p. 51.

[54] *Ibid.*, p. 50. [55] *Ibid.*

[56] They have concluded, however, a series of bilateral readmission agreements with EU Member States, e.g. Morocco with Germany (1998), Spain (1992, 2003), France (1983, 2001), Italy (1998), Malta (2002) and Portugal (1999); Algeria with Italy (2000) and the

role as transit countries to the EU. Signing a readmission agreement would oblige them 'to accept illegal immigrants independently of their nationality if they transited through their territory'.[57]

Nonetheless, the EU has been more successful in developing cooperation on readmission with the Western Balkans, Eastern ENP Partners and to a lesser extent the Russian Federation. Clearly, this is because of a second factor, namely these countries' strong expectations vis-à-vis the EU, be it membership at a later stage (e.g. Ukraine, Moldova, Georgia) or a visa-free regime with the Schengen Member States of the Union (Russia).[58]

The EU's efforts to widen the network of readmission agreements also highlight its readiness to cooperate with authoritarian regimes. Belarus is probably the best illustration in this respect. The EU has frozen its cooperation with Lukashenka's dictatorship since the middle of the 1990s and the country is only theoretically part of the neighbourhood policy and the Eastern Partnership. However, in February 2011 (three months after the crackdown on political opposition in the wake of the presidential elections), the Council of the EU authorized the European Commission to open talks for a visa facilitation and readmission agreement. While presented by the Council as part of a strategy to increase people-to-people contacts with Belarus,[59] this decision is undoubtedly also driven by the desire to fill a gap and conclude a readmission agreement with the only Eastern partner that has not opened negotiations with the EU in this respect.

Over the past decade, the EU has substantially contributed to introducing more restrictive migration policies and control in the neighbourhood. The EU's approach to migration and the corresponding policy toolbox sheds light on two interwoven series of tensions that call into

United Kingdom (2006). Wolff, 'Border Management in the Mediterranean', p. 263; J.-P. Cassarino, 'Dealing with Unbalanced Reciprocities: Cooperation on Readmission and Implications', in J.-P. Cassarino (ed.), *Unbalanced Reciprocities: Cooperation on Readmission in the Euro-Mediterranean Area* (Washington, DC: Middle-East Institute, 2010); and P. Cutitta, 'Readmission in the Relations between Italy and North African Mediterranean Countries', *ibid.*

57 D. Wunderlich, 'The Limits of External Governance: Implementing EU External Migration Policy', p. 1424

58 A. Lobjakas, 'EU–Russia Relations in 2011: A Four Dimensional Space', in A. Lobjakas and M. Mölder (eds.), *EU–Russia Watch* (Tartu: Centre for EU–Russia Studies, 2012), p. 15.

59 Council of the European Union, Council Conclusions on Belarus, 3065th Foreign Affairs Council Meeting, Brussels, 31 January 2011, available at www.consilium.europa.eu/uedocs/cms_data/docs/pressdata/EN/foraff/119038.pdf.

question the ethical nature of EU external action: first, a well-known contradiction between the EU's security and normative or value-based agendas; and secondly, a tension between the increasing devolution of migration control to neighbouring countries and the lack of monitoring exerted by the EU on the way in which democracies in the making (at best) or authoritarian regimes perform such tasks. These tensions embedded in the ENP policy framework are not confined to the neighbourhood region and are spreading to other regions.

3 (Unintended) implications of EU Policies on migration patterns beyond the neighbourhood and negative trans-regionalism

The diffusion of EU migration norms and policy templates to the neighbourhood has wide-ranging consequences on migration patterns beyond the Union's periphery. EU-induced measures primarily affect mobility with the countries adjacent to ENP partners, for instance sub-Saharan Africa in the South, and to a lesser extent Central Asia in the East. Beyond the 'neighbours of neighbours', the implementation of EU migration policies in the neighbourhood has sparse yet reported effects on migration flows with other parts of the world. From examining the *nature* of these effects worldwide and specifically those to sub-Saharan Africa, it can be argued that the externalization of EU migration policies in the neighbourhood has unintended yet disruptive and even harmful implications on migration patterns between the EU's periphery and the rest of the world. This is because EU templates primarily reflect the Union's self-interest rather than ethical principles. The emphasis placed on combating irregular migration has led the Union not only to cooperate with undemocratic regimes in the neighbourhood but also to overlook implications of policies introduced in the neighbourhood for third-countries' migrants. In essence, the 'tendency of the EU to securitise migration issues'[60] has occurred to the detriment of migrants' livelihood strategies, rights and even lives.

Strengthened border controls and the application of stricter migration policies by neighbours as a result of EU pressures did not stop or significantly reduce migration flows to these regions. According to the International Organization for Migration, between 65,000 and 120,000

[60] S. Eylemer and S. Şemşit, 'Migration-Security Nexus in the Euro-Mediterranean Relations' (2007) *Perceptions* 49; cf. also J. Huysmans, 'The European Union and the Securitization of Migration' (2000) 38 *Journal of Common Market Studies* 41.

sub-Saharan Africans enter the Maghreb yearly overland.[61] Only a small percentage of these (20 per cent to 38 per cent) are estimated to enter Europe; at the same time, as noted by de Haas, even migrants from China, India, Pakistan and Bangladesh migrate to the Maghreb and Europe after having flown to West African capitals.[62] Irregular migration thus continues to be a major component of migration to the EU, with estimates varying from 'fewer than 2 million up to 4.5 million' most often cited.[63] However, while they did little to reduce migration flows and to curb illegal migration to the EU, restrictive migration policies across the EU's neighbourhood yielded a number of side effects.

The diffusion of EU restrictive policies to the neighbourhood resulted in a series of reconfigurations of migration routes and sea crossing points to the Union. In the middle of the last decade, migration to the Canary Islands (a Spanish territory) surged in reaction to the new migration laws passed in Morocco and to increased border patrolling in the Strait of Gibraltar. Some 31,000 arrivals were recorded in 2006 from Western Africa, including migrants having sailed to the Canary Islands from Mauritania and Morocco.[64] Another change in migration routes resulted from the restrictive immigration regulations introduced in Libya, a key transit country for those sub-Saharan Africans migrating to the EU.[65] The new migration legal framework in Libya led to a partial shift of migration westwards, towards Tunisia, Morocco and Algeria.[66] At the end of the 2000s and the beginning of the 2010s, the islands of Sardinia (Italy) and Crete (Greece) emerged as new entry points into the EU for migrants crossing the Mediterranean Sea. Over the past year, the bulk of illegal migrants have entered the EU via Spain and the Turkish–Greek border.[67]

[61] International Organization for Migration (prepared by Hein de Haas), *Irregular Migration from West Africa to the Maghreb and the European Union: An Overview of Recent Trends*, International Organization for Migration Research Series 32 (Geneva: IOM, 2008).

[62] De Haas, 'The Myth of Invasion'.

[63] European Commission, Communication to the European Parliament and the Council, COM (2012) 250 final, p. 4.

[64] International Organization for Migration, *Irregular Migration from West Africa to the Maghreb and the European Union*, p. 62.

[65] In the mid-2000s, 70 per cent to 80 per cent of Sub-Saharan Africans migrating to the EU were believed to migrate through Libya as compared to 20 per cent to 30 per cent through Algeria and Morocco. De Haas, 'The Myth of Invasion', 1308.

[66] International Organization for Migration, *Irregular Migration from West Africa to the Maghreb and the European Union*, p. 15.

[67] Approximately 22,500 illegal migrants arrived to the Schengen area from Turkey in the last three months of 2011. L. Peťková, 'EU's Readmission Agreement and Visa

These examples highlight *adaptation strategies* on the part of migrants to adjust to stricter immigration regulations and increased sea and land border surveillance resulting from the externalization of EU norms and policies to the neighbourhood. In turn, constant changes in migration routes have resulted in an 'unintended increase in the area that EU countries have to monitor to "combat" irregular migration', thus making it even more difficult for the EU effectively to reduce illegal migration flows.[68]

Yet, the crucial point raised by the diversification of crossing points and transit routes is not so much the *effectiveness* of EU-induced policies as their *ethical implications*.

The externalization of EU migration policies to the neighbourhood has occurred without consideration of the socio-economic implications for migrants, in particular from Western and sub-Saharan Africa. As pointed out by Nauja Kleist, 'migration is often part of family livelihood strategies, financed by the pooling of family resources with ensuing expectations of remittances or of support for the migration of other family members'.[69] The restriction of legal migration in neighbouring countries as a result of EU pressure thus affects remittance flows and resources of African families, although the exact impact is difficult to assess.

Moreover, a number of examples show that the externalization of EU norms and templates to neighbouring countries has led to human rights violations against migrants. The Commission's legislative proposals on *EU actions* to curb illegal migration have to be compatible with the Charter of Fundamental Rights of the European Union and subject to an in-depth impact assessment on fundamental rights.[70] However, that is not necessarily the case for *EU-induced actions implemented by neighbours*. As noted by Noll, it is especially difficult for undocumented migrants to argue formal violations of human rights law: while their 'bodily presence is a tangible reality, [they are] nevertheless incapable of

Liberalization Talks with Turkey: Backing up Turkey's Protracted Way to the EU', Global Political Trends Center Policy Brief (2012), p. 7.

68 International Organization for Migration, *Irregular Migration from West Africa to the Maghreb and the European Union*, p. 49.

69 N. Kleist, 'Europe Fighting Illegal Migration: Consequences for West African Mobility', Danish Institute for International Studies Policy Brief, October 2011, p. 3.

70 European Commission, 'Commission Staff Working Document: Third Annual Report on the Development of a Common Policy on Illegal Immigration, Smuggling and Trafficking of Human Beings, External Borders, and the Return of Illegal Residents' (EC) SEC (2009) 320 final, 9 March 2009, p. 3.

appearing jurisdictionally'.[71] Yet, the EU has left migrants in the hands of authoritarian governments without much attention being paid to their effective protection. In a number of regions, these are put at risk as a result of EU policies.

For instance, the decisions made on *readmission* have raised serious concerns as to the fate of readmitted persons in countries known for infringing human rights. According to Article 33 of the 1951 Geneva Convention,[72] a country requesting readmission may not send returnees back to a place where they may be under threat. While such a risk is unlikely in those Eastern partners who have concluded a readmission agreement with the EU, as noted by Balzacq these countries have set up similar agreements with states having poor human rights records.[73] For instance, Ukraine has been criticized by the United Nations for sending asylum-seekers back to Uzbekistan.[74] Thus, readmission agreements may lead to infringing the principle of non-refoulement enshrined in UN Conventions and EU legislation. To address these concerns, the European Commission has proposed to strengthen the safeguard of human rights by envisaging the ad hoc participation of non-governmental organizations and international organizations in the Joint Readmission Committees in charge of monitoring the application of the agreements.[75] It also suggests including a provision for the temporary suspension of an agreement 'in the event of persistent and serious risk of violation of human rights of readmitted persons'.[76] In this case, 'the EU could unilaterally stop the application of the agreement by notification to the other contracting Party'.[77]

The conditions of interception and deportation of refugees, asylum-seekers and illegal migrants in Maghreb countries have raised even harsher criticisms by human rights defenders. For instance, in the middle of the last decade Human Rights Watch asked the Spanish government to

[71] G. Noll, 'Why Human Rights Fail to Protect Undocumented Migrants' (2010) 12 *European Journal of Migration and Law* 241 (243).

[72] Convention Relating to the Status of Refugees, 28 July 1951, 189 UNTS 150.

[73] T. Balzacq, 'The Implications of European Neighbourhood Policy in Terms of Border Control', Briefing Paper, Directorate-General Internal Policies, European Parliament, March 2008.

[74] Amnesty International, *Human Rights in Ukraine: Report 2007* (London: Amnesty International, 2008) available at https://www.amnesty.org/en/region/ukraine/report-2007.

[75] European Commission, Communication to the Council and to the European Parliament on Evaluation of EU Readmission Agreements, COM (2011) 76 final.

[76] *Ibid.* [77] *Ibid.*

suspend the deportation of undocumented migrants to Morocco and condemned an excessive use of force by both Spanish and Moroccan border patrols. The non-governmental organization also required an independent investigation on violence perpetrated by Moroccan authorities against migrants storming fences of the Spanish enclaves of Ceuta and Melilla in October 2005;[78] migrants were reportedly abandoned in the desert without any food or water. Libya provides yet another example of human rights abuses. In the mid-2000s, pressure from the EU (in the broader context of Libya's quest for international recognition at that time) prompted the country to strengthen control at its borders and adopt a plan to arrest and return migrants, while it had not ratified the 1951 UN Convention relating to the status of refugees and had no law of asylum.[79] Frequent human rights abuses have been reported either during detention or during the deportation process, sometimes resulting in death. Racism against sub-Saharan migrants is on the rise in Mediterranean societies.[80] In some countries it pre-dated cooperation with the EU on migration management, as shown by the anti-African riots that burst out in Libya as early as 2000. Nonetheless, as indicated by international watchdogs, 'the policies pursued by the European Union in the area of migration [. . .] display complacency and blindness towards continued violations of migrants' rights'.[81] In Libya in particular, violence was perpetrated against African migrants during the 2011 conflict. Sub-Saharan Africans were 'threatened and abused on the grounds that they were or could potentially become mercenaries fighting for Gaddafi'.[82]

In addition, with the decline in possibilities for legal migration and more stringent controls 'a market for irregular migration services has emerged'.[83] The scale of smuggling (defined by the United Nations as a

[78] Human Rights Watch, 'Spain: Deportations to Morocco Put Migrants at Risk. Violence against Migrants in Ceuta and Melilla Requires Independent Investigation', 13 October 2005, available at www.hrw.org/news/2005/10/12/spain-deportations-morocco-put-migrants-risk.

[79] Human Rights Watch, 'Managing Migration Means Potential EU Complicity in Neighboring States', Abuse of Migrants and Refugees', Report No. 2, October 2006, pp. 9–10.

[80] U. Holm, 'North Africa: A Security Problem for Themselves, for the EU and for the US' (2008), Danish Institute of International Studies Report No. 2, p. 27.

[81] International Federation for Human Rights, 'Libya: The Hounding of Migrants Must Stop' (2012), p. 35.

[82] *Ibid.*, p. 33.

[83] J. Salt mentions two different views on the factors explaining trafficking in migrants. Trafficking is assumed to occur either because of the decline in possibilities of regular

crime involving 'the procurement, in order to obtain, directly or indirectly, a financial or other material benefit, of the illegal entry of a person into a State Party of which the person is not a national or a permanent resident')[84] is difficult to assess given the lack of statistical data. However, according to the United Nations Office on Drugs and Crime, 'criminals are increasingly providing highly profitable smuggling services to irregular migrants to evade national border controls, migration regulations and visa requirements. As border controls have improved, migrants are deterred from attempting to illegally cross them themselves and are diverted into the hands of smugglers'.[85] According to the International Organization for Migration, increased surveillance in the Strait of Gibraltar and elsewhere has led to the professionalization of smuggling methods.[86] For instance, in the mid-2000s smugglers started using larger and faster boats instead of fishing boats.[87] Combating smuggling is thus difficult since smugglers constantly change routes and modi operandi in response to changed circumstances.[88] Smuggling thus epitomizes the tensions and paradoxes to which EU migration policy is confronted. The Union has firmly condemned smuggling on a number of occasions and it provides assistance to neighbouring countries in combating trafficking of human beings.[89] Yet, smuggling appears to have emerged as an unintended consequence of EU-induced increased border surveillance at the Union's periphery, which has resulted in the deaths of hundreds of people.

The biggest casualties and human losses indeed occur when illegal migrants try to enter the EU (especially by sea), although statistics are

migration, or weak enforcement of anti-trafficking legislation. J. Salt, 'Trafficking and Human Smuggling: A European Perspective' 1 (2000) *International Migration* 32.

84 Art. 3, Protocol against the Smuggling of Migrants by Land, Sea and Air, United Nations Convention against Transnational Organized Crime, adopted by General Assembly Resolution 55/25 of 15 November 2000, available at www.unodc.org/unodc/en/treaties/CTOC/index.html.

85 United Nations Office on Drugs and Crime, 'Migrant Smuggling', available at www.unodc.org/unodc/en/human-trafficking/smuggling-of-migrants.html.

86 International Organization for Migration, *Irregular Migration from West Africa to the Maghreb and the European Union*, p. 48.

87 De Haas, 'The Myth of Invasion'.

88 'Migrant Smuggling', United Nations Office on Drugs and Crime, available at www.unodc.org/unodc/en/human-trafficking/smuggling-of-migrants.html.

89 EU support is provided through the Thematic Programme on cooperation with Third Countries in the areas of Migration and Asylum set up by Regulation (EC) No. 1905/2006, with an overall funding of €384 million under the 2007–13 financial framework. European Commission, 'Commission Staff Working Document: Third Annual', p. 22

scarce for obvious reasons. In this case, too, the connection with EU policies is deemed quite straightforward. Deaths associated with illegal entry into the EU's territory are increasing since the 'closing of established migration routes and the exclusion from legal mobility flows cause the emergence of new and often more dangerous means of irregular entry'.[90] As emphasized by Thomas Spijkerboer, 'increases in the numbers of fatalities of irregular migrants are related to the tightening of border controls. Thus, these fatalities are a foreseeable consequence of this policy'.[91] Media regularly report on the sinking of boats full of illegal migrants off Turkish, Greek or Italian coasts with dozens of people being killed. As noted by Grant, 'migrant frontier deaths [...] have tended to be seen as a "tragic by-product" of increased immigration control'.[92] This is also because their number is 'high but unknown', although according to an estimate 'as many as one out of four persons attempting to reach Europe by sea had perished during the trip'.[93] In spite of general commitments taken under the Stockholm Programme to avoid the recurrence of tragedies at sea and, in the case of such events, to explore how to better record and identify migrants dying as a result of their attempt to reach the EU,[94] 'there has been less official willingness to examine the evidence, and institute systematic data collection'[95] in Europe than in other parts of the world, including the US.

Migration cooperation developed by the EU with neighbouring countries thus offers a case of negative trans-regionalism and yields perverse effects on either sending or transit regions. This is also because the EU has not yet succeeded in developing a policy approach that would strongly connect not only the external and internal dimensions of migration but also all migration-related aspects of the different geographical frameworks in which EU external migration policy is implemented. This is a key objective for the renewed Global Approach to Migration, especially under the dialogues on migration, mobility and security already negotiated with some Southern Mediterranean partners

[90] N. Kleist, 'Europe Fighting Illegal Migration', p. 1.

[91] T Spijkerboer, 'The Human Costs of Border Control' (2007) 9 *European Journal of Migration and Law* 138.

[92] S. Grant, 'Recording and Identifying Frontier Deaths' (2011) 13 *European Journal of Migration and Law* 135.

[93] Quoted by Grant, *ibid.*, p. 138.

[94] European Council, The Stockholm Programme: An Open and Secure Europe Serving and Protecting the Citizen, OJ (2010) C115/1, Part 6.

[95] Grant, 'Recording and Identifying Frontier Deaths', p. 140.

(e.g. Morocco, Tunisia). Yet, whether this renewed approach will succeed in developing an effective 'overarching framework'[96] for the EU's external migration policy remains to be seen.

4 Conclusion

Moving beyond the legal principles, this chapter has reviewed the set of policy instruments used by the Union in migration cooperation with neighbouring countries and charted the impact of EU actions, in particular regarding the control of migration flows and the prevention of illegal migration.

The chapter has shown that the EU undoubtedly shapes the legal order and the institutional framework governing migration in its neighbourhood. Even though partner countries' motivations for adopting EU norms differ, the EU's influence has yielded similar effects across its periphery. It has led to more restrictive migration policies in both the Eastern and the Southern neighbourhoods. The EU's prioritization of security objectives has altered neighbours' own approaches to migration, resulting in significantly harsher policies. Migration cooperation between the EU and its neighbours also elicits the contradictions underlying the Union's external policy, as illustrated by the EU's engagement with illiberal regimes to combat irregular migration.

Yet, the analysis has primarily unravelled the unintended consequences yielded by the EU's external migration templates.

The first point made in this chapter pertains to the *geographical scope of the EU's influence*. It is not circumscribed to the neighbourhood but is much more global and far-reaching, affecting the 'neighbours of neighbours' and beyond. Certainly, the EU has sufficient leverage not only to spread norms to its neighbourhood but to have them implemented. It is also a key destination for migrants worldwide. Nonetheless, the breadth of EU impact on migration patterns is made possible by the regulatory and governance vacuum at the global level in the migration area. This is implicitly acknowledged in the renewed Global Approach for Migration:

[96] Emphasis in the original text. European Commission, Communication to the Council, the European Parliament, the European Economic and Social Committee and the Committee of the Regions on the Global Approach to Migration and Mobility, COM (2011) 743 final, Brussels, 18 November 2011.

> Dialogue at global level can address some of the shared challenges and concerns. However, it is at regional, national and local levels that each individual and each stakeholder will seize the opportunities brought by migration and by mobility. Migration is now firmly at the top of the European Union's political agenda.[97]

The second point highlighted by this contribution relates to the *unethical effects of the EU's influence* on international migration patterns, and on migrants themselves. This is because EU external migration policy is 'unreflexively eurocentric'.[98] It attempts to promote the EU's priorities and model without much consideration either for the domestic context of implementation or for regional links that connect neighbours to other countries. So far, and in spite of general statements condemning reported abuses of human rights in the neighbourhood, the EU's external migration policy has been primarily driven by the Union's self-interest. Nevertheless, it is also mediated by neighbouring countries' interests and capacities, and affected by the regional context in which they are embedded. Migration policy thus provides an illustration of the way in which ethical discourses and objectives can be distorted by competing security goals and external policy actors.

The third point pertains *to the way in which the EU exerts influence* on international migration patterns. The EU's impact in this case is not direct but develops by ricochet, as a result of EU priorities and norms being adopted by neighbouring countries. While the literature on the subject has primarily placed the emphasis on direct effects, or lack thereof, of EU norms and actions in specific parts of the world, this conclusion opens new research avenues to study the EU's influence worldwide. It indeed suggests the existence of spill-over phenomena (or ripple effects) that may not be limited to the migration policy area but might apply to other spheres of EU external action as well.

[97] *Ibid.*, p. 2.
[98] F. Bicchi, '"Our Size Fits All": Normative Power Europe and the Mediterranean' (2006) 13 *Journal of European Public Policy* 286.

PART III

The EU and the global financial crisis

12

Back in balance? the EU and the challenges of international financial regulation

CHRISTOPH OHLER

1 Introduction

The regulation of financial markets is one of the areas in which the European Union (EU) has been active for nearly forty years playing a decisive role also on the international plane. The internal market for financial services is one of the biggest and most open markets in the world. Yet it is also one of the markets gravely hit by the financial crisis of 2007 to 2009. More than ever before in the history of the EU, the experiences of the crisis showed that financial regulation poses severe challenges. They are owed to the characteristics of financial markets: their international scope, their riskiness and their networked nature. In the second section, the peculiarities of financial markets will be analysed in more detail. Financial market regulation is also an example of a possible field where the intensification of the EU's involvement in the *Geist* of the active paradigm of external relations would be possible. Section 3 will analyse how the standard-setting bodies operate, what influence they exercise and what position the EU has in this context. Yet the advantages of international standard setting do not provide a sufficient answer as to what regulatory objectives the EU should pursue and which regulatory instruments it should use. The underlying uncertainties can be traced back to the question as to which idea of justice should be followed by the EU and, especially, the issue whether the EU can be regarded as an actor of global justice, approached by Andrew Williams earlier in this volume. The internationally acknowledged rationales of financial market regulation are, first, to protect investors and consumers, and, second, to maintain the stability of financial markets. Whereas the idea of justice can be easily grasped with respect to the protection of consumers, the meaning of financial stability seems to be unclear and not immediately convincing. Section 4 will discuss this problem in depth, demonstrating that the concept of financial stability is very broad and implies difficult value judgements. Considering there is no international consensus on the rules that are necessary to assure financial stability, the EU, like other leading economies in the world, plays a major role in developing adequate rules for the problems identified in the wake of the financial crisis and the current debt crisis. Therefore, financial stability must be considered in its full economic context. Hence, sections 5 and 6 discuss the issue of systemic risks and the conflict of regulatory objectives in a market economy.

2 Peculiarities of financial markets

The regulation of financial markets differs from other areas of international economic law because the objects of trade in international financial markets are different from other economic areas.[1] The objects of financial trade are legal obligations created under private law contracts which are part of a domestic legal system.[2] The obligations of both parties are performed by the same instrument: money. Both legal obligations and money come into existence and are considered valid only as far as they are guaranteed by a sovereign legal order. This could be the legal order of the home state of the creditor (or the debtor) or another jurisdiction as the parties to a contract enjoy autonomy and accordingly may choose the applicable law. In contrast thereto, the party autonomy is restricted as far as the *lex monetae* is concerned, i.e. the legal order guaranteeing the monetary side of an obligation.[3] The double guarantee function for the existence and validity of financial products makes financial markets much more dependent on these legal orders as is the case with trade in goods or services.

This peculiarity goes hand in hand with another aspect: to a large extent, trade in financial products depends on confidence between the market participants.[4] Confidence is an economic factor that no legal order can regulate directly. It is conventional wisdom, however, that a legal order may establish the foundations on which such trust may

[1] C. Ohler, 'Finanzkrisen als Herausforderung der internationalen, europäischen und nationalen Rechtsetzung' (2011) *Deutsches Verwaltungsblatt* 1061 (1062).

[2] C. Tietje, 'The International Financial Architecture' (2011) 54 *German Yearbook of International Law* 11 (35).

[3] On the *lex monetae*, see C. Proctor, *Mann on the Legal Aspect of Money*, 6th edn (Oxford University Press, 2005), p. 331; Frank Vischer, *Geld- und Währungsrecht* (Basel: Helbing Lichtenhahn, 2010), p. 180.

[4] T. Padoa-Schioppa, *Regulating Finance* (Oxford University Press, 2004), p. 24.

grow: by a solid monetary constitution, the protection of property rights under the rule of law, the guarantee of free movement of capital and an adequate prudential supervision of all relevant market participants.[5] Another peculiarity is that the markets are moved by expectations which change quickly. Since money and legal obligations can also be exchanged quickly and easily, there is no reason to assume that the financial markets will ever discover the fortunes of slowness.

This last point leads to the question as to why financial markets are so risk-prone. Risks are an inherent and necessary part of any financial business.[6] Therefore, the task of regulation is not to prohibit all sorts of risks, but to prevent excessive risk-taking either by an individual market participant or in the market as a whole. This is particularly relevant for systemic risks which market participants do not internalize in their costs.[7] The regulatory objective is to prevent an accumulation of financial risks the realization of which would gravely affect the functioning of other parts of the economy. If regulators and supervisors ignore the existence and costs of systemic risks, as was the case in the financial crisis of 2007–9, then the breakdown of financial markets will occur unexpectedly and suddenly, causing sharp recession, high unemployment and dramatic shortfalls in public budgets.[8] The EU also had to learn the lesson that a financial crisis may alter its appearance and become a sovereign debt crisis as often happened elsewhere in the past.[9]

3 The logic and limits of international standard setting

3.1 *The governance mode of international standard setting*

The international financial architecture as it exists today reflects the historical and economic experiences of the decades after the First World War. As far as rulemaking within this architecture is concerned, states and other actors like the EU rely to a large extent on non-binding

[5] D. Arner, *Financial Stability, Economic Growth and the Role of Law* (Cambridge University Press, 2007), p. 196; Padoa-Schioppa, *Regulating Finance*, p. 24.

[6] J. Benjamin, *Financial Law* (Oxford University Press, 2007), para. 1.25.

[7] K. Alexander, R. Dhumale and J. Eatwell, *Global Governance of Financial Systems* (Oxford University Press, 2006), p. 24.

[8] Vischer, *Geld- und Währungsrecht*, p. 147.

[9] This is the main thesis of C. Reinhart and K. Rogoff, *This Time Is Different* (Princeton, NJ: Princeton University Press, 2009).

international standards that are developed by highly specialized international groupings like the Basel Committee of Banking Supervision (BCBS), the International Association of Insurance Supervisors (IAIS), the International Organization of Securities Commissions (IOSCO) and, with a coordinating function, the Financial Stability Board (FSB). These bodies have been established since the mid-1970s to develop common regulatory standards and give technical advice to supervisory authorities in all matters of internationally operating financial institutions. Their members are not states as subjects of international law but specialized state organs like ministries of finance, supervisory authorities or central banks.[10] They do not operate on the basis of international treaties but of informal understandings amongst their members.[11] Accordingly, the standard setting bodies do not constitute international organizations in a proper sense,[12] but institutions *sui generis* permitting the conclusion that they constitute relations akin to 'administrative networks'.[13]

The EU became a player in the early seventies when it started to establish the fundaments of the common market. Despite its legislative activities for what later became known as the internal market for financial services, the European Commission only enjoyed an observer status in most of these networks and was not invited to participate as a regular member. The weak external role was mainly owed to the fact that the standard setters were established under the auspices of the G10 (like the Basel Committee) or the G7 (like the Financial Stability Board) which did not provide a membership for the EU. Presumably, another reason was that central banks and supervisory authorities of the Member States considered themselves in charge of regulatory matters. This changed in April 2009 when, under the auspices of the Group of Twenty (G20), and in the wake of the financial crisis, a reorganization

[10] Art. 4 Financial Stability Board (FSB) Charter, available at www.financialstabilityboard.org/publications/r_090925d.pdf.

[11] Cf. Art. 16 FSB Charter; see also Basel Committee on Banking Supervision, 'History of the Basel Committee and its Membership' (August 2009), available at www.bis.org/bcbs/history.pdf.

[12] Alexander, Dhumale and Eatwell, *Global Governance of Financial Systems*, p. 79; S. Emmenegger, 'The Basel Committee on Banking Supervision: A Secretive Club of Giants', in R. Grote and T. Marauhn (eds.), *The Regulation of International Financial Markets* (Cambridge University Press, 2006), p. 226.

[13] A.-M. Slaughter, *A New World Order* (Princeton, NJ: Princeton University Press, 2004), p. 38; R. Weber, 'Multilayered Governance in International Financial Regulation and Supervision' (2010) 13 *Journal of International Economic Law* 683.

took place to broaden the institutional framework.[14] Today, the EU is represented by the Commission and the European Central Bank as members in the Financial Stability Board and as observers in the Basel Committee.

The standard setting bodies are authorized by their members to develop guidelines and supervisory standards but they do not have a mandate to negotiate internationally binding instruments. Also, the standards cannot be qualified as reflecting customary international law.[15] This means that, contrary to the international practice of regulation in goods and services, the regulation of financial markets is a *domaine* of international soft law.[16] From a technical perspective, the missing treaty basis provides a sufficient explanation as to why the standard setters may only adopt non-binding recommendations, and not binding secondary law. But this does not, however, explain why the standard setting procedures were never used as a basis for international state conferences which negotiate and adopt binding treaty law. The reason why this regime was never formalized is supposedly the procedural flexibility it offers and which the members do not want to give up.[17]

The legal impact of international standard setting can be identified on various levels. On a global scale, the International Monetary Fund (IMF) refers expressly to the international standards since their implementation by a country forms one of the assessment criteria for its economic surveillance under Article IV of the Articles of Agreement.[18] The IMF has no formal power to enforce the standards but relies on the disciplinary effect of the surveillance procedure and the reputational

[14] See Preamble of the FSB Charter; on the topic of international legitimacy with respect to the limited number of members, see Alexander, Dhumale and Eatwell, *Global Governance of Financial Systems*, p. 135.

[15] On soft law as a potential source of customary law, see D. Thürer, 'Soft Law', in R. Wolfrum (ed.), *Max Planck Encyclopedia of Public International Law*, online edition, para. 28.

[16] C. Brummer, 'Why Soft Law Dominates International Finance – and Not Trade' (2010) 13 *Journal of International Economic Law* 623; C. Brummer, *Soft Law and the Global Financial System* (Cambridge University Press, 2012); Alexander, Dhumale and Eatwell, *Global Governance of Financial Systems*, p. 134; R. Lastra, *Legal Foundations of International Monetary Stability* (Oxford University Press, 2006), p. 453.

[17] C. Brummer, *Soft Law and the Global Financial System*, p. 63; on the 'club design' of the Basel Committee, see M. Barr and G. Miller, 'Global Administrative Law: The View from Basel' (2006) 17 *European Journal of International Law* 15 (18).

[18] The Financial Sector Assessment Program of the IMF is reflected in Art. 6(1)(d) FSB Charter. See also H. Scott, *International Finance: Law and Regulation*, 2nd edn (London: Sweet & Maxwell, 2008), p. 766.

effect that adherence to the standards should imply. Promoting the adherence to these standards is also part of the work of the standard setters themselves.[19] The proper legal effects of these standards are mirrored mainly in domestic and EU legislation as they are designed to be implemented in binding law.[20] Despite its – originally – weak representation in the standard setting bodies, the European Commission supported their work from the beginning by adopting the standards as a blueprint for EU secondary legislation. The reason why particularly the EU (and not always the rest of the world)[21] accepted the work of the standard setters – without any legal obligation thereto – is to be seen in the ideas of technical craftsmanship, political independence and effective harmonization.[22] To put it in other words: the standards very often reflected best practices[23] which fit well in the context of the internal market, modernized national law and enjoyed a high technical reputation. This is the reason why over many years the European Union (and its predecessor, the European Community) was a 'net importer' of these standards as a basis for its own legislation. Today, the Commission plays an active role in these bodies but there is no evidence that it is able to take the lead or exercise an influence that is stronger than the role of the specialized agencies such as central banks and supervisory authorities.

3.2 *The legal weaknesses of the governance mode*

The informality of the standard setting procedures exhibits its strength and its weakness at the same time. Therefore, some authors stress that the standards allow for efficient, i.e. flexible and rapid, rulemaking.[24] A closer look at the history of the standard setters and a comparison with EU and national legislation reveals, however, that the negotiation

[19] FSB, 'Promoting Global Adherence to Regulatory and Supervisory Standards on International Cooperation and Information Exchange' (April 2011), available at www.financialstabilityboard.org/publications/r_110429.pdf.

[20] Brummer, *Soft Law and the Global Financial System*, p. 115.

[21] See in particular the critical stance of the US administration towards the Basel standards: D. Tarullo, *Banking on Basel* (Washington, DC: Peterson Institute for International Economics, 2008).

[22] Emmenegger, 'The Basel Committee on Banking Supervision', p. 234.

[23] Brummer, *Soft Law and the Global Financial System*, p. 117.

[24] *Ibid*., p. 125; G. Walker, *International Banking Regulation, Law, Policy and Practice* (The Hague: Kluwer Law, 2001), p. 70.

processes – because of the need for consensus – are not always more efficient than domestic procedures. Adopting, for example, the standards under the Basel II Capital Accord[25] took the BCBS nearly seven years – starting in 1999 and ending in 2006. Today, it is also discussed whether the process of standard setting should be framed by international treaties that permit a stronger democratic control by national parliaments.[26]

In theory, international standard setting should result in a sufficient degree of harmonization of domestic laws and create a global 'level playing field' for financial institutions. The reality is different. Since the extent to which international recommendations are followed is in the discretion of each state and also of the EU, effective implementation of standards differs strongly amongst the members. The flexible approach of standard setting is further mirrored in the material content of the standards. Very often, their wording conveys a considerable degree of discretion to the addressees; in particular, when so-called 'core principles' are concerned. Contrary to this, other standards, mostly of a highly technical nature, exist that can be extremely detailed and leave only little room for discretion.[27] As a consequence of the co-existence of such formal and material flexibility, the effective set of domestic regulation in any jurisdiction is a mixture of international standards which were implemented by binding norms and additional EU or national elements. Consequently, the material requirements of supervisory law will not be identical in the various jurisdictions. These regulatory differences do not necessarily contradict the efforts of international standard setting. Rather, they are the unavoidable consequence of a system of informal rule-making. The flexibility adopted by states when implementing the standards can be useful as it permits the adaptation to national legal and economic peculiarities and opens, at least indirectly, the way to regulatory competition.[28] The other side of this coin, at least in the eyes of the financial institutions, is the

[25] Basel Commission on Banking Supervision, 'International Convergence on Capital Measurements and Capital Standards: A Revised Framework, Comprehensive Version' (2006), available at www.bis.org/publ/bcbs128.pdf.

[26] C. Calliess, 'Finanzkrisen als Herausforderung der internationalen, europäischen und nationalen Rechtsetzung', in *Veröffentlichungen der Vereinigung der Deutschen Staatsrechtslehrer*, vol. 71 (Berlin: de Gruyter, 2012), p. 133; W. Höfling, 'Finanzmarktregulierung – Welche Regelungen empfehlen sich für den deutschen und europäischen Finanzsektor?', *Gutachtachten F zum 68, Deutschen Juristentag* (Munich: C. H. Beck, 2010), F 39.

[27] The print version of the document known as Basel II ('International Convergence of Capital Measurement and Capital Standards') of June 2006 has 347 pages.

[28] C. Tietje and M. Lehmann, 'The Role and Prospects of International Law in Financial Regulation and Supervision' (2010) 13 *Journal of International Economic Law* 663.

absence of a *regulatory* level playing field. Similarly, national supervisors tend to consider the national differences as a source of regulatory arbitrage which threatens the proper functioning of their domestic systems.

3.3 *Material challenges: in pursuit of adequate rules*

One of the lessons of the financial crisis has been that efficient rule-making is only one relevant aspect of financial regulation. As such regulation concerns economic and social core interests of most countries in the world, the question is also whether these rules adequately address the real risks inherent in financial markets and effectively protect the public goods involved.[29] In hindsight, the financial crisis of 2007–9 revealed structural weaknesses of the international standards in a material sense and not only with respect to a deficit of global harmonization. This was particularly true for the problem of systemic risks that, by the year 2006, was not even mentioned in the central text of the BCBS, the Basel II capital accord.[30] In the future, the biggest challenge seems to be whether international standards are appropriate for inducing a material regulation that effectively supports international objectives and fits into an extremely heterogeneous economic context on a global scale.

4 Financial stability as an international public good

4.1 *The rationales of financial market regulation*

The generally recognized key objectives of financial market regulation are: enhancing financial stability, protecting customers, avoiding supervisory arbitrage between financial institutions and markets and, finally, supporting economic growth.[31] To secure the accomplishment of these objectives, most jurisdictions share the view that all relevant market participants and products that have been unregulated prior to the crisis should be appropriately regulated now.[32] However, the meaning of 'effectively' or 'appropriately' in this context is unclear, in particular

[29] For an overview of the various approaches, see R. Lastra and George Wood, 'The Crisis of 2007–09: Nature, Causes and Reactions' (2010) 13 *Journal of International Economic Law* 531 (547).

[30] See BCBS, 'Basel II', available at www.bis.org/publ/bcbs118.pdf.

[31] See G20 Leaders Summit, 14–15 November 2008, Washington, DC, para. 5/6, available at http://www.g20.utoronto.ca/summits/2008washington.html.

[32] *Ibid.*, para. 9.

when it comes to technical details of regulation, i.e. capital requirements, the role of deposit insurance, reporting obligations, risk management requirements and other regulatory instruments. Moreover, international standards do not provide an answer to the role of other policy areas intensely related to financial supervision such as monetary and budgetary policy. This question is left open to political decision-making at the level of the G20 where vague compromises tend to disguise the conflicts more than they are able to solve them.

4.2 *Financial stability*

Despite the international dissent in many questions of detail, the recent crisis strengthened the idea of financial stability as an important public good under international law.[33] The concept of financial stability has been enshrined in some legal documents in the past, in particular in the Annex on Financial Services to the GATS.[34] Several EU directives mention financial stability as an objective of banking supervision.[35] And, last but not least, the EU established by year-end 2010 the European System of Financial Supervision with a new set of supervisory authorities whose key objective is to maintain financial stability and to improve cooperation between national supervisors.[36] Agreeing on this principle does not mean, however, that there is already universal consent on the significance in concrete political circumstances.[37] Or to put it in more practical terms, it is easy to agree on the notion that financial stability is indispensable but it is difficult consensually to arrive at concrete measures to restore financial stability once it has disappeared.

[33] C. Tietje, *Architektur der Weltfinanzordnung*, Beiträge zum Transnationalen Wirtschaftsrecht, 109 Martin-Luther-Universität Halle-Wittenberg (2011), p. 28; J. Trachtman, 'The International Law of Financial Crisis: Spillovers, Subsidiarity, Fragmentation and Cooperation', 13 *Journal of International Economic Law* 719 (721); Weber, 'Multilayered Governance in International Financial Regulation and Supervision', p. 693.

[34] Entry 2(a), Annex on Financial Services, General Agreement on Trade in Services.

[35] Recitals 24 and 57, Art. 130(1), Directive 2006/48/EC of the European Parliament and of the Council of 14 June 2006 on Relating to the Taking up and Pursuit of the Business of Credit Institutions OJ L 177/1; Recital 17, Art. 51(3), Directive 2004/39/EC of the European Parliament and of the Council of 21 April 2004 on Markets in Financial Instruments amending Council Directives 85/611/EEC and 93/6/EEC and Directive 2000/12/EC of the European Parliament and of the Council and repealing Council Directive 93/22/EEC OJ L 145/1.

[36] EU Regulations 1092, 1093, 1094 and 1095/2010 of 24 November 2010 OJ L331.

[37] Weber, 'Multilayered Governance in International Financial Regulation and Supervision', p. 693.

This refers particularly to the instruments available, their negative side-effects and their conflict with other economic paradigms, e.g. the risk of moral hazard. The practical difficulties can be demonstrated in three fields, where financial stability plays a dominant role.

4.2.1 Stability of financial markets

First of all, financial stability refers to the stability of the financial system, i.e. the proper functioning of financial markets.[38] In a more qualitative sense financial stability is defined as the capability of financial markets to withstand shocks and the unravelling of financial imbalances.[39] The ethical dimension of this concept is that the creditors of financial transactions bear economic risks which form a necessary part of this kind of business. The purpose of regulation is not to prohibit risk-taking in general but to ensure that the various creditors only take adequate risks corresponding to their capacity to carry the risk burden. This is primarily done to protect all other market participants who do business with this person. In networked markets, which are a characteristic of all financial markets, a breakdown of an important actor could cause massive harm to other participants and in a worst case scenario ruin the overall economy. In a positive sense, only functioning financial markets offer all services at prices which foster economic growth and which fulfil the various demands of households, private businesses and public entities.[40] Therefore, any regulation should emphasize the credit function, the payment and settlement function and the risk transfer function of banks which have to be continued even in times of severe crises.[41]

In European law, Article 127(5) TFEU recognizes that the stability of the financial system is an objective which the European Central Bank (ECB) may pursue within the context of its general monetary policy mandate under Article 127(1) TFEU. This provision has also formed the legal basis for the extensive supply of liquidity by the ECB since the beginning of the financial crisis in summer 2008.[42] The European move was part of a global concerted policy of low interest rates, modest

[38] Cf. Lastra, *Legal Foundations of International Monetary Stability*, p. 92.

[39] European Central Bank, 'Financial Stability Review' (December 2011), p. 7.

[40] Cf. Arner, *Financial Stability, Economic Growth and the Role of Law*, p. 135.

[41] E. Hüpkes, 'Rivalry in Resolution: How to Reconcile Local Responsibilities and Global Interests?' (2010) *European Company and Financial Law Review* 216 (219).

[42] For a similar view prior to the crisis, see René Smits, 'The Role of the ESCB in Banking Supervision', in European Central Bank, *Legal Aspect of the European System of Central Banks* (European Central Bank, 2005), p. 205.

collateral requirements and full tender allotment aimed at preventing the breakdown of banks owing to a shortage of liquidity as had happened during the Great Depression.[43] One of the problems, however, is whether central banks know the point at which the amount of liquidity available to banks should be reduced. Banks translate liquidity into credits to businesses or households or into other investments on the market. The underlying risk is that these credits fuel a new bubble which is not based on sound economic reasoning but on the supply of risk-free money from the central bank only.

4.2.2 Fiscal stability

In some cases, financial stability means fiscal stability, i.e. the stability of revenues and expenditures of a public household, in particular the sustainability of public indebtedness.[44] On a global scale, a majority of industrial nations face rising public debt, with debt ratios reaching more than 180 per cent of GDP in Japan, more than 85 per cent in the United Kingdom and more than 60 per cent in the US.[45] Against this background, it is widely accepted that excessive sovereign debt poses severe risks for financial and monetary stability. The European debt crisis, to take a recent example, is not directly a crisis of the euro as a currency but results from the unsustainable budgetary situation of some Member States. In the EU, this should never have happened had the relevant actors taken the obligations under primary law literally: Article 126 TFEU prohibits excessive deficits because they threaten the normal functioning of monetary policy in the long run.[46] The economic reasoning is that excessive (or unsustainable) deficits put the central bank under pressure to finance the budget deficit which is expressly prohibited by Article 123 TFEU.[47] But that is not the full story: once investors believe that a public debt is not sustainable any more, financial markets come under massive strain as the investors fear substantial losses when the state debtor defaults. As a consequence, the respective state loses access to the markets and becomes unable to revolve its existing

[43] European Central Bank, 'The Implementation of Monetary Policy since August 2007' (July 2009) *ECB Monthly Bulletin* 75 (78).

[44] Tietje, *Architektur der Weltfinanzordnung*, p. 34.

[45] See recent figures of the OECD, available at http://stats.oecd.org/Index.aspx?datasetcode=GOV_DEBT#.

[46] U. Häde, in C. Calliess and M. Ruffert (eds.), *EUV/AEUV Kommentar*, 4th edn (Munich: C. H. Beck, 2011), Art. 126 AEUV para. 2.

[47] With respect to the exemptions to this rule see *ibid.*, Art. 123 AEUV, para. 10.

debt or to generate new funds. Finally, as the case of the euro area demonstrates, Member States and the ECB fear that a disorderly state bankruptcy could produce contagion effects to the disadvantage of other states and investors. Should this scenario become real, it may well undermine the trust which is necessary for the political survival of Economic and Monetary Union (EMU). With a thorough reform of EMU pending, the political answer to these problems so far is the establishment of the European Financial Stability Facility (EFSF) and its successor, the European Stability Mechanism (ESM).[48]

4.2.3 Monetary stability

The economic complexities likewise become evident with respect to the principle of price stability as a central objective of monetary policy.[49] So far, there are three lines of conflict. The first concerns the extent to which other monetary goals may play a role in monetary policy. This refers in particular to the goal of supporting economic growth. Compared to any other central bank in the world, the ECB is under a very strict regime as price stability enjoys primacy over any other monetary goal.[50] The US Federal Reserve System, to take another example, has a triple mandate and must 'promote effectively the goals of maximum employment, stable prices, and moderate long-term interest rates'.[51] These legal differences in the mandate have a strong impact on how monetary policy is carried out.[52]

The second line of conflict refers to the relationship between price stability and stability of the financial system. The recent crisis showed that there is a strong correlation between both goals because the central bank must rely on properly functioning financial markets to implement its monetary policy.[53] But, if a central bank is to have a strong interest in the existence and functioning of credit institutions, does this mean that

[48] C. Ohler, 'The European Stability Mechanism: The Long Road to Financial Stability in the Euro Area' (2011) 54 *German Yearbook of International Law* 47.

[49] Cf. Art. 127 para. 1 TFEU.

[50] Häde, *EUV/AEUV Kommentar*, Art. 127 AEUV, para. 2.

[51] Sect. 2A Federal Reserve Act, 12 USC 225a.

[52] For further analysis, see D. Arner, M. Panton and P. Lejot, 'Central Banks and Central Bank Cooperation in the Global Financial System' (2010) 23 *McGeorge Global Business and Development Law Journal* 1.

[53] For a general overview, see B. Hofmann and A. Worms, 'Monetary Transmission in the EU', in X. Freixas, P. Hartmann and C. Mayer (eds.), *Handbook of European Financial Markets and Institution* (Oxford University Press, 2008), p. 721.

the central bank must even reanimate 'zombie' banks with no perspective for revival? With respect to the prohibition of monetary financing under Article 123 TFEU, a line is drawn between liquidity needs and capital needs of the banking sector and, accordingly, illiquid and insolvent banks.[54] This reflects the generally recognized role of the central bank as lender of last resort.[55] Whereas liquidity needs should be fully covered by the central bank, the recapitalization of banks is regarded as a task of private investors, and if they are not prepared to do so, then this task falls to the competent budget authority.[56] The distinction may be helpful as long as one can be sure that at a given time the difference between an illiquid and an insolvent bank is clearly visible. However, central banks themselves blur the line when they accept assets below investment grade as collateral in their monetary transactions with credit institutions.

Thirdly, there is a lot of uncertainty as to whether a central bank should monitor asset price stability. Price stability, which is clearly a fundamental task of a central bank, is measured as stability of consumer prices but not of asset prices.[57] The reason for this choice is simple. The development of consumer prices is easy to measure, it concerns all participants in the economy on a daily basis and it adequately reflects the risks of inflation and deflation. The development of asset prices can be measured but it is not always clear whether a rise in asset prices constitutes a dangerous bubble or a normal market development. There is also a lot of uncertainty regarding the extent to which the regular instruments of monetary policy are apt to influence the development of asset prices. Clearly, the different macroeconomic approaches between the US and the EU in this respect lead to very different results. The argument generally deployed in the US is that when inflation risk is low the central bank may channel as much money on the market as may be necessary to bolster economic growth. In contrast, the EU considers the growth of credit volume in the market as a potential risk for future price stability; and hence the central bank would probably act more carefully in such a system.

[54] ECB, Convergence Report May 2012, p. 29.

[55] See Arner, *Financial Stability, Economic Growth and the Role of Law*, p. 139; Lastra, *Legal Foundations of International Monetary Stability*, p. 114.

[56] S. Radtke, *Liquiditätshilfen im Eurosystem* (Jena: Jenaer Wissenschaftliche Verlagsgesellschaft, 2010), p. 140.

[57] See European Central Bank, 'Definition of Price Stability', available at www.ecb.int/mopo/strategy/pricestab/html/index.en.html.

5 The complex issue of systemic risk

5.1 *Maintaining stability in all respects*

Based on the assumption that financial stability must be preserved in all the respects discussed above, the analysis must focus on identifying the exact origins of the risks that threaten stability. Therefore, the institutional side of markets needs to be included in the analysis in order to understand the problem of systemic risks.[58]

5.2 *Relevant institutions*

5.2.1 Large, complex and interconnected banks

The relevant institutions are, first of all, the so-called systemically important banks. The idea that large and complex financial institutions exist and that they pose special regulatory problems is not new.[59] Still, the concept was revived after the breakdown of Lehman Brothers in September 2008 as this event resulted in an economic shock of unexpected magnitude. What exactly is the calibre that makes a bank 'important' for the stability of financial markets? Quite a broad range of factors should be considered such as market capitalization, volume of assets, leverage, interconnectedness with other financial institutions or the question whether its business can be easily substituted by other banks after the opening of an insolvency proceeding.[60] The point is that all these factors may be relevant but their particular relevance presumably varies over time.[61] In good times even bigger banks may default without shocking the market. In a bad market environment with a high degree of uncertainty about economic prospects or a low degree of trust, the breakdown of a rather small or less interconnected bank by contrast could be sufficient to trigger panic. In addition, the geographical scope of a systemically important bank can vary considerably, with some banks being relevant on the global level and others restricted to a mere regional importance.

[58] Cf. Alexander, Dhumale and Eatwell, *Global Governance of Financial Systems*, p. 23.

[59] See Financial Stability Board, 'Reducing the Moral Hazard Posed by Systemically Important Financial Institutions' (20 October 2010), available at www.financialstabilityboard.org/publications/r_101111a.pdf.

[60] International Monetary Fund, Bank for International Settlements, Financial Stability Board, 'Guidance to Assess the Systemic Importance of Financial Institutions, Markets and Instruments: Initial Considerations' (Financial Stability Board, October 2009), p. 8, available at www.financialstabilityboard.org/publications/r_091107c.pdf.

[61] *Ibid.*, p. 5.

5.2.2 Market infrastructure

Systemically important are also market infrastructures such as payment and settlement systems.[62] Therefore, they require a high degree of attention by the legislator and by the supervisor. A good example for EU legislation is the Settlement Finality Directive which aims at reducing systemic risk by protecting the proper functioning of payment systems.[63] One could also consider that EU law establishing central counterparties for 'over-the-counter' (OTC) trade in financial derivatives aims not only at more transparency in this part of the market but stabilizes the whole market.[64] Obviously, the central counterparties, once established, will also become systemically important institutions.

5.2.3 States

As can be learnt from the European debt crisis, states may also trigger a systemic risk for the proper functioning of financial markets.[65] This is clearly the case when the debt position of a state has reached a level at which a default would threaten the stability of entire markets or lead directly to the breakdown of creditors, which are systemically important themselves. The case of Greece and other ailing Member States demonstrates that monetary policy and budget policy can end up in a vicious circle of mutual dependence. The ECB purchased government bonds within its open market operations and thereby became a direct creditor of Greece and other Member States. It also accepted those bonds as collateral in its transactions with private banks periodically. Once banks do not have access to the interbank market any more they become dependent on the ECB as their main source of refinancing, at least as long as the latter accepts these bonds as collateral. When a Member State defaults, banks heavily relying on its bonds would effectively have no more access to the credit instruments of the ECB and would run out of liquidity. Also the ECB would suffer from losses as a creditor in the event

62 Alexander, Dhumale and Eatwell, *Global Governance of Financial Systems*, p. 23; Schioppa, *Regulating Finance*, p. 107; Lastra, *Legal Foundations of International Monetary Stability*, p. 143.

63 Directive 98/26/EC of the European Parliament and of the Council of 19 May 1998 on Settlement Finality in Payment and Securities Settlement Systems [1998] OJ L 166/45.

64 Regulation (EU) No. 648/2012 of the European Parliament and of the Council of 4 July 2012 on OTC Derivatives, Central Counterparties and Trade Repositories [2012] OJ L 201/1.

65 Ohler, 'Finanzkrisen als Herausforderung der internationalen, europäischen und national en Rechtsetzung', p. 1064.

of a state insolvency. In this scenario it is extremely difficult for the ECB to argue that the restructuring of sovereign debt is a good idea, at least as long as an orderly insolvency mechanism is missing on the European level. This demonstrates that even under the subtle rules of EU law aiming exclusively at the stability of the monetary system and at full independence of the ECB, the central bank can be trapped by its prior monetary decisions to safeguard the liquidity of the European banking system in any event. Any change of the policy stance towards the ailing Member States would then trigger enormous costs for the ECB itself.

6 Regulatory conflicts of interests in a market economy system

Any regulation of financial markets is confronted with economic conflicts of interests and competing legal values that are of major relevance in an open market economy. Thus, there exist no clear ethical solutions; in fact, these problems require a weighing of political and economic risks.

6.1 *Balance of chances and risks*

It is well established that the problem of moral hazard is triggered when states guarantee the survival of financial institutions.[66] It will occur when states guarantee – even implicitly – the survival of financial institutions at any costs. The effects of such a public guarantee are that the bank managers are prepared to take inappropriate risks since they know that the bank would be saved anyhow. There is also the risk that business partners, in particular capital lenders and depositors, will not realistically assess the risk involved with an investment in such a bank. Under an explicit or implicit state guarantee the investors would assume that their investment is safe, inducing investors to accept excessive risks.

This phenomenon leads to a more fundamental, ethical problem. It is a fact that we have to pay for the costs of all decisions we make. The indissoluble link between a business decision and its economic consequences is particularly obvious with regard to financial markets which are based on the taking and transferring of risks. The risks taken reflect the expectations by the investor to generate profits but they also imply the possibility that the risk materializes and creates losses for the

[66] Arner, *Financial Stability, Economic Growth and the Law*, p. 306; Schioppa, *Regulating Finance*, p. 99; Lastra, *Legal Foundations of International Monetary Stability*, p. 115.

investor. From a very general point of view, financial market regulators should accept that economic risks are not a definite category which is per se a regulatory problem but a phenomenon that is the essence of any market economy. This means that a market economy works only if and to the extent that market participants actually pay for the wrong economic decisions they make. Personal liability of managers and the real possibility of insolvency proceedings for financial institutions are therefore necessary prerequisites for the proper functioning of a market economy.[67] If these instruments do not operate well, any legal system ends up being divorced from the essentials of a market economy.

6.2 *The limits of the (European) regulatory state*

6.2.1 Limits of competence

Within EU law, strict limits exist as far as the competences of the Union are concerned. Under the principle of conferral (or enumerative competences) in accordance with Article 5(1) TEU, the Union may only act if and to the extent that the Member States have conferred the competence for a legislative measure. One would assume that there would not be too many problems in the field of monetary policy, which is an area of exclusive competence of the EU.[68] Yet the European debt crisis revealed that this is not the case since the issues have their origin in the area of fiscal policy which is still a competence of the Member States.[69] Accordingly, the EFSF was based on a private law agreement between the Member States to establish a company under Luxembourg law – a measure clearly outside the scope of the treaties. Its successor, the ESM, will be an instrument of public international law that is only loosely woven into the fabric of the amended Article 136 TFEU. The EU measure to establish the European Financial Stabilisation Mechanism[70] was based on Article 122(2) TFEU, which provides only very little room for manoeuvre. A broad external and internal competence exists only in the field of financial regulation. The external competence is reflected by the ambit of secondary legislation adopted by the organs (compare Article 216(1)

[67] Arner, *Financial Stability, Economic Growth and the Law*, p. 155.

[68] Art. 3 para. 1(c) TFEU.

[69] Ohler, 'Finanzkrisen als Herausforderung der internationalen, europäischen und nationalen Rechtsetzung', p. 1066.

[70] Council Regulation (EU) 407/2010 of 11 May 2010 on Establishing a European Financial Stabilisation Mechanism OJ (2010) L118/1.

TFEU). Internally, the organs rely to a growing extent on Article 114 TFEU; in addition to Article 53(1) TFEU that so far was a legal basis for issuance of European passports, Article 114 TFEU permits the adoption of regulations that can be directly implemented by the European Commission and the supervisory agencies established within the European System of Financial Supervision.[71]

6.2.2 Material limits: fundamental rights and rule of law

Freedom to conduct a business[72] and the protection of property[73] are fundamental rights which the European and the national legislators must respect in the context of financial market regulation as well. Even acknowledging that any of these rights may be limited under a law that pursues a public interest, the principle of proportionality reduces the discretion enjoyed by legislators. The rule of law limits the means available to legislators, too. In this respect, the principle of legal certainty plays an important role.

6.2.3 Factual restrictions

Apart from the constitutional limits of each form of financial regulation, there are factual restrictions which no legislator/regulator can avoid. The first restriction results from cognitive limits of rule-making: supervisory law is to a large extent based on the experiences of the last crisis. Each reform demonstrates the extent of learning from the latest turmoil in the market and what legislators hope to prevent in the near future.[74] But financial market regulation cannot provide an answer to future crises if one assumes that they will appear in a different shape again. Another factual limit is that no legislator can command an adequate degree of confidence in the markets. In a market economy it also cannot order market participants to have particular expectations and abstain from others. It can only take into account that the legal and administrative environment is the fundament on which the confidence necessary for a normal functioning of financial markets may grow. A regulator should also consider that its instruments may have a potentially negative impact on

[71] Directive 2006/48/EC of the European Parliament and of the Council Relating to the Taking up and Pursuit of the Business of Credit Institutions, OJ (2006) L 177.

[72] Art. 16 Charter of Fundamental Rights of the European Union.

[73] *Ibid.*, Art. 17.

[74] Ohler, 'Finanzkrisen als Herausforderung der internationalen, europäischen und nationalen Rechtsetzung', p. 1066.

the competition on the market.[75] Whereas regulatory law in the context of former state monopolies is aimed at establishing markets and opening them for competition, the same is not true for financial markets. Here, the legislator/regulator faces a majority of private institutions, and hence a large number of market participants. Competition in this field is based on prices, the innovative character of products and the quality of services offered. In particular, regulatory capital requirements have a strong impact on the way business is done since the management of banks will avoid transactions that reduce the regulatory capital to an extent that the capital costs are higher than the expected yield under the transaction. The downside of this kind of regulation is that it *can* negatively affect competition between financial institutions. The more detailed capital requirements are and the more they reduce the incentive to make alternative business decisions, the more financial institutions behave in the same way.[76] The same problem occurs in the field of risk management where neither EU law nor international standards require a specific method or prescribe specific procedures. In reality, however, one must assume that the mathematical models used by banks and recognized by supervisors are not so different from each other. This would mean that the risk management systems of various banks resemble each other and translate into an asset structure – on and off balance sheet – that is very similar across the market. When a crisis develops, the conformity of asset structures means that a downturn will catch many institutions at the same time and in the same way. In practice, it is extremely difficult to avoid this regulatory trap since there are good reasons fully to harmonize capital requirements and risk management systems. The price of this trend, however, is that assets with identical risks will be equally distributed over the market place and the risk convergence between financial institutions will grow.

6.3 *The problem of international burden sharing*

Two fields remain in which the processes of informal law-making within administrative networks do not seem to be apt to provide adequate answers to urgent international challenges. These fields concern the

[75] This is recognized for the moral hazard problem of state guarantees. Lastra, *Legal Foundations of International Monetary Stability*, p. 120.

[76] Cf. Christoph Ohler, 'International Regulation and Supervision of Financial Markets after the Crisis' (2010) 3 *European Yearbook of International Economic Law* 19.

problem of international burden sharing in the case of insolvency of either a systemically important bank or a state. Since both scenarios lead to tremendous costs not only for the creditors but also for the public in many other states, there should theoretically be a common interest to tackle that problem. In reality however, international burden sharing is one of the big unresolved problems in international and European law.

6.3.1 Restructuring of globally operating firms

With respect to internationally operating financial institutions a perplexing phenomenon must be faced. They live internationally but they die nationally, as Eva Hüpkes from the Financial Stability Board (FSB) put it once.[77] The reason is that the law of restructuring and insolvency is national, based on the territoriality principle, whereas most financial firms exist under complex corporate structures covering a plethora of jurisdictions.[78] So far, there exist only very basic EU rules for branches of cross-border operating credit institutions.[79] Under public international law there are no obligations to recognize or even support national measures in the area of restructuring and insolvency regulations. This is particularly painful for international groups when the insolvency of a foreign subsidiary endangers the domestic parent or vice versa. Against this background, the recommendations of the FSB for the effective resolution of financial institutions are of high importance.[80] In the case of the insolvency of an international group the question, however, remains unresolved as to who should shoulder the burden of fresh capital injections – even for the sake of financial stability.[81]

6.3.2 Restructuring of sovereign debt

The lack of internationally accepted legal rules is also apprehensible with respect to sovereign debt. If a restructuring takes place, a qualified majority of debtors should agree to the mode and the results of the restructuring. This would normally happen in the form of an international conference where participants negotiate until they reach a compromise on how to restructure the existing debt. In the meantime, the

77 Hüpkes, 'Rivalry in Resolution', p. 221. 78 *Ibid.*

79 Council Directive 2001/24/EC of 4 April 2001 on the reorganisation and winding up of credit institutions *OJ* 2001 L125/15.

80 Financial Stability Board, 'Key Attributes of Effective Resolution Regimes for Financial Institutions' (October 2011), available at www.financialstabilityboard.org/publications/r_111104cc.pdf.

81 Hüpkes, 'Rivalry in Resolution', p. 224.

state would have to maintain its public functions without having access to private capital markets and probably having simultaneously to deal with a deep recession.[82] Therefore, the current discussion in the EU on the role of the EFSF and ESM centres around the political question whether and under which conditions an ailing Member State may receive public financial assistance in order to restore its budgetary position and reform its underlying policies. The exchange of financial assistance against structural reform ('conditionality') reflects the ambivalence between the fear that financial stability could be threatened and the fear that funds could create an incentive to neglect necessary reforms.

7 Conclusion

International standard setting by administrative networks is a necessary and useful element of financial market regulation. Its ambit is limited, though. In a global system of sovereign states, administrative networks neither solve the complex interface between regulation, monetary policy and fiscal decisions of public entities, nor can they provide answers as to who should invest fresh capital when public and private debts need to be restructured. The reason is that these problems require political answers which fall within the competence of governments and parliaments. Yet, as one of the leading economic areas in the world, the political contribution of the EU will be of utmost relevance. Against the background of the ongoing debt crisis in Europe, the challenge for the EU to offer solutions that are acceptable for other parts of the world is a compelling one. Structurally, the problem-solving capacity of the EU is impeded by its strict and rather inflexible constitutional framework under the Treaties. The EU is not an omni-competent state and its powers in several crucial areas are shared with the Member States. This means that many of the tools developed are political compromises and reflect the specific constitutional situation of the EU, as can be shown, for instance, with respect to the EFSF and the ESM. On the international plane, the room for manoeuvre of the EU is particularly limited in the area of fiscal policy. In a material sense, the EU is a laboratory for the Member States to try to solve the tricky issues of international burden-sharing while restructuring systemically relevant financial institutions and dealing with unsustainable sovereign debt.

[82] Arner, *Financial Stability, Economic Growth and the Role of Law*, p. 304.

13

The EU and the euro area in international economic governance: the case of the IMF

JAN WOUTERS, SVEN VAN KERCKHOVEN AND THOMAS RAMOPOULOS

1 Introduction

International economic governance is one of the major contemporary fields of cross-border policy and regulatory efforts. It has gained further significance since the outbreak of the 2008 financial crisis. A significant role within this framework is played by the International Monetary Fund (IMF or Fund). Since the beginning of the European sovereign debt crisis, the relationship between the European Union (EU), in particular the euro area, and the IMF has evolved and shifted considerably. In light of these developments this chapter examines and discusses the potential and limits that the post-Lisbon EU Treaty provisions offer with regard to the external representation of the EU and the euro area in the IMF. This discussion is subsequently approached from the viewpoint of the IMF; in particular, the Articles of Agreement of the latter.

The international financial crisis and the European sovereign debt crisis have given rise to seemingly conflicting economic and political developments in the EU. On the one hand, they have provoked – or at least exacerbated – the problem of diverging economic and monetary interests amongst EU Member States. On the other hand, the crisis has accelerated the ongoing rebalancing of global economic and monetary power in favour of emerging economies, which, in turn, underlines the urgency for EU Member States to improve their coordination and/or representation in international financial institutions and conferences (IFIC), if they are to remain influential, fulfilling the Union's *raison d'être* as elaborated by de Búrca in this volume. Hence, it is important to examine how the relevant EU Treaty provisions that have entered into force with the Treaty of Lisbon could alter EU/euro area performance in the Fund. As argued in this chapter, the euro area, but perhaps not the EU as a whole, is now equipped with the legal tools to improve the effectiveness, visibility and coherence of its external representation. Article 138 of the Treaty on the Functioning of the EU (TFEU) obliges euro area Member States to adopt common positions in international forums and even allows for a unified representation of the euro area in these forums. However, the Treaties stop short of clarifying the relationship between the external representation of the euro area and the EU. They did not formally bestow the euro area with legal personality, thereby handicapping it in becoming fully engaged in IFIC. Still, the Treaties do create a potential for the euro area to shape the agenda and policies of the IMF more successfully.

The same questions are also approached from the perspective of the IMF. First, the feasibility of any change in the representation of the EU and the euro area from the perspective of the IMF Articles of Agreement is analysed. More concretely, the discussion revolves around who can become a member of the Fund and under what conditions. The conditions for changing constituencies are also examined. We argue that the IMF Articles of Agreement would allow the EU/euro area Member States to improve their loose coordination mechanisms, or to join an EU/euro area constituency. However, with regard to the question of a single euro area IMF seat, the IMF Articles of Agreement and practice cast a more negative light. Therefore, a single euro area seat might not be feasible without an amendment of the Articles of Agreement.

2 Europe at the IMF today

All EU Member States are member countries of the IMF. The EU does not have any status in it: it is represented by two of its institutions, the ECB, which has received observer status at the IMF Executive Board,[1] and the European Commission, which only has observer status at the Development Committee of the IMF. Naturally, observers do not enjoy full participation in the decision-making procedures and are for that reason in a disadvantaged position. The ECB, for example, is only empowered to speak during Executive Board meetings on matters of European monetary policy.[2] Thus, the Union and the euro area have to

[1] See Decision No. 11875 (99/1), 21 December 1998, substituted by Decision No. 12925 (03/1), 27 December 2002, as amended by Decisions No. 13414 (05/01), 23 December 2004, 13612 (05/108), 22 December 2005, and 14517 (10/1), 5 January 2010.

[2] A. Ahearne and B. Eichengreen, 'External Monetary and Financial Policy: A Review and a Proposal', in A. Sapir (ed.), *Fragmented Power: Europe and the Global Economy* (Brussels: Bruegel, 2007), p. 140.

rely on their individual Member States to deliver their messages and express the 'European voice' at the Fund.[3] The individual Member States, however, may have little incentive to diverge from their national positions. They often fail to coordinate and support a common European position. This coordination problem is exacerbated by their dispersion amongst several constituencies consisting of a mixture of euro area Member States, EU Member States and third countries (so-called mixed constituencies),[4] further lowering EU and euro area visibility and voice at the IMF.[5] The result is that Europe often finds itself punching below its weight.[6] The European voice is reduced to a whisper despite a joint quota of more than 30 per cent for EU Member States and about 24 per cent for the euro area.[7] EU institutions and observers have been aware of this problem for years.[8] Coordination mechanisms

[3] G. Mahieu, D. Ooms and S. Rottier, 'EU Representation and the Governance of the International Monetary Fund' (2005) 6 *European Union Politics* 499.

[4] G. Mahieu, D. Ooms and S. Rottier, 'The Governance of the International Monetary Fund with a Single EU Chair' (2003) 1 *Financial Stability Review* 173.

[5] For an overview, see J. Wouters and S. Van Kerckhoven, 'The International Monetary Fund', in K. E. Jorgensen and K. V. Laatikainen (eds.), *Routledge Handbook on the European Union and International Institutions: Performance, Policy, Power* (London: Routledge, 2012), pp. 221–33.

[6] L. Bini Smaghi, 'A Single EU Seat in the IMF?' (2004) 42 *Journal of Common Market Studies* 230; R. Smits, 'International Representation of Europe in the Area of Economic and Monetary Union: Legal Issues and Practice in the First Ten Years of the Euro', Proceedings of the Conference 10 Years of European Monetary Union: A Legal Perspective, 29–30 January 2009, p. 12.

[7] Each IMF member is assigned a quota, reflecting its weight in the global economy. This quota determines both the contribution and the voting power of the IMF member country. See Wouters and Van Kerckhoven, 'The International Monetary Fund'; and Bini Smaghi, 'A Single EU Seat in the IMF?'.

[8] Jean Claude Juncker, as President of the Eurogroup, stated that: 'It is absurd for those 15 countries not to agree to have a single representation at the IMF. It makes us look absolutely ridiculous. We are regarded as buffoons on the international scene.' E. Vucheva, 'Eurozone Countries Should Speak with One Voice, Juncker Says', *EUObserver*, 15 April, 2008, available at http://euobserver.com/19/25984. Joaquin Almunia followed a similar reasoning in stating that: '[T]he external representation of the euro should become more consistent if the EU is to make its voice heard in the international arena.' 'Commissioner Joaquín Almunia: Look Back with Pride, Look Forward with Confidence', *European Economy News*, issue 6 (April 2007), available at http://ec.europa.eu/economy_finance/een/006/article_5205_en.htm; and that '[I]ts external representation could be strengthened'. See http://ec.europa.eu/economy_finance/emu10/index_en.htm. See also E. Broussy, 'Article 111 CE', in I. Pingel (ed.), *De Rome à Lisbonne, commentaire article par article des Traités UE et CE*, 2nd edn (Paris: Lichtenhahn, Dalloz and Bruylant, 2010), p. 936, where it is suggested that 'Le souci de cohérence et d'efficacité, poursuivi par les autorités de la Communauté, ne se concilie qu'avec une organisation parlant d'une seule

have been set up in both Washington and Brussels – the group of EU representatives to the IMF (EURIMF) in Washington, DC and the Subcommittee on IMF (SCIMF) under the Economic and Financial Affairs (Ecofin) Council in Brussels. Still, coordination is deemed to be insufficient and there have even been 'occasional problems to fully translate the common lines agreed in Brussels into the statements of EU Executive Directors in Washington'.[9] Proposals to strengthen these coordination mechanisms failed on several occasions.[10] Even after the coming into force of the Treaty of Lisbon, there have been no significant changes in the representation of the EU or the euro area at the IMF.[11] A Union Delegation to the IMF is still to be established representing the EU as a whole (Article 221 TFEU), contrary to current practice at the WTO, UN, FAO, OECD and UNESCO.[12] The EU thus continues to conduct its relations with the IMF in a distant manner. The main coordinating mechanisms – EURIMF and SCIMF – continue to be little more than

voix sur l'euro dans les enceintes internationales.' See further recommendation No. 30 of the High Level Group on Financial Supervision in the EU, 'Report on Financial Supervision in the EU' (de Larosière Report) (25 February 2009): 'In the context of a more ambitious institutional reform, this could imply a consolidation of the EU's representation in the IMF and other multilateral fora'; Smits, 'International Representation of European in the Area of Economic and Monetary Union'; W. Kiekens, 'What Kind of External Representation for the Euro?', OeNB-Seminar, 'The European Convention on the Future of Europe', 2 June 2003; C. Garnier, D. Daco and F. Di Mauro, 'UN–EU Cooperation on Financial Issues: The Role of the European Union at the International Monetary Fund and the World Bank', in J. Wouters, F. Hoffmeister and T. Ruys (eds.), *The United Nations and the European Union: An Ever Stronger Partnership* (The Hague: TMC Asser Press 2006); K. McNamara and S. Meunier, 'Between National Sovereignity and International Power: What External Voice for the Euro?' (2002) 78 *International Affairs* 849; N. Corrales-Diez, 'The EU Representation at the International Monetary Fund', Federal Ministry of Finance (Austria) Working Paper 3/2003 (2003), p. 7. This claim was already advanced before the introduction of the euro; see C. Wyplosz, 'EMU: Why and How it Might Happen' (1997) 11 *Journal of Economic Perspectives* 3 (16).

9 Economic and Financial Affairs (Ecofin), Directorate-General, European Commission, 'EMU@10: Successes and Challenges after Ten Years of Economic and Monetary Union' (2008) 2 *European Economy* 142.

10 For an analysis of these coordination mechanisms, see Bini Smaghi, 'A Single EU Seat in the IMF?'; Eurodad Report, 'European Coordination at the World Bank and the IMF: A Question of Harmony?' (2006); Wouters and Van Kerckhoven, 'The International Monetary Fund'.

11 This is contrary to the early expectations of some authors, such as R. S. Martha, 'The Fund Agreement and the Surrender of Monetary Sovereignty to the European Communities' (1993) 30 *Common Market Law Review* 749.

12 Council Decision 2010/427/EU of 26 July 2010 establishing the organization and functioning of the European External Action Service, OJ (2010) L 201/30.

loose structures where Member States discuss issues pertaining to the work of the IMF. Moreover, they are EU – and not just euro area – coordination mechanisms: all EU Member States participate in the meetings of these Committees despite the fact that only euro area Member States have pooled their monetary policies. Naturally, this effort to coordinate Member States with different levels of integration is prone to produce a cacophony of national positions.

These problems have become yet more pronounced in the wake of the international financial crisis and the European sovereign debt crisis. The crises have brought to the surface and aggravated '[d]ivergence[s] in competitiveness and fiscal performance [. . .] between member-states', which have led to 'strongly diverging national interests among [them]'.[13] It is illuminating that in the recently revived effort to reform the international monetary system, Germany and France have found themselves on opposing sides on the issues of global financial safety nets and the role of Special Drawing Rights as an alternative reserve asset.[14] These differences often paralyse efforts to maintain a common European stance in international macroeconomic, financial and fiscal policies.[15] They have also activated sovereignty reflexes, especially within smaller Member States, which are afraid that a possible further unification of the representation of the EU or the euro area in the Fund would divest them of the possibility to have their opinion heard.[16] Hence, Member States have so far been rather reluctant to increase coordination and discretely oppose a unification of their representation in the IMF.[17]

However, individual Member States realize that it is becoming increasingly difficult to influence international developments on their own and

[13] D. Schwarzer, 'The European Union and the Economic and Financial Crisis: Reforming Internal Governance and External Representation in Turbulent Times', in B. J. C. McKercher (ed.), *Routledge Handbook of Diplomacy and Statecraft* (London: Routledge, 2012), p. 303.

[14] See K. Gnath and C. Schmucker, 'Same Economic Nightmares, Different Solutions: Transatlantic Approaches to International Macroeconomic Policymaking', AICGS Policy Report No. 48, American Institute for Contemporary German Studies, Washington, DC (2011), pp. 20–3.

[15] *Ibid.*

[16] Schwarzer, 'The European Union and the Economic and Financial Crisis', p. 311.

[17] Ahearne and Eichengreen, 'External Monetary and Financial Policy', p. 145; Corralez-Diez, 'The EU Representation at the International Monetary Fund', p. 12; R. Barents, 'Het Verdrag van Lissabon: Achtergronden en Commentaar' (The Hague: Kluwer 2008), p. 584; F.-X. Priollaud and D. Siritzky, *Le Traité de Lisbonne: texte et commentaires, article par article, des nouveaux traités européens (TUE–TFUE)* (Paris: La Documentation Française, 2008), p. 259.

that they could benefit from more coordination or even from a unification of their representation.[18] This has been in particular the case after the international and subsequent European crises. These have accelerated the shift of economic power from advanced economies, in particular the USA and Europe, to emerging economies. Cooperation in Europe's external representation is therefore even more important if it wants to be able to continue co-determining international economic decisions and represent European interests.[19] Broadly speaking, the following three proposals[20] are brought to the table: (i) enhancing existing coordination mechanisms, (ii) bringing all EU/euro area Member States in one or more EU/euro-area constituency, or (iii) establishing a single EU/euro area seat through the succession of Member States' seats to the Union or the euro area (possibly with an adaptation of the quotas).[21] The first question examined below is whether the Lisbon Treaty actually provides the EU or the euro area with the legal tools to establish some kind of unified representation at the IMF, or a more enhanced coordination is the only way forward.

3 The potential and limits of the EU treaties

This section deals with the potential and limits of the EU treaties after Lisbon to improve the representation of the EU and the euro area in the IMF. The Lisbon Treaty has made a small but significant step in the direction of a unified representation of the euro area, but not necessarily of the EU, in the IMF. Article 138 TFEU, which replaced the previous Article 111(4) and (5) TEC, obliges in paragraph 1 the euro area Member States to reach common positions on economic and monetary issues that are the subject matter of IFIC. However, in paragraph 2 it only *enables*

[18] Interestingly, at the Convention on the future of Europe, France and Germany proposed in a joint contribution: 'With respect to the external representation of the euro zone, France and Germany share the view that a single representation in international financial institutions such as the IMF will be the adequate voice of an integrated Europe. A single European seat will increase the weight of the European Union compared to other major actors in the international environment. As first step, it requires strengthening and improving the preparation of common viewpoints in international financial institutions'. French–German contribution to the work of the European Convention on Economic Governance, CONV 470/02, 22 December 2002.

[19] D. Schwarzer, 'The European Union and the Economic and Financial Crisis'.

[20] Kiekens, 'What Kind of External Representation for the Euro?', p. 3.

[21] Wouters and Van Kerckhoven, 'The International Monetary Fund'; Bini Smagi, 'A Single EU Seat in the IMF?'.

('may') the Council to adopt appropriate measures, on a proposal of the Commission, to ensure a unified representation at the IFIC after consulting the ECB.[22] This is in contrast to the former Article 111(4) TEC, which *obliged* the Council to adopt measures regarding representation.[23] Still, the Treaty of Lisbon's reference to a *unification* of the representation of the euro area is new.[24] If read in conjunction with the fact that the new formulation makes no reference to the Union as was previously the case with the Community, it can convincingly be argued that, in recognizing the differing levels of integration within the EU, Article 138 TFEU opens the door for a unified international representation of the euro area.[25] This provision reads as follows:

> 1. In order to secure the euro's place in the international monetary system, the Council, on a proposal from the Commission, shall adopt a decision establishing common positions on matters of particular interest for economic and monetary union within the competent international financial institutions and conferences. The Council shall act after consulting the European Central Bank.
> 2. The Council, on a proposal from the Commission, may adopt appropriate measures to ensure unified representation within the international financial institutions and conferences. The Council shall act after consulting the European Central Bank.

[22] Ahearne and Eichengreen, 'External Monetary and Financial Policy', p. 162 and Bini Smaghi, 'A Single EU Seat in the IMF?', p. 270 argue that the IMF would be the best starting point for consolidating Europe's representation into a single chair as the European preferences are relatively homogenous in this institution. Smits disagrees. Smits, 'International Representation of European in the Area of Economic and Monetary Union', p. 34.

[23] Smits, 'International Representation', p. 4; J.-C. Piris, *The Lisbon Treaty: A Legal and Political Analysis* (Cambridge University Press, 2010), p. 306. Art. 111(4) TEC stipulated: 'Subject to paragraph 1, the Council, acting by a qualified majority on a proposal from the Commission and after consulting the ECB, shall decide on the position of the Community at international level as regards issues of particular relevance to economic and monetary union and on *its representation*, in compliance with the allocation of powers laid down in Arts. 99 and 105' (emphasis added).

[24] For the other differences between the two provisions, see J.-C. Piris, *The Lisbon Treaty: A Legal and Political Analysis*, pp. 305–6. Some of the adaptations brought about by Art. 138 TFEU were already part of the discussion during the Convention on the Future of Europe, Final Report of the Working Group VII on External Action, para. 13; Final Report on the Working Group VI on Economic Governance, CONV 357/02, 21/10/2002, Brussels, WG 17, V.2.

[25] J.-C. Piris, 'It is Time for the Euro Area to Develop Further Closer Cooperation Among its Members', Jean Monnet Working Paper 05/11 (2011), available at http://centers.law.nyu.edu/jeanmonnet/papers/11/110501.pdf.

> 3. For the measures referred to in paragraphs 1 and 2, only members of the Council representing Member States whose currency is the euro shall take part in the vote.
>
> A qualified majority of the said members shall be defined in accordance with Article 238(3)(a).

This provision seems to go beyond just an enhancement of existing coordination mechanisms. In opting for a 'unified' representation of the euro area based on 'common positions on matters of particular interest for economic and monetary union', this article clearly favours the second proposal mentioned above, i.e. the creation of a euro area constituency. It is submitted that the provision even allows for a single euro area seat in the future but this would require overcoming existing legal concerns, as discussed below. Given the focus of Article 138 TFEU on the euro area, the ensuing analysis revolves primarily around the representation of the euro area in the IMF.

The first proposal favours the deepening and strengthening of existing EU coordination mechanisms in the IMF. This, however, would mean leaving untapped the potential created by Article 138 TFEU. First, this provision places the adoption of common positions and measures for a unified euro area representation in IFIC in the hands of the Council – with only the euro area Member States having a right to vote and allowing for a decision to be taken with a qualified majority (Article 138(3)) – and not in loose cooperation mechanisms at a lower level. Secondly, opting for an improvement of the current arrangements would not do away with the existing problems preventing the EU, let alone the euro area, from having a common position and a unified representation in the IMF. In coordination mechanisms all EU Member States would continue participating, although only euro area Member States share a common monetary policy and are ever more integrating their economic policies.[26] In addition, the dispersal of euro area Member States in different constituencies containing non-euro area Member States and third states would continue hampering any serious effort to present a common euro area position.

[26] See European Council, The President, Towards a Genuine Economic and Monetary Union: Interim Report (12 November 2012). Also, European Commission, A Blueprint for a Deep and Genuine Economic and Monetary Union: Launching a European Debate, COM (2012) 777 final, 30 November 2012.

The second option involves grouping euro area Member States in one or more euro area constituencies. Such a development would create the external conditions and the incentive for euro area Member States to comply with their obligations under Article 138(1) TFEU with regard to the IMF. In addition, the possibility offered by Article 138(2) TFEU would materialize in practice. This seems to be the view of the European Commission too, which in its 'Blueprint for a deep and genuine economic and monetary union' suggests the creation of euro area constituencies as a first step towards a unified euro area representation in the Fund.[27] It should be noted here that the creation of a single euro area constituency containing all or most euro area Member States is rather preferable to a rearrangement of euro area Member States in multiple euro area constituencies. This would allow euro area Member States to decide, unencumbered by non-euro area Member States or third states, who will be responsible for conducting the unified representation of the euro area in the Fund.[28] This issue is not addressed directly in Article 138 TFEU or elsewhere in the Treaties. To put it in IMF terminology, at first sight it is not clear under EU law who would become the Executive Director and the Alternate Executive Director of a euro area constituency. Arguments have been made that the ECB is the natural bearer of the external competences in the field of monetary policy.[29] The case for the

[27] European Commission, Communication from the Commission, A Blueprint for a Deep and Genuine Economic and Monetary Union Launching a European Debate; European Commission, A Blueprint for a Deep and Genuine Economic and Monetary Union, 30 November 2012, p. 25 and Annex II, pp. 46–8.

[28] Barents, 'Het Verdrag Van Lissabon', p. 590.

[29] Bini Smaghi, 'A Single EU Seat in the IMF?', p. 263; C. Zilioli and M. Selmayr, 'The External Relations of the Euro Area: Legal Aspects' (1999) 36 *Common Market Law Review* 273. This has been opposed by C. W. Herrmann, 'Monetary Sovereignty over the Euro and External Relations of the Euro Area: Competences, Procedures and Practice' (2002) 7 *European Foreign Affairs Review* 1 (2); Horng looked into the prospects of the ECB as the representative of the euro area at the IMF. He elaborates on the necessary changes of EU law in order to allow for the ECB to take up such role within the IMF. However, his paper was written prior to the Lisbon Treaty. D. C. Horng, 'The ECB's Membership in the IMF: Legal Approaches to Constitutional Challenges' (2005) 11 *European Law Journal* 802; Barents, 'Het Verdrag van Lissabon', p. 579; S. M. Seyad, 'The Lisbon Treaty and EMU', *European Policy Analysis*, 4/2008, p. 3; and Piris, *The Lisbon Treaty: A Legal and Political Analysis*, p. 305 look at the changes between Arts. 127–33 TFEU and the prior-Lisbon Arts. 105–111a and observe that the amendments made are trivial and are unlikely to produce any different legal consequences. Only minor changes and clarifications have been carried out in Art. 127(6) TFEU (previously Art. 105(6) TEC) and Art. 129 TFEU (previously Art. 107 TEC). Only Art. 133

ECB as representative is strong as this institution includes all euro area Member States, has legal personality, and its statute allows it to participate in international monetary institutions.[30] However, the ECB's competences cover solely monetary policy and not the broader range of economic policies dealt with by the IMF. An analysis conducted elsewhere pointed to the European Stability Mechanism (ESM) as an alternative organization that could represent euro area Member States whereas the ECB would be the Alternate Executive Director of the euro area constituency dealing with monetary issues.[31] However, a similar problem arises as with the ECB – the ESM cannot represent the euro area on the full range of economic policies addressed in the Fund.[32] Rather, euro area Member States would have to show flexibility in order to reach a commonly agreed solution on their common representation that would notably take into account the concerns of smaller Member States.

What is also important is that the option of euro area constituencies takes into account the fact that the Treaties do not confer legal personality to the euro area, which would allow it, at least from an EU law perspective, to accede to the IMF replacing euro area Member States. Although, as will be discussed below in this section, it could be argued that though the euro area is in the process of obtaining such a legal personality, it is not quite there yet.

In addition, this option would not violate the allocation of competences of the EU Treaties and respect the obvious limits of Article 138 TFEU. In particular, euro area Member States may have transferred their

TFEU is brand new and provides the Council and the Parliament with the power to lay down the measures necessary for the use of the euro as a single currency. The minor changes in EU law regarding monetary policy allow Horng's views to retain some relevance.

30 Art. 6.2, Protocol on the Statute of the European System of Central Banks and of the European Central Bank, states: 'The ECB and, subject to its approval, the national central banks may participate in international monetary institutions'.

31 A. Giovannini, et al., 'External Representation of the Euro Area', Study for the European Parliament, Directorate-General for Internal Policies, Policy Department A: Economic and Scientific Policy, May 2012, p. 40.

32 The European Stability Mechanism is the financial crisis management mechanism of the euro area tasked with safeguarding the stability of the euro area 'serv[ing] to complement the new regulatory framework for strengthened economic governance of the Union', which also has a major 'essentially preventive' component. See Case C-370/12 *Thomas Pringle* v. *Government of Ireland, Ireland and The Attorney General* [2012] nyr, paras. 58–9.

monetary powers to the European level (cf. Article 3(1)(c) TFEU, classifying 'monetary policy for the Member States whose currency is the euro' as an exclusive competence),[33] but this is not the case for all matters dealt with in the Fund. Consequently, establishing a euro area seat succeeding to the euro area Member States' memberships in the IMF,[34] i.e. opting for the third proposal outlined above, would require a prior EU Treaty reform transferring further competences (economic policy) to the Union, at least for the euro area Member States. Ideally, by the same token, this Treaty reform would also have to grant the euro area legal personality. That said, the euro area will still have to continue conducting its economic policy 'with a view to contributing to the achievement of the objectives of the Union, as defined in Article 3 [TFEU]'.[35] This requirement serves, amongst others, to avoid fragmentation of the internal market and other EU policies, given the already existing split in economic and monetary integration between euro area and non-euro area Member States. All twenty-seven EU Member States would have to agree on such a change. However, this is a time-consuming and difficult exercise with an uncertain outcome, and for which the political appetite of Member States seems to be currently very limited, to say the least. Still, such steps would very much be in tune with the current tendency within the euro area towards 'full [. . .] economic, fiscal and political union'.[36] Notwithstanding such aspirations, a single

[33] This, however, was already the case before the entry into force of the Lisbon Treaty: Arts. 4(2), 118 and 123(4) TEC. See also Herrmann, 'Monetary Sovereignty over the Euro and External Relations of the Euro Area', p. 4; A. Kaczorowska, *European Union Law* (London: Routledge, 2008), p. 91; Kiekens, 'What Kind of External Representation for the Euro?', pp. 2–3.

[34] The possibility of a joint membership of the IMF for euro area Member States *and* the euro area itself (somewhat comparable to the situation of the EU and its Member States in the WTO and the FAO) is not contemplated here. Such an option does not seem to be politically expedient and raises very complex legal questions. It would rather worsen the problem of over-representation of Europe in the Fund (hence be also hardly acceptable to third-member countries) and would not necessarily improve coordination amongst euro area Member States. Furthermore, it is difficult to imagine how quota would be allocated between the euro area and its Member States. Lastly, if the decisive criterion for IMF membership is the exercise of the sovereign right to issue currency and adopt monetary policy, it would be difficult to argue that although this right now resides with the euro area its Member States should also remain members of the IMF.

[35] Art. 120 TFEU.

[36] See European Commission, Communication from the Commission, 'A Blueprint for a Deep and Genuine Economic and Monetary Union Launching a European Debate', COM (2012) 777 final, 30 November 2012, p. 3.

euro area seat lies further in the future and does not appear to be legally feasible or politically practicable at present.

If non-euro area Member States opposed such a treaty reform, another legal avenue for a unified representation of the euro area would be for the euro area Member States to pool their national competences in the area of economic policy outside the scope of the EU Treaties, creating a parallel structure. They could then designate the Commission as their representative in this policy area in the Fund whereas the ECB could continue representing the euro area in monetary policies. In doing so, they would not drift too far away from the institutional design of the EU. This formula is obviously inspired by, but goes further than, the Treaty Establishing the European Stability Mechanism (TESB) and the Treaty on Stability, Coordination and Governance (TSCG) in the Economic and Monetary Union discussed further below.[37] However, this would lead to a further fragmentation of the EU legal order and raise questions with regard to its compatibility with that order. Besides, it may prove difficult to sell to third member countries in the IMF, which would be perplexed by the variable geometry of the EU.

The above discussion has brought to the surface the limitations imposed on the euro area due to its lack of international legal personality and the many decision-making levels within the EU. It would, therefore, seem that *prima facie* from an EU law point of view, the euro area cannot be given full membership status at the IMF in the absence of international legal personality. Still, two observations are due in this respect. First, international legal personality is not necessarily dependent on the granting thereof in the founding treaty of an organization. According to the International Court of Justice, what matters is that the entity in question 'is in fact exercising and enjoying functions and rights which can only be explained on the basis of the possession of a large measure of international personality and the capacity to operate upon an international plane'.[38] Second, especially since the outbreak of the sovereign debt crisis, the euro area is becoming an actor in its own right next to EU structures and institutions, and it is increasingly

[37] With regard to the allocation of tasks outside the framework of the Union to EU institutions by Member States, see Case C-370/12 *Thomas Pringle* v. *Government of Ireland, Ireland and The Attorney General*, paras. 155–77.

[38] ICJ, Reparation for Injuries Suffered in the Service of the United Nations, 11 April 1949, ICJ Rep. 1949, p. 174.

perceived by third parties as one entity.[39] Heads of State and Government of the euro area adopt 'statements', 'agreed lines of communication' and 'press lines'.[40] There are increasing references to 'euro area Member States' with their own emerging 'euro area governance structure', consisting in 'Euro Summits' to be held at least twice a year at the level of Heads of State and Government with a designated 'President of the Euro Summit' next to the Eurogroup, the President of the Eurogroup and the Eurogroup Working Group, which will be chaired by a full-time Brussels-based President.[41] Even more revealing of this trend is the fact that the euro area has undertaken further steps to address the current crisis through the creation of a Special Purpose Vehicle, the European Financial Stability Facility (EFSF) together with Poland and Sweden, which was replaced by a permanent mechanism safeguarding financial stability in the euro area, the European Stability Mechanism.[42] Euro area Member States have also spearheaded the conclusion of the TSCG, which was signed by all EU Member States with the exception of the United Kingdom and the Czech Republic.[43] This Treaty, which lies outside the framework of the EU

[39] D. Schwarzer, 'A Consolidated Representation of Interests in the Context of Europe's Relative Economic Decline: Drivers and Obstacles', in J. Lieb, N. Ondarza and D. Schwarzer (eds.), *The European Union in International Fora* (Baden-Baden: Nomos, 2011), p. 150.

[40] See Statement by the Heads of State and Government of the Euro Area, 25 March 2010, www.consilium.europa.eu/uedocs/cms_data/docs/pressdata/en/ec/113563.pdf (accessed 7 February 2013); Statement on the support to Greece by Euro area Members States, 11 April 2010, www.consilium.europa.eu/uedocs/cms_data/docs/pressdata/en/ec/113686.pdf; Statement of the Heads of State and Government of the Euro Area, 7 May 2010, available at www.consilium.europa.eu/uedocs/cms_data/docs/pressdata/en/ec/114295.pdf; Decision of the Representatives of the Governments of the Euro Area Member States Meeting within the Council of the European Union – Decision of the Representatives of the Governments of the 27 EU Member States, 9614/10 of 10 May 2010; European Financial Stability Facility, Articles of Incorporation, available at www.efsf.europa.eu/attachments/efsf_articles_of_incorporation_en.pdf; Council of the European Union, Statement by the Heads of State or Government of the euro area and EU Institutions, 21 July 2007, available at www.consilium.europa.eu/uedocs/cms_data/docs/pressdata/en/ec/123978.pdf; 21 July 2011, 26 October 2011, 9 December 2011, 30 January 2012, 2 March 2012, 23 May 2012, 9 June 2012; remarks by Herman Van Rompuy on behalf of Euro area leaders, 24 May 2012.

[41] See statement, Euro summit 26 October 2011, paras. 30–3 and, in particular, Annex 1; see also statement 9 December 2011, para. 10.

[42] Treaty Establishing the European Stability Mechanism (ESM), D/12/3, Brussels, signed 2 February 2012, entered into force 27 September 2012. The ESM was inaugurated on 8 October 2012.

[43] Treaty on Stability, Coordination and Governance in the Economic and Monetary Union (TSCG), signed 2 March 2012, entered into force 1 January 2013 for the seventeen

Treaties,[44] strengthens fiscal discipline and introduces stricter surveillance within the euro area, establishing amongst others a 'balanced budget rule'. In light of all these impressive developments, it is no exaggeration to suggest that the euro area is quickly heading towards further integration and is more and more asserting its own actorness. These developments will in the future add force and value to arguments for the unification of euro area representation in the IMF through the succession of the euro area to the membership of its Member States in the Fund.

Regarding the EU as a whole, no specific provisions have been made for increased coordination or a unified position in IFIC. The sole requirement for all EU Member States is that they must treat their exchange rate policy as a matter of common interest (Article 142 TFEU). This article does not deprive them of the right to negotiate independently on a number of IMF issues, but merely rules out the use of currency exchange rates as a beggar-thy-neighbour policy. EU Member States that are not members of the euro area are thus not directly dependent or bound by decisions in the monetary field.[45] In this sense, not much has changed for non-euro area Member States after the Lisbon Treaty.

By way of preliminary conclusion, the euro area is legally able to go for a unified representation at the IMF, a development that would be in accordance with the spirit and letter of Article 138 TFEU. Political and economic realities also call for such a development. The establishment of a single, or at least a few, euro area constituencies would be in full compliance with the EU Treaties and would allow the euro area to advance its interests and arguments in the Fund, overcoming the observed fragmentation in its external representation.[46] For the other EU Member States not much has changed in terms of an obligation to have a unified position or representation in the IMF. A single euro area membership succeeding to those of its Member States could be envisaged in the future, since the euro area seems to be emancipating from the EU, slowly asserting its legal personality and assuming more competences.

Member States that ratified it prior to this date. It has yet to enter into force for Belgium, Bulgaria, Hungary, Luxembourg, Malta, the Netherlands, Poland and Sweden.

[44] However, according to Art. 16, the substance of TSCG is to be incorporated in the EU legal order at most within five years since its coming into force.

[45] Still, EU Member States will have to uphold their obligations from the exchange-rate agreement (ERM II) between them and the euro area to the extent that these Member States participate in ERM II.

[46] D. Smith, 'International Financial Regulation: A Role for the Eurozone?, EU Diplomacy Paper 08/2012, p. 26.

In practice, however, nothing has happened yet and the voice of both the EU and the euro area still largely depend on the individual preferences of Member States and loose coordination mechanisms.[47]

4 The IMF dimension of EU/euro area representation

The previous section dealt with the potential created by the Lisbon Treaty to have a unified euro area representation at the IMF. The question addressed here is whether the IMF itself would allow for such a development. This entails two contingent questions, namely (i) the issue of joint representation of euro area Member States, when these remain individual member countries in the IMF, and (ii) the accession of the euro area to the IMF. The IMF is a country-based organization[48] and it is not clear whether its Articles of Agreement allow for either a euro area constituency with unified representation of the euro area Member States or a euro area membership.[49] From an IMF point of view, two main issues arise with regard to the EU/euro area. First, the EU/euro area take up a large voting share within the Fund, making the IMF less legitimate in the eyes of emerging economies.[50] Second, as euro area Member States have transferred their monetary competences to the Union, it has become very difficult for them to fulfil their individual obligations towards the Fund.[51]

[47] Bini Smaghi, 'A Single EU Seat in the IMF?', p. 236.

[48] Kiekens, 'What Kind of External Representation for the Euro?', p. 4.

[49] In September 1998, the IMF's Executive Board discussed the coming into being of the euro and declared: 'The Fund is a country-based institution and the transfer of monetary powers by members of the euro area to the institutions of the EMU will not affect their legal relationship with the Fund under the Fund's Articles of Agreement. Euro-area members will continue to be members of the Fund in their own individual capacity as countries. All rights of membership will continue to be available to each individual member, and all the obligations that membership in the Fund entail will continue to bind them individually'. 'Concluding Remarks by the Acting Chairman of the IMF Executive Board Meeting 98/101, 21 September 1998', cited in Kiekens, 'What Kind of External Representation for the Euro?', p. 4.

[50] Mahieu, Ooms and Rotier, 'The Governance of the International Monetary Fund with a Single EU Chair', p. 174; Edwin Truman, 'Rearranging IMF Chairs and Shares: The Sine Qua Non of IMF Reform', in Edwin Truman (ed.), *Reforming the IMF for the 21st Century* (Washington, DC: Peterson Institute for International Economics, 2005), p. 202; Lauren Phillips, 'Lead, Follow or Get Out the Way? The Role of the EU in the Reform of the Bretton Woods Institutions', paper prepared for the XXVI G24 Technical Meeting, Geneva, 16–17 March 2006, p. 4.

[51] Kiekens, 'What Kind of External Representation for the Euro?'; K. Regling, 'Strengthening the Economic Leg of EMU', Euro 50 Group Roundtable: 50 years after the Treaty of Rome, 2–3 July 2007.

As to the first proposal outlined above, i.e. increasing the European voice by improving the loose coordination mechanisms, the IMF Articles of Agreement do not raise real problems: EU/euro area Member States are free to coordinate.

The second proposal, gathering all euro area Member States in a single constituency, should also theoretically be possible from an IMF viewpoint. IMF member countries are allowed to join any constituency of their liking. The practice of establishing constituencies is only marginally regulated by the Articles of Agreement. Constituencies are no more than groupings of countries, which are represented by an elected Executive Director. Article XII, section 3(b)(ii) of the Articles of Agreement stipulates that fifteen members should be elected and that these elected Executive Directors then cast the number of votes of the members appointing them.[52] Nowhere in the Articles of Agreement can one find constraints on who could be elected. If the euro area Member States thus join one constituency and vote for a common 'euro area' official, this would be possible and could greatly improve the effectiveness of the euro area's participation in the IMF. If euro area Member States (or even EU Members States for that matter) decide to join their representation and elect a common Executive Director, this would not require any amendment to the IMF Articles of Agreement.

The third and most far-reaching proposal from an IMF perspective is the establishment of a single euro area seat. In this scenario, the euro area itself would accede to the IMF and replace the individual euro area Member States. A single euro area seat would not only solve European coordination and under-effectiveness problems but could as well address some IMF issues. First, the euro area Member States take up a very significant share of votes at the IMF (about 24 per cent). If the euro area itself would join the Fund succeeding its Member States, the joint quota of euro area Member States could be lowered, freeing up quota and votes for the emerging economies. Logically, if the euro area became a member of the IMF, intra-euro area trade would be excluded from the calculation of its quota.[53] A second benefit of a single euro area seat is that it would

[52] See IMF Art. XII, section 3(i). The number is higher today as the number of Executive Directors has been increased.

[53] Ahearne and Eichengreen, 'External Monetary and Financial Policy', p. 164. If the euro area becomes a single member, it is to be expected to receive a lower quota. The opposite holds true in the case of a break-up, as precedents show us. When Czechoslovakia and Ethiopia divided into different countries the sum of the quotas held by the resulting countries was higher than their previous joint one. Their break-up thus resulted in a

solve the other big challenge, namely the emergence of a single-currency euro area.[54] Indeed, as stated above, due to the adoption of the euro and the transfer of national monetary powers, euro area Member States are no longer able to fulfil all their obligations towards the IMF individually. The euro area has a single exchange rate and a single monetary policy, which from an IMF perspective resembles more closely a single country than several individual countries.[55] The euro area Member States can no longer fulfil their individual obligations under Article VII of the Articles of Agreement, which lays down the obligations of member countries regarding current and capital payments regimes and reserve asset policies. The same holds true for the official consultations on monetary policies (Article IV), which necessitate the involvement of the ECB for euro area Member States.[56] In practice, it is the ECB which is solely responsible for the interaction between the euro area and the IMF.[57]

The prospect of euro area membership in the IMF is of course not realistic as long as the former cannot be considered to have international legal personality, as discussed in the previous section. But even assuming legal personality, a potential pitfall remains that the Articles of Agreement do not allow for any other entity than a country to join the IMF.[58] Article II.2 stipulates that membership must be open to other *countries* at such times and in accordance with such terms as may be prescribed by the Board of Governors. These terms, including the terms for subscriptions, must be based on principles consistent with those applied to other countries that are already members.[59]

higher combined voting share than before when they were still one country: see Mahieu, Ooms and Rotier, 'The Governance of the International Monetary Fund with a Single EU Chair', p. 174.

54 Regional arrangements, such as the EMU, pose an important challenge to the IMF: see R. C. Henning, 'Regional Arrangements and the International Monetary Fund', in E. M. Truman (ed.), 'Reforming the IMF for the 21st Century', Institute for International Economics Special Report No. 19 (2005), p. 172

55 Smits, 'International Representation of European in the Area of Economic and Monetary Union', p. 25.

56 Michael Emerson, Piotr Maciej Kaczyński, Rosa Balfour, et al., *Upgrading the EU's Role as a Global Actor: Institutions, Law and the Restructuring of European Diplomacy* (Brussels: Centre for European Policy Studies, 2011), p. 70.

57 Horng, 'The ECB's Membership in the IMF', p. 815

58 International organizations are only envisaged as cooperation partners by the IMF, Art. X, Articles of Agreement.

59 E. Denters, 'The IMF', in J. Wouters (ed.), *International Encyclopaedia of Laws*, vol. 3, *Intergovernmental Organizations* (Alphen aan den Rijn: Wolters Kluwer, 2010), para. 23.

In light of the various regional integration processes of the last decades and the establishment of a diversity of regional organizations (such as ASEAN, EU), the question whether a non-state actor could join the IMF becomes more interesting. The Articles of Agreement do not define the term 'country' but practice suggests that only states can successfully apply for membership. Other entities such as monetary unions are *prima facie* not eligible for membership.[60] The reasons for using 'country' instead of 'state' as a criterion for membership are not entirely clear. One explanation for the use of this concept is that it allows an applicant to become a member even though it cannot be considered a state under international law, as was the case with a number of participants at the Bretton Woods conference which at the time were not yet independent states: Australia, Canada, New Zealand and South Africa were British dominions.[61] Formal statehood may also have been challenged because borders had not been delineated with finality or the applicant government controlled only part of the territory.[62]

Currently, only states are members of the IMF. This is most likely not due to a statehood requirement per se but rather to the inherent right of states to issue their own currency (or the prospect thereof in some cases). Therefore, it has been suggested that the exercise of the sovereign right to issue a currency and adopt a monetary policy is decisive for membership.[63] However, in the case of the euro area, the individual euro area Member States have surrendered this power, which could lead to an interpretation of the Articles of Agreement favouring a possible membership of such a common currency area. Given the lack of international legal personality of the euro area, this could happen through a joint membership of its Member States to the IMF. Nonetheless, the Articles of Agreement do not appear to provide for a joint membership of states.[64]

In what follows, the application of Article II.2 of the Articles of Agreement is examined, with some examples of cases in which the

[60] J. Gold, *Membership and Non-membership in the International Monetary Fund* (Washington, DC: IMF, 1973), p. 45.
[61] *Ibid.* [62] Denters, 'The IMF', para. 24. [63] *Ibid.*, para. 25.
[64] F. Gianviti, 'Comment on Polak and Thygesen', in P. Masson, T. Krueger and B. Turtelboom (eds.), *EMU and the International Monetary System* (Washington, DC: IMF, 1997); Henning, 'Regional Arrangements and the International Monetary Fund', p. 173.

IMF took a rather pragmatic approach regarding its provisions.[65] First, it is interesting to note that the IMF in its balance of payments statistics and on its website states that the term 'country' does not in all cases refer to a territorial entity that is a state as understood by international law and practice. As used there, the term also covers some territorial entities that are not states. The IMF World Economic Outlook treats the euro area as a whole.[66] However, this pragmatic approach does not seem to extend to membership applications. So far, IMF membership is restricted only to widely recognized states. Somewhat disputed entities such as Taiwan[67] are not members. The same is the case with Hong Kong.[68] In contrast, Kosovo, although not globally recognized as a state, joined the Fund on 29 June 2009.

The next question is whether the IMF has already allowed monetary unions to join the Fund. The focus here is on monetary unions which were integrated enough to make it difficult for their members to satisfy their individual obligations towards the Fund. In 1958, Syria and Egypt united and formed the United Arab Republic (UAR). They informed the IMF Managing Director that they wanted to become a single member of the IMF with a single quota and subject to the provisions of the Articles of Agreement.[69] The UAR requested and received approval for a transitional period during which both countries still conducted their relations with the IMF in an individual manner and were allowed to uphold both currencies.[70] The Fund as well continued to hold two separate depositories. However, as both countries decided to unite, they became one country in the eyes of the IMF. Consequently, their combined voting share was lowered.[71] The main difference with the euro area

[65] This analysis builds heavily upon Joseph Gold's work. Most of Gold's cases date from the 1950s and 1960s, in the aftermath of de-decolonization when problems related to country boundaries and currencies were quite common. Gold, *Membership and Non-membership in the International Monetary Fund.*

[66] Bini Smaghi, 'A Single EU Seat in the IMF?', p. 238.

[67] Taiwan was replaced at the IMF by China in 1980 and has not applied to return since.

[68] Hong Kong is not a member but does contribute statistical data to the Fund, as do the Palestinian National Authority and the ECB for the euro area.

[69] Mahieu, Ooms and Rotier, 'The Governance of the International Monetary Fund with a Single EU Chair', p. 176.

[70] Even before this transitional period elapsed, the UAR broke up. K. Bühler, *State Succession and Membership in International Organizations: Legal Theories Versus Political Pragmatism* (The Hague: Kluwer Law International, 2001), p. 57.

[71] The quotas in the 1950s were calculated using a formula of 250 basic votes for every county and one additional vote for each $100,000 hold as quota. The UAR votes were based on the common quota but included only 250 basic votes instead of the 500 basic

is that the individual countries, Syria and Egypt, ceased to exist and the UAR in practice was a single country, although from an IMF point of view it never completely got to that point since the two countries separated again before they finished their IMF transition. No single currency had been adopted before the collapse of the UAR.[72]

Another precedent which probably better resembles the euro area is the case of Lebanon and Syria in the 1940s.[73] The two countries possessed nominally distinct currencies which were in fact a common currency. Their banknotes only differed in the mentioning of either Syria or Lebanon, but they circulated freely and were accepted in both countries. Both countries' monetary and foreign exchange policy was carried out by the Bank of Syria and Lebanon. Apart from monetary policy, the two countries remained politically independent. The question was consequently raised whether it made sense for both countries to hold a single quota at the Fund. Eventually, the Fund decided that, owing to the political independence of the countries, both of them should continue to hold separate quotas as well. The close resemblance with the euro area case casts a negative light on whether the IMF would support a membership application of the euro area. However, euro area Member States have also conferred other competences on the Union.

It follows from the above that precedents are not particularly illuminating on the question of a unified IMF membership for the euro area. The question of IMF membership of monetary unions should be solved by an authoritative interpretation under Article XXIX or by an amendment of Article II of the Articles of Agreement.[74] As laid down in

votes. See Gold, *Membership and Non-membership in the International Monetary Fund*, p. 298. Over the years, basic votes have lost much of their importance: see N. Woods and D. Lombardi, 'Effective Representation and the role of Coalitions within the IMF', Global Economic Governance Working Paper, 2005/17 (2005).

[72] Gold argues that the drafters of the Articles of Agreement had in mind a member with a currency of its own that was subject, at least legally, to regulation by no other country. Gold, *Membership and Non-membership in the International Monetary Fund*, p. 90. There is evidence for this hypothesis in various cases. Experiences with Sudan (1957) and Gold Coast (Ghana) (1957) prove that not having an own currency is probably not a breaking point, although every IMF member is expected to have its own currency in due course.

[73] Gold, *Membership and Non-membership in the International Monetary Fund*, p. 106

[74] The board of Governors can admit a new member by resolution and it is not necessary to amend the Articles for that purpose (Gold, *Membership and Non-membership in the International Monetary Fund*, p. 19). However, Gold referred to members presumably in relation to the admission of new countries to the IMF rather than monetary unions joining it.

Article XXVIII(a), an amendment needs to be approved by the Board of Governors and can be implemented as follows:

> If the proposed amendment is approved by the Board of Governors, the Fund shall, by circular letter or telegram, ask all members whether they accept the proposed amendment. When three-fifths of the members, having eighty-five percent of the total voting power, have accepted the proposed amendment, the Fund shall certify the fact by a formal communication addressed to all members.

IMF Article XXVIII(b) further requires the approval of all euro area Member States whose quota would be lowered. The positive note is that if the euro area Member States agree upon a unification of their membership in the Fund, the other IMF member countries will most likely approve an amendment in light of the opportunities that a lower euro area quota brings about. This was exemplified at the G20 finance ministers meeting at Chengyou on 23 October 2010, where, because of the pressure from the emerging economies, agreement was reached to shift Executive Directors and voting shares from the advanced economies to the emerging economies. This last development could result in a further lowering of the European voice within the Fund, and might hence increase the need for stronger coordination or unification of the representation.[75]

5 Conclusion

Currently, the EU and the euro area are mainly represented at the IMF through their respective Member States, which themselves are represented within a number of different constituencies. This leads to an over-representation in terms of voting shares and under-effectiveness in terms of advancing a strong unified European voice. An additional problem is that the euro area Member States are no longer able to fulfil their individual obligations towards the Fund as they have transferred certain competences (in particular, monetary policy) to the Union. The Lisbon Treaty provides for a potential answer to these problems. It has strengthened the potential for a unified euro area representation at the IMF. For the EU as a whole, though, not much has changed. However, the IMF Articles of Agreement do not allow for any entity other than a country to join the Fund, and the Fund has so far applied this provision rather restrictively. This does not pose any legal obstacle should the

[75] Wouters and Van Kerckhoven, 'The International Monetary Fund'.

EU/euro area Member States decide to improve their existing loose coordination mechanisms or to create a joint constituency. However, for the euro area itself to accede to the Fund, a prior amendment of the IMF Articles of Agreement would have to take place.

So far, the entry into force of the Lisbon Treaty has not led to any changes in the relationship between the IMF and the EU/euro area as the political support for such adaptations has been lacking. Still, other than solving the problems mentioned above, a single euro area seat would also help in other respects. A single euro area seat could allow the euro area to gain access to larger IMF funds, which could then be distributed to the euro area Member States in need of support; something which has gained in significance since the euro sovereign debt crisis. The question remains, though, whether euro area Member States will be able to overcome their internal struggles and whether they are prepared to give up their individual voting share and the power to appoint an Executive Director. Thus, euro area Member States have yet to capitalize on the opportunity offered by the Treaties after Lisbon in order to pool their representation in the IMF. Such a development seems to be a prerequisite in order to safeguard their interests and influence within the Fund, and by extension in international economic governance and law. If they fail to recognize this reality, the traditional role of Europe in co-determining international economic and monetary governance may gradually but unavoidably diminish.

14

The EU's financial transaction tax: shaping global financial governance in its own image?

BART VAN VOOREN

1 Introduction

In the wake of the 2008 financial crisis, taxation of the financial sector has forcefully re-emerged on the European Union political agenda. Since then, several EU Member States and the European Parliament have sought to stimulate this proposal in the form of a financial transaction tax (FTT). What had for years existed as a political Utopia in the minds of grass roots movements reached a legal and political milestone during Commission President Barosso's State of the Union speech on 28 September 2011. There he presented a proposal for an EU Directive on an FTT installed across the twenty-seven EU Member States,[1] through which the Union would prove its feasibility and desirability to the world. The November 2011 G20 meeting under French Chairmanship was then supposed to give the starting shot for working towards its global implementation. However, the aspirations of the former French President were decisively cut short by the Eurozone crisis entering its most acute phase. In the months that followed, the EU's ambitions in the field of FTT withered both outside and within the Union. On the global stage the EU no longer pushed the FTT at the G20 in Mexico,[2] and in June 2012 it became clear that an FTT across the territory of the twenty-seven EU Member States was not feasible either. As a consequence, by September 2012 eleven Member States (Austria, Belgium, Estonia, France, Germany, Greece, Italy, Portugal, Slovakia, Slovenia and Spain) had requested the Commission to outline an FTT on the basis of enhanced cooperation.[3]

[1] European Commission, Proposal for a Council Directive on a Common System of Financial Transaction Tax and Amending Directive, 2008/7/EC, COM (2011) 594 final, Brussels, 28 September, 2011.

[2] Joint letter of President Van Rompuy and President Barroso to the EU Heads of State or Government on the G20 Summit in Los Cabos, Mexico, Brussels, 25 May 2012, EUCO 96/12.

[3] Arts. 20 TEU and 326–34 TFEU.

The proposal to authorize enhanced cooperation followed in October 2012 for the Ecofin Council meeting in November 2012.[4] However, at that meeting a number of Member States declined to give their authorization in accordance with Article 329(1) TFEU, pending a more detailed assessment of its impact on the Internal Market.[5] While the consequences of a partial implementation of the FTT are justifiably questioned,[6] it does show that the idea of the EU spearheading the FTT and therefore setting an example for the world has not yet fully disappeared in the minds of some of Europe's political elites.

With this volume, the editors wish to approach the EU as an *active* actor in the international legal order, by looking at the fashion in which it shapes the subjects and the law surrounding the Union. It is clear that in the short term the Union has not been able to convince its international counterparts of the merits of the FTT. In fact, the FTT remains a divisive issue amongst the EU Member States themselves. This chapter examines two aspects of the research question posed by the editors in relation to the proposed EU Directive for an FTT. First, why is or should the Union be a (pro-)active actor in shaping the international (financial) order through taxing financial transactions? Secondly, how could the proposed EU legislation positively shape the global financial order in the medium term; and how can the Union serve as a model to do so? In responding to these questions it is argued that on the basis of the EU's objectives in the Treaties there is indeed the mission proactively to shape the global (financial) legal order in its own image. On the basis of that argument, the contribution then explores the institutional and substantive aspects of the EU as a legal order of twenty-eight Member States, focusing on how they would permit the effective and successful implementation of a European FTT. On this basis a parallel is drawn with the international financial legal system. The argument is that the Union is a well-placed example to demonstrate the necessary legal characteristics of an FTT at the international level. While it seems clear that legally a global FTT *could* indeed be crafted following the EU model, the chapter concludes with a word of caution, reminding that the legal advances in the global

4 European Commission, Proposal for a Council Decision Authorizing Enhanced Cooperation in the Area of Financial Transaction Tax, COM (2012) 631 final, Brussels, 25 October 2012.

5 EU Council, Economic and Financial Affairs (Ecofin), Commission Communication on tax fraud and tax evasion – Council Conclusions, 13 November 2012, p. 11.

6 J. Kanter, 'Italy and Spain Add Support to a Tax on Financial Trades in Europe', *New York Times*, 9 October 2012

financial system required for a fully fledged FTT to become operational are nothing short of a political, legal and institutional revolution.

2 The Union's mission in global financial governance

The 2001 Laeken Declaration on the future of the European Union strongly asserted a global role for the EU in its characteristically grand language: 'Does Europe not, now that is finally unified, have a leading role to play in a new world order, that of a power able both to play a stabilizing role worldwide and to point the way ahead for many countries and peoples?[7] The European Convention started work soon after that declaration was made. In an early draft produced by the Commission (called the Penelope project), that institution's proposal of December 2002 contained the following provision under the heading 'external economic relations policy':

> Article III-97 External economic action by the Union shall contribute to the harmonious development of the world economy. To that end the Union shall adopt a single position in relations with non-member countries and in international organizations with responsibilities for economic and financial matters. It shall support the effectiveness and transparency of the financial markets in order to reduce financial volatility and speculation at global level.[8]

This Commission proposal took the EU single voice far beyond the comparatively narrow scope of the Common Commercial Policy. However, the call for unified EU representation in global economic governance writ large was not picked up by the Convention. Should this have happened, a straightforward case could have been made that the Union would have a legally binding obligation to implement an FTT, or a global measure with the equivalent effect of reducing financial volatility and speculation.[9] Even so, the Union could still reap great benefits from the successful global implementation of the FTT.[10]

[7] European Council, Laeken Declaration on the Future of the European Union, SN 300/1/01 REV 1, 14–15 December 2001, subheading 'Expectations of Europe's Citizens'.

[8] F. Lamoureux, et al., 'Feasibility Study, Contribution to a Preliminary Draft, Constitution of the European Union', European Commission Working Document, 4 December 2002, available at http://ec.europa.eu/economy_finance/emu_history/documents/treaties/Penelope%20pdf_en.pdf.

[9] B. Van Vooren, 'The EU as a Global Robin Hood: Proposal for a Multilateral Financial Transaction Tax', Centre for the Law of EU External Relations Working Paper 2011/4 (2011), pp. 10–14; available at www.asser.nl/upload/documents/992011_104937cleer2011-4web.pdf.

[10] *Ibid.*

First, success in this regard would be supportive of the Union's self-imposed image of the proverbial value-based international actor.[11] Second, it would do much to provide post-Lisbon legitimacy towards its own citizens through effectiveness as an international actor.[12] An FTT would have as its purpose the financing of global public goods such as the Millennium Development Goals and additional funding to climate change; and therefore respond to calls for a fairer contribution of the financial sector to society writ large.[13] Additionally, such a tax would have a significant regulatory impact towards a more stable financial system which is currently dominated by non-binding soft law.[14] In sum, the FTT would lead to – and require – a sea change to international financial law and governance with the European Union guiding the way in line with its constitutional objectives.

Even though no mission statement for the EU in global financial governance has been included in EU primary law, the more general Treaty obligations in external relations are nevertheless pertinent. A role for the Union whereby it 'stabilizes' the world, and 'points the way ahead' is not merely a moral imperative, but a legally binding obligation embedded in primary law. Article 3(5) TEU states that in its relations with the wider world, 'the Union *shall* [. . .] contribute to peace [. . .] the sustainable development of the Earth, solidarity and mutual respect among peoples, free and fair trade, eradication of poverty [. . .] as well as to the strict observance and the development of international law, including respect for the principles of the United Nations Charter'.[15]

The language 'shall' indicates the binding nature of this mission statement, which has been confirmed by the Court of Justice of the EU

[11] U. Khaliq, *Ethical Dimensions of the Foreign Policy of the European Union: A Legal Appraisal* (Cambridge University Press, 2008); R. Petrov and P. Leino, 'Between "Common Values" and Competing Universals – The Promotion of the EU's Common Values through the European Neighbourhood Policy' (2009) 15.5 *European Law Journal* 654.

[12] On output legitimacy, see F. W. Scharpf, *Governing in Europe: Effective and Democratic?* (Oxford University Press, 1999).

[13] See Commission consultation which ended in April 2011: 'Commission Summary Report, May 2011', available at http://ec.europa.eu/taxation_customs/resources/documents/common/consultations/tax/financial_sector/summary_results_en.pdf.

[14] C. Brummer, 'Why Soft Law Dominates International Finance – and Not Trade' (2010) 13 *Journal of International Economic Law* 623 (627); E. Baltensperger and T. Cottier, 'The Role of International Law in Monetary Affairs' (2010) 13 *Journal of International Economic Law* 911 (935). See also the chapter by Christoph Ohler in this volume.

[15] Emphasis added.

in the *Air Transport Association of America* (ATAA) case.[16] Here the Court affirmed that Article 3(5) TEU imposes a substantive legal obligation on the Union 'to contribute to the strict observance and the development of international law'.[17] Thus, the Union is not just morally, but in fact legally obliged to pursue equality amongst wealthy and poorer nations, to support their development and ensure 'fairness' between them. In doing so, the TEU not only imposes substantive requirements on EU international relations, but also a strong methodological imperative: according to Article 3 TEU and confirmed in Article 21(1) TEU, the EU 'shall be guided by the principles which have inspired its own creation and which it seeks to advance in the wider world [...] respect for the principles of the United Nations Charter and international law'. In other words, the Union must pursue a just and fair global order, entrenched in multilateral solutions based on the rule of law. The global implementation of an FTT through a multilateral, binding international convention requiring unprecedented positive change to international financial governance does exactly that.

3 Institutional and substantive legal features of a global FTT convention

3.1 Central features of the EU proposal

In order to outline how the Union might proactively shape the global financial order on the basis of its internal legislation on the FTT, we must briefly outline the central features of the proposed EU regime. However, as indicated, the Ecofin Council of November 2012 has not yet given its approval to the request for enhanced cooperation in the field of FTT, and thus the Commission is holding publication of its legislative proposal until a new impact assessment has been completed. Nevertheless, unsurprisingly, the Commission has indicated that it will build on its September 2011 text, thus continuing the basic choices made in that proposal for a Directive as outlined in the following paragraphs.[18]

[16] Case C-366/10, *Air Transport Association of America and Others* v. *Secretary of State for Energy and Climate Change* (ATAA case) [2011] ECR I-1133.

[17] *Ibid.*, para. 101

[18] European Commission, 'Commission Proposes Green Light for Enhanced Cooperation on Financial Transaction Tax', press release, IP/12/1138, 23 October 2012.

The proposal for an FTT moved up the EU political agenda in the wake of the 2008 financial crisis. The proposed Directive therefore seeks to ensure that the root causes for the crisis are eliminated in the future, and that the financial sector makes amends for governments having to step in. The first objective is thus that of market correction, namely to change behaviour such as trend-chasing and short-termism which is viewed as negatively impacting, or not reflecting the needs of the real economy. The FTT would therefore complement regulatory initiatives to ensure systemic, macro-economic stability. The FTT does this by limiting perceived excesses across the EU-28 Member States, and create appropriate disincentives for transactions that endanger the stability and efficiency of financial markets.[19] Secondly, the FTT would ensure that financial institutions make a fair contribution to covering the costs of the recent crisis, and to ensure that financial services in the long term contribute equally to government budgets. Concretely, the projected revenue of an EU-wide FTT is projected to be 57 billion euros.[20]

To achieve these objectives the proposed EU Directive would set up a harmonized system that would impact on financial transactions which are not desired for their rationale (speculative), large volume (compared to real economy) or high speed (digital automatic trading). As regards revenue, the proposed EU Directive connects the FTT to the EU negotiations on the Multi-Annual Financial Framework, whereby the revenue generated would be an own source of revenue. With its market correction objective in mind, the EU Directive would install an FTT which is broadly defined in scope as regards products, transactions, types of trade and financial actors, as well as transactions carried out inside a financial group. For example, the definition of financial institutions includes investment firms, organized markets, credit institutions, insurance and reinsurance undertakings, collective investment undertakings and their managers, pension funds and their managers, holding companies, financial leasing companies and special purpose entities. And it makes provision in delegated powers to the Commission so that it may set targets for 'significant' activities of other entities whereby it would also be classed as a financial institution. As regards financial transactions, the proposal includes spot transactions (shares, bonds, currencies) and derivatives transactions (forwards, futures, options,

[19] European Council, Laeken Declaration on the Future of the European Union.

[20] European Commission, Proposal for a Council Directive on a Common System of Financial Transaction Tax, 2011.

swaps, currency derivatives, commodity derivatives, etc.),[21] in the context of both organized markets and 'over-the-counter' (OTC) transactions between financial institutions. This aspect illustrates the EU's choice for a sweepingly broad FTT, but also raises an important question for global implementation. Namely, it is clear that the EU legal order is well-suited for the kind of EU-wide harmonized approach necessary to implement this tax? Indeed, Member States would have been obliged to implement this Directive by 2014 should it have entered into force as planned. This has important implications at the global level. It is questionable whether the 'nature of governance' in the global financial system as it stands can accommodate the level of legal cooperation needed to install this tax. Thus, in what follows we outline that this would require nothing less than a revolution in global financial governance.

3.2 *The functions of the FTT convention in the EU's own image*

The Proposal of the Directive states that 'The present proposal demonstrates how an effective FTT can be designed and implemented, generating significant revenue. This should pave the way towards a coordinated approach with the most relevant international partners'.[22] However, this is easier said than done. If the EU wishes to establish a global FTT, it is argued that it must forcefully support further legalization and institutionalization of the global financial governance system. This is because the level of legally binding harmonization required at the global level is currently simply non-existent in the international financial system. Hence, to install the FTT at the global level, a global, mature international institutional framework is required to oversee its various aspects: a multilateral framework convention on the FTT.[23]

More concretely, the legal and institutional regime of the FTT would at least have to fulfil the following functions, which will be explained in the next section: first, decision-making and steering by political actors during the negotiation of the regime, but also during its lifetime; second, rule-making and rule adjustment at the more technical levels through

[21] European Commission, Impact Assessment accompanying the document Proposal for a Council Directive on a Common System of Financial Transaction Tax and Amending Directive, 2008/7/EC, vol. 1, SEC (2011) 1102 final, Brussels 28 September 2011, p. 39.

[22] European Commission, Proposal for a Council Directive on a Common System of Financial Transaction Tax and Amending Directive, p. 3.

[23] Van Vooren, 'The EU as a Global Robin Hood'.

institutions geared to ensure the dynamic nature of the legal regime, locking into the political level;[24] third, levying the tax in line with substantive principles laid down in the multilateral regime, to be implemented at national level by contracting parties; fourth, administration and management of information for macro-prudential purposes; fifth, dispute settlement between parties through judicial means; sixth and finally, distribution of revenue of the tax in line with the objectives for which the tax is set up. To attain these functions three options could be pursued.

Option 1. Setting up a limited international legal framework which is not an international organization proper, but an intergovernmental conference without independent institutions endowed with decision-making powers. A limited secretariat would serve the needs of the intergovernmental conference, and the framework would at most consist of a legal bringing together of the current actors already active in the sphere of global economic governance. While politically possibly the most feasible avenue, this model could legally *not* properly accommodate an FTT. As indicated in the brief illustration of the proposed EU FTT regime, effective implementation requires a mature, efficient and effective strong legal and institutional order to support the FTT.

Option 2. Setting up a standalone *new* international organization with specific FTT purposes, with legal personality and effective institutions to implement, oversee and manage its complex legal and political system. This regime would coexist with the current international financial institutions and draw on their expertise for substantiating, implementing and overseeing the FTT. While feasible to implement the FTT, it would have the problem of competition and resource duplication, notably with the IMF. This may be a politically viable option to negotiate since the standalone regime would be disconnected from issues such as IMF governance or linkage with the WTO and the Doha Round. However, instituting the FTT would provide an ideal moment for a deeper overhaul of the global economic governance system as a whole, though the FTT might get lost in translation in such an ambitious project.

Option 3. The third and final option is integrating the new legal regime into the International Monetary Fund (IMF). Negotiations on a framework convention for taxation of global financial transactions would most likely trigger a more thorough overhaul of the Bretton Woods system.

[24] Dispute settlement and rule-making evidently overlap, but in this context rule-making is delimited to decisions by 'legislative' institutions of the FTT regime.

It would provide an opportunity to transform the functions of the IMF into a Global Economic Governance Organization (GEGO).[25] The regime would take on the form of the WTO with institutions at its centre, managing a number of agreements: the FTT alongside the Articles of Agreement. Synergy with the WTO dispute settlement could be foreseen, though it could also merely serve as inspiration for the judicial mechanism supporting the FTT regime.

In the following subsections the proposed EU FTT is utilized to explore the six functions a global FTT regime would have to fulfil. In this way, we can consider in greater depth the fashion in which the EU should pursue adaptation of the global financial order to realize the FTT at the international level.

3.3 *Political decision-making: need for G20 reform*

The first function is political decision-making which is required both during the negotiation on the existence and nature of the regime itself as well as during its lifetime; a role for which the G20, though not ideal, is best suited. This body would have a dual role with regard to the FTT. First, political impetus to commence negotiations on the FTT Convention will have to come from this body, since at present it possesses the most political legitimacy in international economic governance. To draw a parallel with the European Union, it would play the role of the European Council, namely to provide the FTT regime with the necessary impetus for its development and to define the general political directions and priorities thereof, without, however, exercising legislative functions.[26] Similarly, the G20 would provide the political impetus and draw the initial chalk lines for the several rounds of undoubtedly challenging negotiations to follow. Subsequently, it would need to establish for itself a firm leading political role during the lifetime of the FTT regime, and this requires a formalized stature for the G20 as an organ of the international organization overseeing the FTT. The European Union would thus in effect need to seek the reproduction of its own governance model at the global level. However, the G20 as a decision-making mechanism is a far cry from Brussels-based institutions.

[25] J. Vestergaard, 'The G-20 and beyond: Towards Effective Global Economic Governance', DIIS Report 2011:04, Danish Institute for International Studies (2011), available at www.diis.dk/graphics/Publications/Reports2011/RP2011-04-G20-and-beyond_web.pdf.

[26] Art. 15(1) TEU.

At this juncture the G20 is a flexible, open-ended, high-level policy-deliberation mechanism that gained political clout because of the 2008 global financial crisis. Legally the G20 is nothing like the European Council. It is not an institution (organ) of an international organization, but rather an informal body without a constituting document, and without formal requirements for membership. It has no formalized voting mechanism, though, similar to the European Council, consensus is the method of choice.[27] Given that it has no real legal existence, no powers have been formally conferred upon it. In terms of organization, it possesses a two-level structure reflecting the political stature of participants in the European Council and the Council of Ministers: (bi-)annual meetings at head of state level, and meetings by the finance ministers and central bank governors. Substantively, the G20 can discuss any matter it chooses because there is no formal link with an international organization with limited conferred competences. The deliverables from summit meetings take on the form of G20 leaders' statements or summit declarations, and it does not produce legally binding instruments. The implementation of its policy agenda depends on formally instituted international organizations (IMF, WTO, OECD),[28] national governments, or other bodies such as the FSB, IOSCO or the Basel Committee. Hence, the G20 is characterized by its informal nature, which would require formalization in support of the FTT.

Given its crucial role during the initiation and mature phases of the FTT legal framework, the present form of the G20 is not suited to decide on something as fundamental as a harmonized global tax to ensure funding for global public goods. First, it does not possess the legitimacy to decide central issues which also concern the 173 non-member countries. This is because it lacks formal rules for membership based on objective indicators, and as a consequence it requires more formal stature. Secondly, it drew its post-2008 political clout from the atmosphere of crisis, with questionable longevity in the long run. Hence, while from a pragmatic perspective the European Union would use the G20 as the forum to initiate the process of negotiating an FTT legal regime, subsequent negotiations would have to be as inclusive as possible and reform the G20 in the process. Because the FTT would essentially imply deep reform to global economic governance, countries excluded from the G20

[27] N. Woods, 'The G-20 Leaders and Global Governance', Global Economic Governance Working Paper 2010/59 (October 2010).

[28] *Ibid.*

could only support this body's central role if the rules for membership of the G20 are clearer and formalized. Hence, in support of the FTT one could agree with the suggestion to reform the G20 into a Global Economic Council (GEC).[29] The GEC would transform the G20 into a more formalized decision-making body within the institutional framework of the existing Bretton Woods institutions.[30] In relation to the IMF, this transformed G20 would be institutionally positioned above the IMF's Board of Governors, which is politically the equivalent of the earlier and first format in which the G20 met, the Ministers of Finance.[31] In this model, the G20 would take on a role and position similar to that of the European Council in the European Union, a role of political steering, grand decision-making and the general direction in global economic governance. Only in this fashion is it possible to attain the geographic inclusiveness that will allow the global implementation of an FTT. A fixed, legitimate, high-level decision-making body mustering the political weight the G20 currently enjoys is integral to that objective.

3.4 *Flexible rule-making and adjustment: a reformed IMF*

In the EU, special legislative procedure is applicable for adopting Council directives, e.g. requiring unanimity in the Council and consultation of the European Parliament. The proposed FTT Directive then foresees that the Commission shall submit a report on the application every five years and for the first time by the end of 2016.[32] On the implementation side, the Member States' legislatures and tax authorities are competent to adopt and implement the necessary rules at a national level to implement the EU directive. At the global level, a similar substantive legislative follow-up would be required. The FTT framework convention thus requires the setting up of institutions which have been conferred the necessary decision-making competence to avoid the regime from quickly becoming obsolete through financial innovation and engineering.

The FTT regime would thus also require institutions with the power to adopt dynamic revisions of the content of the framework agreement as needed. It would be particularly important to have a 'legislative'

[29] Vestergaard, 'The G-20 and beyond'. [30] *Ibid.*, p. 9.

[31] *Ibid.*, p. 44. Vestergaard suggests that it would function as the Board of Governors, whereas I suggest it should be hierarchically placed above it.

[32] Review Clause, Art. 16, European Commission, Proposal for a Council Directive on a Common System of Financial Transaction Tax and Amending Directive, p. 22.

mechanism that deals with financial innovation which might be created in the future across different jurisdictions. However, hard law institutions and instruments currently have a very limited role in the global, multilateral level of financial regulation. The IMF and World Bank do not create regulatory standards, rather 'the sources of international financial law are informal, intergovernmental institutions that set agendas and standards for the global regulatory community'.[33] The global implementation of the FTT would thoroughly uproot that system owing to strong foreseeable demands for hard legal commitments required for its successful global implementation. For example, Basel III is soft law at the global level, agreed upon in a Committee consisting of peers from central banks and financial authorities. Implementation of such duties depends on appropriate national enactment, and it is proverbial that global implementation is 'unequal' across different jurisdictions. The FTT institutions could not replicate this 'peer-to-peer' nature of the standard setting bodies of international finance, and, rather, the institutions of the FTT Convention below G20-level would have to include a ministerial level to make decisions at regular intervals. This would be similar to the EU Council of Ministers, meeting as is considered necessary in line with ongoing policy needs. Further, there would be a lower-level permanent cooperation body for day-to-day management and feedback into the higher decision-making organs. If the FTT regime were to be engrafted on the IMF, the Executive Board could play this role, with the IMF Board of Governors having the 'Council' role. However, the FTT regime would very likely reopen the question of representation in economic governance,[34] notably in light of discussions on formalized G20 membership. The powers of the decision-making bodies would also have to be reconsidered in line with the EU example. Notably, where there is taxation, there are attempts by its subjects to narrow its application. Hence, financial actors are sure to set up original new legal vehicles in order to carry out financial transactions in a fashion which would limit the applicability of the FTT regime. The proposed EU Directive foresees delegated powers to the Commission to ensure that actions by private

[33] C. Brummer, 'Why Soft Law Dominates International Finance – and Not Trade' (2010) 13 *Journal of International Economic Law* 627. See also the chapter by Christoph Ohler in this volume.

[34] On the issue of just representation in the international financial institutions, see J. Wouters, S. Van Kerckhoven and J. Odermatt, 'The EU at the G20 and the G20's Impact on the EU', in B. Van Vooren, S. Blockmans and J. Wouters, *The EUs Role in Global Governance: The Legal Dimension* (Oxford University Press, 2013), chap. 17.

actors to avoid the tax are dealt with in a rapid fashion.[35] Thus, similar powers are indispensable at the global level, yet swift decision-making is not a defining feature of international cooperation – not even in the highly integrated European Union, as the European sovereign debt crisis has sufficiently illustrated.

3.5 *Levying the tax: watershed for the global financial legal order*

The Impact Assessment for the EU proposal on the FTT states that 'there are strong economic (and technical) reasons for a high degree of harmonization and coordination in order to avoid substitution and loopholes'.[36] As a consequence, fundamental legislative decisions have been taken at EU level to be implemented by Member States in accordance with their own legal systems but leaving them no substantive legislative choice on anything else than levying a higher rate than proposed in the Directive. For a global implementation of the FTT, similarly, the multilateral FTT convention should act as a framework convention which lays out central choices on definitions and legal principles, to be subsequently implemented at regional and/or national level. In line with the institutional dimension of rule-making, on the substantive side too this requires a sea change to global financial governance. As Thomas Cottier has noted, 'It seems paradoxical that financial services are among the most regulated businesses in domestic law, but that no rules of such significance exist on the global level for the most advanced global players'.[37] One of the core challenges for a global FTT is this: the Union would not only have to shape the international legal order in its own image in terms of how laws are made (as discussed in section 2.2) but also how they are implemented and enforced. In other words, an EU FTT Directive is possible only because the strength of the legal system set up within the Union guarantees its effective and uniform implementation across twenty-eight EU Member States – a work in progress to this day.[38] Consider just briefly

[35] European Commission, Proposal for a Council Directive on a Common System of Financial Transaction Tax and Amending Directive, p. 7.

[36] European Commission, Impact Assessment accompanying the document, Proposal for a Council Directive on a Common System of Financial Transaction Tax and Amending Directive, 2008/7/EC, vol. 1, p. 44.

[37] T. Cottier, 'Challenges Ahead in International Economic Law' (2009) 12 *Journal of International Economic Law* 3 (7–8).

[38] S. Prechal and B. Van Roermund (eds.), *The Coherence of EU Law: The Search for Unity in Divergent Concepts* (Cambridge University Press, 2008).

the legal effects of legislative instruments in the EU legal order: the Member States have an obligation to implement them in their national laws, and, failing such, the provisions can have a direct effect, with Member States possibly being held liable for lack of implementation. The strength of the EU legal order indeed stems from recruiting individual citizens' interests for the cause of enforcing EU rules through the preliminary reference procedure, alongside the infringement procedure which is the competence of the European Commission. Together, these elements ensure effective implementation of EU law across twenty-eight jurisdictions.

At the global level the challenges multiply owing to the nature of global financial governance: as stated, the FTT requires a level of harmonization currently unknown to the global financial system. In popular discourse, the FTT is, commonly stated, 'simply to apply a low rate' that would hardly be felt by the financial system. In reality, the technical complexities related to setting the tax rate and levying the tax on very different kinds of financial transactions is much greater than this popular sentiment implies. In order to work effectively, the product coverage and the tax rates should be equal across different members of the FTT regime. This to avoid financial institutions relocating to markets with lower tax rates, different definitions of financial transactions or smaller product coverage.[39] Overall, for an FTT to work effectively it is necessary that a global consensus is attained on the tax rate (how high), on the scope of the tax (which instruments to include, e.g. derivatives or not?), the tax base (tax notional value or alternatives?) as well as the taxable event (what is a financial transaction?). The definitions of these principles should be applied equally across all participating Member States, and sufficiently strong legal enforcement should be available. It seems entirely utopian to imagine a legal order of the maturity of the EU legal order being created at the global level.

3.6 *Administration: information for prudential purposes*

In managerial terms, the FTT requires a strong secretariat to provide executive, monitoring and administrative services – at EU level provided mainly by the European Commission. In the context of a global FTT regime, we can use the proposed EU Directive for inspiration on the kinds of tasks the executive of the global regime would need to fulfil.

[39] European Commission, Proposal for a Council Directive on a Common System of Financial Transaction Tax and Amending Directive, p. 18.

First, centralized direct management by the Commission, day-to-day management and long-term follow-up. Second, centralized indirect management, focusing on record-keeping and management of information flows. Third, shared management with the Member States' tax authorities for concrete execution of the international tax regime, including information exchange. Fourth, decentralized management and cooperation with non-participation of third countries. Fifth, the EU Directive also foresees joint management with international organizations, but adds that this is 'to be specified'.[40] These five managerial functions are necessary to ensure accurate and timely levying across the different participating jurisdictions; and they require a strong, international administrative machinery. To avoid resource duplication and competition with the IMF, the best option is a reformed version of that international organization to provide these functions. Recall that the proposed EU FTT Directive has a function in relation to market correction and ensuring stability of the financial system. We shall briefly flesh out this function to illustrate the need for a strong Commission-like executive in the global FTT regime.

Levying a broad-based FTT in itself poses significant technical challenges as regards availability of information across all jurisdictions, but it would also generate large amounts of data on financial transactions, financial actors, and the kinds of linkages between them. This is especially true for a broad FTT as proposed by the EU, which includes transactions which are not traded on centralized markets. Aside from the projected positive impact on stability of financial markets, this kind of information generated by the FTT has huge positive potential from a regulatory prudential perspective. One of the key problems of the 2008 financial crisis was the lack of transparency and the lack of information available to decision-makers on interconnections in the financial system at a macroscopic level. Hence, in order to alleviate further the systemic risk of global financial activities, obtaining better information is essential.[41] According to the IMF, such information should be 'more accessible, more timely, go beyond traditional statistical approaches and should draw on new sources'.[42] The FTT checks all those boxes, and could thus contribute to macro-financial stability through the

[40] *Ibid.*, p. 25.

[41] G. Dell'Ariccia, et al., 'Lessons and Policy Implications from the Global Financial Crisis', IMF Working Paper WP/10/44 (2010), p. 26.

[42] *Ibid.*

novel and comprehensive nature of the information generated by and required to implement a global FTT. Again, to that end the FTT legal framework would have to be equipped with institutions possessing the capacity to manage this information flow. Given that such expertise is most readily present at the IMF, efficiency mandates that this organization be reformed to accommodate the FTT regime. From a prudential perspective then, employing that data for regulatory purposes would require a connection between that reformed IMF and bodies such as the Financial Stability Board (FSB) In fact, the FSB, which is already overseeing work on identification of systemic risk as mandated by the G20, might potentially be explicitly couched in this new institution of global economic governance.

3.7 Dispute resolution and sanctioning following the WTO example

It is indispensable for the global legal regime to ensure that differences in the application of legal principles and definitions are settled in a binding fashion. Diverse definitions and interpretations across jurisdictions on what constitutes a financial transaction, what is a financial institution, and so on, would swiftly create distortion of competition, legal engineering and geographical relocation. Thus the global FTT regime would require a robust system to settle such disputes, with appropriate binding sanctions, which would substantiate lacunae of the global legal regime through successive case law. A binding dispute settlement mechanism as instituted in the WTO in 1994 would be necessary to ensure the smooth application of the FTT, and to ensure parties' continued commitment to the principles laid down in the FTT Convention. Proposing a dispute settlement mechanism under international financial law is not entirely new. In November 2009 the former IMF Chief Economist Simon Johnson proposed the establishment of a dispute settlement mechanism for exchange rate controversies, such as that between the US and China.[43] It is, however, highly unlikely that China would agree to such binding dispute settlement. Nonetheless, Johnson argued back in 2009 that consensus was shifting to the idea that the WTO would have more legitimacy over exchange rates too: first, because smaller and poorer countries can bring and win cases against heavyweights such as

[43] S. Johnson, 'Obama in China: Breaking the Exchange-Rate Deadlock', *New York Times*, 5 November 2009.

the USA and the EU; and secondly, because the WTO also has proven tools for violations of acceptable trade practices with specific sanctions.[44]

Both arguments could be transposed to the FTT context, though the nature of the regime would be different from the perspective of sanctioning. The international trade regime is engrafted on the possibility of allowing infringements of the regime to be counteracted by the suspension of concessions equal to the infringement,[45] and no such reciprocity mechanism would be available under the FTT regime. An alternative means of enforcement would be to employ differentiated tax rates, and deploy higher tax rates for transactions with infringing jurisdictions. Importantly, then, the process by which such infringements and sanctions are established should be sufficiently disconnected from the political institutions of the FTT regime. As the GATT and WTO experience has taught us,[46] only when the reverse consensus principle was adopted, from 1995 onwards, did the system of panels and appellate body reports truly become effective to enforce global trade law in a legal fashion. Hence, while the political institutions might use differentiated tax rates for regulatory and prudential purposes, or politically to punish non-cooperative jurisdictions, such decisions should remain disconnected from the due process by which the global FTT regime could be legally enforced. Otherwise the regime is bound to result in stalemate and non-enforcement of its legal set-up.

In sum, the FTT would require a sufficiently objective, legal process independently to enforce 'a level playing field' in international finance. Probably most feasible is simply to use the WTO as inspiration, independent of the trade regime, and set up this dispute settlement system under a reformed IMF or an autonomous FTT organization. It need not be repeated that this kind of a dispute resolution mechanism would be a watershed for the nature of global financial governance. When thinking more boldly from an institutional perspective, we could even envisage a global economic governance organization as an umbrella over the IMF and the WTO, with broader institutionalized dispute settlement, connecting FTT proceeds to the Doha compromise, and with the G20 as the global economic council to provide political direction of the overall economic system, given that finance and trade are evidently interconnected.

[44] *Ibid.*

[45] A. Lowenfeld, 'Dispute Settlement in the WTO', in *International Economic Law* (Oxford University Press, 2008), pp. 161–212.

[46] Lowenfeld, 'Dispute Resolution in the GATT 1948–1994', *ibid.*, pp. 145–60.

3.8 Distribution of revenue: innovative financing for climate and development

If the tax is introduced at the global level, all countries supposedly carry its burden and should benefit from it. Although levying would occur in the relevant national jurisdictions, the global approach needs to incorporate a mechanism to share the risks and benefits of the system. At the outset of this contribution, we pointed out that the FTT has for many years existed in the minds of grass roots movements under the guise of a 'Robin Hood tax', i.e. taking away from the financial sector and giving back to the poor.[47] This indicates that the perceived benefit of the FTT would not only lie in the taxation of the wealthy, but also the earmarking of revenues for redistributive justice. In proposing the EU Financial Transaction Tax, the Commission has certainly shown itself aware of this debate, but it has not followed that logic. Rather, it has connected this proposal to the ongoing negotiations for the next seven-year multi-annual budget of the EU (2014–20).[48] By doing so, the Commission had been hoping to pave the way for an 'own source' of revenue through taxation directly linked to EU coffers. Hence, the European Commission chose pragmatism over principle, and did not make an explicit connection with financing for development or climate change.[49] By doing so, the Union has lost an important source of political legitimacy to its citizens and grass roots movements across the world. Thus, it would be important to rectify that error in translating the EU proposal to a global message, and it would be crucial for the Union to emphasize the FTT as integral to global redistributive justice. Concretely, the EU could propose directly to earmark FTT income for the financing of the Millennium Development Goals post 2015 and the provision of global public goods such as the environment, health or climate change. The institutions of the FTT Convention would then have the responsibility to accord the proceeds according to the distributive formula laid down in the Convention. Significantly, revenue could be committed to any or all of the following international sources. First, within the United Nations Framework Convention on Climate Change (UNFCCC), the Cancun meeting of 2010 decided to set up the 'Green Climate Fund'. The transitional

[47] See e.g. the Robin Hood Tax proposal, available at www.robinhoodtax.org.

[48] European Commission, Amended Proposal for a Council Regulation Laying Down the Multiannual Financial Framework for the Years 2014–2020, COM (2012) 388 final, Brussels, 6 May 2012

[49] Van Vooren, 'The EU as a Global Robin Hood'.

committee setting up this fund consists of seconded staff from UN agencies, international financial institutions, multilateral development banks, alongside the secretariat of the UNFCCC itself. The fund has as its objective to 'make a significant and ambitious contribution to the global efforts towards attaining the goals set by the international community to combat climate change'.[50] Institutionally and substantively, this fund could provide inspiration for earmarking FTT revenues, or the FTT regime could establish a direct link with this fund and very substantially contribute to its resources. Secondly, funds could be allocated as *resources to the IMF* which would utilize them to support further its lending activities with specific earmarked objectives. The IMF already has special arrangements such as the Poverty Reduction Facilities, the Heavily Indebted Poor Countries Initiative and the Poverty Reduction and Growth Facility. In this field cooperation with the World Bank is already tight-knit, which would continue. However, this option is likely to be the least preferable, since the role of the IMF in development is certainly not viewed as positive by all, whether it be developing countries, Latin American nations or certain Asian countries. Third, the proceeds could serve to fund so-called *debt swaps for development*, whereby heavily indebted poor countries are relieved of a certain amount of their debt burden, and in return receive grants for specific purposes such as health, environment, and so on. Fourth, funding could go to other *multilateral/regional development banks*, the international development agency or the African Development Fund. Such an earmark would be in line with the G20 Pittsburgh communiqué which committed itself to ensuring that the development banks would have sufficient capital to fulfil their core challenges. Fifth, revenue could support *UN Specialized Agencies*, specifically the United Nations Children's Fund, United Nations Environment Programme, United Nations Development Programme, Joint United Nations Programme on HIV/AIDS, United Nations High Commissioner for Refugees, United Nations World Food Programme, and others, depending on the decision as to what public good should be supported by FTT proceeds. Sixth, and finally, one could consider innovative financing through special regimes such as the International Finance Facility for Immunisation (IFFI). This functions through donors providing long-term pledges which are converted by the IFFI by selling bonds on capital markets, and through that mechanism has access to capital

[50] Transitional Committee Fourth Meeting, Report of the Transitional Committee for the Design of the Green Climate Fund to COP 17, TC- 4/3, 18 October 2011, p. 6

more readily available to support its health care objectives. The proceeds of the FTT could take the place of, or figure alongside such long term pledges, and the capital raised in this fashion could be disbursed to donors in accordance with their own mechanism.

These are but a few suggestions, the choice of which partially depends on the legal structure chosen to implement the FTT. Specifically, the relationship to the World Bank and the IMF will be crucial. In the case of the IFFI, for example, the World Bank acts as adviser and treasurer for the charity, which itself is incorporated as a charity in the United Kingdom. Conversely, an IMF-run FTT Convention would require either distribution of funds within its mandate (i.e. lending, debt relief) or a revision of its functions and relationship to, for example, UN specialized agencies and the provision of grants to other donors. In this author's view, establishing links with bodies such as the Green Climate Fund are the most promising avenues for FTT revenue earmarking.

4 Conclusion

In order to examine the extent to which the EU could proactively shape global financial governance, this chapter has drawn a parallel between the European legal order and its institutional set-up and the global financial legal order in order to reach conclusions on their respective receptiveness to the effective implementation of an FTT. The chapter started by examining the normative aspect of this endeavour. Looking at the Treaties, we concluded that the EU indubitably has an ambitious political agenda and legally binding mission statement to shape the international legal order in line with its own values.[51] The FTT is then an excellent case study because of its ambitious nature: to mitigate global risks posed by current excesses in the financial system, to correct imperfect market mechanisms, to ensure a just contribution by the financial sector to public coffers, to provide significant new revenues for the provision of underfunded global public goods; and all this with a global calling. In the next section of the chapter we then found the challenges at the global level are commensurate with the ambition of a global FTT at the EU level. The chapter has demonstrated that if the EU wishes effectively to see the establishing of a global FTT, it must forcefully pursue further legalization and institutionalization of the global economic governance

[51] See the chapter by Joris Larik in this volume.

system, drawing on its own experience. However, while the EU possesses an institutional set-up and a (relatively) effective legal order which has matured over sixty years, the global financial order is relatively fledgling and under-developed. Therefore, by making the EU–international legal order comparison with regard to the various aspects which an effective FTT regime requires, we have pointed to the fact that a global FTT requires setting up an entirely novel international legal regime only matched by that of the EU itself. The FTT would require the G20 to provide initial political impetus to the negotiation of the regime, during which the process would itself have to be transformed into the top political institution of the FTT regime; it would have to become an organ reflecting the membership of the international organization, much like the European Council. Subsequently, the framework convention would have mature institutions to ensure dynamic rule-making adapting the regime to financial engineering and innovation, similar to the Council of Ministers and the European Commission. In substance, the legal regime would require legal effects and a dispute settlement system to ensure harmonious implementation across its contracting parties, not unlike the legal system overseen by the European Court of Justice in cooperation with national Courts of the Member States. Distribution of revenue would occur through classical or more innovative means of financing, with the Green Climate Fund providing important inspiration on concrete avenues of implementing this aspect.

In sum, if the Union were successfully to push for setting up the Financial Transaction Tax Convention, this would lead to an unprecedented change to international financial governance to the benefit of the international economic system. The regime would further introduce legal commitment and a level playing-field, thereby thoroughly changing the international system of financial governance which is currently governed by club-like international networks that generate non-binding instruments and which have failed to contain the financial system from spinning out of control. However, the level of legalization and institutionalization required is so extensive that even the calamity of the 2008 financial crisis could not create the political will for such a watershed change in the global financial order.

Conclusion: messianism, mission, or *Realpolitik*? Some concluding observations on the EU's role in shaping the international legal order

FABIAN AMTENBRINK AND DIMITRY KOCHENOV

1 The Union's many engagements with the international legal order

Reflecting on the contributions in this edited volume covering a wide range of policy areas and activities beyond the borders of the EU's own territory there can be little doubt that the Union is not only firmly established within the international legal order, but is also actively involved in shaping it. This role is arguably a conscious choice rather than an unexpected side-effect of the Union's engagement with the international legal order.

Gráinne de Búrca in her contribution observes that Europe has developed from a project that was 'primarily inwardly focused on repairing and strengthening a damaged continent so as to deliver internal peace and prosperity',[1] to 'enhancing Europe's global economic and political influence and role'.[2] The case studies included in this book certainly support the latter conclusion. Yet one could also argue that from the start European integration was geared towards playing an active role in securing global stability and peace precisely because of the inward focus de Búrca refers to. Evidence for this seemingly paradoxical observation can be found in the grand promise of the Schuman Declaration which opens by stating that 'World peace cannot be safeguarded without the making of creative efforts proportionate to the dangers which threaten it. The contribution which an organized and living Europe can bring to civilization is indispensable to the maintenance of peaceful relations'.[3]

Younger generations of Europeans may be inclined to dismiss this statement as a somewhat inflated proclamation and sentimental

[1] See the chapter by Gráinne de Búrca in this volume. [2] *Ibid.*
[3] Declaration of 9 May 1950.

language.[4] Yet, this would arguably be disregarding the profound stamp that the experience of two World Wars, both of which originated on this continent, left on the generation of politicians that spoke out in support of the idea of European integration. It served as a strong motive for their aspirations, even if the initial project of the European Coal and Steel Community was understandably also partly driven by strategic considerations in some European capitals, probably even bringing mixed results.[5]

It may thus be argued, particularly in the light of Philip Allott's scholarship, that Europe's first active contribution to the international legal order was the initiation of the European integration project itself, opening up an alternative way of building international relations, as opposed to the mainstream approach prevalent until this day.[6] The six founding Member States of the European Communities opened a new chapter of international law and international relations by agreeing upon the curtailing of their sovereignty in favour of the establishment of 'a new legal order of international law',[7] which was fundamentally different from the traditional public international law. It was considered by the European Court of Justice not only to create rights and obligations for its constituting members but also for their nationals. This, once proven workable, has not only led to an increasing number of European states joining the integration process but has also inspired other attempts at regional integration in different parts of the world, even though none of them has (yet) come anywhere near the level of political and legal integration to be found in the EU today. The Union emerged as a cosmopolitan project.[8]

[4] For a general discussion see e.g. the chapter by Gráinne de Búrca in this volume; J. H. H. Weiler, '60 Years since the First European Community: Reflections on Messianism' (2011) 22 *European Journal of International Law* 303; G. de Búrca, 'The Quest for Legitimacy in the European Union' (1996) 59 *Modern Law Review* 349.

[5] E.g. K. J. Alter, 'The Theory and Reality of the European Coal and Steel Community', in S. Meunier and K. McNamara (eds.), *European Integration and Institutional Change in Historical Perspective* (Oxford University Press, 2007).

[6] See e.g. P. Allott, *Eunomia: New Order for a New World* (Oxford University Press, 1991); P. Allott, *The Health of Nations: Society and Law beyond the State* (Cambridge University Press, 2002).

[7] Case 26/62 *Van Gend en Loos* [1963] ECR 1; Case 6/64 *Flaminio Costa* v. *ENEL* [1964] ECR 585.

[8] P. Eleftheriadis, 'The European Constitution and Cosmopolitan Ideals' (2011) 7 *Columbian Journal of European Law* 7; D. Beetham, 'Human Rights and Cosmopolitan Law', in D. Archibugi, D. Held and M. Köhler (eds.), *Re-imagining Political Community* (Palo Alto, Calif.: Stanford University Press, 1998), 58–71. But see F. Amtenbrink, 'The Multidimensional Constitutional Legal Order of the European Union – A Successful Case of

It is beyond any doubt, as Blockmans observes in his contribution, that the 'gradual development of the Union's own external relations and designated institutional architecture'[9] has contributed to the EU's constitutional character beyond what he refers to as the 'Westphalian system of international relations'.[10] The contribution of the Union's very essence to the widening of the boundaries of the possible within the realm of international law and international relations is thus fundamental.

When approached in its dynamics, the picture of the Union's stance vis-à-vis the rest of the world is a rather complex one; taking into account the constituting *raison d'être* referred to above, the EU has refined and intensified its involvement with the international legal order. This has been partially driven by the expanding number of policy fields in which the Union could claim (shared) competence with an external dimension and the corresponding case law of the European Court of Justice on the EU's competence to conclude international agreements.[11] It was also increasingly driven by the explicit formulation of external objectives in Union documents, such as the Laeken Declaration, and the inclusion of explicit objectives in primary law pertaining to the Union's relation to the wider world, namely Articles 3(5) and 21 TEU, which are of essential importance.

As we learn from Joris Larik's contribution, the expression of ambition with regard to the shaping of the international legal order in constitutional documents is by no means a feature unique to European integration and the EU. In fact the latter seems to be what Larik refers to as '"dynamic internationalization" in constitutional law around the world' in which the Union 'expresses itself as to how the international order *ought* to be shaped'.[12] In fact, in this author's view, 'Just as Treaty objectives have been drawn upon time and again to advance the *internal* order of the Union towards a community based on rules and values [. . .] the external objectives of the Union call for nothing other than the active shaping of the *international* order along the same lines'.[13] This

Cosmopolitan Constitution-Building?' (2008) 39 *Netherlands Yearbook of International Law* 3–68.

9 See the chapter by Steven Blockmans in this volume, p. 131. 10 *Ibid.*

11 Reference is made here to the ERTA doctrine developed by the Court first in Case C-22/70 *Commission of the European Communities* v. *Council of the European Communities* [1971] ECR 263. On the conclusion of international agreements by the EU and its Member States, see e.g. C. Hillion and P. Koutrakos (eds.), *Mixed Agreements Revisited: The EU and its Member States in the World* (Oxford: Hart Publishing, 2010).

12 See Joris Larik's contribution to this volume, p. 78 (emphasis added). 13 *Ibid.*, p. 86.

development may be seen as a logical extension of what Sergio Dellavalle has described as the progressive development of interactions within a post-national arena that call for the handing-over to institutions beyond the nation state of 'the elaboration of rules that should guarantee that social interactions are predictable, peaceful and to a large extent co-operative, as well as the reinforcement of social integration that arises from the establishment and implementation of such rules'.[14]

It becomes clear from the contributions in this edited volume[15] that the EU has actively been shaping the international legal order in such areas as the recognition of states,[16] the rule of law,[17] patterns of global migration,[18] the environment[19] and more specifically climate change,[20] international approaches to energy law,[21] including energy sustainability,[22] WTO dispute resolution[23] and global financial governance.[24] These led at times to the most profound changes in the international legal order. To mention only a few examples of the findings in the case studies included in this book: Pech observes that 'the EU may be said to have significantly contributed to the diffusion of a substantive and holistic conception of the rule of law and the progressive solidification of an international consensus regarding its core elements and inextricable links with the principles of democracy and respect for human rights';[25] Blockmans concludes that 'the EU contributes its own rules to the definition of the international law on statehood';[26] and Delcour finds that 'the EU undoubtedly shapes the legal order and the institutional framework governing migration in its neighbourhood'.[27]

[14] S. Dellavalle, 'Lost in Transition? From Domestic Integration through National Constitutions to Supranational Integration through European Costitutionalism', in F. Amtenbrink and P. J. van den Berg (eds.), *The Constitutional Integrity of the European Union* (The Hague: TMC Asser Press, 2010), p. 116.

[15] See also Introduction (sect. 2.2).

[16] See the chapter by Steven Blockmans in this volume.

[17] See the chapter by Laurent Pech in this volume.

[18] See the chapter by Laure Delcour in this volume.

[19] See the chapter by Esther Herlin-Karnell in this volume.

[20] See the chapter by Christina Eckes in this volume.

[21] See the chapter by Peter Van Elsuwege in this volume.

[22] See the chapter by Anatole Boute in this volume.

[23] See the chapter by Tilman Krüger in this volume.

[24] See the chapters by Ohler, Wouters, Van Kerckhoven and Ramopoulos, and Van Vooren in this volume.

[25] See the chapter by Laurent Pech in this volume, p. 110.

[26] See the chapter by Steven Blockmans in this volume, p. 131.

[27] See the chapter by Laure Delcour in this volume, p. 280.

A question that follows from observing the Union's active role in shaping the international legal order is whether the Union pursues a clear and coherent strategy that is grounded in objectives, principles and values agreed upon by the *Herren der Verträge*, and laid down in the primary law of the EU. Moreover, what are the main drivers of the Union's actual engagement with the international legal order? Is the Union putting values first in engaging actively with the international legal order or is it in reality primarily led by its (economic) interests? In short, does the Union put the grub before the moral, to reiterate a famous quote from Bertold Brecht's 1928 play *Die Dreigroschenoper*?[28]

2 First the grubs, then the moral?

What links all contributions on the Union's shaping of the international legal order is not only that they provide evidence for the active engagement of the EU in the different policy fields. They equally illustrate how the values and principles that apply to the Union internally interact with as well as shape the EU's external engagements. In fact Article 3(5) TEU extends the Union's internal core values laid down in the first place in Article 2 TEU to its dealing with the outside world, stating that the Union is to 'uphold and promote its values [...] and contribute to the protection of its citizens'. Article 21 TEU builds further on this approach by stating that the 'Union's action on the international scene shall be guided by the principles which have inspired its own creation, development and enlargement, and which it seeks to advance in the wider world'. This provision includes an impressive non-hierarchical list of values and objectives, ranging from democracy, the rule of law, the universality and indivisibility of human rights and fundamental freedoms, respect for human dignity, the principles of equality and solidarity, the eradicating of poverty, sustainable development, the promotion of an international system based on strong multilateral cooperation and good global governance, to the abolition of restrictions on international trade.

Bart Van Vooren concludes that Article 3(5) TEU implies that 'the Union is not just morally, but in fact legally obliged to pursue equality amongst wealthy and poorer nations, to support their development and ensure "fairness" between them'.[29] In his opinion, 'the Union must pursue

[28] B. Brecht, *Die Dreigroschenoper* (Frankfurt: Suhrkamp, 2005).
[29] Bart Van Vooren's contribution to this volume, p. 332.

a just and fair global order, entrenched in multilateral solutions based on the rule of law'.[30] Leaving the exact Treaty source of this duty undetermined, Andrew Williams goes one step further than black-letter law in his legal-philosophical analysis. He claims that 'the EU represents a plausible vehicle of *interim* global justice',[31] whereby 'interim' reflects the belief that 'the ultimate destination is recognized as unlikely to be reached except in theory'.[32] To be sure, this author explicitly chooses not to provide hard evidence that the EU actually lives up to 'a deep institutional duty (respected and enforced in law) in relation to the distribution of wealth, a duty perhaps enshrined in its legal system',[33] but rather proposes a research agenda for further study.

Taking into account these views of the EU's ethical duties one cannot help but agree with Van Vooren that the Union 'has an ambitious political agenda and legally binding mission statement to shape the international legal order in line with its own values'.[34] At the same time, crucially, the exact scope of the Union's mission statement is anything but clear. Indeed, Articles 3 and 21 TEU refer to some rather broad and open concepts which at least partly lack clear definitions. Referring to the rule of law, Laurent Pech in his contribution points out that 'the EU Treaties say very little about what this principle entails and how the EU should seek to uphold and promote it beyond its borders'.[35] On the one hand, broad and open wording bears the danger of such concepts remaining rather vague, diminishing their effective operationalization in the EU's external sphere. On the other hand, this normative opaqueness also leaves room for the inclusion of values that the Treaties do not as such explicitly identify or link to the Union's external action. Take, for example, Christoph Ohler, who in the context of international financial regulation identifies (economic) objectives such as financial stability, economic growth and prosperity, as well as acting against supervisory arbitrage between financial institutions and markets.[36] Similarly, Bart Van Vooren links global financial governance to the Union's objectives 'in its relation with the wider world' laid down in Article 3(5) TEU.

[30] *Ibid.* [31] See the chapter by Andrew Williams in this volume, p. 39.
[32] *Ibid.*, p. 40. [33] *Ibid.*, p. 39.
[34] See the chapter by Bart Van Vooren in this volume, p. 347.
[35] See the chapter by Laurent Pech in this volume, p. 110.
[36] See Christoph Ohler's contribution to this volume with reference to the G20. See, however, also the reference in Article 21(2)(d) TEU, according to which the EU aims to 'foster sustainable economic, social and environmental development of developing countries, with the primary aim of eradicating poverty'.

Overall, the round-up of values and objectives included in primary Union law that is supposed to determine the Union's engagement with the international legal order can hardly be criticized for an ethical deficit or for a lack of ambition. The 2001 Laeken Declaration clearly encapsulates this ambition as it refers to the Union as a 'power seeking to set globalization within a moral framework' and raises the rhetorical question whether the role of the Union should not be 'that of a power able both to play a stabilizing role worldwide and to point the way ahead for many countries and peoples'.[37]

This strong commitment suggests that the EU takes a rather self-assured position in engaging with the international legal order, assuming that its values that are reflected in its internal substantive norms and procedures are worth pursuing at the international level and, in dealing with other countries, should be adopted by these countries. The most obvious example of the application of this approach is of course the EU enlargement policy. Steven Blockmans observes rather pointedly that the Union's approach to developing conditions and procedures for the recognition of aspirant states has been 'Driven by a sense of moral superiority about [the Member States'] own democratic values and respect for human rights and fundamental freedoms'.[38]

Does this approach provide proof for the claim that the Union pursues 'political messianism'[39] in its engaging with the international legal order? If one follows Joseph Weiler's definition of political messianism as an approach whereby 'the justification for action and its mobilizing force, derive not from process, as in classical democracy, or from result and success, but from the ideal pursued, the destiny to be achieved, the Promised Land waiting at the end of the road',[40] the many references to the values of the EU referred to above may very well carry this characterization. If, however, taken in a more literal sense of the word, the reference to messiansim may be somewhat overstating the aspiration and abilities of the EU in terms of actually delivering on promises it makes to the global community. In the absence thereof, a more accurate but still ambitious description may be that of the EU as a missionary. Namely, Articles 3(5) TEU and 21 TEU highlight the fact that the EU is

[37] Referred to by Joris Larik in his contribution to this volume.
[38] See Steven Blockmans' contribution to this volume, p. 164.
[39] A phrase borrowed from J. H. H. Weiler, '60 Years since the First European Community'.
[40] *Ibid.*

equipped with an ambitious duty not only to defend but actually spread its own values beyond its own territory. Of course this says little about whether and to what extent the Union actually practises what it preaches and what aims it actually pursues in employing this tactic.

In fact it follows from the contributions to this book that in most instances the EU cannot and does not pursue its mission in splendid isolation, but rather at best as an integral part of its external policies that are also geared towards other objectives. Indeed, Article 3(5) itself states that in its relations with the wider world the Union is not only supposed to uphold and promote its values but also its 'interests'. Similarly, Article 21 TEU states that the Union shall define and implement common policies and actions that are inter alia not only to secure its values, but also, crucially, its 'fundamental interests'. The balancing of the Union's values with such interests is addressed by several authors in this volume in detail. Peter Van Elsuwege points to 'the difficulty to reconcile the promotion of the EU's values with the reality that important energy partners are not always the best pupils when it comes to respect for human rights, democracy and the rule of law'.[41] He comes to the conclusion that while 'the EU does not shy away from openly criticizing its most important energy partner [. . .] the "ethical dimension" of the EU's external action faces its limits when this risks undermining the vital interests of the Union'.[42] Anatole Boute outlines similar dilemmas for the EU's external energy efficiency policy, combining climate change with security of supply issues, which 'is characterized by strategic (geopolitical) interests and, at the same time, touches upon moral issues that go to the heart of the difficult equity question that underlies contemporary international climate change and energy security politics'.[43] He also concludes that the EU focus on 'strategic considerations at the expense of the moral goals of this external policy considerably reduces the legitimacy of the EU's exercise of its normative power in relation to its partners'.[44] Tilman Krüger observes that the EU's promotion of judicial decision-making in the WTO was 'not the result of EU attempts to promote a just vision of international (trade) governance per se. Rather, the EU primarily tried to ensure its own vision of, and advantages within, the international legal order'.[45]

[41] See Peter Van Elsuwege's contribution to this volume, p. 232. [42] *Ibid.*, p. 233.
[43] See Anatole Boute's contribution to this volume, p. 239 (n. omitted). [44] *Ibid.*, p. 260.
[45] See Tilman Krüger's contribution to this volume, p. 290.

The pursuit of such strategic interests may clash with the values that the EU claims to promote in its engagement with the international legal order. Christoph Ohler in his contribution finds that '[a]ny regulation of financial markets is confronted with economic conflicts of interests and competing legal values that are of major relevance in an open market economy'.[46] In his view 'there exist no clear ethical solutions; in fact, these problems require a weighing of political and economic risks'.[47] In a similar vein, Christina Eckes in the context of the EU environmental policy refers to a 'tension between the ethically right position and the most effective strategy to achieve the greatest possible effect on the preservation of a public good [that] goes to the heart of the discussion on the Union's debate about its *raison d'être*'.[48] What these findings from case studies highlight is that contrary to what Articles 3(5) TEU and 21 TEU may suggest in their absolute formulation, the actual pursuit of European values carrying with them ethical standards is subject to a balancing of interests for which these two provisions do not provide clear guidelines. Laure Delcour's findings highlight that Union's values may not always be winning over from other Union interests even in policy fields with a strong ethical dimension, such as migration. This author observes the '*unethical effects* of the EU's influence on international migration patterns, and on migrants themselves'[49] and refers to Federica Bicci's rather harsh criticism of EU foreign policy as often being 'unreflexively eurocentric'.[50]

Adding to this, the pursuit of the value agenda of the Union may not only be hampered by competing Union interests but also by the interests of individual Member States, which, as several contributions in this edited volume highlight, continue to engage (alongside the Union) with the international legal order. The rather complex situation at the IMF described by Wouters, Van Kerckhoven and Ramopoulos highlights how this can impact on 'the effectiveness, visibility and coherence'[51] of the external representation of the EU, but as a consequence of this also the pursuit of its values at the international level.

[46] See Christoph Ohler's contribution to this volume, p. 300. [47] *Ibid.*
[48] See Christina Eckes' contribution to this volume, p. 209.
[49] See Laure Delcour's contribution to this volume, p. 281 (emphasis removed).
[50] F. Bicchi, '"Our Size Fits All": Normative Power Europe and the Mediterranean' (2006) 13 *Journal of European Public Policy* 286, p. 287.
[51] See the chapter by Wouters, Van Kerckhoven and Ramopoulos in this volume, p. 307.

While only empirical studies of an array of different policy fields could provide definitive answers, the qualitative findings collected in this volume suggest that in the real world *Realpolitik* tends to catch up with the Union's high-flying value-driven mission stated in primary Union law. The latter is obviously not a plea for altruism – the Union is bound to act, first of all, in the interests of its citizens – nor is it to say that the Union does not at all, or only occasionally, actively promote its values. This complex interplay of values and interests does make it rather difficult to predict in what constellations and to what extent the Union actually promotes its internal values in actively engaging with the international legal order.

3 The Union's active paradigm in engaging with the international legal order

Today's active shaping of the international legal order by the Union can be mapped along several lines, including inter alia the policy fields involved, the actual degree of Union activism, and the types of values which the Union pursues in a given instance. Thus the Union has long developed from only actively shaping the international legal order areas closely linked to its economic activities and related interests, such as trade and the global financial system, to also include issues that can be more directly linked to global common goods, such as democracy, the rule of law, and the protection of the environment. The actual role that the Union plays in the shaping of the international legal order varies, ranging, as has been pointed out in the introduction, from the consequences of the mere existence of this supranational legal order within the sphere of international law to the attempts by the Union to engage in a pro-active co-shaping of the international legal order alongside other actors inside and outside established international organizations. Finally, as the case studies in Parts II and III of the book highlight, the actual approach to shaping the international legal order by the Union and the extent to which it actively pursues its values varies across policy fields. This makes it rather difficult to qualify the EU's active shaping of the international legal order as being coherently and strictly value-driven.

The active shaping of the international legal order is not a recent phenomenon as from the outset the very *raison d'être* of European integration has been the placing of interstate relations between the European states on a new legal footing based on a set of values shared by all Member States, thereby channelling conflicts in a way that had not been attempted before. Yet, as is clearly highlighted throughout this book, this *raison d'être* has been extended to form the guiding principle for shaping the Union's active engagement with the international legal order. It would arguably be too dramatic to claim that the successful export of the values that govern the EU internally are existential for the survival of the European Union. But their defence and promotion at the international level do reinforce what de Búrca refers to as the 'mission legitimacy' of the EU. She argues that 'when the question of Europe's *raison d'être* is raised today, the importance of having a relatively unified European political system to counterbalance the influence of other existing and rising powers has become a more significant part of the answer than was ever previously the case'.[52]

Andrew Williams for his part is absolutely right in pointing out that 'assess[ing] the EU and its legitimacy primarily in relation to its democratic credentials [is] too narrow a scope'.[53] Approaching the vital legitimacy question Gráinne de Búrca proposes a dual-facing mission for the Union, justifying its very existence. Like Janus, this mission boasts two main elements linked to the internal and external action of the EU, consisting in the gradual articulation of a novel transnational relationship between the Member States, their citizens and the EU on the one hand, and the development of the EU's mission and role within the broader global context on the other. This twenty-first-century reading of the purpose of European integration certainly better reflects the Union's own dual ambition not only to promote and defend its values internally but also its dealing with the wider world. The Union's aim to take on responsibility and assume leadership at the global level seems to be falling squarely within this vision.[54] Yet, increasingly relying on the Union's international role for its (internal) legitimacy may not be a viable option.

In fact it is rather doubtful whether the active paradigm of shaping the international legal order based on the EU's mission statement can help to address the long-lasting legitimacy crisis, which has turned into an identity crisis to reach existential proportions in the eyes of some as a result of the global financial and economic crisis and the euro area debt crisis. First, as Andrew Williams has clearly demonstrated: not being a state, even the claims of becoming a possible actor of global justice need a

[52] See the chapter by Gráinne de Búrca in this volume, p. 21.
[53] See the chapter by Andrew Williams in this volume, p. 60.
[54] See the statements by the President of the European Commission in a contribution to the *Guardian*: 'Europe's Rising Global Role', 3 January 2010, www.guardian.co.uk/commentisfree/2010/jan/03/europe-global-role.

serious justification, when stemming from the Union. As such it can be debated whether the Union's engagement with the wider world makes its activities more legitimate in the eyes of its citizens, who are, probably paradoxically, ready to take the viability, worthiness and even goodness of their Member States for granted. What is more, it may be argued that the euro area debt crisis highlights the limits of the upholding of the essential constitutional values and thus the mission statement within the Union. To the extent that the crisis can be linked to the issue of distribution of wealth and more generally to solidarity between the Member States, the deep reluctance in some quarters to come to the rescue of financially failing Member States does not necessarily support the view of the EU as a vehicle of interim global justice that includes the redistribution of wealth. Finally, as is observed by Christoph Ohler in the context of international financial regulation, 'the problem solving capacity of the EU is impeded by its strict and rather inflexible constitutional framework under the Treaties'.[55] These shortcomings potentially affect the credibility of the Union abroad as the latter may not be seen practising what it preaches. Yet, concerning the fact that the Union emerges as a very dedicated missionary there can be very little doubt.

[55] See Christoph Ohler's contribution to this volume, p. 305.

INDEX